Aron Hsiao

SAMS
Teach Yourself

Linux® Security Basics

in 24 Hours

SAMS

201 West 103rd St., Indianapolis, Indiana 46290 USA

Sams Teach Yourself Linux® Security Basics in 24 Hours

Copyright © 2001 by Sams Publishing

International Standard Book Number: 0-672-32091-6

Library of Congress Catalog Card Number: 00-111802

Printed in the United States of America

First Printing: April 2001

04   03   02   01   4   3   2   1

Trademarks

Warning and Disclaimer

ASSOCIATE PUBLISHER
Jeff Koch

ACQUISITIONS EDITORS
Maureen McDaniel
Katie Purdum

DEVELOPMENT EDITOR
Mark Renfrow

MANAGING EDITOR
Matt Purcell

PROJECT EDITOR
Natalie F. Harris

COPY EDITORS
Gene Redding
Mary Ellen Stephenson

INDEXERS
Sandra Henselmeier
Eric Schroeder

PROOFREADERS
Benjamin Berg
Matt Wynalda

TECHNICAL EDITOR
David Bandel

TEAM COORDINATOR
Vicki Harding

INTERIOR DESIGNER
Gary Adair

COVER DESIGNER
Aren Howell

PAGE LAYOUT
Darin Crone
Lizbeth Patterson
Gloria Schurick

Contents at a Glance

Contents

HOUR 17 Introduction to Kerberos 259

HOUR 18 Encrypting Web Data 277

About the Author

ARON HSIAO is a computing entrepreneur and freelance consultant with a 15-year background in UNIX and UNIX-like operating systems. He has worked almost exclusively with Linux since 1994. As an independent contractor throughout the 1990s, Aron helped various dot-com firms with systems installation, network deployment, content production, and Internet marketing. He has also worked as a volunteer in a number of computing-related and educational capacities in his community. Aron has collaborated in the past with Sams Publishing and Que on Linux- and Unix-oriented texts as a technical editor and as an author. Aron served as the About.com guide to Linux from 1997 to 2000.

About the Technical Editor

DAVID BANDEL has over 10 years' worth of Unix system administration experience on a wide variety of systems, including DEC-5000 systems running Ultrix, SUN SparcStations running SunOS 4 and later Solaris 2.x, HP-9000's running HP-UX, RS-6000's running AIX, and Intel systems running SCO OpenServer and Linux. In February 1996, David retired after 20 years of active duty in the U.S. Army, where he was initially introduced to Unix System Administration. While still in the military, he became an avid fan of Linux, which provided the look, feel, and power of Unix on an Intel platform. Currently, David enjoys working as a Unix/Linux consultant, installing firewalls and providing network connectivity, and writing books and articles about Linux.

Dedication

To Ching-Chuan Hsiao, Chu-Ying Hsiao, Wilson Gutzman, and LaBerle Gutzman.

—Aron Hsiao

Acknowledgments

This project was undertaken during an interesting phase of my life, and I couldn't have finished it without the support of others. Thanks for this support go first and foremost to the members of my family, each of whom is always ready to listen and advise. (This includes you, Quincy and Baby—both of you have been very helpful in paradoxically keeping me calm and focused.)

Thanks also go to Carlos, Kelli, and Onyx, my second family, who have invested a great deal in me and my undertakings, especially when phone bills are considered. Finally, this book is quite simply the product of a great deal of patience and hard work on the part of everyone at Sams. Maureen, Kathryn, Natalie, Mark, and everyone else involved—my thanks go to the entire team for sticking with this project until it was done and done right.

Aron Hsaio

Tell Us What You Think!

As the reader of this book, *you* are our most important critic and commentator. We value your opinion and want to know what we're doing right, what we could do better, what areas you'd like to see us publish in, and any other words of wisdom you're willing to pass our way.

As an Associate Publisher for Sams, I welcome your comments. You can fax, e-mail, or write me directly to let me know what you did or didn't like about this book—as well as what we can do to make our books stronger.

Please note that I cannot help you with technical problems related to the topic of this book, and that due to the high volume of mail I receive, I might not be able to reply to every message.

When you write, please be sure to include this book's title and author as well as your name and phone or fax number. I will carefully review your comments and share them with the author and editors who worked on the book.

Fax: 317-581-4770

E-mail: feedback@samspublishing.com

Mail: Jeff Koch
          Sams
          201 West 103rd Street
          Indianapolis, IN 46290 USA

Introduction

In the computing world, *security* is a strange topic. This is because the computing world as we know it has largely become a collection of technologies for the enabling of networks, and our conception of what a network should be is fundamentally opposed to our conception of what good security should be. A network is designed specifically to allow needed data to be retrieved and to allow connections to be made between otherwise unrelated computers and systems. The role of security, on the other hand, is largely to forbid data from being retrieved or to forbid one computer from making a connection with another. Clearly, then, the process of securing a system or a network is one in which context and balance are important. Security must function well enough within your own computing context to provide you and your users with an acceptable balance between allowing and forbidding.

Because of the context-specific nature of this opposition, which is inherent in phrases like *computer security* and *network security*, and because security is a nearly infinitely deep topic for those who care to study it in depth, no one book can ever be the final word on security—no one book can ever be used by every user or system administrator to secure every system.

But Why Is Security Important at All?

When it comes to large Internet servers full of users' credit card numbers or large government servers full of nuclear secrets, it is easy to see why information ought to be protected—why some system-to-system connections and some attempts at data retrieval ought to be forbidden. These types of risks, on the one hand financial and involving hundreds of thousands of individuals and on the other hand national or even global in scale, are easy to see. But what about the typical dial-up modem user, who connects to the Internet to browse the Web or to help the kids with their homework? And what about the small business user who runs a small Web site but hardly feels important or large enough to be a target for international terrorists or organized crime?

Unfortunately, the Internet, like the real world, is not always a friendly place. There are any number of small-time ne'er-do-wells who like to get their hands on just the 10 or 15 credit card numbers your server contains. Even more frighteningly, there are thousands of "script kiddies" roaming the Internet without any motive at all—they enjoy breaking into computer systems and erasing data simply for fun. Often, they're not even knowledgeable hackers, but instead download their exploits (tools used for breaking into other peoples' computers) from security-oriented Web sites.

In fact, these two classes of security threats—the small-time criminals and the clueless script kiddies—actually *prefer* to break into tiny computer systems located in living rooms and small business offices. Why? Because most of the time, these types of systems are the least protected of all. Think about it: Have you taken any measures to protect the computer in your living room from outside attacks? The data on your home computer may not be especially valuable in terms of money, but how would you react if you left your computer connected to the Internet to make a cup of coffee and came back five minutes later to find your hard drive completely blank and unrecoverable, all of your letters, checkbook balancing records, even your Netscape bookmarks gone?

In the case of a small business, the threat is even easier to see. You certainly don't want your Web site taken down if it is your main source of income. More importantly, there are all of those records—the books from your business, built with your blood, sweat, and tears, going back seven years—gone.

In today's world, network security is important for every Internet user and every Internet-enabled small business. Period.

But I'm Using Linux! How Much More Secure Could It Be?

Here are a few facts about the average home or small-business Linux user that are important in this context. The average Linux user

- Is connected to the Internet often or always and may even run a small Web site, FTP server, or e-mail server.
- Runs Linux on standard PC-compatible hardware.
- Has installed a commercial Linux distribution, probably Red Hat Linux.
- Has not taken any security measures beyond those (if any) taken by the makers of the distribution.
- Rarely or never checks the system logs.

If this sounds a lot like you, you're asking for trouble—or you may even be in trouble already. The truth is that most Linux distributions ship in a fundamentally insecure state—with access from anyone nearly always allowed for nearly all services that Linux is capable of handling. Why? Because Linux originates in the world of Unix operating systems, and most distribution vendors still operate as if a competent system administrator is performing all Linux installations and can thus take the necessary steps to secure a system before it goes online.

Unfortunately, this is not always the case. If you feel that most of the items above describe your situation, one more fact is probably clear to you right now: You need to make your system more secure.

That's where this book comes in.

By following a few relatively simple steps and making a few changes in the way your system handles requests for various types of data and connections, you can make your Linux system or Linux network much more secure than it is now.

But Can I Make It Secure Enough?

How Much Security Is Enough Security?

Some veteran Linux users, especially system administrators, are fond of saying that a system can never be "secure enough" to let up on the security focus even a little bit. These individuals are speaking from positions of experience in large organizations with large security needs. For users who aren't computer professionals and can't afford to hire one, a continual focus on security 24 hours a day, 7 days a week simply isn't realistic. In other words, some amount of attention to security must at some point be called "enough."

Luckily, there is some good news for home and small business Linux users in need of security help. Though your system may be an ideal candidate for break-in by a small-time crook or a script kiddie, it is probably not large enough to be the target of a systematic attack from an expert hacker or a group of expert hackers. Therefore, enough security in your case is possible to define, or at least to imagine.

By taking the time to follow a few simple steps, regarded by security experts as the fundamentals of good security policy, and then staying vigilant and aware of your own system and your own Linux installation, you can prevent most attacks and close most vulnerabilities. In short, you can probably preserve your data, your privacy, and your peace of mind. The steps you may need to take, and which are covered in this book, can be summarized as follows:

- Make sure your physical environment does not pose a security risk.
- Install Linux and any updates you can find carefully and with a security-oriented mentality.
- Password-protect everything you can and choose good passwords that are difficult to guess.
- Instruct your file system not to give up any secrets to those who shouldn't have them.
- Turn off any network services you don't use.
- Make the network services you do use more picky about who they'll connect with and what sort of data they'll release.
- Protect your network, if you have one, with firewalling or packet filtering.
- Encrypt any sensitive data you send out across the network and, if necessary, encrypt sensitive data stored locally.

- Log everything and know how to monitor your logs. Audit regularly for vulnerability.
- Maintain good backups and know how to recover if you do get attacked or compromised.

These are the fundamentals of computer and network security. With them, the vast majority of attacks from script kiddies and small-time hackers can be stopped dead in their tracks. For the vast majority of home and small business Linux users, this series of tasks represents enough security.

How This Book Is Organized

The 24 lessons in this book are divided into several parts and can be followed from beginning to end coherently. However, certain users may find that they can skip some of the individual lessons—for example, home users with a single PC and nothing more can skip the lesson on Kerberos authentication—but each of the four major parts of the book contains something of importance to you as a Linux and Internet user, regardless of how you use your system.

The lessons in Part I, "Basic Security for All Roles," discuss some security fundamentals not related to specific network services or role-specific types of security needs. This section contains information that is both the simplest and also the most often overlooked when installing and configuring a Linux system. Physical security (hardware and location), operating system–independent security issues, Linux installation, booting, accounts, passwords, file permissions, and TCP wrappers (the most basic form of network security) are all covered in this part of the book.

The lessons in Part II, "Network Security," discuss issues related specifically to using Linux in networked environments and especially to using Linux as a small server for various types of data services. Firewalling and packet filtering, Kerberos authentication, security related to each individual network service including Web service, and security for X11R6 displays and data streams are covered in this part of the book.

The lessons in Part III, "Data Encryption," go a step further and walk you through the process of encrypting your sensitive data. First you'll learn to encrypt nearly any data stream traveling into or out of your computer system or network, using the SSH secure shell and its tunneling capabilities. Part III also includes lessons on providing encrypted (secure) Web sessions, encrypting your local file system using two different tools, and encrypting your e-mail using PGP (Pretty Good Privacy) and GNU Privacy Guard.

The lessons in Part IV, "Intrusion Detection, Auditing, and Recovery," will help you fortify the changes you've made to your system in the previous lessons. You'll learn to audit your system for remaining security defects, monitor an active system for ongoing attacks or suspicious activity, understand the exploited vulnerability should an attack occur, and recover from an attack should misfortune strike you.

The appendixes in Part V contain data designed to work as a kind of quick reference when working with security issues on your Linux system or Linux network. Of special interest is Appendix D, "Quick Security Checklist," which contains a categorized and simplified checklist of individual security-related items important for home or small-business users. You may want to follow the checklist as you complete each lesson in order to clearly see the ways in which your Linux environment is becoming more secure.

Enough talk. Let's learn how to protect your data.

PART I

Basic Security for All Roles

Hour

HOUR 1

Selecting and Installing a Linux Distribution

In our first hour, we're going to perform a security-minded Linux installation. Before we hit the power switch, however, there are two steps that must be performed first: A distribution must be selected, and the role of the machine in question must be clearly defined. We'll discuss the latter first.

Establishing the Role of the Machine in Question

Before you can install Linux or even select the distribution that matches your needs, you must understand, on a fundamental level, what the machine in question will be doing for you. There are four primary roles for machines in small businesses:

- **Workstation**   A workstation is a machine that primarily will be used by a single local user for running applications, often under the X Window System. This includes tasks such as Web development (not serving or deployment), word processing and spreadsheets, graphic design, and other processes that require human interaction on a regular basis.

- **Server**   There are a number of different types of servers. Network or Internet servers typically handle services like HTTP requests (Web), SMTP requests (e-mail), NNTP requests (net news), and other Internet-oriented protocols. File servers support NFS (Unix), SMB (Windows), or other systems for providing primary storage services across a local area network. Database servers are more rare in small business settings and provide extensive data storage, retrieval, and manipulation capabilities, using a relational database like Oracle or IBM's DB2. Larger servers or servers in very small environments can even handle all of these functions simultaneously. Regardless of the type of server in question, however, the basic concept behind a server is the same: Servers are primarily for providing services across a network, whether the network in question is a local area network or the Internet at large.

- **Infrastructure**   A network infrastructure machine's primary role is to facilitate the functionality of the local network. Among such machines are firewalls and routers, which allow machines in local area networks to share a connection (such as a modem, cable, DSL, or T1 connection) to the larger Internet. These types of machines provide security and either network address translation or IP masquerading for machines on the inside. Also in this category are DNS (domain name service) servers and machines that provide directory services or authentication services (as is the case with Kerberos).

- **Multipurpose**   Clearly, the average small business doesn't have the resources to shell out for a separate Web server, file server, firewall/router, and workstation. This is even more true for the average household. Thus, multipurpose machines are also very common. The multipurpose machine may act as its own firewall with packet filtering, provide routing services for one or two other workstations, and serve Web pages to the outside world (the Internet) and files to a local area network.

Before installing Linux, it is necessary that you understand which of these descriptions best applies to the machine or machines in question, because the expected role (or combination of roles) of the machine will directly influence both the choice of distribution you'll make and the combination of options and preferences that will apply while installing it.

Choosing a Linux Distribution

The process of choosing a Linux distribution for secure installation is different from the traditional choice process. First, the role of the machine in question is suddenly more important that it otherwise would be. More importantly, however, different distributions treat security very differently, even given support for the same roles.

The Features/Security Tradeoff

Once you understand the role the machine in question is going to play, it is useful to understand the features/security tradeoff inherent in all operating systems. This tradeoff is simple: An operating system can have the latest-and-greatest features or it can be secure and stable, but generally not both. This dichotomy is especially pronounced in the Linux community.

Before we look at specific Linux distributions, let's look at this tradeoff a little more closely and discuss some examples.

Workstations Need Features

When choosing a Linux distribution for use on the desktop as a workstation, it is generally features and speed that govern the choice. The average workstation will be connected to a number of input/output devices that are necessary for the work at hand. Input devices like sketchpads or tablets, printers, scanners, and digital cameras or camcorders are all examples of such devices. Entire subsystems like parallel-port or USB support become important above and beyond all else.

Unfortunately, because many of these devices are relatively new to the world of computing, support for the particular device or devices you need to use with a workstation may not exist in Linux kernel releases just a few months old. Even devices supported in user space, such as graphics adapters, may not be supported in older distributions. The X Window System in Linux (provided by XFree86) is constantly evolving to support the latest in graphics hardware. Thus, for exclusive desktop workstation use, the most cutting-edge distribution is often the Linux operating system of choice. Such a distribution usually ships with the latest kernel, the latest version of the X Window System, the latest drivers, and the latest software. Workstation users are often eager to get these "point-oh" releases—the "point-oh" referring to the zero after version numbers like 1.0, 2.0, or 4.0. At times, even pre-release (or, as some vendors call them, "technology preview") versions are useful for desktop workstations.

Servers Need Security and Stability

The situation is markedly different when the machine in question will be a network server or infrastructure machine. Such machines are intimately involved with connections to and from strangers in the outside world via the Internet. These types of machines can thus come into contact with some of the most dangerous or willfully destructive forces in the computing world. In these cases, security becomes very important, with speed coming in (a distant) second and features (a very distant) third. This is especially true for network infrastructure machines like firewalls, whose sole purpose is to provide security and network functionality. USB support and the capability to use GIMP with a sketchpad are absolutely unimportant for a dedicated Web server or a domain name server. On the other hand, a few minor vulnerabilities or stability bugs are completely intolerable.

Thus, for any role other than workstation, a point-oh release isn't a good idea. This kind of early release isn't yet widely tested; numerous outstanding bugs and vulnerabilities are likely to remain, and these won't be fixed until the point-one, point-two, or later releases. In fact, many administrators have the general policy of using the final release of a previous generation product for production machines. For example, if the current version of operating system Foo-Bar is 3.1 and the last pre-3.0 release was version 2.9, the server will be deployed with 2.9 because this is the "most fixed" version of 2.0 before new features were added for 3.0. While this logic doesn't always hold true in the industry, it illustrates the point nicely.

Similarly, entire distributions that have a reputation for staying on the bleeding edge can be a bad idea (though not necessarily) simply because they tend to include newer (and thus less well-tested) features in the operating system.

Multipurpose Machines and the Tradeoff

For the multipurpose machine, which might act as a server, a workstation, a firewall, or some combination of the three, the tension is obvious. It is up to you to decide whether cutting-edge features or security and stability are more important for the tasks at hand. Here are some things to keep in mind:

- Some features are convenient but not necessary. Though it is nice to have support for features such as universal serial bus or USB, it isn't always necessary. If your machine is more a server than a workstation, you may want to consider carefully whether some features are really necessary. For example, USB printers and USB removable storage devices are common now, but parallel versions of these types of devices are also often available at similar cost and are supported by well-tested kernels. On the other hand, USB support in Linux is still relatively new.

- Some features aren't needed at all. If the current kernel doesn't support your sound hardware or the 3D capability of your graphics hardware, but your machine is serving Web pages and handling e-mail and you only use it interactively for word processing and Web browsing, these features aren't needed. If you're worried about security, never go cutting edge to get features you won't use.

- Earlier isn't always better. In some cases, the cutting edge will actually have benefits. For example, if cutting-edge kernel versions support your SCSI controller well, but earlier kernel versions are a little unstable with it, you may need to consider whether the added stability is worth a security tradeoff.

- Be willing to invest in security. If the only thing preventing you from using a distribution with a 2.2.18 kernel instead of a pre-2.4.0 beta-test kernel is your previously unsupported sound card, which you desperately need for sound editing, consider simply buying a sound card that will be compatible with the older and better-tested distribution. If you can save yourself a security-related headache by spending the cost equivalent of two pizzas, the money will be well spent.

Choosing from the Major Linux Distributions

It is unfair to categorically classify each vendor and Linux distribution with respect to security and features, because each release from each vendor is its own animal entirely. A vendor that is conservative during one release may take a few risks with the next one. However, there are some reasonably justified stereotypes and a few incontrovertible facts that can be applied when discussing Linux distributions.

Of course, there are far too many Linux distributions to count, much less discuss in a single hour, so we'll stick to the majors in this text: Red Hat Linux (Mandrake Linux), Caldera OpenLinux, SuSE Linux, Slackware Linux, and Debian GNU/Linux (Corel Linux).

Note that in terms of the features/security tradeoff we were discussing earlier, this list is ordered from generally most feature-oriented to generally most security-oriented. After reading about each of these systems, it will be up to you to decide which distribution meets your needs, based on the role your machine is to play and the features you require. Again, keep in mind that these are only guidelines based on typical experience. Any particular release by any of these vendors can vary to some degree from past or future performance.

Red Hat Linux and Mandrake Linux

Red Hat is the leading Linux vendor, enjoying a true majority in terms of installation numbers across the Linux community. Over the years, Red Hat has established itself as an excellent workstation distribution (though this dominance isn't as exaggerated as it once was) by including more features earlier on than any other vendor. For example, Red Hat was the first to ship a distribution based on the second major release of the GNU C library with the Red Hat Linux 5.0 release. More recently with the Red Hat Linux 7.0 release, Red Hat was first to market with XFree86 4.x support and system tools that are ready for kernel 2.4. Unfortunately, both Red Hat Linux 5.0 and Red Hat Linux 7.0 received mixed reviews from users, some of whom experienced few or no problems and some of whom experienced pronounced problems.

Mandrake Linux is based on Red Hat Linux and thus shares many of the same benefits and liabilities. Generally, Mandrake Linux tends to fix many bugs and security vulnerabilities present in the most recent Red Hat releases, but of course they also add a few of their own thanks to the modifications made.

Red Hat Linux generally has not been secure when shipped; many services are enabled by default, and no default connection or packet filtering policies have been constructed out-of-the-box. On the other hand, users of these systems can make use of the Bastille Linux scripts to aid in closing security holes not related to bugs in the software. Bastille Linux can be found at http://www.bastille-linux.org. For those running Red Hat Linux, Red Hat keeps a current list of security advisories and updates at http://www.redhat.com/support/errata/.

To summarize, Red Hat Linux and Mandrake Linux are excellent cutting-edge distributions, but each will require attention of the kind this book presents before a system is secure. Furthermore, it is vitally important with either of these systems that the user stay on top of the updates available from the vendor Web sites, which repair security and stability-related programming errors in such cutting-edge software as they are discovered. Avoid the early point-oh releases of Red Hat Linux unless you absolutely require a feature provided by such a release. You can read more about Red Hat Linux at http://www.redhat.com.

Caldera OpenLinux (eDesktop and eServer)

Caldera has made its name selling what it calls "Linux for business" through corporate deals and on retail shelves. Either version of OpenLinux can be used as either a workstation or as a network server platform; the difference between the two lies primarily in third-party applications included with the eServer product and with the support options available.

Caldera also has a history of innovation in the Linux community. Caldera is responsible for developing the original version of the RPM package manager, later to be made famous by Red Hat. Caldera introduced one of the first graphics-based installers (Lizard) and was the first major distribution to ship with KDE as the default desktop (in OpenLinux 1.3).

Caldera's platform is among the most readily networked in the Linux community, shipping with all traditional services but also making available to customers some additional services such as OpenLDAP (a directory services protocol), SQUID (a proxy server), and NetWare for Linux.

1

In contrast to Red Hat, Caldera's point-oh releases generally don't make it into wider circulation to the degree that Red Hat's early releases do. Caldera is also more conservative when it comes to including cutting-edge versions of some critical system components. Thus, Caldera has a slightly better record in terms of security and stability than does Red Hat. On the other hand, Caldera's products also do not install with any real default security policy, and there is no Bastille Linux–comparable product for OpenLinux. For those using OpenLinux-based products, Caldera keeps an active list of security advisories and updates at `http://www.calderasystems.com/support/security/`.

Security-conscious users should avoid Caldera's Technology Preview product series; these products are Caldera's equivalent of beta-test software and are designed for testing purposes only. The features found in Technology Preview products will generally find their way into official system releases once the bugs and vulnerabilities have been worked out.

To summarize, OpenLinux eDesktop and eServer are network-oriented products with a reasonable track record for security and stability. No default security policy exists, however, so the user will need to pay attention to details in securing either system after install. You can read more about Caldera OpenLinux eDesktop and eServer at `http://www.calderasystems.com`.

SuSE Linux

SuSE Linux was popular in Europe before becoming very popular in the U.S. It has since become one of the more popular Linux distributions, partially because of its ease-of-use and strength and partially because of the wide array of software packages included in the retail box.

Like Caldera, SuSE shies back a little bit from the bleeding edge generally walked by point-oh and sometimes even later releases of Red Hat Linux operating systems, though SuSE doesn't spend as much time before major releases testing things as does the Debian project.

SuSE seems to have paid more attention to Linux security than has Red Hat or Caldera; SuSE Linux includes some tools (for example, port scanners) that have definite security uses and that are not included on distribution CDs from other vendors. The YaST administration tool used by SuSE also has some explicitly security-oriented options related to firewalling and packet filtering. On the other hand, some users have complained that SuSE places configuration files in unusual places, in anticipation of automated management by proprietary tools. SuSE keeps a fairly active list of security advisories and updates at `http://www.suse.com/us/support/security/`.

To summarize, SuSE strikes a good balance between delivering features early and giving software a chance to mature. SuSE also pays some attention to security with its shipped product. On the other hand, SuSE still doesn't ship in what could be called a well-secured state, and manual configuration of the sort this book is concerned with may be difficult. You can read more about SuSE Linux at `http://www.suse.com`.

Slackware Linux

Slackware Linux is one of the oldest Linux distributions and remains popular for precisely the same reason it did early on: Slackware attempts to be simple, straightforward, and text file oriented. This makes it very much like traditional BSD systems and the ideal system for competent system administrators who prefer to use vi and emacs for administrative tasks rather than proprietary tools like Caldera's LISA or SuSE's YaST.

Slackware is slower to release distributions based on the latest technologies, waiting instead for individual software components to mature after major releases before including them in release distributions. Slackware ships without a real security policy, but also exercises some restraint when it comes to making services available in the default install. However, Slackware is a smaller operation than many of the other distributions and thus is slower and less vigilant in watching for security problems and reporting them to users. Thus, it is up to the Slackware user to understand which services are in use and to monitor each of their development cycles independently for security advisories on a package-by-package basis.

To summarize, Slackware Linux is a distribution for competent Linux users. This eliminates much of the unnecessary noise created by proprietary distributions. Slackware can be made very secure and is very conservative with software versions, but it requires vigilance and competence on the part of the user or administrator to make it so. You can read more about Slackware Linux at `http://www.slackware.com`.

Debian GNU/Linux and Corel LinuxOS

Debian GNU/Linux is also sometimes known as the reference Linux distribution because it is the de facto GNU Linux operating system. GNU stands for "GNU's Not Unix" and is a reference to the Free Software Foundation, responsible for much of the code from which Linux operating systems are built, as well as for providing Linus Torvalds with the software license that has made Linux both free and famous. In keeping with this tradition, Debian has a long history of including only free software without proprietary or unusual extensions or modifications in its releases. Because of this, Debian GNU/Linux is traditionally very difficult to use, even more so than Slackware Linux.

It is therefore fitting that Debian is also by far the most conservative of the Linux distributions, having only recently released a distribution based on the new GNU C library and

1

the 2.2 kernel years after the other major distributions did so. Because of this, Debian is comparatively the most feature-poor of the distributions in terms of device support or support for current commercial Linux software. On the other hand, because of its very extended beta-test cycle and conservative approach, Debian therefore is also by far the most stable and secure (in terms of bug count) Linux operating system available. Debian GNU/Linux users can find a list of recent security advisories at http://www.debian.org/security/.

Debian is distinctive in that it is currently the only Linux operating system to offer an automatic upgrade path that can preserve for the most part the security status of the system being upgraded, avoiding the need for a complete re-install and re-editing of the myriad text files involved. Debian is also the only current distribution to fully support the Apple Macintosh in an official release. Both 68K Macintosh machines and PowerPC Macintosh machines are supported.

Corel Linux is based on Debian GNU/Linux, but uses a different installer developed by Corel for ease-of-use and presents a different desktop system to the user. Though Corel LinuxOS is gaining market share among desktop Linux users, the original Debian distribution is more likely beneficial to security-conscious users because Debian's security and bug tracking lists are much more extensive.

To summarize, Debian is feature poor for the desktop but easily the best choice among major Linux distributions for machines that will act as network servers or part of a network infrastructure. Support for Macintosh means that small businesses with old Macintosh hardware can put it to work on the network rather than having to retire it. The learning curve for Debian GNU/Linux is high, but the extremely large collection of supported packages and the easy upgrade system in some ways make up for other deficiencies. You can learn more about Debian GNU/Linux at http://www.debian.org.

Security-Minded Linux Installation

Security begins with installation. Though problems with the typical user's installation choices can usually be repaired later to make a system more secure, it is much easier for most users to simply install Linux correctly to begin with than to try to correct problems later.

This section will assume that you understand the basics of Linux installation. If you've installed Linux in the past and have been able to boot into your new system, this means you. Rather than walk through installation in depth, we'll just touch on those aspects of installation that are important for security reasons. The steps that follow may or may not be presented in the correct order, depending on the distribution you've chosen. You therefore will need to adapt the rest of this hour to suit your circumstances.

Step 1: Get Linux Straight from the Source

The first and most important step in performing a secure Linux installation is to ensure the integrity of your source or your source media. Never install Linux from an unlabeled, home-burned CD that you got from somewhere or other or someone with whom you're not closely acquainted. Many Linux users' groups are full of these types of CDs, passed around free to whoever wants a copy. Unfortunately, there is no way for you to ensure absolutely that the material has not been tampered with. You'll never have a secure Linux installation if you begin with a compromised install source.

In general, it is best either to purchase your install media in sealed retail packaging or to download Linux yourself and install it. When downloading or installing via FTP or NFS, be sure to download the install source either from the official server for the distribution in question or from an approved mirror site. Never download and install Linux from an unapproved or unlisted mirror just to save download time. You might well regret it later. Links to lists of official mirror sites for the distributions discussed in the previous section of this hour are shown in Table 1.1.

TABLE 1.1   Primary Site and Links to Mirror Site Lists

Vendor	Primary URL and URL to List of Mirror Sites
Red Hat	`ftp://ftp.redhat.com`
	`http://www.redhat.com/mirrors.html`
Mandrake	`ftp://ftp.sunsite.uio.no/pub/unix/Linux/Mandrake`
	`http://www.linux?mandrake.com/en/ftp.php3`
Caldera	`ftp://ftp.calderasystems.com`
	`ftp://ftp.calderasystems.com/pub/OpenLinux/MIRRORS`
SuSE	`ftp://ftp.suse.com`
	`http://www.suse.com/us/support/download/ftp/int_mirrors.html`
Slackware	`ftp://ftp.slackware.com/pub/slackware`
	`http://www.slackware.com/getslack/`
Debian	`ftp://ftp.debian.org`
	`http://www.debian.org/misc/README.mirrors`
Corel	`ftp://ftp.corel.com/pub/linux/CorelLinux/`
	(no official mirrors available)

1

In general, it is best to own a local copy of your chosen distribution. Thus, if you download it or do a Net install, be sure to burn a CD-R or save the distribution to tape. This will enable you to restore needed binaries from media later if necessary without having to rely on a working network connection.

Step 2: Define Multiple Partitions

It is infinitely more convenient to create a single large partition for your Linux file system than to follow traditional Unix-world practices and separate your file systems across partitions. However, there are a number of security benefits that can be achieved by separating file systems across multiple partitions. Among them are the following:

- **Avoiding some attacks directly**   There are some exploits that directly use world-writable directories like /tmp to gain root access for an intruder when such directories are on the same physical device as other parts of your file system. Thus, it is best to isolate world-writable file systems from the rest of the file systems on your machine.

- **The capability to mount some areas with execution restricted**   On all but the most open systems, there is rarely any legitimate reason for allowing executable files to be launched from locations outside of a binaries (bin) directory. Areas like user accounts (/home) and temporary storage (/tmp) can be isolated and mounted with the noexec flag to prevent any user from launching binaries from them.

- **The capability to mount some areas with SUID/SGID disabled**   SetUID (SUID) and SetGID (SGID) binaries are programs marked with permissions that cause them to run under the identity of their owner or group, rather than of the caller. This functionality is necessary for certain binaries that must access hardware directly, but such binaries should never be world-executable and should never be found outside the /sbin, /bin, or /usr/X11R6 directory. By separating these file systems and using the nosuid flag, we can prevent unauthorized SUID/SGID access. More information on the SUID/SGID file attributes can be found in Hour 7, "File System Security."

- **The capability to mount some areas as read-only**   It is easy to understand why some areas of the file system should never be easily writable. Among them are directories like /sbin, /bin, and /etc, which don't change often and are never changed without the administrator's attention. With separate partitions, these areas can be remounted as read-only once the boot process has finished.

Of course, if a cracker is somehow able to obtain root-level access to your system, each of these measures can be defeated, one by one. However, they do help to prevent an intruder from gaining root-level access in the first place, and they will stop many of the more clueless script kiddies dead in their tracks.

The partition scheme shown in Table 1.2 is one possible example, and we'll work with it a little later, once the install is more or less complete. Note that using this many partitions will require that you create an extended partition. These values are flexible and will depend on your disk size (a large modern disk is assumed here) and the plans you have for your installation. Change them as necessary to suit your needs.

TABLE 1.2   One Possible Partition Scheme for Secure Linux

File System	Size	Special Treatment
/boot	5MB	None; necessary for booting on some systems. Be sure to keep this partition below cylinder 1024 with most versions of LILO.
/ (root)	150MB	None yet. Hour 4, "The Boot Process," explains how to mount this as read-only if desired.
/tmp	500MB	No SUID/SGID, no execute.
/usr	2000MB	No SUID/SGID. Any remaining trees normally found in root (/) that require write capability will be moved here, and a symlink will be created in root so that root can later be mounted read-only if desired.
/home	varies	No SUID/SGID, no execute. This is the most secure route; workstation users may choose to change the noexec for convenience.

The methods for implementing special treatments for each file system will be discussed later in this hour.

The size values given may need to be adjusted to better fit your own needs. If you will be installing a lot of third-party application software or large commercial libraries of multimedia (such as clip art), you may want to increase the size of the /usr partition. Note that personal user files (documents) are generally stored on the /home partition in /home/user.

Step 3: Install and Enable only the Essentials

In the olden days of Linux, installing the operating system was a definite pain. This was largely because there weren't many distribution choices, so many users were forced to assemble their own Linux, and the distributions that did exist, such as Slackware Linux or Debian GNU/Linux forced a user to choose which packages to install, one by one.

This process required hours of work, but there was one beneficial side effect: The administrator of the system knew every piece of software present, and thus only those components that were absolutely necessary were installed.

Fortunately or unfortunately, these days the most popular distributions have streamlined the process considerably: Users generally choose from a short list of roles such as Standard Installation, Development Workstation, or Server when selecting packages. If you're knowledgeable enough to know what packages you will and won't need in your system, the best idea is to instruct the installer (when possible) to allow you to select by hand the packages or groups of packages you need. There are a few things to keep in mind when making the selection:

- Development tools are a bad idea. Unless you plan to do software development on the system, install few or no development tools. Installing C and C++ compilers and related tools on non-workstation systems is certainly unwarranted in nearly all cases. If you need to compile some software before placing the system into service, compile the software on a separate workstation machine and copy the files to the server machine over the network.

- Don't install XFree86 on a server. Since the X Window System uses a network protocol to communicate, it is fundamentally network aware and thus also fundamentally as vulnerable as any other network service to malicious attacks. If you won't be doing desktop application work on a given machine, don't unnecessarily increase the risk level associated with the machine by running X on it.

- Limit the number of services you install. In general, if you're sure you won't ever use a given service on the machine, don't install it. For example, for a machine that will act only as a firewall/router to connect your LAN to the Internet, there is no reason to install Apache, WuFTPd, NFSd, or other network services.

- Do the same for applications at large. If you're installing for a machine that will have no desktop or workstation functionality, avoid installing applications, games, or unnecessary software packages. There's a great deal of software on the average Linux CD, but the vast majority of it is designed for desktop workstation users. Don't install software you won't use on your server or network infrastructure machine; there's no functional need, and you may unknowingly install a program that presents a risk of compromise.

- Avoid excessive user-space hardware support. Take care also to avoid installing user-space support for hardware devices you don't plan to use. Generally, such binaries will either be SUID/SGID or will employ some trick in order to interoperate directly with hardware. Any binary that has permission in any way to access hardware can conceivably pose a threat to system security.

- Read package descriptions carefully. Understand what each package you're installing does. If you have the time, read each package description, or visit the package's home page to understand what it's for. Certainly avoid installing system-level packages you can't identify or don't understand, and be wary of any package whose description says that it must be run with the SUID or SGID bits set. If you're truly unable to determine whether a system-level or service-oriented package is necessary in your case, make note of it and what it's for. You can always install it later if you need it and have the install source media available to you.

Don't panic too much about making a mistake during package install, especially when it comes to selecting packages on an individual basis. This is only a preventative measure; most of what comes in the next 23 hours is more important in terms of system defense. In hours 4 and 5 especially, we'll take some time to disable services that have been installed but aren't needed.

Step 4: Finish Separating File Systems, Fix `/etc/fstab`

Once you've completed the software installation, booted into your new installation, and logged in (as `root`), you can implement the security measures related to multiple file systems on separate partitions that we discussed earlier. This process sounds more complicated than it actually is; following these steps, it won't take more than five or ten minutes to complete.

If you're running at runlevel 3 (multiuser) or 5 (X support), you'll need to drop down to maintenance mode before making these changes. It's easy enough to do, and you should become familiar with the command, because we'll discuss it several times in this book. As `root`, from a command prompt, enter

```
# shutdown now
```

After a few moments, you'll find yourself at a console login prompt; you are now ready to proceed.

Rearrange Files and Trees as Necessary

Remember that we may want to preserve the capability to mount our root (`/`) partition as read-only. However, some directory trees that we haven't created separate partitions for, such as `/var` and `/opt`, may need write capability for Linux to function properly at runtime. Thus, we'll make a directory for these trees in `/usr` and copy these trees there, making symbolic links afterward, thereby enabling us to mount `root` as read-only if we want to.

```
# mkdir /usr/root-write
# cp -dpR /var /opt /usr/root-write
# rm -rf /var /opt
# ln -s /usr/root-write/var /var
# ln -s /usr/root-write/opt /opt
```

The root partition can now safely be mounted as read-only once the boot process has completed, enabling us to give the file system some measure of protection later. It is also a good idea to protect the network-oriented binaries in /usr/sbin. This is easy enough to do:

```
# mkdir /usbin
# cp -dpR /usr/sbin/* /usbin
# rm -rf /usr/sbin
# ln -s /usbin /usr/sbin
```

The binaries in all three major system binary directories, /sbin, /bin, and /usr/sbin, can now be mounted read-only after boot and thus can be protected to some degree against modification. Remember that, if you've installed the X Window System on the machine, then you have an SUID binary (the X server) on your /usr file system. Since we're going to mount this with the nosuid option, this file at least will have to be moved to the root file system, where such binaries are allowed.

```
# cp /usr/X11R6/bin/XF86_SVGA /bin
# rm /usr/X11R6/bin/XF86_SVGA
# ln -s /bin/XF86_SVGA /usr/X11R6/bin
```

Note that you'll need to change the name of the binary to match the name of the X server used by your graphics hardware. For XFree86 3.x users, the name of the server will always begin with XF86_. For XFree86 4.x users, the name of the server is somewhat different, so the command is slightly different as well.

```
# cp /usr/X11R6/bin/XFree86 /bin
# rm /usr/X11R6/bin/XFree86
# ln -s /bin/XFree86 /usr/X11R6/bin
```

Now that the X server has been moved to the root partition, it can be started with the SUID bit set while at the same time the /usr partition is protected.

Edit /etc/fstab to Reflect the Changes

Now that the files and directory trees are all sorted out, we can perform our first real bit of securing by editing the mount list in /etc/fstab. This file controls which file systems are mounted during the boot process and what options are used to mount them. Installed as described in this hour, the /etc/fstab file as created by the distribution installer (barring comments and spacing) might look something like the file in Listing 1.1.

LISTING 1.1   The `/etc/fstab` File Created by the Installer

```
# Special file systems or mounts

devpts     /dev/pts     devpts   gid=5,mode=620          0 0
/proc      /proc        proc     defaults                0 0
/dev/hda7  swap         swap     defaults                0 0

# Devices that can be mounted and unmounted

/dev/cdrom /mnt/cdrom   iso9660  user,noauto             0 0
/dev/fd0   /mnt/floppy  auto     user,noauto,umask=0     0 0

# Linux file systems

/dev/hda1  /            ext2     defaults                1 1
/dev/hda2  /tmp         ext2     defaults                1 2
/dev/hda3  /boot        ext2     defaults                1 2
/dev/hda5  /usr         ext2     defaults                1 2
/dev/hda6  /home        ext2     defaults                1 2
```

Note that each of the Linux file systems is mounted with the `defaults` for ext2 file system options. The default behavior is to allow executables to be forked, even with SUID or SGID permissions. Our changes to this file are shown in Table 1.3.

TABLE 1.3   New Options for Partitions

Partition	File System	Options to Replace `defaults`
/dev/hda2	/tmp	noexec
/dev/hda3	/boot	nosuid, ro
/dev/hda5	/usr	nosuid
/dev/hda6	/home	noexec

After the changes are made, only the `root` ext2 file system will show `defaults` in the options column. The updated file is shown in Listing 1.2.

LISTING 1.2   The `/etc/fstab` File with New ext2 Options

```
# Special file systems or mounts

devpts     /dev/pts     devpts   gid=5,mode=620          0 0
/proc      /proc        proc     defaults                0 0
/dev/hda7  swap         swap     defaults                0 0

# Devices that can be mounted and unmounted
```

LISTING 1.2   continued

```
/dev/cdrom   /mnt/cdrom   iso9660   user,noauto          0 0
/dev/fd0     /mnt/floppy  auto      user,noauto,umask=0  0 0

# Linux file systems

/dev/hda1    /            ext2      defaults             1 1
/dev/hda2    /tmp         ext2      noexec               1 2
/dev/hda3    /boot        ext2      nosuid,ro            1 2
/dev/hda5    /usr         ext2      nosuid               1 2
/dev/hda6    /home        ext2      noexec               1 2
```

Note that the distribution installer has also created entries for the CD-ROM drive and floppy drive. These entries may or may not be desirable to you. Although in most homes and small businesses a CD-ROM or floppy drive won't represent a large security problem, a conservative security attitude suggests that disallow should be the default answer for any question. There are two changes that can be made here; the simplest is to remove the user flag from both device entries and the umask=0 flag from the floppy device entry. The resulting file is shown in Listing 1.3.

LISTING 1.3   A Slightly More Secure /etc/fstab

```
# Special file systems or mounts

devpts       /dev/pts     devpts    gid=5,mode=620       0 0
/proc        /proc        proc      defaults             0 0
/dev/hda7    swap         swap      defaults             0 0

# Devices that can be mounted and unmounted

/dev/cdrom   /mnt/cdrom   iso9660   noauto               0 0
/dev/fd0     /mnt/floppy  auto      noauto               0 0

# Linux file systems

/dev/hda1    /            ext2      defaults             1 1
/dev/hda2    /tmp         ext2      noexec               1 2
/dev/hda3    /boot        ext2      nosuid,ro            1 2
/dev/hda5    /usr         ext2      nosuid               1 2
/dev/hda6    /home        ext2      noexec               1 2
```

The changes shown in Listing 1.3 have the effect of preventing non-root users from issuing mount commands for the floppy and CD-ROM drive. The umask=0 option causes any mounted floppy to be world-writable; this has been removed as well.

In order to truly establish peace of mind with respect to the /etc/fstab file, you may want to remove any unnecessary lines altogether. Removing the /dev/cdrom and /dev/fd0 lines (or lines that refer to other removable devices) isn't too big a liability for most administrators; mount commands must then simply be issued at the command prompt.

Test the Changes

You should now be able to reboot into your new system and verify that non-SUID segments of the file system do not allow SUID binaries to be executed and programs cannot be forked from non-executable segments of the file system.

In order to perform such tests (and for the rest of this text), it will be helpful to be able to change the properties of any mounted partition on-the-fly. As root, you can do this with the mount command and the remount option; supply the properties you wish to enable or disable as extra options after remount. For example, you might want to make the root file system read-only for a moment:

```
# mount -o remount,ro /
```

To make it read-write again but at the same time prevent SUID execution, you would issue this:

```
# mount -o remount,rw,nosuid /
```

The other file systems can be remounted with new options in much the same way. Simply replace the / with the mount point of the file system in question. In Hour 4, we'll use this technique as part of the boot process to allow for a read-only root file system. For now, use it if you need to do so to verify that your options are correctly set.

Step 5: Install All Current Updates

Once you've finished installing from the source media and fixing up the file system options in /etc/fstab, proceed immediately to the distribution vendor's Web or FTP site, download all current updates and fixes, and install them. This is perhaps the single most important step in a secure Linux installation, but it is also the most often overlooked.

Stated another way, the need is easy to understand: The security updates at your vendor's site exist because someone's system or network has already been exploited using each of the vulnerabilities they fix.

You certainly don't want to join those who have already been violated. Don't let your system be compromised by a problem that's already been corrected. In case you've forgotten, the security advisories URL for each vendor is shown in Table 1.4. Note also that many vendors have additional updates on their Web or FTP sites related to stability rather than security; these should be installed as well.

TABLE 1.4 URLs for Security Advisories

Vendor	URL
Red Hat	http://www.redhat.com/support/errata/
Mandrake	http://www.linux-mandrake.com/en/security/
Caldera	http://www.calderasystems.com/support/security/
SuSE	http://www.suse.com/us/support/security/index.html
Slackware	None; security-oriented mailing list details at http://www.slackware.com/lists/
Debian	http://www.debian.org/security/
Corel	http://linux.corel.com/support/updates.htm#linuxos

Note that you should save any downloaded security updates you install to permanent media so that you can re-install them later if necessary without having to go online first.

Summary

This hour, we've covered three main topics: understanding the role of your machine, selecting a distribution, and performing the installation in a security-conscious manner.

Most home or small business machines fit into one of four basic roles. The role you plan for your machine will affect the basic approach you take toward the security versus features tradeoff. The roles are

Workstation   A typical desktop machine.

Server   A machine dedicated to providing network services.

Infrastructure   A machine used for firewalling, routing, or DNS.

Multipurpose   A machine used for more than one of these tasks.

When selecting a distribution, consider the role of your machine and the security versus features tradeoff. The major distributions are

Red Hat   Features first, point-oh releases, risky.

Caldera   Features first, more conservative than Red Hat.

SuSE   Some features emphasis, some security options.

Slackware   Difficult but cleaner and more conservative.

Debian   Difficult, multiplatform, very conservative.

Most users do not install Linux with any particular attention to security. A security-oriented installation is slightly different; the major tasks to complete when installing Linux with a security-oriented focus are

Verify   Is your source media legitimate? Make sure that it is.

Partition   Separate file systems for control and defense.

Eliminate   Don't install X or GCC when not needed.

Choose   Don't install packages you won't use or don't know.

Options   Set /etc/fstab options for mounted file systems.

After coming to an understanding of your machine's role, selecting a distribution to match it, and installing with the attitude of a discriminating administrator, you're ready to tackle more explicitly security-related tasks.

After powering on and before your system ever sees Linux, a multitude of tasks are performed. Pay attention to the settings in your motherboard, SCSI, and other BIOS programs, set jumpers carefully, and choose the correct boot order and your system will be less vulnerable to a locally caused compromise.

Q&A

Q Which distribution is the most secure?

A Generally speaking, the Debian GNU/Linux distribution is the most conservative of Linux distributions. This doesn't mean that Debian GNU/Linux is necessarily more secure than any other distribution, but rather that Debian GNU/Linux is tested more before it goes into full release.

Q What sizes should I use for my partitions?

A There is no right or wrong answer here; the sizes you use are based entirely on your own preferences and needs. Typically, the root (/) partition will function easily with less than 100 megabytes. You should be willing to dedicate more space to the partition(s) hosting the /usr and /tmp trees. The size of the /home file system will vary, depending on the number of users (and user files) you plan to accommodate.

Q I have already installed my preferred version of Linux, and it isn't one of those you've listed. Can I still use this book?

A Absolutely, though you may have to hunt a little in some cases to track down the locations of files we'll discuss, especially if you don't have access to some of the higher-level tools we'll discuss, such as Linuxconf.

Q I have already installed Linux on a single partition as a unified file system and don't want to re-install. Can I still use this book?

A Absolutely, though you won't gain any of the security benefits of separating your file system across multiple partitions.

New Terms

read-only file system   A file system that has been mounted with the read-only (ro) flag and therefore cannot be altered by anyone, not even root.

SGID   A program attribute that causes a program binary to run as though it were launched by a member of the group that owns it.

SUID   A program attribute that causes a program binary to run as though it were launched by the user who owns it.

HOUR 2

BIOS and Motherboards

During this hour, we're going to step outside Linux for a moment and work on what a PC-class computer does before it gets around to starting an operating system. There are important security issues that must be addressed before we concern ourselves with Linux. This hour covers the following issues:

- Password protection of the system BIOS
- Pre-boot password protection by the BIOS
- BIOS boot device order
- Secondary BIOS programs
- External or attachable device issues
- Controlling access to flash BIOS update capabilities

Once you've finished the hour, you'll be aware of and will have taken care of various software security issues that exist outside any specific operating system.

Linux Security Before Linux Is Loaded

Most users associate the word "security" with operating system issues only—commands, configuration files, network access, remote crackers halfway around the world, and so on. Indeed, most serious attacks, including large-scale attacks that make news headlines, occur this way. So why concern ourselves with what happens before the operating system is loaded?

The truth is that a large number of compromises also occur in the local context, meaning that the system is compromised by somebody who is sitting right in front of it. Any sufficiently determined attacker can eventually compromise any system with which he is in physical contact. After all, throwing the Web server out the tenth-story window is one of the easiest ways to maliciously take it offline. Still, any steps you can take to increase the effort needed to access your data are helpful to your cause as the system administrator.

Though these issues aren't necessarily Linux-specific per se, they're certainly part of a holistic approach to Linux system security. After all, what good is security inside Linux if your computer never gets that far?

The System BIOS

It's true that the operating system is what really runs the computer, but have you ever wondered just how the computer knows to load an operating system in the first place? After all, it's a complicated process. The display must be switched on, and the hard drive must be queried for the operating system software—in our case, Linux. After that, the operating system software must be started.

All of the tasks that occur between power-on and the operating system's final takeover are handled by software contained on a read-only memory chip on your computer's main circuit board (also called the *motherboard*). The software in question is called the Basic Input/Output System, or BIOS for short. Even though the list of BIOS tasks is short when compared to the number of tasks Linux will perform once it has been loaded, most system BIOS programs are highly configurable. Nearly every PC made within the last decade has a configurable BIOS, and it is with this BIOS configuration that we need to concern ourselves.

Three major options are available in most modern BIOS programs that need to be audited and perhaps fixed with security in mind. They are BIOS password protection, boot password protection, and main BIOS boot order configuration. Before you can change them, however, you'll need to enter your BIOS software's setup mode.

Entering Setup

Unfortunately, there's no standard way to enter the BIOS setup program. Many original equipment manufacturer (OEM) motherboards commonly used by home computer builders and smaller computer shops contain the standard American Megatrends Incorporated (AMI) or Award BIOS system. These BIOSs generally display a message when the machine is first started that gives instructions for entering the BIOS setup program. Such a message may be similar to any of these:

- DEL to enter SETUP
- INS to enter SETUP
- F1 for SETUP
- ALT+F1 for SETUP, ALT+F2 for FLASH

The key word in this case is SETUP, which refers to the BIOS configuration program we're trying to access. If you can see a power-on message relating a specific keystroke to SETUP, enter the keystroke while the message is being displayed, and you should find yourself in the BIOS configuration program. Other keystrokes, which lead to functions like the FLASH utility, are not directly related to configuring BIOS setup options.

If your system displays no such message and is manufactured by one of the larger retail computer makers, you may find that your system BIOS does not allow access to the configuration program without the use of a special BIOS setup disk that must be inserted before the computer is powered on. Other computers may require that you boot into Windows and use a Windows-based configuration utility to configure your BIOS. If this is the case with your system, perform these steps now.

Finally, some systems display no such message and include no obvious setup disk or software, but instead have hidden keystrokes. Some IBM machines, for example, require that the user hold the F1 key down while the computer is switched on. The key must be held until the BIOS configuration program actually appears on the display or it will not be run. If you find that your system offers no clear method for BIOS configuration access, try pressing each of the Delete, Insert, and F1 keys during the memory check. If none of these work, try each of them again, this time holding each one down as the system is switched on.

If in doubt, consult your computer or motherboard's manual for instructions on entering the BIOS configuration program.

Navigating Setup

There is no generally accepted standard or uniformity between the user interfaces of various BIOS configuration programs. Some of them, like the AMI WinBIOS, are mouse based and present the user with a Windows-like interface. Others, like the more popular Award BIOS, require the user to navigate with the directional arrows and the Enter key.

Because each BIOS is different, you'll have to spend a few minutes on your own becoming accustomed to the way in which your own BIOS configuration program works. Most newer BIOS configuration programs contain at least the following sections, though the names of each section may vary a little:

- BIOS Setup or General Setup (sometimes separate)
- Chipset Setup
- Integrated Devices Setup
- PCI Devices Setup
- Power Management Setup

Each of these sections contains a number of options related to the type of device or the subsystem in question. If you're unable to get an understanding of what's in your BIOS configuration program, consult the manual for your motherboard or computer system for in-depth details.

BIOS Password Protection

Any BIOS program worth its salt will include an option to password protect the BIOS configuration program itself, and this is the first option we're going to tackle. Once a BIOS password has been set, no one will be able to enter your system's BIOS configuration program without first entering the password that protects it. This is important for several reasons:

- If the BIOS isn't password protected, the other settings we're going to change in the interest of security can be easily changed back to their original settings by anyone who can figure out how to enter your BIOS configuration program.
- A password-protected BIOS prevents often ham-handed service technicians or even meddling family members from making detrimental changes to your system hardware without your knowledge.
- Some older BIOS programs can actually be used maliciously themselves. For example, some older versions of the AMI BIOS popular on 386, 486, and early Pentium systems contain software that can be used to erase your hard drive completely. BIOS setup programs containing similar features should always be password protected.
- Many current BIOS programs include tools to update the flash memory on your motherboard. The term *update flash* is really code for "erase the current BIOS program and install a new one from the manufacturer." This is a risky process even

when performed by a technician. In the hands of a malicious user, flash update capability can render your motherboard completely unusable. Most manufacturers will exchange a mis-flashed motherboard under warranty, but it is likely that others will not.

Generally, the option related to the BIOS password can be found in the BIOS Setup, Security Setup, or General Setup section. You'll have to enable the option and supply a password that will be used for the purpose at hand.

Be sure to select a password you'll remember. Once you've set your BIOS password, you won't be able to enter BIOS setup again without it, even to turn off password protection. On some systems, you can clear the BIOS configuration settings (and thus the password) by opening up your computer's case, finding a small set of jumper posts among the many that appear on most motherboards and shunting them together. This process is a delicate and time-consuming one, however, and may not always work.

On a few systems, there is no way at all to get back into the BIOS configuration program if you've forgotten your password. On systems like this, a forgotten password means a new motherboard or, worse (as is the case with some laptops), a new machine altogether.

> If your computer system or motherboard includes no BIOS password-protection option, it may be time to get a new system or a new mother-board altogether, unless you're sure that your physical environment is very secure. This is especially true if your BIOS includes flash update or hard drive low-level format capability. BIOS password protection is fundamental.

Boot Password Protection

In addition to password protecting the BIOS configuration program, it's a good idea to password protect the boot process if the system doesn't need to be able to boot automatically after power failures. When the boot process has been password protected, any user who powers the system on will be prompted for a password before any operating system is ever loaded from any device. Such a password is your first line of defense against unwanted access.

For example, imagine that you leave your office for lunch and, while you're gone, someone else who has physical access to your computer attempts to break in to it. Linux user accounts are password protected, but suppose this person simply power-cycles the machine by switching it off and then back on again? Suddenly, your system is unprotected. On an average computer system, any knowledgeable person can at that point simply insert a floppy, bypass the Linux user accounts altogether, and have at all of your data.

If you password protect the boot process itself, however, this can't occur. A malicious user wouldn't be able to make the machine start again without the password.

On a large percentage of current computer systems, the boot password is automatically enabled when the BIOS password is enabled, and the passwords are the same. If this is the case on your system, you're all set. If not, look for a boot password option, usually near the area where you found the BIOS password option.

If you forget your boot password, it's not as big a deal as forgetting your BIOS password, because you can always go back into the BIOS configuration program and choose a new boot password. Of course, this applies only if your BIOS and boot passwords are separate options.

If your motherboard or computer system doesn't provide boot password capability at all, you may want to consider replacing it, but it's not nearly as serious an issue as is a missing BIOS password option. The next BIOS configuration option we're going to discuss will also help to mitigate the negative effects of a missing boot password option.

Be sure to save any changes you make to your BIOS when you exit; otherwise, none of the new settings will take effect.

Boot Order Configuration

In the BIOS Settings, Boot Settings, or General Settings section of the BIOS configuration program, most systems include a series of options that look something like this:

- Boot order: A, CDROM, SCSI, C

On some other systems, the question might be presented as a series of options rather that a single option list. In these cases, boot order configuration might look more like this:

- First boot device: Floppy Drive A
- Second boot device: CD-ROM Drive
- Third boot device: External Adapter
- Fourth boot device: Hard Drive C

In either case, the default settings for most systems will look something like what you see above. The settings shown here mean that each time your computer is started, the BIOS will perform the following steps following the Power-On Self Test (POST):

- Check to see if a floppy drive exists. If so, see if a disk has been inserted. If a disk has been inserted, try to start an operating system from it.

- If no operating system could be started from the floppy drive, check to see if a CD-ROM drive exists. If so, see if a disk has been inserted. If a disk has been inserted, try to start an operating system from it.

- If no operating system could be started from the CD-ROM drive, check to see if there are PCI cards in the system to which data storage devices are connected. If so, pass control of the boot process to the first card found.

- If no such devices are found or no operating system could be started from them, try to load an operating system from the hard drive.

Notice that in this sequence, the hard drive is the last device checked for an operating system, meaning that anyone who wants to bypass the Linux user accounts password protection and get right at your data can simply insert a bootable floppy or CD-ROM disk and go to town. The external adapter query sounds hard to understand, but all it really means is that if you have a SCSI card or secondary IDE expansion card in your system, the BIOS will try to boot devices on these cards as well.

In the interest of security, we don't want to allow anyone to boot from any device other than the hard drive. This way, if the system is allowed to boot at all, it must boot into your Linux installation where logins to user accounts (and therefore all data) are password protected. The boot order setting you're looking for will look more like this when you're done:

Boot order: C Only

Or, if your system separates the options, they might look more like this once you've secured the boot order:

- First boot device: Hard Drive C
- Second boot device: Disabled
- Third boot device: Disabled
- Fourth boot device: Disabled

Under the settings above, only the hard drive will ever be used to boot the system. A malicious user can insert a floppy disk in hopes of bypassing your Linux passwords and getting at your data, but your system will ignore the floppy disk altogether. Similarly, if the system is a net-boot system and the BIOS includes a Network Boot option, use Network Boot as the only boot device.

Here, too, different BIOS setup programs vary. Some BIOS configuration programs are very flexible with regard to boot order, while others are much less flexible. If you don't have the option of disabling all other devices' boot capability altogether, try to disable as many of them as you can and ensure that the first hard drive, usually referred to as the C drive, is listed first in the boot order.

Users who use SCSI hard drives as their primary means of storage may need to leave the SCSI or external adapter option in the boot order, depending on the BIOS software present. Beware, however, that in cases like this, your SCSI controller may become a risk if you have SCSI CD-ROM drives, floppy drives, or other removable storage in the chain. Try to ensure that your primary SCSI hard drive is the first SCSI ID on the first SCSI controller in the system to avoid allowing a malicious user to boot using other devices.

If your system BIOS does not include the capability to manipulate boot order but always tries the floppy first, you may want to consider a new motherboard or system, though you may find that some strategies in Hour 3, "Physical Security," will help you overcome this limitation to some degree. If you have no need for a floppy device at all, a simpler (and cheaper) idea is to remove the floppy drive altogether.

Secondary BIOSs

So far, we've concerned ourselves with securing the BIOS program that is built into your system's motherboard and which controls things like the initial power-on process and the system's IDE devices. If you have any PCI IDE controllers, or any SCSI controller, however, there is a good chance that your system has one or more external BIOSs, which control the additional device(s).

This is a problem because external BIOSs of this type are not generally password protectable. Some of the nicest SCSI controllers, such as those made by Adaptec, BusLogic, and Mylex, suffer from this problem. Using one of these BIOSs, a malicious individual can alter the boot order without having to enter the main system BIOS at all.

For example, a user might have a system that looks like this:

- IDE devices: none
- SCSI ID 0: Hard Drive

- SCSI ID 1: CD-ROM Drive
- SCSI ID 2: Jaz Drive

This user intends for the system to load Linux from the SCSI hard drive each time the system is powered on. However, a malicious user can enter the SCSI BIOS and instruct the controller to ignore the device at ID 0 during the boot process. Suddenly, the CD-ROM drive becomes the first boot device, and the malicious user has again gained control of the boot order. Any removable storage device connected to a card with its own BIOS can be a culprit: CD-ROM drives, magneto-optical drives, Zip and Jaz drives, and even a few tape drives are all equally dangerous in this regard.

Is there a solution for this situation? Yes and no. If you can enable a boot password for your system, the problem is mitigated to some degree, since the BIOS configuration programs for these external cards can generally be reached only after the primary BIOS has initialized itself. However, this means that you must trust a user either completely or not at all. There is no way to accommodate any user who is "trusted enough" to know the boot password and start the system but is not trusted enough to play with the boot order.

One possible solution is to use two separate add-on cards: one with a BIOS and the other without. All removable devices are moved to the card without the BIOS so that they can never be made bootable. Many manufacturers offer versions of their cards without BIOS chips on them. Additionally, some cards include a jumper or switch setting to electronically disable the BIOS altogether. Of course, this route incurs extra expense, but it may be the only way to solve the problem.

If you decide to use the two-card solution described here, be sure that the BIOS on the first card won't act as the BIOS on the second card as well, leaving the problem completely unsolved. Some add-on card models will do this.

Some older SCSI controllers with onboard BIOSs can be converted to controllers without BIOSs simply by removing the BIOS ROM. The BIOS ROM in such cases will usually be labeled as such and will be socketed. If after you remove the chip Linux fails to communicate with the SCSI card, this trick won't work with your particular SCSI card; in this case, carefully re-insert the BIOS chip to restore functionality.

Of course, if you don't need any of the devices on your add-on card to be bootable, as is the case when you're using an internal IDE hard drive, then the problem goes away, since you can configure the boot order in your main (password-protected) BIOS to always try the IDE hard drive first. This creates a second possible solution to the add-on card problem described. Even if your primary hard drive storage will be connected to your add-on card, simply ensure that there is at least one IDE hard drive in the system and that it can be used to boot Linux. Even a small drive will do—just enough to hold the /boot file system tree or the kernel. The root device itself can still be the drive connected to your add-on card. Unfortunately, this requires that yet one more disk device be installed in a system, often using a precious drive bay.

External/Attachable Devices

An additional possibilitywith SCSI cards complicates the issue considerably. Most SCSI cards have both internal and external connectors, and many modern SCSI cards are automatically terminated, meaning that no changes must be made to the card itself in order for devices to be attached to the external connector. This creates a rather large security problem during the pre-boot BIOS stage. If you plan to use an automatically terminating SCSI card with a bootable BIOS and want your system to be secure locally between main BIOS password entry and operating system start, then you must boot from an IDE drive, as was discussed in the last section, unless your SCSI chain is completely full. Why? Because of the external connector.

With an automatically terminating external connector, any malicious individual can bring his own bootable device and simply plug it into the back of your system. Even if you have all of your removable SCSI devices connected to a non-bootable controller, you're out of luck if the malicious individual brings his own boot device to the party and changes the boot order in the SCSI BIOS to include it.

Generally, if your SCSI chain is full or your controller requires modification before the external connector will work, you're reasonably protected against this kind of activity, since adding an external device in such a case will likely result in an unbootable system until the device is disconnected again. Still, given the limitations of the PC architecture, the most secure policy at this point is always to maintain at least one small IDE drive with enough space to hold the kernel. Once the kernel boots, it can be instructed to look for the root file system and any additional file systems on any other device present in the system.

Controlling Flash BIOS Updates

One of the most convenient features of modern PCs can also be one of the most danger-ous. A *flash BIOS* is a BIOS chip that can be overwritten using special software. This capability is useful because it allows significant motherboard upgrades and bug-fixes to be supplied by the manufacturer without requiring that you ship the hardware back to the factory for changes. Not only motherboards have this feature; the BIOS chips on many SCSI and IDE controllers have such a feature. In fact, some hard drives have their own small BIOS system with flash capability.

Unfortunately, all of this flashing is not necessarily a good thing. While the flash process is supposed to require special programming software, the hardware tricks used by such software can also be employed by a malicious user. If a flash BIOS is overwritten not by a new BIOS program but rather by garbage or zeroes, your system's motherboard, SCSI controller, or hard drive is dead for all intents and purposes and must be sent back to the manufacturer. One or two motherboards now include an automatic recovery feature, but using the feature is a complex process, often requiring that you open your computer and set several hard-to-reach jumpers, as well as have Internet access on a second machine in order to obtain a replacement BIOS program.

Rather than go through such headaches, it is better to simply disable flash BIOS writes altogether wherever possible. Most motherboards allow the user to completely disable flash BIOS writes with a single jumper or switch setting; consult your computer system or motherboard's manual for details. If it is not listed in the manual, take the cover off the case, get a flashlight, and look for a chip on your motherboard with a sticker on top of it, usually labeled with a name such as Award, AMI, or Phoenix. This is the BIOS chip. Once you've located it, you'll often see a small jumper or switch nearby on the board that is labeled in white lettering with "flash disable" or "write disable" or some-thing similar. Changing the position of the jumper will disable flash BIOS updates.

For SCSI controllers, PCI IDE controllers, hard drives, and other devices with their own upgradable onboard software, check your manual for jumper settings to disable flash BIOS writes.

It isn't always possible to disable flash BIOS writes for every device, but where possible it should be done in the interest of security and convenience.

Summary

This hour you learned that before your computer ever loads an operating system, a pro-gram called the BIOS must decide where the operating system must be loaded from. If a malicious user can gain control over the boot process and boot his own operating system disk rather than yours, your data is compromised. To avoid this, you've taken the following steps:

- Password protected the BIOS configuration program itself
- Password protected the boot process
- Changed the boot order to prevent floppy and CD-ROM boots
- Disabled or secured secondary BIOSs where possible
- Disabled flash BIOS update capability where possible

Though these steps are not directly related to Linux per se, they are an important part of a holistic approach to security that addresses both remote and local vulnerability as well as the operating system and the hardware to run it.

Q&A

Q I still haven't figured out how to enter my system's main BIOS configuration program. What can I do?

A If you can't get any of the keys we discussed to work and you're unable to find any reference to BIOS setup in your documentation, it's time to contact the manufacturer for instructions. Your computer almost certainly has a BIOS setup routine somewhere. All computers since the 80386 machines have had them.

Q My computer system doesn't have the capability to password protect the BIOS configuration. Is it really that important?

A If there is any chance at all of a user coming into physical contact with your system, yes. Though it is true that any user who comes into contact with your computer can theoretically walk off with it, take it home, remove the hard drive, and extract the data from it using his own hardware, such a long process is certainly more difficult than simply enabling the floppy drive and booting into your data. The prospect of physical theft followed by two hours' hard work in order to get at your data may deter a criminal. On the other hand, the prospect of ten seconds of floppy noise is unlikely to deter even a very lazy criminal. Anyway, why make life any easier for the crooks?

Q I'm not using a PC at all. I'm using hardware platform X. How does the material in this hour apply to me?

A In the most direct sense, it doesn't. The details about BIOS configuration discussed here really apply only to the PC architecture. However, the underlying concept applies to everyone: understand what your system does between power-on and operating system boot and be sure that your data isn't compromised *before* Linux ever gets a chance to load. Unfortunately, some systems are even worse than PCs in this regard. For example, if you're a Macintosh 68K Linux user, there's little that you can do, since Penguin, the Mac booter for Linux, requires that you boot into MacOS before starting Linux.

New Terms

BIOS   Also known as the Basic Input/Output System, this is the program that controls the way your system will boot.

boot order   The list of devices, in order, that your BIOS will search for an operating system at power-on.

flash memory   A type of memory commonly used to hold BIOS programs for various types of hardware. Leaving flash memory enabled can be risky because it means that a malicious user can do permanent damage to expensive components of your system.

IDE   An abbreviation for Integrated Drive Electronics. IDE-type hard drives are inexpensive and are the most common type of storage device on PCs. IDE also is commonly referred to as ATA.

ISA   An acronym for Industry Standard Architecture, an old expansion bus system used by nearly all 386 and many 486 computer systems. VESA, a 32-bit local extension to ISA, is also found on many 486 computer systems, but is rarely found on Pentium or later systems.

jumper   A small piece of plastic containing a copper clip, used to connect two jumper posts on a circuit board in order to change some aspect of the board's behavior.

motherboard   Also commonly referred to as a *mainboard*, a motherboard is the main circuit board in a PC computer. The motherboard contains the CPU (for example, a 486 or Pentium chip), expansion bus (such as PCI or ISA), the BIOS, and all hardware related to basic input and output.

PCI   An abbreviation for Peripheral Component Interconnect, a modern expansion bus system used by many 486 and all later PC systems.

POST   Power-On Self Test, the series of memory and device tests performed by the BIOS when a PC system is switched on.

SCSI   An acronym for Small Computer Systems Interface, a high-performance parallel communications interface for storage devices, scanners, printers, and other computing devices. SCSI devices are most common on server systems.

HOUR 3

Physical Security

This hour we will finish securing aspects of your computer that lie outside the direct influence of Linux, focusing on what is called physical security. *Physical security* refers to aspects of computer security that have to do with the physical placement of the machine itself, the machine's operating environment, and the degree to which the machine is protected from hardware-level compromise.

Why Is Physical Security Important?

Physical security is important because a physical attack is perhaps the most fundamental kind of attack. The types of actions we're referring to when we speak of physical attacks can include things such as the following:

- Simply hitting the reset switch or power button
- Using a floppy drive or CD-ROM drive on a machine that does not support good BIOS security
- Damage to or theft of important machine components, especially those that store data
- Theft of an entire machine

In the home environment, physical attacks are both less likely and more difficult to defend against should you be unlucky enough to be the target of burglary or theft. Still, some steps can be taken to prevent such problems.

In the small office, on the other hand, physical security is one of the most important concerns. While large corporate installations are typically closed to public entrance and are well guarded both by humans and by various forms of electronic security, the typical small business can afford no such luxuries. Thus, it is especially important for the small business user to focus on physical security as an important step in preventing data loss or service interruption.

Location, Location, Location!

The simplest way to provide good, solid physical security is to choose a secure location for your system's installation. What this means in simple terms is that if a system doesn't need to be physically available to the public, don't let it be. There are a few simple axioms that, when followed closely, can prevent nearly all physical attacks involving systems that do not need to be publicly accessible.

- **Keep your server and other machines in the back room**

  If you run a small business with enough floor space, it may seem impressive to display your Web server to your customers. However, if possible, keep all of your computer systems in a back room. When spatially possible, run monitors, keyboards, and mice on extended cabling to public areas. Keeping the processing units themselves in a back room and away from public hands solves nearly every problem discussed in this hour.

- **Secure the environment**

  Of course, no midnight thief is going to consider the back room to be off limits. Ensure that the environment in which your system runs is well secured day and night. Invest in high-quality locks as well as in an alarm system when possible, and be sure to lock up and enable the alarm whenever you leave the area, even if it's just for a 10-minute trip to the sandwich shop.

- **Secure the power controls**

  If your environment is locked tightly but your Web server is down due to loss of power, your customers are still cut off from your services. Know where your building's power sources are. Old buildings especially may have circuit breakers or fuses in odd or publicly accessible locations. A padlock for the breaker box is an inexpensive investment that can prevent all kinds of juvenile pranks, innocent accidents, or malicious attacks.

- **Invest in a continuous power system**

  When possible, invest in a continuous power system (or *battery backup*, as they are sometimes called) to mitigate the problem in the case of unexpected power failure. Even if you've locked your box tightly, you're helpless if the power company decides to work on your block's main line for an hour, cutting the power in the process. Having a solid, regularly tested continuous power system online can keep service up through any minor brownouts and can give you time to notify users, shut down, and prevent data loss in the event of a sudden brownout.

All of these steps should be combined with a holistic attitude toward your computing environment. Be mindful of the physical circumstances surrounding your equipment and of the public at large as a potential danger. It is time to think of security in terms of your computer's physical components, in addition to its cyber-existence.

3

Strategies for Difficult Locations

Unfortunately, not every computer can be sequestered in a locked room. Some machines must even be made available for unattended public use. Though this is certainly risky, there are some steps that can be taken to improve security and reduce the odds that service interruptions or data loss will occur.

The Power Cycle

The simplest form of physical attack against a publicly accessible system is a power cycle—the unexpected loss of power to the system, resulting either in a reboot or unattended "off" time. Incidents of this kind usually aren't even malicious, but are caused instead by clumsy or unaware users or visitors to your place of business or by unaware children in your home.

This type of incident generally is caused by easy access to reset and power buttons, which lie on the front of most computer cases and can be triggered easily by a stray elbow, finger, purse, or other solid object. There are several possible solutions to the power cycle issue, each slightly more severe than the one before:

- **Politeness**

  The most common method for small businesses to handle this problem seems to be to place a note over the switch in question that says "Do NOT hit this switch!"

- **Prevention**

  In spite of the fact that it is the most popular solution, simple politeness is a bit silly in this context. A more proactive step that is also sometimes seen is the placing of strong tape over the switches in question alongside the note.

- **Force**

  The ideal solution for these types of switches is to forcibly disconnect them. Then, they can be hit, whether by accident or purposefully, without causing any interruption or data loss whatsoever.

Simply put, the last option, force, is preferable when security is really a concern. Though it's not as easy as simply placing a note or tape over a switch, it's certainly more effective. In truth, it is not as hard to disable these switches as one might think. The following are a few methods:

- **Use BIOS features**

  Many BIOS configuration programs on newer energy-saving ATX motherboards have an option to control power features, including in some cases system power and reset. Often, both functions can be completely disabled in the BIOS setup without having to make physical system modifications at all.

- **Disconnect the reset switch**

  In most cases, disabling the reset switch is simply a matter of opening the case and unplugging one small cable lead from the system motherboard. Simply follow the lead from the switch itself to its other end and give the cable a gentle tug. In some cases, the arrangement is physically different, and no cable is present. In such cases, the switch must be removed altogether.

- **Disconnect the power switch (ATX)**

  If your system is a newer ATX system, the power switch on your system operates simply by making a momentary connection across two jumper posts. To disable the power switch and place your system into a permanent-on state, simply follow the lead from the switch to the motherboard and pull the cable off as you did with the reset switch. Then place a standard jumper shunt over the two posts to which the cable was connected; this will create a permanent-on setting.

- **Remove the power switch (AT)**

  On an older AT-style case, you must be more inventive because of the wide range of possible power switch configurations that have appeared over the years. In some cases, the solution is as simple as unbolting the switch from the front of the case and taping it elsewhere on the inside of the case, left in the on position. In more extreme cases or on older power supplies, it may be impossible to disable the power switch without modification to the power supply itself, which is best not attempted unless you're very familiar with electrical circuitry.

There is one other potential interruption to the power supply for a machine that is routinely used by the public, and that is the wall plug itself. Your computer must have power, after all, and that power comes through a cord that plugs into 120 volts on one end and the back of the machine on the other.

Here it is best to use your own discretion. If you are relatively sure that most of your power cycle vulnerability lies in unintentional accidents by otherwise trusted individuals, simply disabling the reset and power switches should prevent most service interruptions. Beware the janitor's power-waxer or the clumsy customer's shoe, however: Either could unplug your machine and create the very power cycle problem we're trying to prevent. To that end, you may choose to take additional steps:

- **Secure the power cable to the back of the machine**

  This can be done in a variety of ways, but one of the most effective is to use glue to attach the cable to its socket permanently. Take care not to get glue on the metal contacts, or your newly glued power cord may not work at all!

- **Plug the other end of the cable in somewhere else**

  Use a long cable and plug the 120-volt side of the cable into a socket in another room or somewhere out of view and easy reach so that the temptation to unplug the cable from the wall socket is minimized. Any home hardware store will also sell a wall-type cable clamp that can firmly affix a cable to a wall or floor; use something like this right next to the wall plate to ensure that the cable can't be pulled out by jerking it.

- **Protect the length of the cable**

  Don't run the cable across the floor. Run it to the outlet in conduit against the wall, under the carpet, in a rubber cable guide, or in some other apparatus that will prevent both accidental tripping and a jerk from the janitor.

Unfortunately, these measures protect against only incidental or unintended loss of power from cable interruption. All cables, however, are clippable—there is no way to prevent malicious interruption of power when someone has physical access to the machine. Therefore, the ideal policy is still to separate the machine physically and securely from any individuals whom you don't know or fully trust.

Boot Devices

We covered this once in the previous hour when discussing BIOS issues, but the problem of bootable devices can be explored even further here. If you are unable to password-protect your BIOS or fix your boot order completely, your system is vulnerable to being hijacked by someone with his own boot disk. To prevent these types of attacks from occurring, concentrate on securing these devices specifically.

- **Lock floppy drives**

  Many computer accessory dealers sell a small device called a *floppy drive lock*. This device is a small piece of plastic shaped more or less like a floppy disk with a keyhole on one end. When inserted into a floppy drive and locked, the plastic unit prevents a floppy disk from being inserted until the device is unlocked and removed again.

- **Disable CD-ROM drive eject buttons**

  Some newer CD-ROM drives, especially those from big-name manufacturers, ship with a jumper- or switch-operated feature to allow the user to completely disable the frontal eject button while leaving software eject intact. Even in the absence of such an option, you may be able to disable the button manually with a little tinkering, though doing so will likely void your warranty. Once the button has been disconnected or disabled, a CD can be inserted only after the user has logged into Linux and issued the eject command.

- **Consider removing such drives altogether**

  If there's no reason to have removable storage on a publicly accessible system, by all means remove the device. Any computer system will operate perfectly well with no floppy drive or CD-ROM drive, though a few BIOS configuration changes may be necessary. Remove the drive and put a blank faceplate in its place; this is the ultimate form of floppy or CD-ROM drive security.

If finances allow it, you may even consider using diskless clients for public access machines and mounting needed file systems using NFS or some other network file system hosted in another, more secure room or environment. That way, even if the system is stolen or damaged physically, the data on your boot drive and file systems remains intact.

Locking Down "the Box"

Every measure we've discussed so far is moot if a thief or malicious individual simply picks up your "box" and walks away with it when you're not looking. It makes little sense to spend money on cable clamps, uninterruptible power supplies, floppy drive locks, and other security paraphernalia if your box itself is vulnerable to simple theft. There are several possible ways to solve this problem, which are listed here and which involve progressively more expensive equipment.

- **Lock the back room**

  This method of securing your box costs little or nothing. If you're keeping your machine in a secure room, simply ensure that the room has a lock and that it stays locked at all times. Even when you're on the premises, the circumstances can easily get out of control, and a five-minute absence can translate into a several-thousand-dollar loss from your secure but unlocked room.

- **Use an adhesive cable lock**

  Cable locks come in various shapes, sizes, and installation methods. The most common of these is a thin but strong steel cable with an incredibly powerful adhesive block on each end. One end is glued to the table, the other to the machine. Such cables are generally thick and strong enough to act as a serious deterrent to theft.

- **Use a thicker, invasive cable lock**

  Some site administrators have gone a bit further with the cable lock, drilling a hole in the computer case's sheet metal and another large hole in the edge of the table or desk. A bicycle combination lock with a thick steel cable or even a chain is then threaded through the holes and locked.

- **Use an alarm cable lock**

  Several computer accessory manufacturers sell alarm lock systems that are similar to cable locks described above but that are electrified and connected to an alarm system. If the cable is ever cut, an audible alarm sounds.

> In addition to locking down the box, it is also a good idea to lock the box so that a malicious individual with a few minutes and a screwdriver can't simply open the case and make off with your hard drive and, thus, your data. Some cases include built-in locking mechanisms of high quality, while others do not. The easiest way to lock an unsecured box is to drill a set of strategically placed holes and then use a standard padlock to secure the major parts of the case.

Access Auditing

Even assuming that you've taken many of the measures mentioned so far in this hour, it is still important at all times to be aware when trying to ensure the security of a computer installation. The most important type of awareness in the case of physical security is access auditing. *Access auditing* is the process of knowing who has physical access to your machine and when. This list is important for two reasons:

- If you understand who will have physical access to the machine, you can make some guesses with regard to the degree of suspicion and caution you should have.

- If your system is ever compromised physically or stolen, having a ready list of individuals who had physical access to the computing environment can help to expedite the discovery of the responsible party.

Many users at this point think to themselves, "nobody but me has access to this machine!" Unfortunately, this is not always the case, especially in the small business setting. The list of individuals who have access to your equipment may include any of the following:

- Landlords, property management personnel, or anyone else involved in the ownership or management of your business location.

- Cleaning, maintenance, or janitorial personnel either hired by you or hired by building management or ownership.

- Service workers, repairmen, and other individuals who are brought in on a limited or one-time basis to make repairs or to solve problems.

- Delivery personnel, vending machine operators, or supply runners to whom you have given a door key for early-hour or after-hours work.

- Any other employees or family members who have a key to the area either for after-hours work or because they live there.

Unfortunately, there is one last group of individuals you must also consider: any friends, acquaintances, or family members of those individuals already listed—especially those who regularly accompany those individuals on their rounds or to work.

As you can see, this list can quickly grow to involve individuals you may not have considered in relation to your computing equipment. If you find that your list is very large or that some of the individuals in question can't be fully trusted with your data or your equipment, stronger security measures are called for.

Keep this list up-to-date at all times. Be vigilant, or you may come to the office one day to find that your equipment is no longer working.

Summary

This hour, you've learned to consider the physical environment as an integral part of a holistic approach to Linux security. The basic steps to be taken are

- Lock away all systems in isolation when possible.

- Prevent power cycle issues by disabling reset and power buttons, securing the power cable, and installing battery backups.

- Lock floppy and CD-ROM drives or remove them altogether if they aren't needed.
- Install a cable lock of some kind to prevent your entire box from being stolen.
- Lock your case as well.
- Keep an active list of those individuals who have physical access to the machine in question.

Be aware and be vigilant!

Q&A

Q Is there any way to impose absolute, guaranteed physical security?

A Unfortunately, no. Any door can be kicked down, given a sufficient amount of force, and any cable can be cut with sufficiently large cable cutters. The idea, however, is to make the criminal's job as difficult as possible and to prevent non-criminals from accidentally interrupting your service.

Q My CD-ROM drive doesn't have the capability to disable only the eject button, but it can disable the eject function altogether. Can this work?

A Yes and no. If you never need to use more than one CD, power up the drive, insert the CD, disable eject, reinstall the drive, and you're good to go. However, if you simply disable eject completely on an empty drive, why not remove the drive entirely, thereby both removing temptation and saving electricity?

Q Are there any more secure ways to allow for publicly accessible machines?

A Yes! If the application you need to provide is text based, consider purchasing a dumb serial terminal to run the application. These are often very inexpensive and can be configured easily with Linux using a serial port. If you need to provide access to graphics (X11), consider either building your own inexpensive X-terminal using an old PC, Linux, and XFree86 or even purchasing an X-terminal from a Unix hardware vendor. In either case, your important data can stay sequestered physically in another secure room.

Q I use Linux at home and am primarily concerned about Internet security. Does this hour apply to me in any way?

A It may, though some of it is already true in the home context. Obviously, you want to know who comes in to your home at all times. Still, some modifications, such as disconnecting the reset switch and investing in a continuous power system, can prevent unwanted accidents that might otherwise result in data loss. If you plan to run a server of any kind in your home, these issues are important as well, especially if you have young children around who might be tempted to play with the server system.

3

New Terms

cable lock   In the security context, a device designed to keep a computer system firmly attached to the physical environment in which it is installed. Cable locks come in various sizes and some are equipped with audible alarm systems.

continuous power system   Also known as a battery backup in some cases, a continuous power system allows your system to continue to operate through brownouts and short blackouts.

floppy drive lock   A disk-shaped device with a key lock protruding from one end. When inserted into a floppy drive and locked, a floppy drive lock prevents unauthorized disk insertions.

physical security   The security of the physical environment surrounding a computer system—rooms, locks, and users.

power cycle   The process of disconnecting power from the computer and then adding power again. A power cycle generally has the effect of restarting the system.

HOUR 4

The Boot Process

This hour we're going to focus for the first time on securing a system on which Linux has already been installed and is running. We will concentrate on the remainder of the system boot process as it plays out once LILO and later the Linux kernel have been loaded and are in control of the system. Security issues during the boot process include the following:

- Forbidding the passing of kernel arguments via LILO
- Implementing password protection via LILO
- Choosing the correct runlevel for the machine's primary role and editing runlevels where necessary

The Linux Loader

The Linux Loader, or LILO as it is more commonly known, is the program responsible for loading the Linux kernel once the BIOS has passed control of the computer to the operating system. Most Linux users have seen one or both of the following lines of output during boot:

```
LILO boot:
Loading linux...
```

These lines are displayed by the LILO program before the Linux kernel is started. The first line of output above is the boot prompt, which allows the user to choose a kernel image to boot or to pass arguments to the kernel. The second line of output is what might be displayed if a kernel labeled linux is loaded.

The capability to pass arguments to the kernel is a useful one. For example, when an incorrect change to system libraries or a loss of data due to power issues occurs and renders the system unbootable through normal means, the user can pass arguments to the kernel to boot into maintenance mode:

LILO boot: **linux single**

The single argument starts Linux in a special, stripped-down, root-only mode designed to allow system administrators to make repairs to parts of the operating system otherwise needed for the boot process or normal system function. The single-user mode is analogous in many ways to the Safe Mode of the Windows operating system. However, it can pose a security risk by altering normal operating system functionality as you've configured it and presenting users instead with a root-only password prompt.

Even more dangerous, however, is the init= argument, which allows the user at the LILO prompt to specify an alternate init program for the operating system. The init program is a special program designed to be run first on Unix-like systems. Init is reponsible for starting all services, including things as basic as the login prompt and password verification. A user at an unsecured LILO prompt might just as easily enter something like this:

LILO boot: **linux init=/bin/bash**

This line is particularly risky because it is a full system compromise in a single, simple line. When the init argument is set to /bin/bash, the Linux kernel will start bash (the shell) as the first process rather than init, meaning that no services will be started, no password prompts will be presented, and the offending user will be dumped immediately into a root shell!

> Don't assume that this section doesn't apply to you simply because you never see a LILO boot: prompt when you start your computer. There is a good chance that LILO is still managing your boots. To see if this is the case, try holding down the left Shift key just before your computer begins to load the operating system from the hard drive. If you see the LILO boot: prompt now, you're vulnerable to these types of attack.

Clearly, steps need to be taken to secure the LILO booter. Luckily, the LILO booter uses a flexible configuration file normally found at /etc/lilo.conf that can accept two important security-oriented arguments. Most distributions do not secure LILO for you in advance, so be sure to follow this section closely.

The `/etc/lilo.conf` File

The /etc/lilo.conf file is separated into two main sections. The first section, global settings, occurs at the top of the file and includes keywords that apply to every kernel image or operating system that LILO is managing. Changes made to this global section of the configuration file will apply to every kernel image in your list of bootable images.

The second section of the file begins with the first image= or other= keyword and continues through the end of the file. A new imagebegins each time the image= or other= keyword reappears; the keywords below each image refer to the particular kernel image in question. A sample /etc/lilo.conf file is shown in Listing 4.1.

LISTING 4.1   Sample /etc/lilo.conf File

```
#
# Global section of /etc/lilo.conf
#
boot = /dev/hda
install = /boot/boot.b
prompt
timeout = 100
default = linux
#
# List of images in /etc/lilo.conf
#
other = /dev/hda1
        label = win
image = /boot/vmlinuz-2.2.16
        label  = linux
        root   = /dev/hda4
        vga    = 775
        append = "hdc=ide-scsi"
        read-only
image = /boot/vmlinuz-2.4.0-t9
        label  = linux-new
        root   = /dev/hda4
        vga    = 775
        append = "hdc=ide-scsi"
        read-only
#
# end /etc/lilo.conf
#
```

4

Most Linux systems will have at least one kernel image listed, often called `linux` by default. Dual boot systems generally will also have one or more `other=` images as well, which allow LILO to manage booting for Windows. The file shown in Listing 4.1 is an insecure LILO configuration; any user who sees a `LILO boot:` prompt is free to boot the system or to send arguments to the kernel, which could fully compromise the system.

The password Keyword

The first order of business in securing this LILO configuration file is the addition, when needed, of the `password` keyword. This keyword allows the system to require that the user enter an administrator-supplied password before booting some or all of the images managed by LILO. There are two ways to use the `password` keyword:

- If placed at the top of the file, in the global configuration section, all boot attempts, regardless of kernel image, will require that the user supply a password.
- If placed in an `image=` section of the file, for example, just above the `read-only` keyword, a password will be required to boot the image. No other images are affected.

For example, we'll change our file to require that the password `A4ni77a*` be entered before any image in the system can be booted. The new `/etc/lilo.conf` file is shown in Listing 4.2.

LISTING 4.2   Updated `/etc/lilo.conf` File

```
#
# Global section of /etc/lilo.conf
#
boot = /dev/hda
install = /boot/boot.b
prompt
timeout = 100
default = linux
password= "A4ni77a*"
#
# List of images in /etc/lilo.conf
#
other = /dev/hda1
        label = win
image = /boot/vmlinuz-2.2.16
        label  = linux
        root   = /dev/hda4
        vga    = 775
        append = "hdc=ide-scsi"
        read-only
```

LISTING 4.2 continued

```
image = /boot/vmlinuz-2.4.0-t9
        label  = linux-new
        root   = /dev/hda4
        vga    = 775
        append = "hdc=ide-scsi"
        read-only
#
# end /etc/lilo.conf
#
```

Because the `password=` keyword has been placed before the first `other=` keyword in the global configuration section of the file, the listed password will be required to boot any image.

The `restricted` Keyword

The next order of business in securing this LILO configuration is to add the `restricted` keyword to the configuration file. The `restricted` keyword allows a password-protected image to be booted without a password unless command-line arguments are being sent to the kernel. Like the `password` keyword, the `restricted` keyword can be placed into the `/etc/lilo.conf` file in one of two ways:

- If placed at the top of the file, in the global configuration section, all kernel images will be restricted and no kernel arguments will be passable without first supplying the password related to the image in question.

- If placed in an `image=` section of the file, for example just above the `read-only` keyword, no arguments will be passable to that particular kernel without first supplying the password. Other kernel images remain unaffected.

As an example, let's change our file so that all images are completely restricted. The new `/etc/lilo.conf` file is shown in Listing 4.3.

LISTING 4.3 Updated `/etc/lilo.conf` File

```
#
# Global section of /etc/lilo.conf
#
boot = /dev/hda
install = /boot/boot.b
prompt
timeout = 100
default = linux
password= "A4ni77a*"
```

LISTING 4.3   continued

```
restricted
#
# List of images in /etc/lilo.conf
#
other = /dev/hda1
        label = win
image = /boot/vmlinuz-2.2.16
        label  = linux
        root   = /dev/hda4
        vga    = 775
        append = "hdc=ide-scsi"
        read-only
image = /boot/vmlinuz-2.4.0-t9
        label  = linux-new
        root   = /dev/hda4
        vga    = 775
        append = "hdc=ide-scsi"
        read-only
#
# end /etc/lilo.conf
#
```

This new `/etc/lilo.conf` file will allow any image to be booted without a password
unless kernel arguments are supplied. If the user attempts to enter kernel arguments,
LILO will require that the user enter the related password before proceeding.

Putting password and restricted Together

Of course, not all situations are as simple as the one just described. Sometimes it is useful to allow some images to boot without a password (unless arguments are supplied)
while protecting other images. Listing 4.4 provides an example of this type of configuration.

LISTING 4.4   Both restricted and password Arguments

```
#
# Global section of /etc/lilo.conf
#
boot = /dev/hda
install = /boot/boot.b
prompt
timeout = 100
default = linux
password= "A4ni77a*"
```

LISTING 4.4   continued

```
#
# List of images in /etc/lilo.conf
#
other = /dev/hda1
        label = win
image = /boot/vmlinuz-2.2.16
        label  = linux
        root   = /dev/hda4
        vga    = 775
        append = "hdc=ide-scsi"
        restricted
        read-only
image = /boot/vmlinuz-2.4.0-t9
        label  = linux-new
        root   = /dev/hda4
        vga    = 775
        append = "hdc=ide-scsi"
        read-only
#
# end /etc/lilo.conf
#
```

4

The important thing to understand in this example is that all images remain password protected. However, the `linux-new` image will always require a password, while the default `linux` image will require a password only if additional arguments are supplied to the kernel. Because the first image is marked as restricted, it will boot automatically after 10 seconds (100 tenths of a second) if no additional input is given at the `LILO boot:` prompt. The default image and prompt delay are given by the `default=` and `timeout=` keywords, respectively.

This scenario allows for automatic rebooting while maintaining security by preventing unauthorized passing of kernel arguments.

The `prompt` and `timeout` Keywords

One more minor security issue needs to be addressed in a discussion of the LILO boot loader. The `prompt` and `timeout` keywords give the system administrator the ability to decide what will happen to the system in case of an unexpected power cycle. This is important because in some cases it is undesirable for an unexpectedly rebooted system to be placed immediately online once again. The system administrator may want to have the opportunity to inspect things personally before an unexpectedly rebooted system goes back online, in case the reboot was due to a break-in and parts of the system have been compromised.

On the other hand, if you run a Web server that needs to be available to users as much as possible, you may be willing to take that risk and instead want all unexpected power cycles to be followed by an automatic boot back into Linux. There are three basic methods for using or not using the prompt and timeout keywords.

- If neither prompt nor timeout is present, the system will automatically load the default image during boot, without presenting the LILO boot: prompt or waiting for input from the user.
- If prompt is present but timeout is not, then a booting system will stop at the LILO boot: prompt and will not continue until human intervention occurs.
- If both prompt and timeout are present, then a booting system will stop at the LILO boot: prompt for as many tenths of a second as are set in the timeout argument. For example, a timeout value of 3600 is 360 seconds, or six minutes. Once time has run out, if no human intervention has occurred, LILO will load the default image and boot as it normally would.

Your policy for using prompt and timeout will vary with your intended use of the machine and the degree to which you plan to be suspicious of reboots. You must use your own judgement about the situation to come to some decision.

If an unexpected reboot would be almost impossible in your case, such as if you have a solid system and a high-quality battery backup, you may want to stick to a very cautious policy regarding unexpected reboots. In situations where unexpected reboots are so unlikely, there is a much greater chance that such an event represents some kind of foul play.

Of course, any cracker who is able to compromise a system so fully that he is able to reboot it can likely also edit the /etc/lilo.conf file again and remove such protective measures. Still, it often pays to be conservative regarding security.

Saving Changes

Before changes to your /etc/lilo.conf file take effect, you must rewrite your system's boot sector. To do this, simply issue the lilo command:

```
/sbin/lilo
```

You'll see a list of labels that refer to the images configured in the lilo.conf file. Each of them will be a bootable label at the LILO boot: prompt next time you boot the system.

Permissions for `/etc/lilo.conf`

One final step you'll want to take with the `/etc/lilo.conf` file is to prevent non-root users from being able to read it, especially if you've configured a boot password for one or more images. To do this, issue the following command:

```
chmod 600 /etc/lilo.conf
```

This command sets the file's permissions so that only `root` is able to read from or write to the `/etc/lilo.conf` file. For details on file system permissions, see Hour 7, "File System Security."

The Init Program and the `/etc/inittab` File

The final aspect of the boot process proper that we're going to address this hour is the configuration file for the init process. You may remember that init is the process responsible for taking control of the system once the kernel has been started; init launches services, provides login prompts, and performs other very basic Unix-type services.

The format of the `/etc/inittab` file itself is beyond the scope of this hour, but there are two simple changes that security-minded users might want to consider to make init defaults a little less vulnerable.

Default Runlevel

The init process uses a series of abstractions known as *runlevels* to help it determine which services ought to be run on a given system at a given time. Most Linux distributions use similar runlevels for similar roles; the most common runlevel definitions are shown in Table 4.1. Note that Debian GNU/Linux uses a different set of runlevels, documented briefly in the `/etc/inittab` file.

TABLE 4.1 Common Runlevel Definitions

Runlevel	Description
0	(Procedural) System halt: When the system enters runlevel 0, all processes will be stopped.
1	Single user or maintenance: Network interfaces are started, but no services are started; only `root` is allowed to log in and only on the console. This is the runlevel entered when the word `single` is passed to the kernel as an argument at the `LILO` `boot:` prompt.
2	Multi-user, minimal: Network interfaces are started, and some local services are started to allow for user logins on the console, but most network services (for example, NFS and Web) are not started.

TABLE 4.1 continued

Runlevel	Description
3	Multiuser, full: Network interfaces and desired network services are started. User logins and user requests are allowed both locally and remotely.
4	Unused or user-specified.
5	X11: Network interfaces and desired network services are started. User logins and user requests are allowed both locally and remotely. The X Display Manager or a substitute is started and the system boots into X11R6.
6	(Procedural) Reboot: When the system enters runlevel 6, all processes will be stopped, and a cold reset will occur.

In Hour 1, "Selecting and Installing a Linux Distribution," you learned that many systems that provide only network services do not need X capability, and thus X need not be installed. However, there are some situations in which X will be installed but will rarely be needed to actually run.

In such cases, many current distributions will still set the default runlevel to 5, X11 mode, even though for the most part the X Window System will not be used on the machine. This is a bad thing; in Hour 15, "Securing X11R6 Access," you'll learn that X is actually a network stream like any other and is therefore subject to attack. Because of this, you don't want X running by default but doing nothing most of the time on a network server machine.

Thus, on machines that fit this description, you'll want to edit the /etc/inittab file using your favorite editor and change the first non-comment line in the file. Generally, it will look like this:

```
id:5:initdefault:
```

This line is telling the init program to boot the system using runlevel 5 and to start all services (including X11R6) normally associated with runlevel 5. To change this, simply delete the number 5 and replace it with number 3, referring to full multi-user support:

```
id:3:initdefault:
```

After this change has been made, your system will boot to a console login prompt rather than an X login prompt, thereby securing via closure what might otherwise be an unnecessary potential security problem. Of course, you will still be able to start X from a console using the startx command after you've logged in.

The Three-Key Smash (Ctrl+Alt+Del)

The "three-key smash" has been around in computing since the DOS days. Originally, the combination of Ctrl+Alt+Del was used as a way to perform a soft-reset of an MS-DOS machine. Linux users have preserved this tradition; most Linux distributions now configure this keystroke to reboot the machine at any console.

For a machine that must be in physical contact with the public, however, the ability to perform a soft reboot simply by hitting Ctrl+Alt+Del is an unwanted one. Since most distributions currently handle this keystroke in the /etc/inittab file, simply look for a line like this and comment it out with a hash character (#):

```
ca:12345:ctrlaltdel:/sbin/shutdown -r now
```

The specific line on your system may be slightly different, but the key is to look for a line that contains the keyword ctrlaltdel after the second colon. Once this keystroke has been commented out, users will no longer be able to perform soft reboots using a simple keystroke. Instead, root will have to log in and shut down the system or reboot it by hand.

Summary

This hour, you've learned to secure your boot process by making LILO suspicious of kernel arguments and by changing a couple of typical problem spots in the /etc/inittab file. The steps covered include

- Using the password keyword in /etc/lilo.conf to password-protect kernel images and the boot process in general.
- Using the restricted keyword in /etc/lilo.conf to allow password-protected images to boot without intervention when no additional kernel arguments are supplied.
- Editing the prompt and timeout values in /etc/lilo.conf to reflect your policy and needs with regard to unexpected reboots.
- Editing the /etc/inittab file to avoid starting X at boot on systems that do not need X running all the time.
- Editing the /etc/inittab file on systems that will be available for physical public use to remove the Ctrl+Alt+Del soft reboot keystroke.

Now that these steps have been taken, you're done with "pre-Linux" security and ready to move on to the real meat and potatoes of securing a Linux system in the hours that follow.

Q&A

Q I can't seem to edit either `/etc/lilo.conf` or `/etc/inittab`. Every time I try to do so, I get a message saying that I don't have permission.

A Now that Linux is installed and running in multi-user, you must be working as the `root` user to make changes to these files and to perform most of the other tasks we're going to cover in this book. Log out and log back in again as the `root` user, or use the `su` command to become `root`.

Q The `/sbin/lilo` command failed. What do I do now?

A Carefully check your `/etc/lilo.conf` file for syntax and spelling errors. Consult the `lilo.conf(5)` manual page if necessary. To get more diagnostic output when running the command, use the `-v` argument. If all else fails, undo the changes you've made and start over again.

Q My runlevels don't seem to match the runlevels you describe. X still starts by itself. What do I do?

A First, go back over the `/etc/inittab` file and look for comments that refer to the X Display Manager or to launching X11R6. If you can find them, use them as a guide, along with the `inittab(5)` manual page to help you make the necessary changes. Some distributions start X instead as a service in the `/etc/rc.d` or `/etc/init.d` hierarchy. We'll cover these directories in the next hour. You may also find that administration tools native to your Linux distribution give you the option of disabling the X Display Manager.

New Terms

default runlevel   The runlevel under which the system will start if no specific runlevel has been passed as an argument to the init process.

global   A kind of keyword that is supplied only once at the top of the `/etc/lilo.conf` file but that affects all images listed later in the file.

image   An entry in the `/etc/lilo.conf` file that refers to a bootable operating system. An image specification begins with either the `image=` or `other=` keyword and will contain any number of other keywords, depending on how the operating system is to be handled by LILO.

init   The program responsible for starting services once the kernel is running, from basic services such as login prompts on consoles to high-level services like X, file, and Web servers.

kernel arguments   Arguments passed to the kernel on the command line through the
`LILO boot:` prompt. These can be used to alter the default behavior of the kernel or of
init, posing a grave security risk.

LILO   The Linux Loader, a program designed to accept control of the computer system
from your system BIOS, load the Linux kernel, and pass control of the system to it.

runlevel   An abstraction that init uses to decide which services should be started each
time the machine boots.

three-key smash   Three keys (Ctrl, Alt, and Del) that, when pressed together, traditionally cause a system reboot to occur. Most Linux distributions continue to follow this tradition by default.

4

Hour 5

System and User Fundamentals

This hour, we're going to tackle three major tasks that can best be thought of as security-oriented system administration fundamentals. They aren't necessarily the most exciting things you'll learn, but they are important nonetheless and should be covered before the more service-specific information contained in later hours.

First, we're going to create or edit three important configuration files related to user security in the general sense. Then we'll streamline the daemon and server init process, learning to edit the directories responsible for starting the services in question. Finally, we'll take a look at user accounts and learn how to create accounts with an emphasis on security.

/etc/securetty, /etc/shells, and .bash_logout

There are three basic configuration files that don't really fit anywhere specific in a discussion of Linux security, so we're going to cover them now. All three of these files are really important only if you are allowing remote user shell logins via a service like Telnet, but it's a good idea to secure them just for the sake of correctness.

The /etc/securetty file lists the tty devices on which root logins can occur. These devices are listed one per line and in order to be secure should include only local consoles. A sample /etc/securetty file is shown in Listing 5.1.

LISTING 5.1   Sample /etc/securetty File

```
tty1
tty2
tty3
```

Obviously /etc/securetty is not a terribly complicated file. This particular listing will allow root logins on the first three virtual consoles on the local machine and nowhere else. It is a good idea to remove everything but one or two tty devices from this file. If you are using a 2.4 kernel with devfs support enabled, it is a good idea to remove everything but one or two vc devices from the file.

If no devices are listed (the file is empty), root access in multi-user runlevels will be available only through the su command.

The /etc/shells file and /etc/skel/.bash_logout file really work together. The problem is simple: When a user logs out of a text-mode shell, we want Linux to clear the display so that no data that may have been left on the screen by the user will be visible to other users. These two files provide the means to accomplish this.

First, /etc/skel/.bash_logout is edited. The file $HOME/.bash_logout is sourced by the bash shell each time a user logs out. Thus, any commands it contains will be executed each time a user logs out. The template from which the $HOME/.bash_logout file is created when new accounts are added is /etc/skel/.bash_logout. To this file, we add a single line:

```
/usr/bin/clear
```

This will cause the display to be cleared as the user logs out. Note that changes to /etc/skel/.bash_logout will be reflected only in the accounts of users created after the file is edited.

The /etc/shells file determines which default shells will be available to users through the chsh command. Many distributions provide a long list of available shells, but this is undesirable in a secure system; shells have been known to generate just as many security problems as other components in a system, and it's much easier to monitor and update one shell than six or seven. More to the point, only the first default, bash on Linux systems, is ever likely to be used by most users. Thus, the /etc/shells file should be changed to contain a single line:

```
/bin/bash
```

This will ensure that all users log into a similar baseline shell environment and that the default .bash_logout file will be sourced and the screen cleared at logout time.

The SysV-Style Init Process

We discussed the init process a little bit in Hour 4, "The Boot Process," but now it's time to really dig in and ensure that we understand and control what's going on during system initialization. It's going to get a bit dense for a moment, but bear with me; by the time we're done with init, you'll find it a simple service to edit.

In the /etc/inittab file, which controls the startup process for your Linux system, you'll likely find a block of entries somewhere that looks similar to the one shown in Listing 5.2.

Listing 5.2 Calls to SysV-Style Scripts

```
l0:0:wait:/etc/rc.d/rc 0
l1:1:wait:/etc/rc.d/rc 1
l2:2:wait:/etc/rc.d/rc 2
l3:3:wait:/etc/rc.d/rc 3
l4:4:wait:/etc/rc.d/rc 4
l5:5:wait:/etc/rc.d/rc 5
l6:6:wait:/etc/rc.d/rc 6
```

Notice that each of these lines is run only if the system is starting at the specific runlevel, the runlevel shown between the first two colons (:) on the line. Based on the runlevel, init then calls a central script, in this case /etc/rc.d/rc, and passes to this script the current runlevel of the system as an argument.

This central script uses the information about the current runlevel to call an entire series of scripts located in a specific directory dedicated to the current runlevel. On this particular system, the script directories in question are probably numbered /etc/rc.d/rc0.d

through /etc/rc.d/rc6.d. Other Linux distributions place these directories at /etc/
rc0.d through /etc/rc6.d or even /sbin/rc0.d through /sbin/rc6.d, but in all cases,
the functionality is the same.

Simply put, when your system is started in runlevel 3, init will run every script located in
/etc/rc.d/rc3.d (or equivalent) as a part of the startup process. These scripts are run in
alphabetical order, and each script performs a specific task. One might start the network
interfaces, while another brings up the Web server, and another might start sendmail. To
edit the system initialization process, you only need to add or remove shell scripts in a
specific runlevel directory that perform the functions you want.

> A few older Linux distributions and even one or two less popular current
> Linux distributions use a more BSD-like configuration in which one or two
> larger scripts perform all system initialization. These include, for example,
> /etc/rc.d/rc.S for single-user modes, /etc/rc.d/rc.M for multi-user modes,
> and /etc/rc.d/rc.inet for network services.
>
> Editing the init process on these types of distributions is much more difficult
> and requires that you understand shell scripting and can navigate and edit
> each script by hand. These types of init configurations aren't covered here.
>
> If you aren't fluent enough in Linux to be able to edit shell scripts by hand,
> you should probably switch to a more popular distribution that follows the
> SystemV-style script structure we're discussing in this hour—for example, Red
> Hat Linux, Debian GNU/Linux, Caldera OpenLinux/eDesktop/eServer, or SuSE
> Linux.

Because much of the functionality across runlevels is duplicated and most Linux users
want similar functionality as a part of system initialization, most or all of the scripts in a
fresh install's runlevel directories are actually symbolic links to a standard set of scripts
in a central location, usually /etc/rc.d/init.d, /etc/init.d, or /sbin/init.d. So that
the order in which these scripts are executed can be controlled, their symbolic link names
are altered slightly. For example, Listing 5.3 shows the partial output from an ls -l
command executed in /etc/rc.d/rc3.d.

LISTING 5.3 Some Script Links from /etc/rc.d/rc3.d

```
lrwxrwxrwx  1 root  root  17 May  3 22:58 S01network -> ../init.d/network
lrwxrwxrwx  1 root  root  16 May  3 22:58 S05syslog -> ../init.d/syslog
lrwxrwxrwx  1 root  root  17 May  3 22:58 S05urandom -> ../init.d/urandom
lrwxrwxrwx  1 root  root  17 May  3 22:58 S15portmap -> ../init.d/portmap
lrwxrwxrwx  1 root  root  14 May  3 22:58 S16inet -> ../init.d/inet
lrwxrwxrwx  1 root  root  18 May  3 22:58 S20netmount -> ../init.d/netmount
```

LISTING 5.3 continued

```
lrwxrwxrwx  1 root  root   20 May  3 22:58 S21nis-client -> ../init.d/nis-clien
lrwxrwxrwx  1 root  root   13 May  3 22:58 S26ipx -> ../init.d/ipx
lrwxrwxrwx  1 root  root   13 May  3 22:58 S30amd -> ../init.d/amd
lrwxrwxrwx  1 root  root   13 May  3 22:58 S30ntp -> ../init.d/ntp
lrwxrwxrwx  1 root  root   13 May  3 22:58 S35lpd -> ../init.d/lpd
```

Notice that the symbolic links have been named in a way that forces them to be executed in a specific order. Notice also that each of these links is simply a symbolic link to a universal script located in ../init.d. The names of the scripts should be familiar: S15portmap brings up the portmapper, S16inet starts the Internet daemon, S35lpd starts the print daemon, and so on. Each directory, rc0.d through rc6.d, contains a series of these symbolic links. The links appearing in any one directory depend on which services should or shouldn't be started (or killed) for the runlevel in question.

This arrangement is called a SystemV-style init configuration after the format used by the popular System V release of Unix. In Linux, it's often called simply a SysV-init configuration for short.

Finding and Disabling Unnecessary Services

If you've checked your own rcN.d directories, you've probably noticed that quite a few services seem to be started for each runlevel, especially for multi-user runlevels controlled by the rc3.d and rc5.d directories. It is very likely that you won't be needing all of them, and it is in the interest of better security that you turn off those services you won't be needing.

To turn off a service in a given runlevel, simply remove the symbolic link. For example, to disable the xfs font server in runlevel 5, remove the script associated with it from rc5.d:

```
cd /etc/rc.d/rc5.d
mkdir disabled
mv S90xfs disabled
```

Of course, the path to rcN.d should be adjusted to match the path on your system, and the name S70xfs should be adjusted to match the name of the xfs symbolic link in your own case. Be sure not to remove the original script in the init.d directory, or you'll affect the service in all runlevels, rather than just in the runlevel you intend to edit.

Some of the services we're about to see may seem fairly harmless, tempting you to leave them enabled even if you don't use them often or don't really need them. Avoid this temptation.

Even services like the auto-mount daemon, amd, which is responsible for allowing Linux to automatically access CD-ROM drives and floppy drives without manual mounting, have been the cause of complete system compromises. Though updates to problem services are generally made available quickly through distribution vendors once problems are discovered, you should view each service as a potential violation.

In short, if you don't absolutely need it, turn it off.

To determine which scripts are necessary and which are not, you need to be able to identify the service and the role of the service related to each script. Some of the most common scripts are shown in Table 5.1.

TABLE 5.1 Common Scripts in init.d

Script	Disable?	Description
alsasound	yes(1)	Starts the Advanced Linux Sound Architecture, necessary for supporting some sound cards.
amd	yes	Starts the auto-mount daemon responsible for automatically mounting floppy and CD-ROM discs, rather than forcing the user to use the mount command.
atalk	maybe	Starts services for AppleTalk networks.
atd	yes(1)	Starts the one-time user command scheduler.
cron	no	Starts the cron daemon.
fonttastic	yes(1)	Starts the fonttastic font server used by many commercial Linux applications.
gpm	yes(1)	Starts General Purpose Mouse support for console pointing device access.
httpd	maybe	Starts the httpd daemon, also known as the Web server, usually Apache on Linux systems.
inet	no	Starts the Internet daemon, responsible for handling, directing, accepting, or denying incoming network requests.
ipx	maybe	Starts IPX network services for systems operating on Novell networks.
keytable	no	Enables standard keyboard mappings.
ldap	maybe	Starts the Lightweight Directory Access Protocol for systems using directory services.
lpd	maybe	Starts the print daemon, useful for accepting print jobs from remote sources for local printers.

TABLE 5.1 continued

Script	Disable?	Description
mta	maybe	Starts the mail transfer agent, or SMTP daemon, usually sendmail on a Linux system. May also be called sendmail or qmail on some systems.
netmount	maybe	Mounts network file systems listed in /etc/fstab.
network	no	Starts system network interfaces.
nfs	maybe	Starts NFS services for systems acting as file servers to other Linux machines.
nis-client	maybe	Starts client services for systems using Yellow Pages (yp) or Network Information Services (nis) directory access.
nis-server	maybe	Starts directory services for systems providing Yellow Pages (yp) or Network Information Services (nis) directories.
ntp	no	Synchronizes system clock with the outside world.
portmap	maybe	Starts the portmapper; necessary for services that use rpc, such as NFS.
samba	maybe	Starts the SMB/NMB services for sharing files and print services with Windows network users.
syslog	no	Starts the system logger.
xdm	yes(1)	Starts the X Display Manager for X11R6 authentication.
xfs	maybe	Starts the XFree86 X Font Server for supplying fonts to other systems across the network.

Key:

yes	This service can generally be removed with few effects beyond loss of convenience.
yes(1)	This service can often be removed with little or no loss to network functionality, but at the expense of some user-level functionality. Use your own discretion. For example, you may want to disable xdm on a server system where X is rarely used.
maybe	This network-oriented service should be removed if you do not need the functionality it provides. Normally, only one or two "maybe" scripts will remain active on a single system, depending on which services the system provides.
no	This service is essential either to system functionality or to network functionality and should not be removed.

5

If you're unsure whether or not a given service can be removed, simply try the system without the service. If you don't miss it after a few days, chances are you didn't really need it in the first place. Exceptions to this rule are the logging daemons started by syslog—logs are important for security!

There are so many different Linux distributions and so many different script possibilities that it's impossible to give a good account of all of them in Table 5.1.

Because of this, you're likely going to have to use your common sense when trying to identify at least one or two of the scripts on your system. One thing that may help you is to look at the script itself using a pager:

```
more /etc/rc.d/rc3.d/S20network
```

Generally, you'll find that distribution vendors have included helpful comments and descriptions in each of the scripts that are accessible this way. These can help you to decide whether or not a given script and its related service are right for you.

Be sure to restart your system after any changes to cause the rcN.d directory to activate your new init services configuration.

Reenabling Disabled Services

If you need to reenable a previously disabled service, simply restore the symbolic link to the central script in question, taking care to place it within the order of services started. For example, to reinstate the xfs daemon for runlevel 5, you might use

```
cd /etc/rc.d/rc5.d
mv disabled/S90xfs
```

If you have to re-create a symbolic link rather than simply move it, and you're unsure about which order to start the service in, use your common sense. For example, network daemons should be started after the network itself is started but before services that depend on a daemon are started. If you don't get it right the first time, you can always slide it around until you get it right:

```
cd /etc/rc.d/rc5.d
mv S90xfs S50xfs
```

Eventually, you'll find a working configuration again.

If you would like to disable and reenable services for test purposes while the system is running, you can generally call each of the scripts in the init.d directory by hand with one of three arguments:

start   Starts the service if it isn't already running.
stop   Stops a running service.
restart   Stops a running service and then starts it again, usually to adopt new changes made to configuration files.

> For example, to shut down the samba service temporarily to see if your network can do without it, you'd use this:
>
> ```
> /etc/rc.d/init.d/samba stop
> ```
>
> If you find that you really need it, you can start it again with a command like this one:
>
> ```
> /etc/rc.d/init.d/samba start
> ```
>
> This trick will work with most Linux distributions that use a SystemV-style configuration. Note that any changes made this way are not permanent and will disappear when the system is rebooted. These types of changes are therefore for testing only.

Creating User Accounts Securely

Now that services are all up and running (or not running) as you'd like them to be, it's time to take a look at user accounts. Though many small-system administrators never give this process a second thought and simply proceed with the adduser command once Linux installation is complete, the creation of accounts must be as secure as the rest of the system if compromise is to be avoided.

In fact, before adding users, it is important to ensure that shadow passwords are active on the system. Then, because each vendor's implementation of adduser varies, and some adduser commands don't even function, security-minded administrators will add each user by hand to ensure that all information for the user account is entered correctly.

Shadow and MD5

Before taking the time to create user accounts, you should ensure that both shadow passwords and MD5 encryption are installed and running on your system. If no related package is available with your distribution, MD5 passwords may be foregone, but if your distribution doesn't support shadow passwords, you should upgrade to a newer distribution immediately. Shadow provides a way to protect your user passwords against public access; without shadow, your /etc/passwd file contains all of your user passwords, visible to the entire world—a huge security risk!

To see if shadow passwords are active on your system, check for the existence of an /etc/shadow file, which should be readable by root alone:

```
$ cat /etc/shadow
cat: /etc/shadow: Permission denied
```

If instead you find that there is no shadow file present or that the shadow file is readable by a normal (non-root) user, then shadow either is not installed or is incorrectly installed on your system.

Many older versions of shadow that shipped with Linux systems are exposed to a serious compromise risk by a buggy /bin/login binary, which can be exploited by a cracker to gain root access on your system.

If your distribution is over a year old, be sure to check your distribution vendor's Web site for security updates to the shadow package or, better yet, acquire a more recent Linux distribution.

Nearly all current distributions install shadow passwords by default, and many of them install MD5 encryption by default as well. If you can't find the /etc/shadow file, check your distribution CD or FTP site. In most cases, if your distribution medium contains a package called shadow or something similar, just installing it with rpm or dselect will be enough to install and activate shadow passwords on your system. To be sure, take a look at your /etc/passwd file. If you see anything other than an x in the second field of any user's entry, use the pwconv program to update the /etc/passwd and /etc/shadow files correctly.

Adding a User, Step 1: /usr/sbin/groupadd

The default group behavior in most Linux distributions is to place all user accounts in a single group, usually group 100, called users. Clearly, forcing all users' files to be owned by the same shared group is a risk to the integrity of each user's data. Thus, it is wiser to give each user a private group—a group to which only the user in question will belong.

To do this, choose a number for the user's group and call /usr/sbin/groupadd to create the group. In the interest of clarity, it is best to give all user accounts numbers within a certain range (for example, from 6000 to 6999) that is higher than all existing group ID numbers and is set aside exclusively for users. To find the highest group number used so far, issue this command:

```
cat /etc/group | cut -d: -f3 | sort -n
```

Once you've chosen a group number for the new user, call the groupadd binary to create the new group, supplying the user's chosen login name as the final argument:

```
/usr/sbin/groupadd -g 6001 johnB
```

Depending on how the users group is used on your system, you may also want to add the user to the list of members for the users group. To do this, simply edit the /etc/group file with vi or a similar editor and append the user's login name to the comma-separated list of users members.

Adding a User, Step 2: `/usr/sbin/useradd`

Now that a group has been created for the new user, we can create a login account for him. The default account creation behavior in most Linux distributions is also not very secure, so it is not a good idea to use high-level tools or even the `adduser` script to create accounts. Instead, we're going to use the comparatively low-level `useradd`. The `useradd` command is fairly easy to use; simply supply the `-u` (user ID number), `-g` (group name), `-d` (home directory) and `-m` (make home directory) arguments, followed by the name of the user to create.

Continuing with our example, since we created group number 6001 called `johnB`, our `useradd` command will look like this:

```
/usr/sbin/useradd -u 6101 -g johnB -d /home/johnB -m johnB
```

This will create a user called `johnB`, place him in the group called `johnB` that has a matching number, place his home directory at `/home/johnB`, create the home directory, and copy all of the template files from `/etc/skel` to it.

Adding a User, Step 3: `passwd` and `chage`

Now that you've created the user's group, account, and home directory, the user can log in. However, no password has yet been assigned to this account—an unacceptable security risk unless the user will be logging in and choosing a password immediately.

On larger systems, it may be necessary to install a random password generator, but on smaller systems it's generally enough for the system administrator to assign an interim password, which will last until the first time the user logs in:

```
passwd johnB
```

Choosing this interim password isn't enough, however. We want to be sure that `johnB` changes the password immediately to something of his own choosing. More to the point, we also want to make sure than `johnB` will change his password every so often so that the password doesn't become stale and more easily guessable. This is done with the `chage` command, which controls account "aging" on Linux systems. Possible arguments to the `chage` command are shown in Table 5.2.

TABLE 5.2 Possible Arguments to the `chage` Command

Argument	Description
`-m N`	N = The number of days the user must wait between password changes, or 0 to disable the counter.
`-M N`	N = The number of days after which the user must again change his password, or 0 to allow passwords to exist indefinitely.

TABLE 5.2 continued

Argument	Description
-d N	Indicates that the password was last changed N days after epoch (January 1, 1970). This number is normally maintained automatically.
-I N	N = The number of days of inactivity (no logins) after a password has expired before the account is locked due to neglect, or 0 to allow an account to be accessed any number of days after the password has expired.
-E MM/DD/YY	The month, day, and year on which this account will expire, or -E 0 if the account should never expire.
-W N	N = The number of days in advance to warn the user of pending password expiration.

Here's a sample command for dealing with password management:

```
chage -m 0 -M 90 -d 0 -I 0 -E 0 -W 10 johnB
```

This command forces johnB to change his password immediately upon first login. It also forces him to change his password every 90 days thereafter, giving him 10 days advance warning before a change will be required.

> It is a good idea to set all of these options explicitly when calling chage, because some older versions of Pluggable Authentication Modules (PAM), which is responsible for password management in most recent Linux distributions, don't acknowledge any of these settings unless they're all explicitly set to some value.

Once this change has been made, johnB's account is both complete and securely created, and he can log in at any time.

Summary

In this hour, we covered some security-oriented fundamentals related to normal system administration and account management, including

- Correct use of the /etc/securetty, /etc/shells, and /etc/skel/.bash_logout files for increased security.
- Editing of the SysV-style init script directories to enable or disable launching of various services during system startup.

- Correct methods for securely adding user accounts, including the creation of user-private groups and password and account expiration dates.

- The importance of shadow, md5, and PAM to modern Linux distributions as a method for maintaining the integrity of the system passwords database.

With each of these topics covered, we're now ready to tackle in-depth security configuration in the hours that follow.

Q&A

Q My system doesn't use a SysV-style init script configuration. How do I start and stop services?

A In general, the only way to enable and disable startup services on non-SysV init systems is to follow the init process logically and edit the necessary shell scripts by hand.

Q Aren't there any graphical tools to manage SysV-style init scripts?

A Yes, there are many of them for X users, plus several text-mode tools. Unfortunately, each distribution chooses to use a different tool to manage these init scripts, so in the interest of creating a distribution-independent text, we didn't discuss any of them.

Q Isn't it really a bad thing to force users to change passwords regularly?

A There is some debate on this issue. One school of thought says that a user who isn't ever forced to change his password will begin to use the same password from system to system and for years on end, clearly leaving every account he holds vulnerable.

The other school of thought says that users who change their passwords often are less likely to choose securely, since they need more help in remembering so many recent passwords.

As a system administrator for your own systems, it's up to you to decide.

5

New Terms

adduser   A vendor-supplied script that makes use of several user management commands such as useradd, groupadd, and chage to automate the process of adding new users. Some adduser scripts historically have been less than optimal.

shadow   An extension to the normal password handling capabilities of a Unix-like system that stores user passwords in the non–public-readable /etc/shadow file rather than the public-readable /etc/passwd file.

SysV-Init   A style of init script configuration that places a series of symbolic links pointing to centralized service scripts across a number of directories, one for each run-level, usually named `rc0.d` through `rc6.d` on Linux systems.

user-private group   A group created solely to hold a single user with a matching user-name and UID. This is done to prevent a situation in which all users share the same GID.

Exercises

1. Write a small `bash` script to automate the process of adding users as we've discussed it in this hour. The script should create user-private groups and expiration properties that you as an administrator can live with.

2. Using the name of each script and the comments at the top of each script as clues, try to identify each script in the `/etc/rc.d/init.d` or `/etc/init.d` directory—what service it starts and the role of that service in your system.

HOUR 6

TCP/IP Network Security

Security is the focus of every hour in this book, but if there's one chapter here that's more important than all of the others, it's this one, which concerns itself with securing the core of the Linux TCP/IP service request–handling mechanism.

TCP/IP stands for Transmission Control Protocol/Internet Protocol and is the basic network technology used by Unix-like systems and the Internet as we know it today. You may have heard the term "wide open" or "port scan" in discussions about Internet or TCP/IP security. These terms have a lot to do with the configuration of two aspects of a network-enabled Linux system: the inetd daemon responsible for handling nearly all incoming network requests and the TCP wrappers package, which enables you to accept or deny requests on a system-by-system or network-by-network basis.

Toward the end of this hour, we're also going to look at configuring the system logger to report the right kinds of events in the right ways. This will allow you as an administrator to maintain a more secure system and understand what happened if something goes wrong.

Securing `inetd`, the Internet Daemon

You probably understand already that most network services on Unix-like systems are associated with a specific daemon. For example, File Transfer Protocol sessions are managed by `in.ftpd`, Telnet or remote login requests are handled by `in.telnetd`, network file system requests are handled by `nfsd`, and so on.

But you probably also have noticed that most of these daemons don't run all the time. In fact, of all major network service daemons, only two, `httpd` and `sendmail`, routinely are run on a continuous basis. When an incoming FTP or Telnet request is received, who's responsible for starting `in.ftpd` or `in.telnetd` to handle the connection?

The answer to this question is `inetd`, a daemon whose major responsibility is to listen to a broad range of network ports and start service daemons dynamically in response to incoming requests. For smaller systems, this is a boon representing a significant amount of saved memory that would otherwise have been dedicated to keeping a large number of service daemons running all the time.

Why `inetd` Is Risky

The design of `inetd` allows many services to be multiplexed in a way through a single request broker, saving memory and resources. But on most smaller systems, the vast majority of the network services `inetd` is capable of managing are never used. Most homes and small businesses don't run a network time server, a network news (Usenet) spooler, a Unix-to-Unix copy program (UUCP) node, or even a diskless boot server.

What most Linux users don't realize is that Linux distributions traditionally have left all of these services on in the `inetd` configuration, meaning that all of these types of requests, when received across the network, will be serviced by your system. Even though many of them are password protected or employ some other minimal means of protection, any accepted network connection at all should be viewed as a potential system compromise.

Of course, we already know that this is the nature of networks. Since they are designed to accept incoming connections from at best uncertain sources, they are always risky from an absolute security standpoint. In the case of `inetd`, however, the risk should be minimized.

The `/etc/inetd.conf` File

Luckily, the configuration file for such an essential and central network daemon as `inetd` is surprisingly clear and simple. All configuration for the daemon resides in the

/etc/inetd.conf file, which is read each time the inetd daemon is launched or restarted.

In all but the most special of circumstances, all that needs to be done to secure the inetd daemon is to comment out judiciously with a hash mark (#) all incoming request types that shouldn't be managed by inetd any longer. Each line in the file is a complete rule composed of a series of whitespace-separated keywords or lists. The format is

```
service socket-type protocol flags user server args
```

The meaning of each of these fields is shown in Table 6.1.

TABLE 6.1   Fields in a Line from /etc/inetd.conf

Field	Description
service	The name of the service the line relates to. Many of these (such as ftp or telnet) will seem familiar to you, while some more esoteric services may not.
socket-type	Refers to the type of network socket involved; stream and datagram sockets are the most common. Other types are documented in inetd(8).
protocol	Specifies which type of low-level TCP/IP protocol is used in a particular connection. Most services use either tcp or udp packets, and a complete list of protocols can be found in /etc/protocols.
flags	Any subset of several available arguments, which vary depending on the socket type and protocol in use.
user	The user who will own the connection's process. This is helpful in some cases because a few services don't require full root permissions, meaning that they can be run more securely.
server	The path to the actual program to which inetd will pass control of the incoming connection request, such as in.telnetd or in.ftpd.
args	Any arguments that should be passed to the server program.

6

While all this may look very daunting and is certainly covered in greater detail in any book on the TCP/IP protocol suite, our interest this hour is only in the first field of each line—the name of the service in question.

Simply put, your job is to move through the /etc/inetd.conf file one line at a time, commenting out any services that you don't recognize as being services you intend for your system to provide. For example, take a look at the /etc/inetd.conf snippet in Listing 6.1.

LISTING 6.1   Snippet from Pristine `/etc/inetd.conf`

```
ftp    stream tcp nowait root        /usr/sbin/tcpd in.ftpd -l -a
telnet stream tcp nowait root        /usr/sbin/tcpd in.telnetd
shell  stream tcp nowait root        /usr/sbin/tcpd in.rshd
talk   dgram  udp wait   nobody.tty /usr/sbin/tcpd  in.talkd
```

This section of the `/etc/inetd.conf` file is concerned with four common services. Let's assume, for the moment, that you intend to provide only one of them on your system: File Transfer Protocol. Are any of the others needed? The `telnet` service is for incoming login requests via Telnet, which you don't want to allow. The `shell` service allows remote systems to execute shell commands on your system—certainly not something you intend to make available to the outside world. The `talk` service handles incoming requests for user-to-user chat via the ancient instant messenger–like BSD `talk` program—also not needed.

Clearly, you can comment out the three services you don't want from this section of the file without suffering any loss in terms of functionality. The updated snippet is shown in Listing 6.2.

LISTING 6.2   Updated `/etc/inetd.conf` Snippet

```
ftp     stream tcp nowait root        /usr/sbin/tcpd in.ftpd -l -a
#telnet stream tcp nowait root        /usr/sbin/tcpd in.telnetd
#shell  stream tcp nowait root        /usr/sbin/tcpd in.rshd
#talk   dgram  udp wait   nobody.tty /usr/sbin/tcpd  in.talkd
```

Of course, the entire `/etc/inetd.conf` file on an average Linux system is much longer than this. In fact, many software packages for Linux will add their own services to `/etc/inetd.conf`. For example, if you choose to run an electronic bulletin board system or discussion room, you may find that these types of software packages have added several lines to the file.

> Some services may have more than one line in the `/etc/inetd.conf` file, each with a different socket or protocol configuration. In such cases, to disable a service, simply comment out every line that bears its name.

Even though the length of the `/etc/inetd.conf` file and the variety of services it manages may make it seem daunting and important, there is a little secret among system administrators: Commenting out a service should be the rule rather than the exception. In nearly all cases, you can comment out every service in the file other than those that you explicitly plan to provide—including those marked as "internal"—without any noticeable loss of functionality. Doing so is more than just helpful. In today's Internet-centric world full of script kiddies, it's essential.

> Instead of rebooting Linux each time you change `/etc/inetd.conf`, try issuing the following command to cause just the `inetd` server to restart itself:
>
> `killall -HUP inetd`
>
> Issuing this command as `root` normally will cause any changes you've made to `/etc/inetd.conf` to take effect immediately.

Just remember that, when it comes to `/etc/inetd.conf`, the rule is this: If in doubt, comment it out. After all, if you want to re-enable a service later, it's a simple matter of removing a hash mark.

The `/etc/services` File

You may have been wondering just where the service names in the `/etc/inetd.conf` file come from. They're contained in the `/etc/services` file, which associates a human-readable name with a port. It is the port that is really important to Linux when it comes to handling service requests but, of course, humans don't like to remember long lists of numbers.

In most cases, feel free to leave the `/etc/services` file alone. It isn't important for TCP/IP security in the same way that the `/etc/inetd.conf` file is, but there is one way in which it can be helpful.

Any TCP/IP-enabled Unix-like system can respond to incoming connections on a large array of network ports. These ports can be thought of as a sort of switchboard for connection requests. The request will be routed to a specific daemon such as `in.ftpd` or `httpd` according to which daemon is listening to the port in question or which daemon has been assigned that port by the `inetd` server. Each common TCP/IP service has been assigned a default port by the Internet Corporation for Assigned Names and Numbers (ICANN). For example, Web service (HTTP) normally resides on port 80, and File Transfer Protocol normally answers on port 21.

Though it won't challenge a knowledgeable cracker at all, some reduction in the number of unwanted connection attempts to a specific service can at times be achieved by altering the port on which the service in question is listening for requests. Once you've

6

changed the port on which a service is listening, any user attempting to connect must supply both a port number and a hostname in order to connect. For example, if you alter Telnet services on my-system.net to listen on port 2401 instead of port 23, anyone connecting via Telnet will have to use a command such as this:

```
telnet my-system.net 2401
```

If the remote user fails to specify the new port on the command line, he will see something like this:

```
$ telnet my-system.net
Trying my-system.net...
telnet: Unable to connect to remote host: Connection refused
```

It would thus appear to the casual observer that your system doesn't accept Telnet connections at all. To change the port on which a service will listen, simply edit the port number(s) in the second field of the service(s) you want to move and restart the inetd daemon, using the technique described earlier. For example, compare the file snippets in Listings 6.3 and 6.4 and note the change in the port numbers for the FTP service.

LISTING 6.3   /etc/services, Original Ports

```
chargen     19/tcp      ttytst source
chargen     19/udp      ttytst source
ftp-data    20/tcp
ftp         21/tcp
ssh         22/tcp
ssh         22/udp
telnet      23/tcp
```

LISTING 6.4   /etc/services, Modified Ports

```
chargen     19/tcp      ttytst source
chargen     19/udp      ttytst source
ftp-data    20/tcp
ftp         9124/tcp
ssh         22/tcp
ssh         22/udp
telnet      23/tcp
```

Now, though the FTP data connection is still on its original port, the incoming FTP request connection is on port 9124 rather than the default port, meaning that users will need to know which port to connect to in order to FTP to your system. This kind of weak security-oriented measure is commonly known as security by obscurity.

Most of the lower ports below 500 are either reserved by ICANN or are in common use, so when deciding on your own ports, it's best to pick a large number—usually somewhere in the thousands. You may want to avoid ports 6699, 7777, 8888, and other repeating-number ports, which are now commonly in use by Napster, as well as port 6346, the default for Gnutella.

Though modifying /etc/services may seem like a good idea, there are a couple of caveats.

First, the list of ports contained in /etc/services is guaranteed only to affect those services managed by the inetd daemon. Services that usually are started on a standalone basis by the rcN.d scripts discussed in Hour 5, "System and User Fundamentals," may not obey the port hints specified in /etc/services.

Next and more importantly, remember that altering the ports in the /etc/services file leads only the casual observer to think that a given service isn't available. Crackers will use a piece of software called a port scanner to get a list of every active port in your system before trying to break in, so changing default ports won't help under those circumstances. In the end, the inconvenience of having to remember at which alternate ports your services lie may outweigh any security-oriented benefit.

You'll have to use your own discretion and judgement with regard to your specific circumstances for modification of the /etc/services file.

Using TCP Wrappers Properly

You may have noticed in Listing 6.1 that server programs listed in the last field of each line in /etc/inetd.conf aren't actually what you might have expected. For example, in the case of the FTP service, rather than just listing the path to a binary such as /usr/sbin/in.ftpd, the file actually contains the path to another binary, /usr/sbin/tcpd, which is then followed by the correct server program. If you examine your own /etc/inetd.conf file, you should find that this is the case with the majority of external services.

6

If you don't find any references to /usr/sbin/tcpd in your /etc/inetd.conf file, and the /usr/sbin/tcpd binary isn't present on your system, your system is not protected by TCP wrappers.

Check your distribution media's package list immediately and install TCP wrappers now. If no such package is available for your distribution, upgrade now!

TCP Wrappers Explained

The /usr/sbin/tcpd binary is the core of a security measure called *TCP wrappers*, included and installed by default with every Linux distribution for a number of years. TCP wrappers provide an absolutely essential extra layer of security for the services managed by inetd.

When TCP wrappers are installed, instead of simply calling the in.telnet daemon for an incoming Telnet connection, inetd instead will call /usr/sbin/tcpd, supplying the correct server, in.telnet, as an argument. The /usr/sbin/tcpd program checks the identity of the requesting system against a list of rules that specify who is allowed to connect and who isn't. If the requesting system is in /usr/sbin/tcpd's list of denied systems for this type of service, the connection will be refused.

In short, TCP wrappers provide a way for you to disallow incoming connections from specific systems before the requester even gets the chance to enter a login or password. In the most basic sense, this prevents a ham-handed cracker on an unknown system somewhere from connecting over and over and over again until he is able to guess a working login/password combination.

TCP wrappers also help to mitigate a more serious threat, however: security bugs or flaws. As the Internet and Internet services evolve, new bugs always are being found in the daemons that provide these services. Some of these bugs are harmless, but many of them are security flaws. For example, many older daemons were subject to various kinds of buffer overruns. In the simplest sense, a buffer overrun is a way of breaking into a system that is willing to present a login prompt regardless of whether a valid login/password combination can be discovered or not.

Clearly, any security measure that will allow you as the administrator to accept or deny a connection according to the remote system's identity before any real interaction or authentication can take place is a helpful and important measure.

Healthy Paranoia (The /etc/hosts.deny File)

The first of the two configuration files that govern the behavior of /usr/sbin/tcpd is the /etc/hosts.deny file. This file gives a list of rules that specify which remote systems should be denied requests to various services. It is best to think of this file as the general rule for incoming connections.

The TCP wrappers software is actually quite complex and flexible; the full specification of the format for /etc/hosts.deny can be found in hosts.deny(5) but, for our purposes, the basic format of a line in the file can be described this way:

```
service : host(s) [ : action ]
```

The `service` is any one of the program names that might be passed from `inetd` in response to an incoming connection request. The `host(s)` are those hostnames or IP numbers to which this rule applies. An optional `action` can be supplied and will be executed by the shell when this rule is triggered.

A number of special words and wildcards are available to make formatting of the configuration file more convenient. These wildcards are shown, along with their meanings, in Table 6.2.

TABLE 6.2   Some TCP Wrappers Special Words

Word	Description
ALL	Wildcard; matches any hostname or service name.
KNOWN	Wildcard; matches any user with a known name or any host for which both name and address are known.
LOCAL	Wildcard; matches any hostname that does not contain a dot character.
PARANOID	Wildcard; matches any host whose name does not appear to match its address.
UNKNOWN	Wildcard; matches any connecting host whose identity can't be determined.
EXCEPT	Operator; allows administrator to use a phrase like ALL EXCEPT N.N.N.N when configuring hosts or ALL EXCEPT in.ftpd when configuring services.

With these keywords, we're now ready to assemble a general "deny" policy for incoming connections. On a local area network that wants to provide services only to other machines on the local network (and never to machines from the Internet), the following single line is all that is needed in the `/etc/hosts.deny` file:

```
ALL : ALL
```

This is indeed a paranoid setting. This means that all connection requests from all hosts anywhere will be denied. This is a very safe `/etc/hosts.deny` file. Of course, we did want to allow machines from the local network to access services, and we may also want to allow for things like anonymous FTP from the outside world, so we need to create a few exceptions. Though we could mangle the `/etc/hosts.deny` file with multiple rules and the `EXCEPT` operator, another file has been created just for the purpose of making exceptions to the rules defined in `/etc/hosts.deny`.

Sparing Exceptions (The `/etc/hosts.allow` File)

The `/etc/hosts.allow` file follows the same format used in the `/etc/hosts.deny` file, but its purpose is the inverse. Any incoming connection requests that match a rule in

`/etc/hosts.allow` will be allowed, superceding any matching rules in `/etc/hosts.deny`.

One important exception we want to create is for machines on the local network. Assuming that your local network is built using the `192.168.1` subnet (so that all machines in your network have an address like `192.168.1.N`), you would add the following rule to your `/etc/hosts.allow` file to allow any host on the local network to connect to any service currently managed by `inetd`:

```
ALL : 192.168.1.
```

This line will match any system whose reported IP number is in the `192.168.1` subnet. Now, suppose you also wanted to grant this kind of general-purpose access to a single trusted system on the Internet known as `berts-bar.outdoorbars.net`. You could amend the line to read:

```
ALL : 192.168.1. berts-bar.outdoorbars.net
```

Now, suppose you also need to grant connection requests for FTP because you're running an anonymous FTP server, and you also want to accept all incoming talk requests because you enjoy chatting with whoever happens to dial you up. In that case, you would add the following:

```
in.talkd in.ftpd : ALL
```

Now your system is willing to accept incoming connections for `in.talkd` and `in.ftpd` from anyone. However, you're still a little wary. Specifically, you're not sure you want to grant access to anyone whose host identity can't be determined. You would amend the line to read:

```
in.talkd in.ftpd : ALL EXCEPT UNKNOWN
```

Finally, suppose you remember that you sometimes find yourself using a system on a separate network whose hostname is `wks9.xyz.com`, and that you do at times need to Telnet from that machine to this one. You add one final line to `/etc/hosts.allow` to allow for this connection as well:

```
in.telnetd : wks9.xyz.com
```

Now you've constructed your set of exceptions to the blanket deny rule. The complete file with your comments is shown in Listing 6.5.

LISTING 6.5 The Sample `/etc/hosts.allow` File

```
# Allow all local connections and connections from Bert
ALL : 192.168.1. berts-bar.outdoorbars.net
```

Listing 6.5 continued

```
# Allow talk and ftp from any identifiable source
in.talkd in.ftpd : ALL EXCEPT UNKNOWN

# Allow telnet from one specific host
in.telnetd : wks9.xyz.com
```

With your paranoid /etc/hosts.deny in place and your small list of exceptions, your inetd daemon and all services it manages are much better protected than they were before.

More TCP Wrappers Tricks

There is one more important trick that can be performed with TCP wrappers: the optional execution of a shell command when a rule is triggered. Though the possibilities are limitless, we're going to make only one simple change to the /etc/hosts.deny file to aid in maintaining a secure system.

Recall that the /etc/hosts.deny file we constructed was very simple and contained only the following line:

```
ALL : ALL
```

Wouldn't it be nice to add a shell command to this rule that caused a log entry to be made each time the rule was triggered? That way, we could see in the log when unauthorized connection attempts were made. The amended line is a little more complex and looks like this:

```
ALL : ALL : ( /bin/echo \
"$(/bin/date +'%%b %%d %%H:%%M:%%S') %H TCPW: %d \
>> /var/log/secure )
```

The shell command has been spread across multiple lines using the backslash (\) escape and then enclosed in parentheses to ensure a clean subshell. The net effect of the line is to cause an entry like this one to echo to the /var/log/secure file when the rule is triggered:

```
Oct 25 00:14:23 myhost TCPW: in.telnetd
```

This log entry would indicate that on October 25 at nearly a quarter past midnight, someone attempted to connect via Telnet and the connection was denied.

You may have noticed that the format given to the date command in this example is slightly off. Specifically, each format string in date is marked by two percent symbols (%%) rather than just a single percent symbol (%). This is done intentionally; /usr/sbin/ tcpd contains a number of format strings of its own (such as %H for server hostname and

6

%d for daemon name), but we wanted these strings passed on to the shell, so we escaped each percent symbol that should remain with an additional percent symbol.

 Some TCP wrappers installations are compiled with an optional flag that alters shell command behavior slightly. If you find that the example above doesn't work for you, you may need to insert the word spawn after the semicolon and before the left parenthesis to indicate that a shell should be spawned.

For complete details on executing shell commands from /etc/hosts.deny and /etc/ hosts.allow and for a list of format strings supported in these shell commands, please see hosts.deny(5) or hosts.allow(5).

Using `tcpdchk` and `tcpdmatch`

If this all seems a little confusing and you'd like a quick and easy way to test your /etc/hosts.allow and /etc/hosts.deny configurations, you're in luck. Two utilities are included to aid in the construction of working rule files.

The tcpdchk file simply reads both of your rule files and ensures that there are no problems with them. Possible problems include both incorrect syntax and inconsistencies between /etc/hosts.allow, /etc/hosts.deny and other files like /etc/inetd.conf. To run the checker, simply enter the following:

```
tcpdchk
```

If there is no output, your files are correctly formatted, and tcpdchk was unable to find any obvious problems or warnings. If there were problems or warnings, you will get a clear, concise, but brief list of them, which should help you to correctly format and configure the two files.

The tcpdmatch utility is used once tcpdchk has verified your syntax to see if your rules actually do what you intended for them to do. The syntax is simple:

```
tcpdmatch daemon host
```

For example, to see what would happen if the host at 192.168.1.59 were to make a Telnet request to the system, you'd use

```
tcpdmatch in.telnetd 192.168.1.59
```

In each case, tcpdmatch will give you a list of each triggered rule, in the order in which it was encountered. You'll also be informed if any shell command was executed. Be sure to test a reasonable number of sample cases using `tcpdmatch`, especially if your `/etc/hosts.deny` or `/etc/hosts.allow` file begins to get complex or lengthy.

Logs, `syslogd`, and Security

The `syslogd` daemon is your historian on a Linux system. Each time a program or service wants to make a log entry, it connects to `syslogd` and supplies details about what type of log entry is being made, as well as the log entry itself. When an attack has been attempted or (even worse) successful, it is only by studying your logs that you will be able to understand what has happened, who did it, and how you can fix the problem.

At this point, we're not terribly concerned with all the inner workings of `syslogd` or the ways in which it allows you to log things. We simply need to be sure that enough information is being logged for us to have something to look at later on.

Log Everything

The behavior of the system logger is controlled by the `/etc/syslog.conf` file, which contains a set of rules that will direct different types of log entries to different files in the system. Our concern here is to ensure that everything is being logged somewhere and that authorization- or emergency-related log entries are also being logged somewhere special.

To ensure that everything is logged to the `/var/log/messages` file, find the line that refers to the file and edit it to look like this:

```
*.*         -/var/log/messages
```

If you're uncomfortable modifying the set of messages that will be sent to `/var/log/messages`, you can create a new entry at the end of the file:

```
*.*         -/var/log/everything
```

The dash (-) in front of the pathname for each log file instructs `syslogd` not to call `sync` after each entry to this specific log. Create a separate log for convenience that holds only authorization and emergency information. This is convenient later when you only want to see log entries that might be directly security related:

```
auth.*;authpriv.*;*.emerg     /var/log/secure
```

You will now have at least one "everything" log and one authorization log. Most Linux distributions now install and run (via `cron`) automatic log-rotating software to keep system logs from eating too much space. If you find that this is not the case on your system, visit a Linux software site such as `freshmeat.net` and download and install a log rotater of your own.

6

Log Elsewhere

If you're on a local area network, it is ideal that you maintain logs across systems as well. For example, if you have two hosts—pokey (a desktop machine) and webftp (the server)—consider duplicating webftp's log entries on pokey. To continue our example, you might also choose to add the following two lines to your /etc/syslog.conf file:

```
*.*                        @pokey
auth.*;authpriv.*;*.emerg  @pokey
```

This way, you'll have duplicate logs, and if webftp gets compromised and its logs are erased, you can still inspect them on pokey and try to find out what happened.

Of course, you'll have to instruct pokey to accept log entries from webftp. To do this, you'll have to edit the init.d/syslog script on pokey so that it calls syslogd with the -r option, thereby instructing it to accept messages from other systems.

Summary

In this chapter, you learned about the two pillars of TCP/IP security: the inetd daemon and the TCP Wrappers package, at the core of which lies /usr/sbin/tcpd.

First, you learned to configure the inetd daemon with security in mind by editing /etc/inetd.conf and /etc/services and changing them to suit your needs. In the case of /etc/inetd.conf, a few hash marks (#) to comment out services out is enough to make things secure. In the case of /etc/services, you learned how to move services from port to port, should you choose to do so.

Then you learned that the TCP wrappers program /usr/sbin/tcpd allows you as a system administrator to decide who gets to connect and who doesn't, simply on the basis of host identity. You then learned to construct a paranoid /etc/hosts.deny file with a few exceptions listed in /etc/hosts.allow for systems that should have permission to use various services.

Finally, after learning about inetd and TCP wrappers, you made some simple changes to your /etc/syslog.conf file to ensure that you have good logs at all times, preferably on several different systems.

Q&A

Q **There are many services that I can't identify in /etc/inetd.conf and /etc/services. Couldn't you have presented a table with a description of each one?**

A Unfortunately, not really. Though a small set of services are common across all TCP/IP-enabled systems, there are many, many services that can appear in `/etc/inetd.conf` and `/etc/services`, having been added and being used by various applications. It is folly to try to track down and document them all. Instead, simply know in certain terms what you want to offer to the outside world and offer only that.

Q **I changed my File Transfer Protocol server's port from 21 to something else, and now I can't connect to the system with `ncftp`, even when I specify the correct port.**

A Some early or beta versions of `ncftp` version 3 that shipped with Linux distributions always tried to connect to the default port, whether or not another port was specified explicitly. Either use the traditional `ftp` client or upgrade to a newer version of `ncftp`.

Q **The "paranoid" policy for `/etc/hosts.deny` seems just that—paranoid. Isn't it unnecessarily strict?**

A In a word, no. You should always know exactly who should and who shouldn't be able to connect to your system for each service you offer. If a given service should be offered to everybody, it's easy enough to add one line for that service with an `ALL` wildcard to `/etc/hosts.allow`. Note that there may be some compile-time differences related to the `PARANOID` word in the `hosts.allow` and `hosts.deny` files on various distributions. See the `hosts_access(5)` manual page for details.

New Terms

`inetd`   The Internet daemon. This daemon is responsible for managing most of the incoming network requests on a Linux system and for starting the specific individual servers to handle such requests.

paranoia   The cardinal virtue in the world of network security. A basic philosophy of paranoia means that you deny first and make exceptional allowances on a case-by-case basis rather than allowing first and making exceptional refusals on a case-by-case basis.

security by obscurity   A weak type of security that tries to employ the ignorance and incompetence of a would-be attacker in your defense. It is never very useful as a primary means of security, but it can be helpful in a holistic, "every-little-bit-counts" approach.

`syslogd`   The system logger. This daemon is responsible for accepting log entries from various types of Linux software or services and routing these log entries to various files, as specified in the `/etc/syslog.conf` file.

6

TCP wrappers   In essence, the /usr/bin/tcpd binary and related configuration files. This small and efficient piece of software allows all incoming requests for all services managed by inetd to be connected or denied connection based on connecting host identification and the requested service type.

TCP/IP   Transmission Control Protocol/Internet Protocol, the basic network technology used by Unix-like systems and by the Internet at large.

Exercises

1. Try temporarily editing /etc/inetd.conf and /etc/services to accept Telnet requests both on the default port and on port 5001, just to get a feel for the way in which the two files interact.

2. Construct a good, paranoid /etc/hosts.deny file and a functional set of exceptions to go in /etc/hosts.allow that suit your circumstances. Test your new configuration thoroughly with tcpdcheck and tcpdmatch and then test it again by trying to trigger the rules from a remote system.

Hour 7

File System Security

This hour, we're going to learn to use the security-oriented features of the Linux file system. In terms of its user interface, the Linux file system can be described as Unix-like. It is a permissions-based file system, meaning that access to various system resources is determined by ownership and access rights explicitly granted by the system administrator. This file system security model can generally be made to work very well. However, it can't work for you if you don't understand how it functions and take steps to employ it properly.

Understanding Permissions

The Linux file system security model works by assigning two sets of properties to each file in the system. These properties are stored automatically on the disk, along with the file to which they apply. Since most devices in the system are also referenced by a file (known as a *device node*), this security model applies to many raw devices as well. The two sets of properties given to each file or each device are known as *ownership* and *access rights*.

File Ownership

Each file must be owned by exactly one user and exactly one group. To see evidence of this, use the `ls -l` command to get a directory listing. A sample directory listing is shown in Listing 7.1.

LISTING 7.1   Sample Output of the `ls -l` Command

```
total 1531
drwxr-xr--   2 root     root          1024 Nov  8 14:04 junk
-rw-r--r--   1 lenny    users        29065 Nov  1 15:52 fiona.jpg
-rw-rw-r--   1 jeff     jeff       1560558 Jul 25 23:09 lpg28539.pdf
-rwxr-xr-x   1 root     uucp            32 Nov  8 13:31 temp-script
```

In this listing, there are three files: `fiona.jpg`, `lpg28539.pdf`, and `temp-file`. Their ownership can be described as follows:

- The directory `junk` is owned by the superuser, `root`, and belongs to the superuser group `root` as well.
- The file `fiona.jpg` is owned by the user called `lenny` and by the group called `users`.
- The file `lpg28539.pdf` is owned by the user called `jeff`, who also has his own user-private group, which owns the file, called `jeff`.
- The file `temp-script` is owned by the superuser, `root`, and belongs to the group called `uucp`.

Any user listed in the `/etc/passwd` file can be the owner of a file, also known as the file's user. Similarly, any group listed in the `/etc/group` file can be the group owner of a file, also known simply as the file's group. What exactly does user and group ownership mean for security?

Access Rights

Take another look at Listing 7.1. You may notice that each file's directory entry begins with a series of symbols that looks something like this:

`-rw-r--r--`

This block of symbols describes the access rights specification for the file in general, more commonly known as the file's *permissions*. These access rights or permissions give Linux instructions for handling all user requests to access the file, given the context of its user and group ownerships. There are 10 permission properties, and thus a permissions list is always 10 characters long. It is formatted according to the following rules:

- The first character position in the list indicates a special file type.
- Positions 2–4 give permissions for the file's user.
- Positions 5–7 give permissions for the file's group.
- Positions 8–10 give permissions for everyone else—any user who neither is the user of the file nor belongs to the group that owns the file.

A number of different characters can occur in the first position:

- A d indicates that the file is a directory.
- A b indicates that the file is a system device that uses block input/output to talk to the outside world (usually a disk).
- A c indicates that the file is a system device that uses sequential character input/output to talk to the outside world (examples include serial ports and sound devices).
- A dash character (-) in the first position indicates that the file is a normal file without special properties.

Positions 2–4, 5–7, and 8–10 each apply to the user, the group, and everyone, respectively:

- **Read access:** The first character in each range (characters 2, 5, and 8) controls read access to the file. The presence of an r indicates that the user, members of the group, or everyone is allowed to read data from this file. The presence of a dash instead of an r indicates that read attempts will be denied for the role in question.

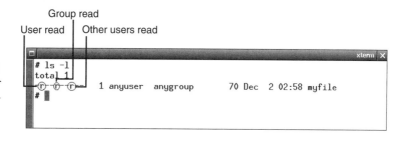

FIGURE 7.1

Characters 2, 5, and 8 control read access for user, group, and everyone, respectively.

- **Write access:** The second character in each range (characters 3, 6, and 9) controls write access to the file. A w indicates that the user, members of the group, or everyone is allowed to write data to this file. The presence of a dash instead of a w indicates that write attempts will be denied for the role in question.

7

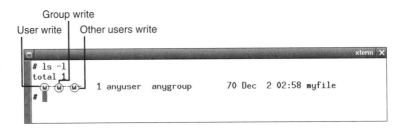

Figure 7.2

*Characters 3, 6, and 9
control write access
for user, group, and
everyone, respectively.*

- **Execute access:** The third character in each range (characters 4, 7, and 10) controls execute access to the file. An x indicates that the user, members of the group, or everyone is allowed to execute this file if it is a program or a shell script. The presence of a dash instead of an x indicates that execute attempts will fail for the role in question.

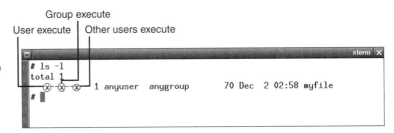

Figure 7.3

*Characters 4, 7, and 10
control execute access
for user, group, and
everyone, respectively.*

In order for a script to be executed, a user or group member must have both read and execute permission for it. The same does not hold true for binary executables, for which no read access is required in order for execution to take place.

When the file in question is a directory rather than a normal file, a few special details apply to read, write, and execute permissions:

- **Read access:** The presence of an r in position 2, 5, or 8 indicates that the user, members of the group, or everybody, respectively, will be allowed to list the contents of this directory. The presence of a dash instead of an r indicates that directory list attempts will fail.

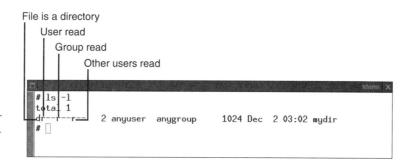

FIGURE 7.4

Characters 2, 5, and 8 control read access for user, group, and everyone, respectively.

- **Write access:** The presence of a w in position 3, 6, or 9 indicates that the user, members of the group, or everybody, respectively, will be allowed to create or delete files stored in this directory. The presence of a dash instead of a w indicates that file create or delete attempts in this directory will fail.

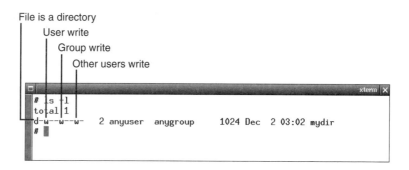

FIGURE 7.5

Characters 3, 6, and 9 control write access for user, group, and everyone, respectively.

- **Execute access:** The presence of an x in position 4, 7, or 10 indicates that the user, members of the group, or everybody will be allowed to execute files in this directory and to make this directory their current working directory—for example, using the cd command. The presence of a dash instead of an x indicates that attempts to execute files in this directory or to make this directory the current working directory will fail.

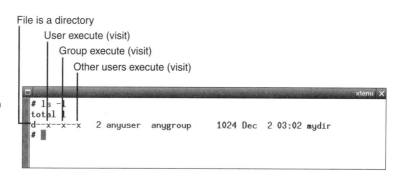

FIGURE 7.6

Characters 4, 7, and 10 control execute access for user, group, and everyone, respectively.

7

Only a file or directory's user can change its access permissions, even if the file is
writable by everyone or the directory in which the file resides is writable by everyone.
Of course, the superuser, root, is the exception here: root can set permissions for any
file or directory in the system, regardless of ownership or existing permissions.

Permission Examples

While these rules are often confusing at first, in practice they are actually quite simple to
understand. The best way to learn about them is to study examples. Let's step through
the entries in Listing 7.1 again, one by one.

```
drwxrwxr--   2 root      root       1024 Nov  8 14:04 junk
```

Because the character in the first position for junk is a d, we know that junk is a directory. The permissions in positions 2–4 are rwx, meaning that the user root will have permission to list all of the files in junk, to create new files or delete existing files in junk,
or to make junk his current working directory.

The permissions in positions 5–7 are also rwx, meaning that members of the group root
will have identical access concerning the directory called junk—to list the directory, create new files or delete old ones, and to make junk their current working directory.

The permissions in positions 8–10, however are only r--, meaning that users who are
not root and do not belong to the group root will have permission only to list the
directory. These users will not have the ability to create or delete files in junk, to run
executable programs in junk, or to make junk their current working directory.

Let's look at another entry or two from Listing 7.1:

```
-rw-r--r--   1 lenny     users      29065 Nov  1 15:52 fiona.jpg
```

In this case, the first position is a dash (-), meaning that the file fiona.jpg is a normal
file without special properties. The file is readable by everyone: the user lenny, members
of the group users, and (because there is an r in position 8) by anyone in general. The
file is writable only by the user lenny. The file is owned by the group users, but because
there is no w in position 6, members of users will not be able to write to fiona.jpg.
Finally, fiona.jpg is not executable by anyone at all.

One last test case from Listing 7.1:

```
-rwxr-xr-x   1 root      uucp       32 Nov  8 13:31 temp-script
```

The file temp-script is also a regular file. It is readable, writable, and executable by
the user, root. Members of the group that owns the file, uucp, can read the file and
execute it, but they cannot write to it. All other users can also read from and execute
temp-script but cannot write to it.

> Permissions are checked from left to right when a user attempts to access a file. For example, assume that the file `fiona.jpg` in the example above actually had the following permissions:
>
> `-r--rw-r--`
>
> Even if `lenny` is a member of the group `users`, he will not be able to write to the file, since he is denied write permission in the leftmost match.

Modifying Permissions

The user of a given file or directory can change the permissions of the file using the `chmod` command. There are two modes in which `chmod` can function: a symbolic mode, which uses characters to modify a file's permissions, and a numeric mode, which uses a series of three numbers to modify a file's permissions.

Using `chmod` in Symbolic Mode

Each invocation of `chmod` in symbolic mode can be used to either add (enable) or remove (disable) permissions with respect to one or several files. When the plus (+) or minus (-) mode is used in symbolic mode, permission modifications are made while leaving existing, unreferenced settings intact. When the equals (=) mode is used, permissions are set explicitly to the set of permissions specified. The syntax is one of the following:

```
chmod [ugoa]+[rwx] file [file...] (add permissions)
chmod [ugoa]-[rwx] file [file...] (remove permissions)
chmod [ugoa]=[rwx] file [file...] (set permissions)
```

u represents a permissions change for the user, g for members of the file's group, o for other users (neither user nor group member), and a for everyone (user, members of the group, and other users). To illustrate how `chmod` works, we'll go over a few examples.

```
chmod ug+x file1.txt file2.txt
```

In this case, both `file1.txt` and `file2.txt` gain execute permission for the user and members of the file's group.

```
chmod o-rw privatefile.doc
```

Here, other users (neither user nor group owner) lose both read and write permissions for `privatefile.doc`.

```
chmod ug=rwx,o=rw publicfile.wpd
```

7

In this example, `publicfile.wpd` will now be readable, writable, and executable by the user and members of the related group. Other users will be allowed to read from the file and write to the file but not to execute the file as if it were a program.

Using `chmod` in Numeric Mode

In numeric mode, `chmod` uses a series of single-digit numerals to determine permissions for a file explicitly. The syntax for using `chmod` in numeric mode is as follows:

```
chmod NNN file [file...]
```

The first N represents permissions for the user, the second for members of the file's group, and the third for all other users. The digit is either a zero (0) or a single-digit sum of the values related to the permissions assigned. These values are shown in Table 7.1.

TABLE 7.1   Values for `chmod` Numeric Mode Permissions

4	Indicates that read permission should be present for the file or directory.
2	Indicates that write permission should be present for the file or directory.
1	Indicates that execute permission should be present for the file or directory.

When you are using `chmod`'s numeric mode, each of the three numeric digits must be a digit, 0–7, constructed as a sum of the permissions the user wants to grant to this file. Let's look at some more examples.

```
chmod 710 script*.sh
```

In this case, any file matching the shell pattern `script*.sh` will be given the following permissions: read, write, and execute for the user; execute only for members of the related group; no permissions (no read, write, or execute) for other users who neither are the user nor belong to the related group.

```
chmod 664 file.txt
```

Here, the file `file.txt` has been given read and write permissions for the user, read and write permissions for members of the related group, and read permission for everyone else in the system.

The most public permissions specification (read, write, and execute for everyone) when given via `chmod`'s numeric mode looks like this:

```
chmod 777 myfile
```

By contrast, the most closed permissions specification (no read, no write, and no execute for anyone at all) is given by

```
chmod 000 myfile
```

System administrators tend to be more fond of the numeric mode of chmod because it is quicker and more obviously related to the format of umask (which we're going to discuss in the next section), while users tend to prefer chmod's symbolic mode because it more closely resembles the output of the ls -l command.

Using umask to Set Default Permissions

Clearly, the permissions given to various files throughout the system have a great effect on the security of data owned by any given user. However, it would be annoying (and nearly impossible) to set permissions explicitly on every file in a system, one by one, and then to maintain such discipline for new files as each file is created. Distribution vendors and package maintainers have already taken great pains in most cases to set correct permissions for various system files when they are installed to secure defaults. Therefore, it generally isn't necessary to step through all files on a Linux system one by one, setting permissions by hand.

Luckily, it is also possible to create a default setting for new file creation within scripts or user accounts. This is done via the umask shell command. To see your current umask value, enter this command without arguments:

```
# umask
137
#
```

This output indicates that the current default umask value for this user's shell environment is 137. As was the case with chmod's numeric mode, this value is a series of three numbers that represent user permissions, group member permissions, and other user permissions.

Notice, however, that these values do not seem to make sense in that context. A chmod value of 137 would cause new files to have only execute permissions for the user, write and execute permissions for members of the group, and full permissions (no security) for everyone else.

In reality, this is because umask values are inverted with respect to the chmod values listed in Table 7.1. That is, while chmod specifies which permissions to add, umask specifies which permissions to remove. Thus, a umask value of 137 specifies the following:

- The user should have only execute permissions removed by default from a newly created file.
- Members of the file's group should have execute and write permissions removed by default from a newly created file.
- Other users should have all permissions removed by default from a newly created file.

7

For example, a `umask` value of 137 means that any newly created file in the shell environment will have the following symbolic permissions in `ls`-style output:

```
-rw-r-----
```

For security purposes, it is desirable to remove all non-user permissions from newly created shell files. Thus, the user will have to add permissions manually via `chmod` if extra permissions should be granted. The `umask` value that accomplishes this is 177, which results in symbolic permissions like this:

```
-rw-------
```

With permissions like this, only the file's user will be able to read from or write to the file. All other users will have no permission to operate on the file whatsoever. The user can easily change this via `chmod` if desired, but the default creation permissions remain more secure. To set the new `umask` value, simply pass 177 as an argument to the `umask` shell command:

```
umask 177
```

Of course, entering the command like this will affect the `umask` value in the current shell only for as long as the shell is running. When the shell is exited, the changes will be lost and all new invocations of the shell will have the original `umask` value. To make the changes permanent, you'll need to append the `umask` command to the `/etc/profile` file, which `bash` sources each time it is launched:

```
echo 'umask 177' >>/etc/profile
```

All login shells will now by default have a `umask` value of 177 when the user begins.

> When making changes to files this way using the shell append (>>) operator, be sure to include both greater-than symbols, without extra space between them. The following two commands are very different:
>
> ```
> echo 'umask 177' >>/etc/profile
> echo 'umask 177' >/etc/profile
> ```
>
> The first command adds a line to the end of the `/etc/profile` file, and the second command deletes the original `/etc/profile` file and creates a new one containing only one line.

Adding a `umask` call to the end of `/etc/profile` changes the default value for login shells but doesn't affect non-login shells, such as those often seen in `xterm` windows. To affect these kinds of shells, the `umask` command must be added to the end of the

`$HOME/.bashrc` file, which is sourced for non-login shells. To change the default `$HOME/.bashrc` file for new accounts to reflect the updated `umask` value, append a line to the file in `/etc/skel`:

```
echo 'umask 177' >>/etc/skel/.bashrc
```

Note that these changes only affect the `bash` shell; if you've chosen to include other shells as options on your system, you'll have to make similar changes for them as well.

Special Cases, Risks, and Solutions

The permissions picture is actually a little more complicated than what we've painted so far. Though the basics remain the same, there are some special cases that require special treatment in the context of a security-conscious Linux system.

Extra Directory Permissions

In addition to the permissions covered so far, there are two interesting special cases for directories.

The first special case is known as the *sticky bit*, named after a kind of functionality no longer in use. When applied to the other permissions of a directory (non-user, non-group), the sticky bit creates a special situation: Users with write permission will be able to create files in the directory and modify and delete files that they have created. Files created and owned by other users, however, will remain off limits. The sticky bit can be enabled using the the symbolic mode of `chmod` as follows:

```
chmod o+t mydirectory
```

You will know that the sticky bit is set because a letter `t` will appear in the execute-other permission in `ls` output.

The second special case is the SGID bit when applied to a directory. When this property is applied to a directory, any file created within the directory (including a new directory) will be created with the same group ownership as the parent directory. This is useful for situations requiring more subtle group file management techniques.

Device Nodes

Recall that there are some types of files that actually refer to system devices, rather than files on the disk that contain user or program data. These types of files are commonly known as *device nodes* and reside in the `/dev` directory. If you visit `/dev`, you'll notice that there are a lot of them, especially if you're using one of the common Linux distributions.

7

Linux kernel 2.4 implements a new method called `devfs` for managing device nodes. When using `devfs` with kernel 2.4, device nodes exist only in memory in a virtual file system rather than on disk and are automatically assigned initially secure permissions by the kernel.

Luckily, most distribution installers do a reasonably good job of configuring ownership and permissions for system device nodes. However, there are one or two instances in which we should reevaluate and possibly correct device node permissions:

- It is important to ensure that disk devices have their permissions correctly configured. Accidentally granting a non-root user raw access to a disk device is a sure way to get hacked, violated, or crashed quickly.

- It is also important in the case of any devices that seem to grant public permissions (any permission for other users).

In the case of disk devices, the only safe policy is to ensure that only the superuser, root, has read and write access to the device node. The `chmod` value that corresponds to these permissions is 600. To make the change, simply visit `/dev` and use a shell wildcard:

```
# cd /dev
# chmod 600 sd* hd*
```

This will cause all IDE and SCSI disks to give read and write permissions only to `root`. Note that this does not mean that normal users won't be able to use the hard drive; it means only that normal users won't be able to format the hard drive or steal data that they don't otherwise have permission to access.

Now we need to make sure that no device nodes give unrestricted read or write access to other (anonymous) users. This can be accomplished with a single `chmod` command in symbolic mode:

```
chmod o-rwx *
```

In general, there is no real drawback to doing this. There are very few cases in which it is a good idea to give all users access to devices. However, there are exceptions. A few special devices, such as `/dev/null`, `/dev/zero`, and `/dev/random`, should have some permissions available to anonymous users:

```
chmod a+rw /dev/null /dev/zero /dev/random
```

If you are wary about changing permissions on so many files at once, you can get a list of all files that have anonymous permissions by using `ls` and `grep` together with simple patterns:

```
ls -l | grep '^.......r..'
ls -l | grep '^........w.'
ls -l | grep '^.........x'
```

The first command above will match all files that allow public read access. The second matches all files that allow public write access. The third matches all files that allow public execute access (this should be rare for device nodes). Once you have such a list, you can change permissions on the nodes one by one.

> Some device nodes are actually symbolic links to other device nodes. Symbolic links have a unique permissions format:
>
> lrwxrwxrwx
>
> All symbolic links are of type l and grant permission for full read, write, and execute to all users. The actual behavior of the link being referenced then depends on the permissions of the file to which the link points.

SUID/SGID Executables

Perhaps the single largest complicating factor in the Linux permissions system is the SUID (set user ID) property. Normally, when a program is executed, the program's process will be owned by the user. Thus, the program is able to access only files that normally grant the user access. However, when a special property called SUID is set for a given program binary, the program will behave very differently.

When an SUID binary is run, its process is not owned by the user who launched it, but rather by the user who owns the program binary file. Thus, a program file that is owned by root but is publicly executable will in essence become the root user each time it is run.

A similar property called SGID causes a program's process to take on an identity matching its group ownership in a similar fashion. One common SUID/SGID (both properties enabled) binary is /usr/sbin/pppd, which is responsible for dial-up Internet connections using analog modems:

```
# ls -l /usr/sbin/pppd
-rwsr-sr-x   1 root     root        161792 Nov  8 13:31 /usr/sbin/pppd
```

Note that instead of the usual x symbol in the permissions for user and group members, an s, indicating SUID and SGID, is present instead.

Obviously, this type of thing is a security risk: Any program with the SUID or SGID property is like a potential rogue root user and must be treated with extreme caution. Bugs in programs that are usually run as SUID/SGID are very common starting places for exploits that render a system defenseless against attack. Unfortunately, the

7

SUID/SGID properties are useful because they allow programs like /usr/sbin/pppd, for example, to access system networking resources and the modem device—to which normal users don't generally have access. Without SUID/SGID properties, the /usr/sbin/pppd program would be available only to the root user, meaning that normal users could not initiate a dial-out connection.

Setting SUID/SGID with chmod

The chmod command can be used to set or clear the SUID/SGID properties for a file. In symbolic mode, the related character is s and can be applied only to a program binary that already shows the x property for the user. For example, to set the /usr/sbin/pppd program to SUID/SGID status, use

```
chmod ug+s /usr/sbin/pppd
```

To clear the SGID status but leave the SUID status intact, use

```
chmod g-s /usr/sbin/pppd
```

The numeric mode can be used as well to specify SUID/SGID properties. Instead of using a series of three digits, four digits must be used when specifying SUID/SGID properties. If four digits are present, the first will automatically be used for special properties. A value of 4 represents the SUID property, and a value of 2 represents the SGID property. To set a program to public read, write, and execute for user and group, read and execute only for others, with SUID and SGID set, you'd use

```
chmod 6775 myfile
```

Eliminating Unnecessary SUID/SGID Permissions

Because of the implications for system security, it is imperative that any SUID/SGID programs that are not absolutely needed be weeded out of a system immediately. To find SUID/SGID binaries in your file system, simply use the find command with the -perm argument to specify the permissions to look for:

```
find / -perm +6000 -follow
```

This command causes find to search the entire set of mounted file systems for files whose permissions include either SUID or SGID binaries (zero matches all values; see find(1) for details). The additional -follow argument causes symbolic links to be followed as well, just in case.

Once you have the list from this command, use manual pages and common sense to determine which SUID or SGID binaries should retain this special status. Most of the binaries of this sort will be in /usr/sbin and will be network-related items such as traceroute or /usr/sbin/pppd, which strictly speaking don't need SUID/SGID properties on many systems. If you won't be using pppd as a normal user (or at all) or are willing to use su to run traceroute, you can easily disable the SUID/SGID property on these binaries. The same holds true for a large number of binaries you'll locate.

Checking for Anomalous SUID/SGID Instances

As a matter of course, you should check often for "unexplained occurrences" of SUID or SGID permissions. The easiest way to do this is to maintain a list of all known SUID/SGID binaries on your system. Once you have settled on which binaries are to have SUID/SGID and which aren't and you've adjusted permissions accordingly, write this list to a file that is readable only by root in /etc:

```
# find / -perm +6000 -follow > /etc/splist
# chmod go-rwx /etc/splist
```

Then, create a cron job or script that will be run routinely that checks the system for new SUID/SGID binaries and immediately notifies root or some other active user when such binaries turn up. One sample script fragment is shown in Listing 7.2.

LISTING 7.2   Sample SUID/SGID Script Check Fragment

```
for BINFILE in $(find / -perm +6000 -follow); do
    if [ "$(grep $BINFILE /etc/splist)" = "" ]; then
        echo $BINFILE | mail -s "New SUID/SGID!" root
    fi
done
```

This script simply searches again for any SUID/SGID binaries and compares the newly generated list to the old one kept in /etc/splist. If any new binaries have turned up, it sends a warning message to the root account's email box containing the path to the offending file.

Keep SUID/SGID Binaries Current

It is very important to ensure that all SUID/SGID binaries that are allowed to remain be updated whenever bug or security fixes occur. To fail to keep such programs up-to-date is to take large security risks with your data and system.

Append-Only and Immutable Files

7

The Linux ext2 file system provides one extra set of properties that may be useful in the context of security. These properties are called *file attributes*, and they are controlled by the chattr command. The chattr command is used like this:

```
chattr [+|-|=]modes file file...
```

modes is one or more characters that represents special file attributes understood by various versions of the ext2 file system. Only two modes interest us here:

- The a (append) mode prevents all non-append access to the file. In short, nobody will be able to read from the file, and nobody will be able to open it for random access writes.

- The i (immutable) mode prevents any kind of file modification whatsoever from occurring.

These two modes are logically mutually exclusive. They supersede all normal permissions information, and they can only be set or cleared by root.

The lsattr command is a special version of the ls command, which displays ext2 attributes instead of traditional file permissions. More information on chattr and lsattr can be found in chattr(1) and lsattr(1), respectively.

Read-Only root File System

There are some areas of the file system that shouldn't need to be modified at all during the normal course of system activity. For example, there is no good reason for most of the binaries in /sbin, /bin, and /usr/sbin to be changed at runtime; any modification attempts of this sort are almost certainly not benign. Though the permissions-based security model generally works well, there is one additional radical step that can be taken to prevent unauthorized changes to the most sensitive parts of the system. This step is the remounting of the root file system as read-only; we prepared for it to some degree in Hour 1, "Selecting and Installing a Linux Distribution."

Beware that mounting a root file system as read-only can be inconvenient at times and can interfere with compatibility in some cases. It is also unlikely to help security at all in the event that a user is able to obtain root user access. On the other hand, a read-only root file system can also help prevent attacks from clueless "script kiddies" who don't really understand what they are doing, but are instead following step-by-step attack instructions that someone else has written.

Provided your partitioning and file system mounting have isolated your root file system to some degree as was described in Hour 1, you should be able to move to a read-only file system at runtime simply by logging in as root and entering

```
mount -n -o remount,ro /
```

This call to mount causes the root file system to be remounted with the new ro property, which refers to a read-only file system. Once you have executed this command, you will

notice that you can't create, delete, or edit files stored anywhere on the root device, even
when working as the superuser. To go back to a write-capable root file system, use

```
mount -n -o remount,rw /
```

Of course, if you plan to use a read-only file system as a matter of course, you'll want to
automatically remount the file system as read-only at boot time. Some users of read-only
root file systems choose to edit existing init scripts to make this change, but each distribution is different, making such changes tricky and unportable. By far the easiest way
to go read-only is to add a script to your init.d folder like the one shown in Listing 7.3.

LISTING 7.3   /etc/rc.d/init.d/read-only

```bash
#!/bin/bash

# The purpose of this script is to remount the root
# file system as read-only toward the end of the boot
# process.

case "$1" in
 start)
   echo "Preparing to go read-only on /; will sleep for"
   echo "twenty seconds to allow everything to settle down."

   sleep 20

   echo -n "here we go... "

   mount -n -o remount,ro /

   echo "done"
   ;;

 stop)
   echo "Remounting / as read-write."
   mount -n -o remount,rw /
   echo "done."
   ;;

 *)
   echo "use $1 start|stop"
   exit 1

esac

exit 0

# end read-only
```

7

After marking this script as executable, link it into the runlevels that you want to be affected by it, usually runlevels 3 (multi-user with network) and 5 (multi-user with X and network):

```
ln -s /etc/rc.d/init.d/read-only /etc/rc.d/rc3.d/S99ro
ln -s /etc/rc.d/init.d/read-only /etc/rc.d/rc5.d/S99ro
```

Generally, there is no need to go read-only for runlevel 1 because it is for maintenance only and thus should be accessible only to root anyway. However, when dropping from a higher runlevel to runlevel 1 for maintenance, it is convenient to have the root file system automatically remounted as read-write. This can be done with another symbolic link:

```
ln -s /etc/rc.d/init.d/read-only /etc/rc.d/rc1.d/K99ro
```

Since the symbolic link starts with the letter K, the init scheme on the system will call the script with the stop argument when entering runlevel 1.

In some cases, you may find additional minor compatibility or scripting problems with your distribution or other software you've installed. These will have to be handled on a case-by-case basis, but there is always a way to configure a Linux system so that the root file system, in the end, can be mounted as read-only if so desired.

> Any file system that is sensitive and normally doesn't need to be modified very often can be mounted as read-only. The easiest way to do this for non-root file systems is to edit the /etc/fstab file, placing the ro option in place of the default flag or at the end of the list of existing options.

Options for `mount` and `fstab`

One more aspect of file system security must be covered before this hour draws to a close: options for the mount and fstab commands, which are very closely related.

The /etc/fstab file, as discussed in Hour 1, tells Linux which devices contain file systems and where these file systems should be mounted. The fourth field in the /etc/fstab file is the options field. It contains a comma-separated list of options that can further enhance the control of the system administrator over mounted file system options. A number of these options are shown in Table 7.2.

TABLE 7.2   Most Common `fstab` Mount Options

Option	Description
user	Says that regular (non-root) users will be able to mount and unmount this file system.

TABLE 7.2   continued

Option	Description
noauto	Prevents Linux from automatically mounting this file system at boot time. Instead, it must be mounted by hand.
errors=N	Specifies what to do in case of ext2 file system errors. If N is continue, the file system will continue to operate. If N is remount-ro, the file system will be remounted as read-only. If N is panic, errors will cause a system panic (total halt).
umask=N	Mounts a Windows (FAT) file system with the supplied umask value for the entire file system. Remember that a umask value specifies permissions that are not present, so a umask of 000 means that the file system will be readable and writable by everyone!
uid=N	Mounts a Windows (FAT) file system as though user with numeric user ID N owns all files.
gid=N	Mounts a Windows (FAT) file system as though group with numeric group ID N owns all files.

Table 7.2 provides only a very small subset of all available fstab options; for a complete list, see fstab(5), mount(8), and file system documentation in the /usr/src/linux source tree.

These options (with the exception of user and noauto) can also be supplied to the mount command with the -o option.

Summary

In this hour, you learned about basic security issues and techniques related to the Linux file system, including

- File permissions and how they work.
- Proper use of the chmod command in both symbolic and numeric modes.
- Using the umask command to change the default properties given to new files created from the shell or shell scripts.
- Device nodes, what they are, and what permissions they should have.
- The special SUID/SGID case and how to mitigate the risks involved in using SUID/SGID binaries.
- How to mount file systems, especially the root file system, as read-only to prevent unauthorized modification.

The information you learned in this hour forms the basis of non-network Linux security and should become second nature to any Linux user.

7

Q&A

Q **I'm still a little confused about how permissions work. What about scenario *foo*? Scenario *bar*?**

A The best way to learn about permissions and get a feel for the way they work is to make a temporary directory, for example off of the /tmp tree, and to play with them. Try creating some files and directories, using su and chmod to give them various permissions and to test these permissions against various identities. Through experimentation, you'll get a better feel.

Q **I changed the permissions as suggested in the /dev directory and now I don't have sound, I can't access my floppy, my mouse doesn't work, and my 3D games can only be run by root.**

A This is an intended side-effect of the permissions change. If you need sound for non-root users, feel free to go back and change permissions for the /dev/dsp and /dev/audio devices to make them available to all users. The same thing applies to the /dev/fd0 device or to other devices you want made public.

The idea is to implement an unspoken policy of "deny now, allow later" and to allow this to guide your actions and thinking. If you need a device to be publicly accessible and are willing to trade the risk for the benefit, by all means, use chmod to give back the necessary permissions.

Q **I know that the small letter s in permissions output means that SUID or SGID permissions are set, but there are some files on my system with a large s in permissions output. What does this mean?**

A The large S is an essentially meaningless combination. It means that the SUID or SGID bit is set for this file, but that the execute bit for the related role is not set. This means, in essence, that the binary would run as SUID or SGID if it could, but since no execute permission exists, it can't.

Q **Is there any way to give or remove permissions to a whole disk or file system at a time?**

A Yes. Use the execute permission flag (x) on file system mount points. For example, if you have a hard drive file system mounted on /drives/bpdisk and you want only root to have access to this file system, simply make sure that the mount directory, /drives/bpdisk, is owned by root and then remove group and other read, write, and execute permissions from the mount directory.

Q **I want to use a read-only root file system, but when I try, I get unexpected errors or some programs or system resources don't work properly.**

A This is because some program or daemon is still assuming that it has write capability on a file somewhere in the `root` file system. Remount the `root` file system as write-capable, allow the system to run, and use the `find` command to see which files on the `root` file system are being modified. Then, move them off of the `root` file system with symbolic links and try mounting as read-only again.

New Terms

`chmod`   The program used to alter or set file permissions.

device node   A special file in the `/dev` directory that usually refers either to a system device or a low-level service.

group   The group of accounts associated with a given file.

other users   All user accounts that are not the user owner and do not belong to the file's group. Other common terms include "anonymous" users and "world" users, as in "this file is world read/write" or similar phrases.

permissions   Flags that grant or deny various types of access to a given file, depending on who the file's owner is and which group is associated with the file.

SGID   An executable flag that indicates that the process of the program in question will always be associated with the same group associated with the program's binary file.

SUID   An executable flag that indicates that the process of the program in question will always be owned by the owner of the program's binary file.

`umask`   A numeric flag (in a format similar to the `chmod` flag) that determines the permissions given to new files created from within the shell.

user   The user who owns a given file. Only users logged in to this account can alter permissions for the file.

7

Hour **8**

Extra File System Security Tools

This hour, we'll pick up where Hour 7, "File System Security," left off, exploring a few extra tools to improve the security of your Linux file system. There are two basic types of tools we'll consider:

- Access control list mechanisms, which enable permissions to be specified on a much more user-specific and flexible basis than the traditional Unix-like file system allows.

- Tools for permanent deletion, which ensure that data in deleted files is not only not easily available, but is actually *erased* from the disk completely.

Though these measures are extreme compared to simple permissions maintenance, as discussed in Hour 7, they can at times be necessary, especially in circumstances under which maximum file system security and flexibility are required.

POSIX Access Control Lists for Linux

Though the permissions system in the native Linux file system is adequate for many purposes and users, you might have noticed a significant limitation in its capabilities: Permissions can only be specified for three roles:

- The user (owner) of the file, a login account with which the file in question is associated
- The group of the file, one of the groups from /Etc/Group with which the file in question is associated
- Everybody else, as a catch-all group

Again, for most users on small systems, this traditional permissions structure is adequate and provides all the security that is needed. However, there are times when more flexibility is needed. At times like this, a tool called an *access control list*, or *ACL*, is needed.

A Sample Scenario Needing ACL Capability

The problem with the traditional paradigm is that specific permissions cannot be assigned for several different users. For example, consider a situation in which we have five users—joe, marcy, fred, patrick, and dirck—and two groups—workers and drivers. We want to give the following permissions shown in Table 8.1 to each of them.

TABLE 8.1 Sample Scenario Needing ACL Capability

Users	Groups	Permissions Granted	Description
joe		rwx	Read, write, and execute
marcy		rw-	Read and write
fred		r--	Read only
patrick		r-x	Read and execute
dirck		--x	Execute only
	workers	rw-	Read and write
	drivers	r--	Read only
(others)		---	No permissions
(others)		---	No permissions

Notice that for each user and group, the set of permissions we want to grant is different, and each of these users needs permissions that we don't want to give to the world at large (everybody). Under the traditional permissions system, we could perhaps give file ownership to joe, and then give him u=rwx permissions. We could perhaps create a group called marcy, of which marcy is a member. We'd give group ownership to marcy and grant g=rw permissions. For everyone else, we could give o-rwx. However, this leaves out fred, patrick, and dirck, as well as both important groups. Because of the complexity of the situation, the traditional permissions model is woefully inadequate.

Using access control list capability, this list of users and required permissions could easily be implemented. Therefore, in situations that require this much flexibility, an ACL is generally the solution of choice.

POSIX ACLs for Linux

The POSIX ACLs for Linux package is one such package. It consists of a set of patches to the Linux kernel and ext2 file system utilities along with a number of separate utilities. All can be downloaded at http://acl.bestbits.at in source releases built around various kernel versions.

The package amends the Linux kernel to store an extra quantity of metadata for each file; this new metadata contains the extended permissions information provided by the ACL utilities. To install the POSIX ACLs package for Linux, you'll need the components shown in Table 8.2.

TABLE 8.2   Required Downloads for ACL Installation

Item	Description
Linux kernel source	You must have a supported version of the Linux kernel source available. As this text is being written, the supported kernels are 2.2.17 and 2.4.0 (test9, although the patches also work with test10).
Extended attrs patch	The extended attributes patch extends the virtual file system layer in the kernel source to allow for additional attributes.
ACL patch	The access control lists patch for the kernel source uses the additional attributes in the extended attributes patch to store access control list information.
e2fsprogs source	You must have a supported version of the ext2 utilities source available. As this text is being written, the supported version of e2fsprogs is 1.19.
e2fsprogs patch	This patch amends the e2fsprogs source to include additional command-line arguments for e2fsck, which have to do with access control list metadata.
fileutils source	You must have a supported version of the GNU file utilities source code available. As this text is being written, the supported version of fileutils is 4.0z.
fileutils patch	This patch amends the GNU file utilities so that extended permissions information is preserved in file utility operations.
ACL utilities source	This is the source code for the extra utilities used to configure ACL information for files.

> Sources for the Linux kernel can be found at `ftp://ftp.kernel.org`. Sources for `e2fsprogs` and `fileutils` can be found at `http://e2fsprogs.sourceforge.net` and `ftp://ftp.gnu.org/pub/gnu/fileutils`, respectively.

In order to install the ACL patches, you must also be familiar with the process of compiling and installing a new Linux kernel. Information on the process of compiling and using a new Linux kernel can be found in the Linux Kernel HOWTO at `http://www.linuxdoc.org/HOWTO/Kernel-HOWTO.html`. The necessary steps for successful installation are

1. Extract the kernel source:

   ```
   cd /usr/src; tar -xzvf ~/linux-2.4.0-test9.tar.gz
   ```

2. Apply the `ea` (extended attributes) kernel source patch downloaded from the POSIX ACLs site:

   ```
   cd linux
   patch -p1 <~/linux-2.4.0test9-ea-0.7.0.patch
   ```

> If you download your patches via Netscape, be sure that you save them with the `.gz` extension and use `gunzip` to extract them before trying to apply them. Netscape routinely drops the `.gz` extension, even though the file in question might not have been decompressed yet.

3. Apply the `acl` (access control lists) kernel source patch downloaded from the POSIX ACLs site:

   ```
   patch -p1 <~/linux-2.4.0test9-acl-0.7.1.patch
   ```

4. Compile and install the kernel and modules:

   ```
   make clean; make xconfig; make dep; make bzImage
   make modules; make modules_install
   ```

   Be sure to enable the CONFIG_FS_EXT_ATTR, CONFIG_FS_EXT_ATTR_USER, CONFIG_EXT2_FS_EXT_ATTR, and CONFIG_POSIX_ACL options, as shown in Figures 8.1 and 8.2.

FIGURE 8.1

New extended attributes options.

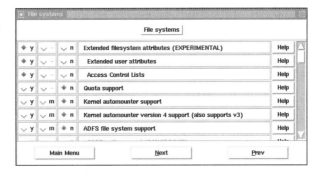

FIGURE 8.2

New ext2 file system options.

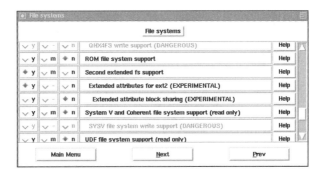

5. Extract the e2fsprogs source:

```
cd ~; tar -xzvf e2fsprogs-1.19.tar.gz
```

6. Apply the e2fsprogs patch:

```
cd e2fsprogs-1.19
patch -p1 <~/e2fsprogs-1.19ea-0.7.1.patch
```

7. Compile and install the e2fsprogs package:

```
./configure; make && make install
```

8. Extract the fileutils source:

```
cd ~; tar -xzvf fileutils-4.0z.tar.gz
```

9. Apply the fileutils patch:

```
cd fileutils-4.0z
patch -p1 <~/fileutils-4.0z-acl-0.7.0.patch
```

10. Compile and install the fileutils package:

```
./configure --prefix=/; make && make install
```

11. Extract the ACL utilities source:

```
cd ~; tar -xzvf acl-0.7.1.tar.gz
```

12. Compile and install the ACL utilities package:

```
cd acl-0.7.1
./configure; make && make install
```

13. Edit your /etc/lilo.conf to include the new kernel if necessary and install the new lilo.conf configuration by running /sbin/lilo:

```
vi /etc/lilo.conf
/sbin/lilo -v
```

> The ACL utilities installer tries to install some localization data into the $PREFIX/share subtree. If your install seems to fail on LC_MESSAGES directories, you can simply ignore the error and continue without any ill effects in most cases.

After you've completed the listed steps and rebooted with the new kernel, POSIX-compliant access control lists are available and enabled on your Linux system.

Syntax for the `setfacl` Command

The two important commands to remember when dealing with POSIX access control lists are `setfacl`, used to set or clear permissions in files with access control list properties, and `getfacl`, used to display permissions in files with access control list properties.

The `setfacl` command is used to add or remove access control list restrictions to a given file or directory. The three basic syntaxes for `setfacl` are as follows:

```
setfacl [-m|-x] u:[user]:[+|^]permissions file [file...]
setfacl [-m|-x] g:[group]:[+|^]permissions file [file...]
setfacl [-m|-x] o:[+|^]permissions file [file...]
```

These three forms of the `setfacl` command correspond to the modifications on a per-user basis, modifications on a per-group basis, or modifications for everybody (other users), respectively. In all cases, the `-m` argument is used to modify or add permissions, whereas the `-x` argument is used to remove permissions. If a specific `user` or `group` is supplied, and this user or group is not the existing user or group via traditional permissions, action will take place in the set of special ACL permissions. Consider the list of examples shown in Table 8.3.

TABLE 8.3 Sample `setfacl` Commands and Descriptions

Command	Description
setfacl -m u::rwx file	Gives read, write, and execute permissions to the user of the file in question.

TABLE 8.3   continued

Command	Description
`setfacl -m g::rwx file`	Gives read, write, and execute permissions to the group of the file in question.
`setfacl -m u:john:rwx file`	Gives read, write, and execute permissions to the additional user `john`.
`setfacl -m g:grunts:r file`	Gives only read permission to the additional group `grunts`.
`setfacl -m o:r file`	Gives only read permission to other users.
`setfacl -m u:john:^x file`	Removes execute permissions for user `john`.
`setfacl -m g:grunts:+w file`	Adds write permissions for the group called `grunts`.
`setfacl -x u:john file`	Removes special permissions granted to user `john` entirely.
`setfacl -x g:grunts file`	Removes special permissions granted to the group called `grunts` entirely.

Clearly, the ACL gives much more flexibility in terms of security. Read, write, and execute permission can be granted and denied to multiple users in addition to the user of the file in question, and the same holds true for groups.

Syntax for the `getfacl` Command

The `getfacl` command simply displays the current list of access control list permissions for a file or list of files. The basic syntax is simple:

```
getfacl file [file...]
```

For example, consider the following command and resulting output:

```
$ getfacl myfile
# file: myfile
# owner: jerry
# group: users
user::rwx
user:tando:rw-
user:tami:r--
group::r--
group:maint:rwx
other:---
$
```

In the case of `myfile`, the owner of the file is `jerry`, and the group is `users`. The owner has read, write, and execute permissions; members of the file's group have only read permissions. Additional users `tando` and `tami` have been granted read and write and just read permissions, respectively. An additional group, `maint`, has been given read, write, and execute permissions. All other users and groups have no permission at all.

The algorithm used for calculating permissions when traditional permissions and ACL permissions conflict is documented fully in `acl(5)`, but it can generally be simplified to the following two rules:

1. Permissions are checked from left to right. That is, user permissions supersede group permissions, and group permissions supersede other permissions.

2. Traditional permissions supersede ACL permissions when granting access, but in all other cases ACL permissions supersede traditional permissions.

Default Permissions (`getfacl`, `setfacl`, and Directories)

The ACL software can also allow for default permissions functionality similar to that offered by `umask` (see Hour 7), but on a much more flexible directory-by-directory basis. The `setfacl` syntax for creating default permissions is the same as the syntax used normally by `setfacl`, except that the letter d must precede each set of permissions:

```
setfacl [-m|-x] d:u:[user]:[+|^]permissions dir [dir...]
setfacl [-m|-x] d:g:[group]:[+|^]permissions dir [dir...]
setfacl [-m|-x] d:o:[+|^]permissions dir [dir...]
```

The default permissions assigned to a directory do not apply to the directory itself. Rather, they are the permissions that will be applied to files created within that directory by default. For example, consider the following series of `setfacl` operations on a directory called `myfiles`:

```
setfacl -m d:u::rw myfiles
setfacl -m d:g::r myfiles
setfacl -m d:o: myfiles
setfacl -m d:u:jerry:rw myfiles
setfacl -m d:g:workers:r myfiles
setfacl -m d:g:admins:rw myfiles
```

Each of these lines sets a default permission for the directory `myfiles`. Thanks to the permissions specified here, all files created in my files will, by default, have the following set of permissions:

- The user will have read and write permission.
- The group will have read permission.
- The additional user `jerry` will also be granted both read and write permission.
- Members of the additional group `workers` will be granted read permission.
- Members of the additional group `admins` will be granted both read and write permission.
- All other users will have no permissions to act on the file in question.

Default permissions lists are inherited; if a subdirectory called yourfiles is created within myfiles, yourfiles will have all the permissions specified by the myfiles default list, and this default list will also apply to files created within yourfiles.

ACL Mask Permissions

When experimenting with ACLs, you might notice a new set of permissions, known as *mask permissions*, in the output of the getfacl command. The mask permissions do not apply to a specific user or group, but rather indicate the maximum set of permissions that can be granted to any additional groups or users in the ACL list, regardless of the explicit permissions granted. To set the mask permissions, use

```
setfacl -m m:[+|^]permissions file [file...]
```

The idea of mask permissions can seem a little confusing at first, but it's really quite a simple idea. Suppose you have granted the following permissions to a file called texasmap:

```
setfacl -m u:jacob:rwx texasmap
setfacl -m u:marlowe:rwx texasmap
setfacl -m u:newton:rwx texasmap
setfacl -m u:parson:rwx texasmap
setfacl -m u:zendor:rwx texasmap
```

Five users other than the file's user have been granted read, write, and execute permission. Suppose, however, that from time to time the file texasmap is used on a Web site, and, during these moments, you as the system administrator want to remove all write permissions for this file. The chmod command can be used to remove write access for the file's user and group ownership, but not for these additional users. The setfacl command can be used to remove write permissions for each of them one by one, but this is a lot of work. Of course, the work is doubled when you need to re-enable write permission afterward. The solution lies in mask permissions:

```
# setfacl -m m:^w texasmap
# getfacl texasmap | grep mask
mask:r-x
#
```

This call to the setfacl command removes write permission from everyone in the access control list (other than the official user and group), even if some of the additional users or groups have explicitly been granted write permission. This is because the mask permissions, currently at r-x, dictate the maximum permissions any ACL entry can grant. To re-enable write permission for users with sufficient permission, use

```
# setfacl -m m:+w texasmap
# getfacl texasmap | grep mask
mask:rwx
#
```

As the output of the getfacl command shows, write access is now available again to those with permitting ACL entries.

Copying ACLs Between Files

Clearly, access control lists enable a system administrator to create long, flexible lists of access parameters for any file or directory in the system. In fact, some lists for important files can stretch to multiple entries. Because it would be inconvenient to have to construct multiple complex setfacl commands over and over again for several files, the ACL commands allow an easy mechanism for copying one file or directory's access control list directly to another file or directory.

To copy an ACL from file1 to file2, use the -S argument for an absolute ACL specification from standard input:

```
getfacl file1 | setfacl -S- file2
```

This copy and many more different types of copy operations are described in the examples section of the setfacl(1) manual page.

Caveats and Considerations

Unfortunately, ACLs are still not a part of the standard Linux kernel or of many Unix-like operating systems. Consequently, there are a number of contexts in which the functionality of ACL information might not be as expected:

- **Standard kernels** Most importantly, any kernel that does not support ACLs will ignore all ACL data, even though file systems can still be mounted. This means that, for example, booting from a floppy boot disk with a standard kernel will effectively render all ACL permissions moot.

- **NFS** The NFS (network file system) protocol doesn't allow for ACL functionality, so ACL permissions won't work as expected over NFS. Thus, exported file systems should not rely on them. The kernel-based NFS daemon has at least been patched to make educated guesses when ACL data is present, but the userspace NFS daemon has not.

- **Samba** Samba will respect ACL permissions on shared file systems, so administrators need not worry about ACL and Samba.

- **Backups** Many backup utilities, including afio and tar, will not preserve extended data of the type present in ACL-enhanced ext2 file systems.

- **Non-ext2 file systems** The getfacl and setfacl utilities do not function on non-ext2 file systems, even under patched kernels. Other file systems, such as vfat or minix, simply are not capable of this type of security functionality.

8

One final note should be repeated here. Although ACL data will not hurt or damage your ext2 file system in any way, and an ACL-enhanced file system will function correctly with non–ACL-enhanced kernels or ext2 utilities (except with regard to ACL permissions), the ACL software adds an argument to the /sbin/e2fsck binary. The -X argument will purge all ACL data from an ext2 file system. Thus, in order to completely remove all trace of ACL metadata from a file system, use

```
/sbin/e2fsck -X /dev/hddevice
```

Other than to purge ACL-enhanced permissions from the file system in question, there will be no visible effects on the files present. All Linux-style (that is, user, group, and other) permissions will be preserved in such a purge.

Secure File Deletion Tools

You can probably imagine a situation in which it would be a disaster if a hacker or even a normal user were to somehow obtain data from a previously deleted file. Most users assume that when a file is deleted, it is gone forever. Unfortunately, this isn't generally the case. The data is no longer accessible via the same filename, but it might actually remain otherwise intact on the raw disk device for days, weeks, or even months before being overwritten by newer data. Even after data is overwritten, it might still be recoverable using special tools and knowledge.

Clearly, it is important to destroy data that needs to be destroyed. In this sense, permanent file deletion tools can be thought of as a paper shredder for your Linux files. The command traditionally responsible for this type of functionality is the wipe command. (wipe is not included with most versions of Linux.) There are several versions of wipe for Linux that can be downloaded and compiled.

Perhaps the simplest and quickest, bcwipe, is available from http://www.jetico.com. The bcwipe utility is not open source, but source code is available, and the utility is free for non-commercial use. It works by overwriting data to be wiped with different bit patterns and random data a number of times to ensure that the original data is indeed completely wiped out. The bcwipe utility can also operate on entire block devices, for example, if you need to erase an entire hard disk securely.

The open source counterpart to bcwipe is wipe, available from http://wipe.sourceforge.net. It functions similarly in principle to bcwipe but lacks the capability to erase entire partitions or devices and isn't as portable as bcwipe seems to be. If you have problems compiling wipe, you might also want to look into bcwipe.

Another open source secure deletion utility called overwrite boasts similar features and can be downloaded from http://www.kyuzz.org/antirez/overwrite.

In theory, all these utilities will prevent a malicious user or organization from collecting data from your storage devices that you had thought was deleted and unrecoverable. They represent an important component in file system security, and you should always take care to securely delete any files you want completely removed, rather than simply deleted, from your Linux file system.

Summary

In this hour, we looked at a POSIX-compliant extension to the Linux permissions file system security model, known as an access control list. Using access control lists, we learned to do the following:

- Download and install the POSIX ACL implementation for Linux and ext2.
- Add multiple users and per-user permissions to the ACL properties list for a Linux file or directory.
- Add multiple groups and per-group permissions to the ACL properties list for a Linux file or directory.
- Remove users or groups from the ACL properties list for a Linux file or directory.
- Understand and set default ACL permissions for a Linux directory.
- Understand and use the ACL permissions mask to control maximum permissions for all ACL properties applying to a given file or directory.

We also learned about so-called secure delete tools or permanent delete tools, which actually erase data being deleted on a hard drive, rather than simply marking space as available once again.

Q&A

Q **Which set of permissions is effective in the event that normal permissions and ACL permissions seem to be in conflict?**

A Actually, they are never in conflict. Because the set of normal permissions is always included in the ACL permissions list as `user::`, `group::`, and `other::`, the traditional set of permissions becomes a completely integrated subset of ACL permissions.

Q **Can the `setfacl` command be used to set ACL permissions recursively?**

A Yes. Use the `-R` argument, just as you would when using the standard `chmod` command, to recurse into subdirectories and apply permissions to multiple files.

Q **Is there any way at all to back up an ext2 file system and preserve ACL permissions when restoring?**

A Yes, but the process is kludgy and will require scripting. The following command can be used to output ACL data recursively for an entire directory tree:

```
getfacl -R /path/to/list
```

After this output has been saved to a file, this file can be used to restore ACL data to the directory tree in question with

```
setfacl -B /path/to/data-file.acl
```

By combining these two commands, a backup process can extract ACL data to a file before writing to streaming media, save the ACL data file to the streaming media along with other files, and, finally, use the ACL data file after restore to reconstruct ACL permissions.

Q **Secure deletion is often used in conjunction with file encryption. Why isn't encryption mentioned here?**

A For encryption information see Hour 19, "Encrypting File System Data," and Hour 20, "Encrypting E-Mail Data."

New Terms

access control list (ACL) A more flexible set of permissions properties than is available via the standard Linux permissions paradigm.

permissions defaults A set of permissions given the default label, which will be assigned by default to any newly created file within the directory in question.

permissions mask A set of permissions which defines the maximum permissions granted to any entry in the ACL list, regardless of explicitly specified permissions.

secure delete A method of removing files from the file system, which attempts to completely erase the magnetic patterns and traces left by the file, rather than simply making the space it occupied available once again.

HOUR 9

Making the Most of Pluggable Authentication Modules (PAM)

This hour, we're going to study basic configuration of PAM for Linux. PAM, or the Pluggable Authentication Modules system, is a complex authentication system that stretches across most of the restricted services (services requiring authentication) in any Linux system. Luckily, PAM is generally shipped in a fairly secure configuration with most Linux distributions, so a little touch-up here and there is all that is needed to ensure that general-purpose authentication is secure on your Linux box.

If PAM is not a component of your Linux distribution by default, you should consider upgrading to a newer distribution. Using PAM not only can make your system more secure, but it can also help to resolve a myriad of inconvenient compatibility conflicts between security necessities such as shadow and MD5 and services that need to access these files. You can check for PAM support on your system by checking for the existence of any of these files or directories:

`/etc/pam.conf`

`/etc/pam.d/`

`/lib/libpam.so.*`

`/usr/lib/libpam.so.*`

If any of these exist, you're probably in good shape with respect to PAM-enabled authentication services. Make no mistake: There's almost no point in trying to use shadow passwords without PAM installed as well, and shadow is more than essential for a secure system.

How PAM Is Configured: The Basics

PAM configuration is located either in a single, central file at `/etc/pam.conf` or in a series of smaller files named after the services they relate to in `/etc/pam.d/`.

In order to fully follow this discussion of PAM configuration, you should try to "follow along" by examining your own configuration files and the PAM modules reference guide, a part of the official PAM documentation located at `www.us.kernel.org/pub/linux/libs/pam/Linux-PAM.html/pam.html`.

PAM configuration is based on a "stack" model. There is a given list, or *stack,* of required actions for any single service that must be completed before access to the service in question is granted. Each action in the stack is supplied on a single PAM configuration file line, which contains exactly one each of the following: a module type, a control flag, a module, and—depending on whether `/etc/pam.conf` or `/etc/pam.d/` is used—a service name.

Each line contains a module type. A module type can be thought of as a specifier for one of four basic contexts within which a PAM stack entry can operate. These module type contexts are shown in Table 9.1.

TABLE 9.1   PAM Module Type Context Names

Type	Description
auth	This stack entry's action is related to user authentication, for example, when asking the user to enter a password for login.
account	This stack entry's action is related to user account management, for example, when checking to see whether a user's account or password has expired.
session	This stack entry's action is related to connection or session management, for example, logging information about the user's login session to the system log.
password	This stack entry's action is related to password management, for example, when updating a user's password as stored in the system /etc/shadow file.

Each line also contains a control flag. A control flag can be thought of as a specifier for one of four basic levels of necessity. It defines the importance of the stack entry in question for the authentication process as a whole. This will determine how PAM will proceed after evaluating any action that has taken place. The control flag levels of necessity are shown in Table 9.2.

TABLE 9.2   PAM Control Flag Necessity Levels

Level	Description
requisite	This stack entry's action *must* be completed successfully to continue processing actions. If not, the service request will fail, and no more actions in this context will be processed.
required	This stack entry's action must be completed successfully. If not, the service request will fail after the rest of the action stack has been processed.
sufficient	This stack entry's action alone is enough to cause a service request to be accepted unless an earlier, required action has not been completed successfully. If the request is accepted based on a successful action, no further actions in the stack will be processed.
optional	If no other action has proven successful or unsuccessful, the success of this stack entry's actions—or the lack thereof—will determine the stack's response to the authentication request.

In addition to the module type and control flag, each stack entry in an /etc/pam.conf file contains a service name supplied by the program requesting authentication. Also present in every stack entry are an authentication module used to control this type of authentication and arguments, which are to be supplied to the authentication module. The format of these elements together in a single stack entry in the /etc/pam.conf file is as follows:

```
service module-type control-flag module [arguments]
```

A PAM configuration file, therefore, is simply a list of these stack entries, one per line, which define the entire set of authentication procedures for a Linux system. When new services are installed on a Linux system that require new authentication techniques, they will normally include additional PAM modules, specific to the service in question, along with documentation on how the module is to be used. The new service and modules can then quickly and easily be incorporated into the existing authentication framework.

How PAM Works: The Basics

The functionality of the PAM system is actually fairly basic. Any service that requires authentication is linked against the PAM libraries included with Linux. For example, try the following:

```
# ldd /bin/login
libcrypt.so.1 => /lib/libcrypt.so.1 (0x40020000)
libpam.so.0 => /lib/libpam.so.0 (0x4004d000)
libdl.so.2 => /lib/libdl.so.2 (0x40055000)
libpam_misc.so.0 => /lib/libpam_misc.so.0 (0x4005a000)
libc.so.6 => /lib/libc.so.6 (0x4005d000)
/lib/ld-linux.so.2 => /lib/ld-linux.so.2 (0x40000000)
#
```

Notice that the login program, used by programs such as getty and in.telnetd to authenticate users and log them in, is linked against the PAM libraries.

When a specific service such as login requires user authentication, it employs the PAM routines to complete this authentication. These routines look at the PAM configuration files for stack entries with a matching service name. It then processes these entries in the order in which they are found, one by one.

To help you to understand the way in which PAM works, let's take a closer look at one service's authentication procedure. For the login service, for example, a default configuration might look something like Listing 9.1.

LISTING 9.1   Section of /etc/pam.conf for login

```
login     auth       required    pam_securetty.so
login     auth       required    pam_pwdb.so
login     auth       required    pam_nologin.so
login     auth       optional    pam_mail.so
login     account    required    pam_pwdb.so
login     session    required    pam_pwdb.so
login     session    optional    pam_lastlog.so
login     password   required    pam_pwdb.so
```

On many newer systems, the PAM configuration is split among a number of files stored in the /etc/pam.d/ directory. Each file is named after the service it handles, and the service identifier is therefore omitted from each action inside the file. For example, the file equivalent of Listing 5.4, the /etc/pam.d/login file, might contain

```
auth        required        pam_securetty.so
auth        required        pam_pwdb.so
auth        required        pam_nologin.so
auth        optional        pam_mail.so
account     required        pam_pwdb.so
session     required        pam_pwdb.so
session     optional        pam_lastlog.so
password    required        pam_pwdb.so
```

In the end, the result is the same. If the /etc/pam.d/ directory exists, it will be used exclusively, and the /etc/pam.conf file will be ignored.

Because each of these rules belongs to the login service, the entire stack will be processed each time a user attempts to log in. Let's step through the stack rules one by one. Refer to the PAM modules reference guide mentioned earlier for extensive descriptions of each module and its properties. The actions will proceed in this order:

1. The pam_securetty.so module checks to see that the requested user is allowed to log in at the console in question by comparing the user's login location against the /etc/securetty file. This action is required; if it fails, the authentication request will be rejected after all other actions have been completed.

2. The pam_pwdb.so module is called to see whether the user has entered the correct password. This action is also required.

3. The pam_nologin.so module is called to see whether the file /etc/nologin exists. If so, the file is displayed, and the action will fail, eventually preventing the user from logging in. This action is also required.

4. The pam_mail.so module is called to see whether the user has any new mail. This action is optional, so the user will be allowed to log in based on the results of other actions whether or not any new mail is present.

5. The pam_pwdb.so module is called again, this time in the account context, which causes it to check for password or account expiration. If the account has expired, or if the user's password has expired and the user refuses to enter a new one, the action will fail. This action is required for login.

6. The `pam_pwdb.so` module is called yet again, this time in the session context, causing it to enter the login attempt in the system log. This action is required, meaning that if the system is unable to record the login, the user will not be allowed to enter.

7. The `pam_lastlog.so` module is called to update the user login history in the `/var/log/lastlog` file.

8. The `pam_pwdb.so` module is called one last time to replace the user's password in the `/etc/shadow` file, in case the password has been updated (see step 5) during the login process. This action is also required, meaning that if the system is unable to complete it, the user will not be allowed to log in.

This stack of actions represents the entire authentication process for user logins, from beginning to end. If it seems a bit cloudy at this point, try referring to the *PAM System Administrator's Guide* for exhaustive detail. However, the best way to learn is to begin working with PAM directly.

Putting PAM to Work: Expiring Passwords

Now that you understand, at least to some degree, how PAM works, we're going to modify a few PAM service stacks. The first one we're going to modify is the password service, which is responsible simply for updating a user's login password. It is important that all user passwords be well-chosen passwords. They should be longer than one or two characters and avoid containing any dictionary words at the very least.

Most distributions now include reasonably good password selection enforcement by default—managed by PAM—but we're going to describe one possible `/etc/pam.d/passwd` file just in case you find this not to be the case on your distribution.

First, we need to verify the presence of the `pam_cracklib.so` module somewhere on the system. Assuming your file database is intact, you should be able to discover whether or not `pam_cracklib.so` and the needed dictionaries are present simply by entering

```
locate pam_cracklib.so dict | grep crack
```

If with this command you are able to locate both `pam_cracklib.so` and a crack terms dictionary file or set of dictionary files, you should, in theory, be able to enable good password enforcement. Just comment out the existing lines in your `/etc/pam.d/passwd` file with a hash mark (#) and replace them with the ones in Listing 9.2.

LISTING 9.2 Enforced `/etc/pam.d/passwd` File

```
password required pam_cracklib.so type=user retry=3
password required pam_pwdb.so use_authtok
```

If you have an /etc/pam.conf file instead of the /etc/pam.d/ directory, search through the file for lines beginning with the text passwd. Comment them out and replace them with the lines shown in Listing 9.3.

LISTING 9.3 Enforced passwd Lines for /etc/pam.conf

```
passwd password required pam_cracklib.so type=user retry=3
passwd password required pam_pwdb.so use_authtok
```

Note that if you have MD5 passwords, you might need to append a space and the word md5 to the end of the second line in either case.

These changes will cause the PAM system to demand better passwords of users rather than accept bad passwords without complaint. The theory behind this small passwd stack is as follows:

- When a user enters his desired password, check the password against a dictionary of common terms. This task is performed by the pam_cracklib.so module and is required in order to proceed in the stack.

- Ask for a good password up to three times before giving up altogether (the retry=3 argument).

- If the user enters a good password (the pam_cracklib.so module completes successfully), update the authentication token (the password) using the pam_pwdb.so module (responsible for managing the password database).

This simple change allows a system administrator to demand good password selection from his or her users without having to know what the passwords are or to install third-party software or aftermarket password utilities.

Putting PAM to Work: Enforcing wheel

It is traditional on Unix-like systems to allow certain actions to occur only if the user in question is a member of the wheel group, reserved by convention for users with system administration type access. Among the actions usually restricted to wheel is the su command, which allows one user to take on the user ID of another user, most often the root user.

Many users are surprised to learn that the wheel group is not enforced by default on Linux systems, meaning that any user at all can execute the su command and use it to log in as root if the password is known. Clearly, the ability to execute su to completion is a security risk in the hands of normal users. Let's remedy the situation.

> If you're not aware of the wheel group, don't worry—it's not hard to imple-
> ment. The wheel group is simply a way of restricting access to some sensitive
> services (such as su) to a small group of users who have been given adminis-
> trative privileges. You probably have a wheel group in your /etc/group file
> already. If not, simply add one with groupadd and then add users as neces-
> sary to the wheel group to create your administrator class. For example, if
> you want frank, mary, and joe to be administrators, the wheel entry in your
> /etc/group file might look like this:
>
> wheel::1:frank,mary,joe
>
> This line makes frank, mary, and joe members of the wheel group. Then,
> using simple techniques such as those documented in this section, you can
> grant access to services such as su only to these users.

We're going to amend the /etc/pam.d/su file, which controls the authentication behavior of the su command, to the following behavior:

- Allow only members of the wheel group to use su at all.
- Require all users, even root, to enter a password when trying to use su to gain
  root-level access.
- Log all su uses.

The updated /etc/pam.d/su file looks like the one shown in Listing 9.4.

LISTING 9.4   Updated /etc/pam.d/su File

```
auth        required    pam_warn.so
auth        requisite   pam_wheel.so group=wheel
auth        required    pam_pwdb.so
account     required    pam_pwdb.so
password    required    pam_pwdb.so use_authtok
session     required    pam_pwdb.so
```

This /etc/pam.d/su file is obvious in its use of the pam_pwdb.so module, well documented in the PAM users guide and used often throughout the other PAM configuration
files. New here, however, is the pam_wheel.so module, which simply checks to make
sure that the user is a member of the wheel group. Because it is marked as requisite, if
the stack entry fails (when the user is not a member of wheel), the stack exits immediately in failure without continuing. Thus, only members of wheel will even be asked to
enter a password. All others will be denied from the beginning.

> If you want to implement wheel and protect su against access from non-wheel members, you should also take another step: Change ownership of the su binary to the wheel group and remove public execute permissions, as follows:
>
> chown root.wheel /bin/su
>
> chmod 4750 /bin/su
>
> Refer to Hour 7, "File System Security," for more information on the chown and chmod commands.

9

Putting PAM to Work: Other Authentication

Perhaps the most important of the PAM configuration files is the one that could otherwise be known as the default file. The other file controls authentication to all services not explicitly configured under other service names. Thus, it is important that the other file be securely configured because it is, in some sense, the last line of defense when handling an as-of-yet unknown or unconfigured service.

The /etc/pam.d/other file recommended by the PAM documentation is perhaps the simplest, easiest, and most secure. It is shown in Listing 9.5.

LISTING 9.5 Secure /etc/pam.d/other File

```
auth        required    pam_warn.so
auth        required    pam_deny.so
account     required    pam_warn.so
account     required    pam_deny.so
password    required    pam_warn.so
password    required    pam_deny.so
session     required    pam_warn.so
session     required    pam_deny.so
```

This file is very simple. For all module types, the control flag is the same, required, and two modules are called. First, pam_warn.so is called to log information about the attempt in progress. Then, pam_deny.so is called to simply return a failure and prevent any kind of connection or authentication from taking place. Therefore, any service that uses PAM must be explicitly configured to allow authentication, or attempts will fail.

Summary

In this hour, we covered the basics of PAM configuration. We learned that PAM configuration is really just a series of stack entries. Each time a service requests PAM's help, the PAM routines simply call all the stack entries related to that service, in order. The process of adding authentication procedures for new services to the system is therefore as easy as adding a few new stack entries in the PAM configuration files.

Each stack entry in a PAM configuration file contains a module type to determine the context in which the stack entry will be run and a control flag to determine its importance. A module is also supplied that contains the actual code to process the task at hand.

Though PAM configuration can seem complex at first, it is actually not too difficult to master, and the online PAM documentation located at `www.us.kernel.org/pub/linux/libs/pam/Linux-PAM-html/pam.html` can help quite a bit.

Q&A

Q Is there a comprehensive list of all PAM modules in existence?

A There might be, but I've never seen it. Many different services include PAM modules of their own as a part of their source distribution, so it's doubtful whether a truly comprehensive list could ever be assembled.

Q Should I create a `wheel` group on my system? How is `wheel` usually used, beyond the `su` command?

A It's probably not needed on a smaller system with only a few users and only one administrator, but on a larger system with multiple administrators and even more users, `wheel` can be an important step in overall security. As far as just how `wheel` is used—there are different philosophies and conventions. Your best bet is to look at several books on Unix system administration.

New Terms

control flag   One of four levels of importance that determine how PAM will proceed when the results of the current action have become clear.

module type   One of four directives that refer to the contexts in which PAM stack entries will be processed.

restricted service   Any service that provides access to system or network resources in such a way as to pose a potential security threat in the hands of an unknown user.

Resources of this type therefore require that a user authenticate himself before access is granted.

wheel   A group used by convention on many Unix-like systems to restrict permission for performing sensitive tasks to a small number of users who are members of the group.

Exercises

9

1. Modify the `/etc/pam.d/su` file or `su` service further to simply log all attempts to use it and then deny access, meaning that `root` commands can only be executed from `root` logins. (Preserve a backup of the `/etc/pam.d/su` file so that you can restore it afterward.)

2. Modify the `/etc/pam.d/chsh` file or `chsh` service further so that only members of `wheel` are allowed to use the `chsh` utility, preventing unsecured access to alternative login shells.

3. Using the online PAM documentation, modify the `rsh`, `rlogin`, and `rexec` files to cause PAM to ignore personal `.rhosts` files, using only the system-wide file at `/etc/hosts.equiv` instead.

PART II

Network Security

Hour

HOUR **10**

Using `ipchains` for Firewalling and Routing

This hour we're going to learn to configure basic firewalling and routing capabilities of Linux. These techniques are most useful when a dedicated firewall system is used between an internal network and an external network, but can also help to improve network security on any host. We'll begin with important kernel options and then continue with the `ipchains` utility, which controls the behavior of the firewalling and routing capabilities in the kernel.

Packet filtering is an art, rather than a science, and skill in packet filtering is heavily dependent upon a user's basic knowledge of TCP/IP networking. It is recommended that readers not familiar with TCP/IP consult a basic TCP/IP reference manual before trying to tackle packet filtering.

This hour only applies to users of the 2.2 kernels, for whom `ipchains` is the correct firewalling or filtering management utility. Users of 2.4 kernels should instead pay attention to Hour 11, "Using `iptables` for Firewalling and Routing," which covers similar systems and utilities in the late 2.3 and the new 2.4 series of kernels.

Network Security and the Kernel

Before attempting to construct any firewalling or filtering rules using ipchains, we need to compile support for this type of network functionality into the Linux kernel. Rather than try to prescribe a set of "do" or "don't" rules for the networking options in the 2.2 kernel, this text will defer to the canonical kernel's defaults as a foundation. These defaults are reasonably sane.

By default, most distributions ship with a kernel already capable of cooperating with ipchains configuration. However, these stock kernels are also very bloated and "open"—nearly every option available has been enabled in order to match any possible contingency or installation size. Generally speaking, this is bad for security. Some options tend to place ethernet cards into promiscuous mode, whereas others require special administration in order to be secure.

Therefore, although it is likely *possible* for you to use ipchains without compiling a new canonical kernel, it is not *recommended,* for reasons related to network security. In the end, you be the judge. If your system is relatively low-traffic with regard to the Internet at large, ipchains and a stock distribution kernel might be all that you need. On the other hand, moderate traffic systems should definitely make an attempt to be more conservative.

Do *not* confuse the kernel source included in a Linux distribution with the official kernel source from ftp.kernel.org. The kernel sources included in most Linux distributions are preconfigured to match the binary kernel included with the distribution. Following defaults in this distribution-supplied kernel source therefore leads to a significantly different result from following defaults in canonical kernel distributions.

In addition to those networking options that are enabled by default in canonical kernel-sources, the items in Networking Options, shown in Table 10.1, should be enabled, in order to work with ipchains configuration.

TABLE 10.1 Kernel Options Related to ipchains Firewalling

Option	Description
CONFIG_FIREWALL	Required; if not enabled, no other filtering or firewalling options will be available.
CONFIG_IP_FIREWALL	Required; enables IP packet filtering. This is the fundamental option related to ipchains and must be enabled.

TABLE 10.1   continued

Option	Description
CONFIG_IP_MASQUERADE	Optional (recommended); needed if you plan to forward packets seamlessly between a private internal network and the public external Internet at large. In short, enables Linux to act as a router.
CONFIG_IP_MASQUERADE_ICMP	Optional (recommended); when used in conjunction with masquerading, enables ICMP packets to be masqueraded as well—important for network performance and notification issues.
CONFIG_IP_ALWAYS_DEFRAG	Optional (highly recommended); prevents certain kinds of attacks when using masquerading. Invisibly enabled behind the scenes in later 2.2 kernels.
CONFIG_IP_ADVANCED_ROUTER	Recommended; if not enabled, none of the advanced router options will be available.
CONFIG_IP_ROUTE_VERBOSE	Recommended; causes extra logging about suspicious packets to take place, thereby helping to notify administrators of possible attack attempts.
CONFIG_IP_TRANSPARENT_PROXY	Optional; enables ipchains to transparently redirect local network traffic destined for a remote host to a local port for proxy.

For all other options, try to respect the canonical kernel defaults, which are reasonably conservative. Don't enable anything that is normally disabled unless you are certain that you need the related functionality and have read documentation on how to correctly administer it.

> Some readers might plan to use additional packet types, such as IPX or AppleTalk, with the same ethernet hardware that will be passing TCP/IP packets. Be very aware that ipchains rules apply only to TCP/IP; no matter how protective and closed your ipchains rulesets are, they cannot prevent attacks over IPX or AppleTalk running on the same interface.
>
> Therefore, if you plan to run AppleTalk or IPX on a machine that will also be connected to the outside (Internet) world via TCP/IP, it is suggested that you install two ethernet cards. One will connect to the outside world and will be filtered via ipchains. The other will be for the internal network only and will handle these additional packet types.

After a new kernel has been compiled, installed, and verified as functioning correctly, you're ready to proceed with ipchains's rule configuration.

Using `ipchains`

With `ipchains`, as is the case with any complex system, the devil can be in the details. Really, however, the basic logic behind `ipchains` is simple. The user defines a series of rules that determine what should happen to a network packet. Each rule is one in a *chain* of rules that process all incoming, outgoing, or forwarded packets on a system. More explicitly, the contexts surrounding rules and chains are as follows:

- There are three chains, or collections of rules. They are the *input* chain, the *forward* chain, and the *output* chain. When a packet is received by the filter, it will always be matched against the rules in the input chain. If a packet is to be forwarded by the filter to another host, it will be matched against the rules in the forward chain. If a packet is to be sent onward by the filter, it will be matched against the rules in the output chain before being sent.
- The rules in each chain are order-dependent. When a packet is processed, it is matched against the rules in the related chain, from first to last. Order is therefore important!
- The user can create new chains, name them, and place rules in them as desired. These chains must then be "called" by the user, in order for them to have any effect.

If you can grasp these three basic ideas, understanding the rest of `ipchains` isn't nearly as remote a prospect as many users assume it to be.

Understanding `ipchains` Rules

Of course, we've left something out here. Just what does a rule look like? Fundamentally, a rule has three major components. The first is the name of the chain to which the rule should belong. The second can be thought of as the rule's *matcher*—a criterion or series of criteria that dictates which packets are matched, and therefore, when this rule should be used. The third and final component is the *target*, the actual task that will be carried out when a rule matches a packet. There are seven possible targets, as shown in Table 10.2.

TABLE 10.2 Seven Targets Used by `ipchains`

Target	Description
ACCEPT	When a matched rule sends a packet to the ACCEPT target, the packet is allowed to pass through the network filter to the system, just as it would have if no filter had been in place.
DENY	When a matched rule sends a packet to the DENY target, the packet is filtered out of network traffic on the system and is never heard from again.

TABLE 10.2 continued

Target	Description
REJECT	When a matched rule sends a packet to the REJECT target, the packet is filtered out, and an ICMP message is sent notifying the sender that the packet was not accepted and has therefore been dropped.
MASQ	When a matched rule sends a packet to the MASQ target, the packet is masqueraded for routing to or from the outside world. This functionality requires that the CONFIG_IP_MASQUERADE kernel option be enabled.
REDIRECT	When a matched rule sends a packet to the REDIRECT target, the outbound packet is redirected transparently to the specified *local* network port. This functionality requires that the CONFIG_IP_TRANSPARENT_PROXY kernel option be enabled.
(user chain)	When a matched rule sends a packet to a named user chain instead of one of the predefined targets listed here, processing of rules for this packet will jump from the current chain of rules and begin traversing the named user chain of rules. In a sense, this can be thought of as a kind of subroutine call involving chains.
RETURN	Used only at the end of user rule chains; when the end of a chain is reached, the rule sends the packet back to the original calling chain for further processing, beginning where the calling chain previously left off. The traversal of that chain is then completed. In a sense, this can be thought of as returning from a subroutine chain of rules.

Each rule can match multiple packets depending on the criteria supplied to `ipchains`, but each rule can send packets only to a single one of these targets.

Calling Syntax for the `ipchains` Utility

One single utility, `ipchains`, is used to add rules to chains, to remove rules from chains, and to create new chains. Therefore, the syntax for `ipchains` is relatively complex. The calling syntax looks like this:

```
ipchains CMD [chain] [rule-spec|num] [options]
```

The basic list of commands known to the `ipchains` utility is shown in Table 10.3.

TABLE 10.3 Common `ipchains` Commands

Command	Description
-A (append)	Appends one or more new rule(s) to the end of the specified chain.
-D (delete)	Deletes the numbered or matching rule from the specified chain.
-R (replace)	Replaces the numbered or matching rule in the specified chain.
-I (insert)	Inserts one or more new rule(s) in the specified chain just before the numbered rule given.

TABLE 10.3 continued

Command	Description
-L (list)	Lists all rules in the selected chain or, if no chain is supplied, list *all* rules in all chains.
-F (flush)	Flushes (deletes) all rules in the specified chain.
-N (new chain)	Creates a new chain with the specified user-supplied name.
-X (delete chain)	Deletes the specified user-created chain.
-P (policy)	Sets the blanket policy for the specified chain to the given target.
-C (check)	Checks the given packet to see whether it matches a rule in the specified chain.

In addition to a command, ipchains will often require options, for example, in order to construct match criteria for an appended rule. The most commonly used ipchains options are shown in Table 10.4.

TABLE 10.4 Common ipchains Options

Option	Description
-p [!] protocol	Specifies the protocol matched by this rule, one of icmp, tcp, udp, or all. The exclamation mark (!) inverts the matching logic; when used, it should be surrounded by a space on either side.
-s [!] addr [[!] port]	Specifies the source address and port matched by this rule. Ports can be specified either in numeric range (NNN:NNN) or symbolic (as per /etc/services) form. If the packet type is ICMP, then port is one of the ICMP service names given by ipchains -h icmp.
-d [!] addr [[!] port]	Specifies the destination address and port matched by this rule. Ports can be specified either in numeric range (NNN:NNN) or symbolic (as per /etc/services) form. If the packet type is ICMP, then port is one of the ICMP service names given by ipchains -h icmp.
-i [!] interface[+]	Specifies the network interface matched by this rule. If present, the plus (+) character indicates that the rule should match all interfaces of the same type as the supplied interface.
-j target	Dictates that, when matched, this rule should send the packet to this target (refer to Table 10.1 for a list of possible targets).
-l	Dictates that, when matched, this rule should cause information about the packet to be logged.
[!] -y	Dictates that this rule should only match TCP packets that are initiating a connection. When preceded with an exclamation mark (!), it will match only TCP packets that are in response to already open connections.

For commands that expect an address to be supplied via -s or -d, a default of 0.0.0.0/0 (matches all addresses) will be used if no address is supplied by the user.

> Many users with basic TCP/IP knowledge do not recognize the slash and following number on IP specifications like 0.0.0.0/0 or 192.168.1.0/24. This slash and following number are called the *network mask*.
>
> The number following the slash indicates the number of bits (from "left" to "right" in a sense) that are significant. For example, the IP 255.255.255.255, the largest possible IP number in ipv4, is represented by four 8-bit words, each containing 11111111 or the decimal number 255. These four 8-bit words, taken together, represent 32 bits of data. In a configuration file or when supplying IP addresses to `ipchains` that will need to match a range of IP addresses, it is convenient to use a form such as
>
> 192.168.1.0
>
> However, in such circumstances, we also want to indicate that we do not mean a host specifically assigned the address 192.168.1.0, but rather that only the first three numbers (192.168.1) are significant or fixed. The last digit is a kind of wildcard. Therefore, we specify
>
> 192.168.1.0/24
>
> This means that the first 24 bits (196.168.1) are significant and that the last 8 bits (the number "0" in this case) are not and can match any number.

A Simple Ruleset That Works

Now that we have at least documented the command syntax of `ipchains` and the logic upon which it operates, we can begin to actually add rules that will govern packet filtering in real life. This process is a tedious one, and it might take you some time to get it correct, especially with very complex rulesets. The sample one presented here is reasonably secure for most systems or private networks with a limited number of internal users. Try to follow the logic of each rule as it is presented, and you'll be well on your way to creating your own rules to match your particular circumstances.

> Because the process of adding rules to the kernel's table of rule chains requires repeated calls to the `ipchains` command, it's a good idea to make your changes to a script file as you follow along with the remainder of this chapter. You'll likely want to make any rule or chain changes permanent anyway, and keeping them in a script will enable you to do this.

The idea behind this simple ruleset is to create a few circumstances in which we accept incoming packets and to deny everything else. We won't bother with trying to filter outgoing packets, thus making the assumption that everyone on the "inside" is trusted and not committing illegal acts.

DNS is perhaps the most fundamental service of all on today's Internet, so let's allow nameserver lookups to occur. Assuming that our nameserver's IP address is stored in the environment variable DNS and that our system's IP is stored in the variable MYIP, we add the following rules:

```
ipchains -A input -p TCP -s $DNS domain -j ACCEPT
ipchains -A input -p UDP -s $DNS domain -j ACCEPT
```

These two lines create rules for the input chain (incoming traffic) making both TCP and UDP packets acceptable as long as they come from the domain service (see /etc/ services) of our nameserver.

We also want to be able to browse the Web on this system, so let's accept TCP packets that aren't connection initiation attempts:

```
ipchains -A input -p TCP ! -y -j ACCEPT
```

Now, finally, let's also allow FTP to work. The file transfer protocol is odd because it generally tries to open a connection back to a port on the requesting system using the ftp-data service. Ports below 1024 should be protected, as should ports between 6000 and 6255, which can be used by X. When all is said and done, we'll have to use two calls to ipchains to specify two different port ranges. The addition for FTP looks like this:

```
ipchains -A input -p TCP -s 0/0 ftp-data \
-d $MYIP 1024:5999 -j ACCEPT
ipchains -A input -p TCP -s 0/0 ftp-data \
-d $MYIP 6255: -j ACCEPT
```

Now, finally, we want to make sure that we deny any packets that we haven't explicitly allowed:

```
ipchains -A input -i ! lo -p ! ICMP -j DENY -l
```

This line creates a rule that denies all packets other than ICMP packets (used for message-sending like ping responses) from all sources that do not come in on the loopback interface (lo). It then logs information about any dropped packets so that we know when there is "funny business" happening on the network.

To check our new rules, the -C argument can be used. The syntax associated with -C is similar to the syntax used for -A, so it is easy to use once you've created a few rules.

For example, to see if a connection to the local machine from `206.144.232.16` on port 80 can be established:

```
# ipchains -C input -i eth0 -s 206.144.232.16 www -d $MYIP www -p tcp
denied
#
```

The output of the `ipchains` program, in this case the word `denied`, fortells the fate of the hypothetical packet in question. It is a good idea to use the `-C` argument to check your rules as you create them.

Masquerading

If your machine is more than just a single host, but is instead a link between your internal network and the outside world, then things get a little more interesting. In order to masquerade, you must have at least two network interfaces. Usually, this will be `eth0` and one of `ppp0` or `eth1`. Though it is possible to configure a masquerading system with only one hardware interface using aliasing, this technique can put ethernet hardware into promiscuous mode and is therefore not recommended.

First, you'll need to instruct the Linux kernel to enable IP forwarding, which is disabled by default in 2.2 kernels. To do this, write a 1 into the `/proc/sys/net/ipv4/ip_forward` file:

```
echo 1 > /proc/sys/net/ipv4/ip_forward
```

This change will go away each time you reboot, so you might need to insert it into an init script to make the change permanent. Next, we will amend the script full of calls to `ipchains` we just made to accommodate the new role of the machine in question. If we still operate under the assumption that all the users on the internal network are trusted to behave, the changes are minimal. First, we need to add three new calls to `ipchains` for forwarding requests:

```
ipchains -A input -i eth1 -s $INT -j ACCEPT
ipchains -A forward -s $INT -j MASQ
ipchains -A forward -j DENY -l
```

These three lines assume that your internal interface is `eth1`. The first line simply enables all communication between this machine and other machines on the internal network. The second two lines enable masquerading for all packets on the local network while forbidding and logging all other forwarding attempts.

Notice that we've added a second variable—the IP range of the local network, complete with mask value. For some common examples, see Table 10.4.

10

TABLE **10.4** Common IP Range Values for Internal Nets

Host	INT Value	Host Masquerades For
192.168.1.1	192.168.1.0/24	192.168.1.1–192.168.1.254
192.168.1.1	192.168.0.0/16	192.168.1.1–192.168.255.254
10.1.1.1	10.1.1.0/24	10.1.1.1–10.1.1.254
10.1.1.1	10.1.0.0/16	10.1.1.1–10.1.255.254
10.1.1.1	10.0.0.0/8	10.1.1.1–10.255.255.254

After these changes are made, the system on which the rules are created will act as a reasonably secure router for other systems on the internal network.

Port Forwarding

Chances are that there is at least one service you'd like to provide to the outside world from behind your minimal firewall. In order to enable machines in the outside world to connect to a port on your internal network, some translation must clearly take place because IP addresses in your internal network are not valid in the larger Internet.

With Linux kernel 2.2 versions, this type of translation is accomplished with the kernel masquerading code and a utility called `ipmasqadm`, or IP MASQerading ADMinistration tool. The syntax of `ipmasqadm` is very simple, and looks like this:

```
ipmasqadm portfw -a -P tcp -L $MYIP port -R server_ip port
```

For example, assume that there is a Web server running on a machine on the internal network. The machine's IP address is `192.168.1.14`, and the Web server is running on the standard port. You want to make this Web server available to the outside world, also at the standard port. The command you'd use is

```
ipmasqadm portfw -a -P tcp -L $MYIP 80 -R 192.168.1.14 80
```

Assuming masquerading for the internal network and incoming TCP connections on this interface and port has already been enabled via `ipchains`, this command is all that is needed to enable port forwarding for port 80 to `192.168.1.14`'s port 80.

Putting It All Together

To make things a little more clear, let's put everything we've done so far together. A sample `bash` script that makes use of all the rules we've created so far is shown in Listing 10.1.

LISTING 10.1   Sample ipchains Script

```
#!/bin/bash

# Clear out all existing rules
ipchains -F

# Edit to reflect your networks
INTERNAL=eth1
EXTERNAL=eth0

# Add your IP number here
MYIP=

# And your internal network plus mask here if applicable
INT=192.168.1.0/24

# And your Web server's address here if applicable
WEB=192.168.1.14

# Find the nameservers in /etc/resolv.conf; allow lookups
for DNS in $(grep ^n /etc/resolv.conf|awk '{print $2}'); do
    ipchains -A input -p UDP -s $DNS domain \
-j ACCEPT
    ipchains -A input -p TCP -s $DNS domain \
 -j ACCEPT

done

# Allow ping responses in as well
ipchains -A input -p ICMP -s 0/0 echo-reply \
    -d $MYIP -j ACCEPT

# Allow active ftp-data connections for file transfer
ipchains -A input -p TCP -s 0/0 ftp-data \
    -d $MYIP 1024:5999 -j ACCEPT
ipchains -A input -p TCP -s 0/0 ftp-data \
    -d $MYIP 6255: -j ACCEPT

# Allow other TCP connections we initiated
ipchains -A input -p TCP ! -y -j ACCEPT

# And deny everything else that isn't on loopback
ipchains -A input -i ! lo -p ! ICMP -j DENY -l
# Now, enable masquerading if necessary
if [ "$INT" != "" ]; then
    echo 1 >/proc/sys/net/ipv4/ip_forward
    ipchains -A input -i $INTERNAL -s $INT -j ACCEPT
    ipchains -A forward -s $INT -j MASQ
    ipchains -A forward -j DENY -l
fi
```

10

LISTING 10.1   continued

```
# And set up port forwarding to our Web server
if [ "$WEB" != "" ]; then
    ipchains -A input -d $WEB www -s 0/0 www -p TCP -j ACCEPT
    ipmasqadm portfw -a -P tcp -L $MYIP 80 \
        -R $WEB 80
fi

# end script
```

Although this script is simple and provides no defenses against "bad" users on an internal network, it is fairly secure with respect to the outside world and avoids unnecessary complexity. More sophisticated or paranoid examples for using ipchains can be found in the ipchains HOWTO document at www.linuxdoc.org/HOWTO/IPCHAINS-HOWTO.html.

You might have also noticed that this ipchains configuration doesn't allow for incoming connection requests for most services on the local machine. For example, it doesn't allow the local system to run an FTP server. It's generally a bad idea to allow connection requests for services that aren't going to be made available. Rather than enable incoming packets for every port in our script from the start, you should add lines as necessary to allow incoming requests for services you plan to make available on the local host. Remember to use /etc/services as your guide.

Summary

In this hour, we learned the basics of IP firewalling, packet filtering, and forwarding with Linux 2.2 kernels using the ipchains utility. Specifically, we covered

- The list of kernel options necessary to make use of the ipchains utility and packet forwarding
- The basic logical process behind the functionality of the ipchains command
- Construction of a simple yet reasonably secure ruleset, which also enables forwarding when the machine in question is acting as the gateway between an internal network and an external one
- Simple-case port forwarding, such as when running a Web server from behind the firewall

Although the script we created here is a simple one, you should now have enough knowledge to construct very complex or very paranoid ipchains configurations given patience, determination, and a willingness to refer to the ipchains(8) manual page often.

Q&A

Q **With the use of TCP wrappers described in Hour 6, "TCP/IP Network Security," is the use of `ipchains` and packet filtering really necessary?**

A In a sense, it's up to you. Certainly if you're running a system that is acting as a router between an internal private network and the outside world, you'll need `ipchains` to administer forwarding and protect the internal network. If you're using a standalone machine, it isn't strictly necessary, but it does provide one more measure of security and logging.

Q **What happened to `ipfwadm`?**

A The `ipfwadm` utility was used only for 2.0 kernels. Even better, the `iptables` utility, which also performs a similar function, is only for 2.4 kernels. When writing this text, the decision was made to document packet filtering and forwarding techniques for 2.2 and 2.4 kernels only. Three chapters on the same basic topic seemed like too many, and the 2.0 series of kernels and accompanying distributions are beginning to show their age anyway, both in terms of security and in terms of performance.

Q **An Internet user has told me that the `ipchains` script in this chapter isn't very secure and that I should use the script from `http://www.foo.bar` instead. It's a lot longer, and I don't really understand it. Should I use it?**

A Probably not, for two reasons. First, the script in this hour, although not *as paranoid as possible*, is really secure enough for smaller systems. This is especially true if all hosts on the internal network are similarly configured and TCP wrappers are installed and properly configured all around.

Second, you should never install a script of this sort that you don't understand from a user you don't personally know. If you understand exactly what the script does, then the decision about whether to use it is up to you, but if not, you might actually be opening your system up to attack without realizing it.

Q **I'm using a dial-up network. This script doesn't work because it needs a specific IP address for the local host. What should I do?**

A You'll have to make the necessary modifications yourself. There are two options. First, you could remove references to destination addresses using the `-d` argument and the port in the MASQ rule, meaning that only the source would be important.

A second choice is to incorporate this script into a `ppp-up` or other script that launches your dynamic connection. You can use the following command expansion to extract the IP number from an active interface:

```
MYIP=$( /sbin/ifconfig $INTERFACE | grep inet | \
awk '{ print $2 }' | cut -d: -f2 )
```

After you have extracted the IP from the running interface, you should have no problem incorporating it into a script.

10

New Terms

chain   A list of rules that are applied for a given context. Three chains are automatically defined at all times: `input`, `forward`, and `output`.

packet filtering   A kernel feature that allows incoming network packets to be discarded based on a number of administrator-supplied criteria.

port forwarding   A method for allowing packets reaching a network port on an external interface to be forwarded to the same port on an internal interface, thereby allowing network services to be provided from behind a firewall.

rule   A list of criteria that, when applied, instruct the kernel to either discard or accept one specific group, family, or source of network packets.

Exercises

1. Assume that a second local network is connected to `eth2` and uses the IP addresses `10.1.1.1` through `10.1.1.50`. Add lines to the script to enable the system to act as a router for this second internal network as well.

2. Add a line to the script that prevents any packets from being sent out that seem to have an address belonging to the local network. This offers minimal protection against suspicious activity from local users.

HOUR 11

Using `iptables` for Firewalling and Routing

This hour, we're going to learn to configure basic firewalling and routing capabilities of Linux. These techniques are most useful when a dedicated firewall system is used between an internal network and an external network, but can also help to improve network security on any host. We'll begin with important kernel options and then continue with the `iptables` utility, which controls the behavior of the firewalling and routing capabilities in the kernel.

Packet filtering is an art rather than a science, and skill in packet filtering is heavily dependent upon a user's basic knowledge of TCP/IP networking. It is recommended that readers not familiar with TCP/IP consult a basic TCP/IP reference manual before trying to tackle packet filtering.

This hour applies only to users of the 2.4 kernels, for whom `iptables` is the correct firewalling or filtering management utility. Users of 2.2 kernels should instead pay attention to Hour 10, "Using `ipchains` for Firewalling and Routing," which covers similar systems and utilities in the 2.1 and 2.2 series of kernels.

What Is `iptables`? What Happened to `ipchains`?

The `iptables` command is a successor to the `ipchains` command associated with 2.1 and 2.2 revisions of the Linux kernel. The `ipchains` command was rebuilt to make some things (like forwarding between interfaces or routing) more clear when dealing with packet filtering.

Users familiar with `ipchains` already might find that `iptables` is a cinch to learn. It is also true that `iptables` is much more flexible than `ipchains` in many ways, allowing the administrator more control over little details such as logging levels. Some late 2.3 and early 2.4 kernels include `ipchains` backward-compatibility as a compile-time option, but a move to `iptables` is desirable because of the added functionality and flexibility `iptables` can offer.

Network Security and the Kernel

Before attempting to construct any firewalling or filtering rules using `iptables`, we need to compile support for this type of network functionality into the Linux kernel. Rather than try to prescribe a set of "do" or "don't" rules for the networking options in the 2.4 kernel, this text will defer to the canonical kernel source's defaults as a foundation. These defaults are reasonably sane.

There aren't very many distributions shipping with 2.4 kernels as this text is being written, but generally speaking, distribution maintainers have a tradition of shipping kernels with nearly every networking option available compiled into them. Although this means that such kernels are likely ready "out of the box" for `iptables` and packet filtering, it also means that the security quotient of your system might be lowered if you choose not to recompile your kernel. For example, some possibly unnecessary networking options tend to place ethernet hardware into promiscuous mode, whereas others require special administration or knowledge in order to remain secure.

Therefore, although it might be possible for you to use `iptables` without compiling a new canonical kernel, it is not recommended for reasons related to network security. In the end, you be the judge. For example, if your system is relatively low-traffic with regard to the Internet at large, `iptables` and a stock distribution kernel might be all that you need. On the other hand, moderate traffic systems should definitely make an attempt to be more conservative.

In addition to those networking options that are enabled by default in canonical kernel sources, the Networking Options items shown in Table 11.1 should be enabled as well, in order to work with `iptables` configuration.

Do not confuse the kernel source included in a Linux distribution with the official kernel source from `ftp.kernel.org`. The kernel sources included in most Linux distributions are preconfigured to match the binary kernel sent with the distribution. Following defaults in this distribution-supplied kernel source therefore leads to a significantly different result from following defaults in canonical kernel distributions.

TABLE 11.1 Required Networking Options

Option	Description
CONFIG_NETFILTER	Required; activates the submenu under which all other packet filtering options are enabled or disabled.
CONFIG_IP_NF_CONNTRACK	Optional (recommended); needed if you plan to seamlessly forward packets between a private internal network and the public external Internet at large. In short, it enables Linux to act as a router.
CONFIG_IP_NF_FTP	Optional (recommended); when used in conjunction with connection tracking, enables problematic FTP connections to be masqueraded as well.
CONFIG_IP_NF_IPTABLES	Required; enables the fundamental packet filtering mechanism in the Linux 2.4 series kernels.
CONFIG_IP_NF_MATCH_STATE	Optional (recommended); when enabled, allows for rules based on connection-state matches.
CONFIG_IP_NF_MATCH_LIMIT	Optional; allows for a limit on logging when excessive numbers of log entries would otherwise be made. Can also be used to prevent denial of service attacks by slowing repeat connection rates.
CONFIG_IP_NF_MATCH_UNCLEAN	Optional; enables the kernel to make guesses about which packets might be bad or suspicious and filter based on this decision.
CONFIG_IP_NF_FILTER	Required; creates the default filter table used by `iptables` for the INPUT, OUTPUT, and FORWARD tables. For most users, `iptables` is pointless without this option.
CONFIG_IP_NF_TARGET_REJECT	Optional; useful if, for example, you want to send ICMP messages to hosts whose packets are being dropped.
CONFIG_IP_NF_NAT	Optional (recommended); needed if you plan to seamlessly forward packets between a private internal network and the public external Internet at large. In short, enables Linux to act as a router.

TABLE 11.1   continued

Option	Description
CONFIG_IP_NF_TARGET_MASQUERADE	Optional (recommended); a special case for network address translation wherein all existing connections are dropped if the interface goes down. Useful for dynamic connections.
CONFIG_IP_NF_TARGET_REDIRECT	Optional; a special case for network address translation allowing a system to accept all packets locally. Useful for setting up transparent proxies.
CONFIG_IP_NF_TARGET_LOG	Optional (recommended); allows for packet logging functionality similar to (but more flexible than) the functionality offered by ipchains via the -l option.

For all other options, unless you know what you are doing, try to respect the canonical kernel defaults, which are reasonably conservative. Don't enable anything that is normally disabled unless you are certain that you need the related functionality and have read documentation on how to correctly administer it.

Some readers might plan to use additional packet types, such as IPX or AppleTalk, with the same ethernet hardware that will be passing TCP/IP packets. Be very aware that iptables rules apply only to TCP/IP; no matter how protective and closed your iptables rulesets are, they cannot prevent attacks over IPX or AppleTalk running on the same interface.

Therefore, if you plan to run AppleTalk or IPX on a machine that will also be connected to the outside (Internet) world via TCP/IP, it is suggested that you install two ethernet cards. One will connect to the outside world and will be filtered via iptables. The other will be for the internal network only and will handle these additional packet types.

After a new kernel has been compiled, installed, and verified to function correctly, you're ready to proceed with iptables rule configuration.

Using iptables

As was the case with ipchains, and as is the case with any other complex system, the iptables devil can be in the details. The basic logic behind iptables is simple, although an extra layer of functionality has been added since the days of ipchains.

When using `iptables`, the user defines a series of rules that determine what should happen to a network packet. A chain of rules processes various types of network packet activity. Each chain is one of a group of chains belonging to a specific table. The relationship of rules, chains, and tables is as follows:

- There are three major tables in the new packet filtering code. They are the filter table, the nat table, and the mangle table. Each table contains a series of rule chains that will be used to process packets in a given context.

- The *filter table* is the default table example; no other is specified when calling `iptables`. The filter table contains the INPUT, FORWARD, and OUTPUT chains, which are processed for incoming, forwarded, and outgoing packets, respectively. These chains are similar to the same chains in the `ipchains` tradition.

- The *nat table* handles network address translation (including functionality related to masquerading) and contains the PREROUTING, OUTPUT, and POSTROUTING chains, which are processed for incoming forwardable packets, locally generated packets, and outbound forwardable packets, respectively.

- The *mangle table* is used for special packet mangling and contains two chains, PREROUTING and OUTPUT, which are similar to the chains in the nat table with the same names. We won't concern ourselves with the mangle table in this text.

- The rules in each chain are order-dependent. When a packet is processed, it is matched against the rules in the related chain, from first to last. Order is therefore important!

- The user can create new chains, name them, and place rules in them as desired. These chains must then be called by the user in order for them to have any effect.

Users of ipchains or the older ipfwadm might notice that the new `iptables` command has incorporated functionality from several other separate commands, bringing all packet filtering functionality in Linux under the umbrella of a single command.

When you have mastered IP `iptables`, you will have a firm grasp on the functionality of Linux packet filtering as an entire topic.

Understanding `iptables` Rules

Of course, we've left something out here. Just what does an `iptables` rule look like? Fundamentally, a rule has four major components. The first and second are the table and chain to which the rule should belong. For example, if no table is specified, then it is assumed that the specified chain is a member of the filters table. The third component of a rule can be thought of as the rule's *matcher*—a criterion or series of criteria that dictates which packets are matched, and therefore, when this rule should be used.

The fourth and final component is the *target*, the actual task that will be carried out when a rule matches a packet. The `iptables` command is extensible via kernel modules and therefore includes support for many more targets than the `ipchains` command did. The most common targets are shown in Table 11.2.

TABLE 11.2 Most Common `iptables` Targets

Target	Description
ACCEPT	When a matched rule sends a packet to the ACCEPT target, the packet is allowed to pass through the network filter to the system, just as it would have if no filter had been in place.
DROP	When a matched rule sends a packet to the DROP target, the packet is filtered out of network traffic on the system and is never heard from again. This target is analogous to the DENY target when using `ipchains`.
REJECT	When a matched rule sends a packet to the REJECT target, the packet is filtered out by the filter and an ICMP message notifies the sender that the packet was not accepted and has therefore been dropped. In order to use the REJECT target, you must have enabled it in the kernel or have the related module loaded.
MASQUERADE	When a matched rule sends a packet to the MASQUERADE target, the packet is masqueraded for routing to or from the outside world. This target can be used only in the POSTROUTING chain of the nat table. In order to use the MASQUERADE target, you must have enabled it in the kernel or have the related module loaded.
SNAT	When a matched rule sends a packet to the SNAT target, the packet's source address is translated for routing to or from the outside world. This target can be used only in the POSTROUTING chain of the nat table and is typically used in place of MASQUERADE for routers with a static IP. When using SNAT, the `--to` option is also supplied, along with the address or range of addresses representing the new packet source.
DNAT	When a matched rule sends a packet to the DNAT target, the packet's destination address is translated for routing to or from the outside world. This target can be used only in the PREROUTING chain of the nat table and is typically used for configuring transparent proxies or performing port forwarding. When using DNAT, the `--to` option is also supplied, along with the address or range of addresses representing the new packet destination.
LOG	When a matched rule sends a packet to the LOG target, information about the packet is logged. A number of extended options can be supplied with the LOG target, the most common of which is `--log-prefix`, to control the text string that precedes every log entry. In order to use the LOG target, you must have enabled it in the kernel or have the related module loaded.
(User chain)	When a matched rule sends a packet to a named user chain instead of one of the predefined targets listed here, processing of rules for this packet will jump from the current chain of rules and begin traversing the name user chain of rules. In a sense, this can be thought of as a kind of subroutine call involving chains.

TABLE 11.2 continued

Target	Description
RETURN	Used only at the end of user rule chains; when the end of a chain is reached, this rule sends the packet back to the original calling chain for further processing, beginning where the calling chain previously left off. The traversal of that chain is then completed. In a sense, this can be thought of as returning from a subroutine chain of rules.

Each rule can match multiple packets depending on the criteria supplied to `iptables`, but each rule can send packets only to a single one of these targets.

Calling Syntax for the `iptables` Utility

The `iptables` utility not only incorporates all the functionality formerly present in `ipchains`, but incorporates functionality from other utilities such as `ipmasqadm` as well. Therefore, the syntax for `iptables` can be extremely complex, and you should consult `iptables(8)` for a complete enumeration. The syntax can usually be simplified, however, to the following:

```
iptables [-t table] CMD [chain] [rule-spec|num] [options]
```

The basic list of commands known to the `iptables` utility is shown in Table 11.3.

TABLE 11.3 Common `iptables` Commands

Command	Description
-A (--append)	Appends one or more new rule(s) to the end of the specified chain.
-D (--delete)	Deletes the numbered or matching rule from the specified chain.
-R (--delete)	Replaces the numbered or matching rule in the specified chain.
-I (--insert)	Inserts one or more new rule(s) in the specified chain just before the numbered rule given.
-L (--list)	Lists all rules in the selected chain or, for example, if no chain is supplied, list all rules in all chains.
-F (--flush)	Flushes (deletes) all rules in the specified chain and table.
-N (--new-chain)	Creates a new chain with the specified user-supplied name.
-X (--delete-chain)	Deletes the specified user-created chain.
-E (--rename-chain)	Renames the specified user-created chain.
-P (--policy)	Sets the blanket policy for the specified chain to the given target.
-C (--check)	Checks the given packet to see whether it matches a rule in the specified chain.

11

In addition to a command, iptables will often require options, for example, in order to construct match criteria for an appended rule. There are a vast number of options for iptables, many of which depend on kernel compilation choices. The most commonly used iptables options are shown in Table 11.4.

TABLE 11.4   Common iptables Options

Option	Description
-p [!] protocol	Specifies the protocol matched by this rule, one of icmp, tcp, udp, or all. The exclamation mark (!) inverts the matching logic; when used, it should be surrounded by a space on either side.
-s [!] addr[/mask]	Specifies the source address or range of addresses matched by this rule.
--source-port [!] port	Specifies the source port or range of ports matched by this rule. Ports can be specified either as a numeric range (NNN:NNN) or in symbolic (as per /etc/services) form.
-d [!] addr[/mask]	Specifies the destination address or range of addresses matched by this rule.
--destination-port [!] port	Specifies the destination port or range of ports matched by this rule.
--icmp-type [!] type	Specifies the type of ICMP message matched by this rule. Only applies when ICMP protocol has been specified.
-i [!] interface[+]	Specifies the incoming network interface matched by this rule. If present, the plus (+) character indicates that the rule should match all interfaces of the same type as the supplied interface. This option is only valid in the INPUT, FORWARD, and PREROUTING chains.
-o [!] interface[+]	Specifies the outgoing network interface matched by this rule. This option is only valid for the OUTPUT, FORWARD, and POSTROUTING chains.
-j target	Dictates that when matched, this rule should send the packet to this target (see Table 11.1 for a list of common targets).
[!] --syn	Dictates that this rule should only match TCP packets that are initiating a connection. When preceded with an exclamation mark (!), matches only TCP packets that are in response to already open connections.

For commands that expect an address to be supplied via -s or -d, a default of 0.0.0.0/0 (matches all addresses) will be used if the user supplies no address.

Many users with basic TCP/IP knowledge do not recognize the slash and following number on IP specifications like 0.0.0.0/0 or 192.168.1.0/24. This slash and following number are called the *network mask*.

The number following the slash indicates the number of bits (from "left" to "right" in a sense) that are significant. For example, the IP 255.255.255.255 (the largest possible IP number in IPv4) is represented by four 8-bit words, each containing 11111111 or the decimal number 255. These four 8-bit words, taken together, represent 32 bits of data. In a configuration file or when supplying IP addresses to `ipchains` that will need to match a range of IP addresses, it is convenient to use a form such as

192.168.1.0

However, in such circumstances, we also want to indicate that we do not mean a host specifically assigned the address 192.168.1.0, but rather that only the first three numbers (192.168.1) are significant or fixed. The last digit is a kind of wildcard. Therefore, we specify

192.168.1.0/24

This means that the first 24 bits (196.168.1) are significant and that the last 8 bits (the number 0 in this case) are not and can match any number.

11

State-Based Matches

New with `iptables` is the capability to create rule matches based on packet states, using the `state` module. The format for creating rules based on state matches is

```
iptables -m state --state [!] [state,state...]
```

The four matchable packet states are shown in Table 11.5.

TABLE 11.5 State Module Matches

Match	Description
NEW	Matches packets that initiate a new connection.
ESTABLISHED	Matches packets that belong to an already open connection, and are thus sent in reply to other packets.
RELATED	Matches packets that are related to another connection, for example the data connection for file trasfer protocol exchanges.
INVALID	Matches packets that don't make any sense within the context of the existing connection or packets that couldn't be successfully received for some reason.

The capability to match packets based on state information using `iptables` and kernel 2.4 greatly simplifies the packet filtering process.

A Simple Ruleset That Works

Now that we have at least documented the command syntax of iptables and the logic upon which it operates, we can begin to actually add rules that will govern packet filtering in real life. This process is a tedious one and it might take you some time to get it correct, especially with very complex rulesets. The sample one presented here is reasonably secure for most systems or private networks with a limited number of internal users. Try to follow the logic of each rule as it is presented, and you'll be well on your way to creating your own rules to match your particular circumstances.

> Because the process of adding rules to the kernel's table of rule chains requires repeated calls to the iptables command, it's a good idea to make your changes to a script file as you follow along with the remainder of this chapter. You'll likely want to make any rule or chain changes permanent anyway, and keeping them in a script will allow you to do this.

The idea behind this simple ruleset is to create a few circumstances in which we accept incoming packets and to deny everything else. We won't bother with trying to filter outgoing packets, thus making the assumption that everyone on the "inside" is trusted and not committing illegal acts. We can use connection state matching to begin our simple ruleset by explicitly enabling all non-inbound TCP traffic:

```
iptables -t filter -A INPUT -m state \
--state ESTABLISHED,RELATED -j ACCEPT
```

Because state matching works only with TCP packets, we'll still need some additional rules for UDP packets. DNS is perhaps the most fundamental service of all on today's Internet, so let's allow nameserver lookups to occur. Assuming that our nameserver's IP address is stored in the environment variable DNS, we add the following rules:

```
iptables -t filter -A INPUT -p udp -s $DNS \
--source-port domain -j ACCEPT
```

These four lines create rules for the default filter table's INPUT chain (incoming traffic) making all TCP packets related to existing connections and UDP packets related to the domain service (see /etc/services) acceptable. Since we've already allowed TCP packets for established and related connections, no additional work is required for outbound Web or FTP traffic.

Now we want to make sure that we deny any packets that we haven't explicitly allowed. In the process, it would be nice to make some logs as well. To do both, we add

```
iptables -N logdeny
iptables -t filter -A logdeny -j LOG \
--log-prefix "iptables: "
```

```
iptables -t filter -A logdeny -j DROP
iptables -t filter -A INPUT -i ! lo -m state \
--state NEW,INVALID -j logdeny
```

First, we created a new user-defined chain called `logdeny`. This chain simply logs a packet and then drops it. Then, we add a rule to the `INPUT` chain that checks any incoming packets on real interfaces to see if they initiate new connections or are invalid. If so, the packets are sent to the `logdeny` chain where they are then logged and dropped.

Masquerading and NAT

If your machine is more than just a single host, but is instead a link between your internal network and the outside world, then things get a little more interesting. In order to masquerade or perform normal network address translation, you must have at least two network interfaces. Usually, this will be `eth0` and either `ppp0` or `eth1`.

First, you'll need to instruct the Linux kernel to enable forwarding, which is disabled by default in 2.4 kernels. To do this, write a 1 into the `/proc/sys/net/ipv4/ip_forward` file:

```
echo 1 > /proc/sys/net/ipv4/ip_forward
```

We should also instruct the kernel to drop packets that come in on mismatched interfaces—for example, packets with internal IP numbers on the external interface:

```
echo 1 > /proc/sys/net/ipv4/conf/all/rp_filter
```

These changes will go away each time you reboot, so you might need to insert them into an init script to make the change permanent. Next, we will amend the script full of calls to `iptables` we just made to accommodate the new role of the machine in question. If we still operate under the assumption that all the users on the internal network are trusted to behave, the changes are fairly minimal.

We're going to assume that the variable `EXTERNAL` holds the name of your external network interface and that the variable `MYIP` holds your static IP number, if you have one.

Assuming you have made the `/proc` file system changes to IPv4 described earlier, it is only necessary to add the rule that actually rewrites the packets in question so that communicating hosts will recognize them. There are two commands to do this; one of them will likely apply to your situation, whereas the other will not:

```
iptables -t nat -A POSTROUTING -o $EXTERNAL \
-j MASQUERADE
iptables -t nat -A POSTROUTING -o $EXTERNAL \
-j SNAT --to $MYIP
```

The first of the two commands that uses the `MASQUERADE` target is for users who have a dynamically allocated external IP that is subject to change. (This could be due, for example, to connection difficulties.) When using `MASQUERADE`, if the interface goes down at all, even if just for a moment, all connections are dropped. The other command that uses the SNAT target will attempt to keep connections open if the interface goes down for a moment, operating on the assumption that, when it comes back up, the IP number will be the same.

After these changes are made, the system on which the rules are created will act as a reasonably secure router for other systems on the internal network.

Port Forwarding

Chances are that there is at least one service you'd like to provide to the outside world from behind your minimal firewall. In order to enable machines in the outside world to connect to a port on your internal network, some translation must clearly take place because IP addresses in your internal network are not valid in the larger Internet.

With Linux kernel 2.4 and the advent of iptables, no additional software is required. Instead, port forwarding of this type can be accomplished using the DNAT target for destination network address translation. Using iptables, the basic syntax for port forwarding is as follows:

```
iptables -t nat -A PREROUTING [-p protocol] \
-d $MYIP --dport original_port \
-j DNAT --to destaddr:port
```

The logic behind this type of rule is as follows: Inbound packets, being processed by the PREROUTING chain in the nat table, which were destined for the local network's outside IP on the specified port, will be mangled and delivered to the new destination address and port. In the case of a local Web server running on 192.168.1.14, using default http ports, the result would be

```
iptables -t nat -A PREROUTING -p tcp \
-d $MYIP --dport http -j DNAT --to 192.168.1.14:80
```

This command would enable port forwarding to the Web server, enabling it to operate from behind the firewall. Before incoming connections would be allowed, however, one additional line must appear in our iptables script, just before we block all NEW and INVALID packets:

```
iptables -t filter -A INPUT -p tcp -source-port www -j ACCEPT
```

This line allows connections from any source to be initiated on the www protocol port as listed in the /etc/services file.

Putting It All Together

To make things a little more clear, let's put everything we've done so far together. A sample bash script that makes use of all the rules we've created so far is shown in Listing 11.1.

LISTING 11.1   Sample `iptables` Script

```
#! /bin/bash

# Clear out all existing rules and user-created chains
for TABLE in filter nat mangle; do
    iptables -t $TABLE -F
    iptables -t $TABLE -X
done

# Add your own IP here
MYIP=

# And your internal network plus mask here if applicable
INT=192.168.1.0/24

# And your Web server's address here if applicable
WEB=192.168.1.14

# Edit to reflect your network(s)
INTERNAL=eth1
EXTERNAL=eth0

# Allow any traffic that we initiated
iptables -t filter -A INPUT -m state \
--state ESTABLISHED,RELATED -j ACCEPT

# Find the nameservers in /etc/resolv.conf; allow lookups
for DNS in $(grep ^n /etc/resolv.conf|awk '{print $2}'); do
    iptables -t filter -A INPUT -p udp -s $DNS \
    --source-port domain -j ACCEPT

# Allow incoming Web if necessary
if [ "$WEB" != "" ]; then
    iptables -t filter -A INPUT -p tcp \
    --source-port www -j ACCEPT
fi

# Deny and log everything else that isn't on loopback
iptables -N logdeny
iptables -t filter -A logdeny -j LOG \
--log-prefix "iptables: "
iptables -t filter -A logdeny -j DROP

iptables -t filter -A INPUT -i ! lo -m state \
--state NEW,INVALID -j logdeny

# Now, enable network address translation if necessary
if [ "$INT" != "" ]; then
    echo 1 >/proc/sys/net/ipv4/ip_forward
    echo 1 >/proc/sys/net/ipv4/conf/all/rp_filter
    if [ $EXTERNAL = ppp0 ]; then
        iptables -t nat -A POSTROUTING -o $EXTERNAL \
```

11

LISTING 11.1   continued

```
                -j MASQUERADE
     else
         iptables -t nat -A POSTROUTING -o $EXTERNAL \
             -j SNAT --to $MYIP
     fi
fi

# And set up port forwarding to our Web server
if [ "$WEB" != "" ]; then
    iptables -t nat -A PREROUTING -p tcp \
        -d $MYIP --dport http -j DNAT --to $WEB:80
fi

# end script
```

Although this script is simple and provides no defenses against "bad" users on the internal network, it is reasonably secure with respect to the outside world while at the same time avoiding unnecessary complexity.

You might have also noticed that this `iptables` configuration doesn't allow for incoming connection requests for most services on the local machine. For example, it doesn't allow the local system to run an FTP server. It's generally a bad idea to allow connection requests for services that aren't going to be made available. Rather than enable incoming packets for every possible service, you should add lines as necessary to allow incoming requests for services you plan to use. Remember to use `/etc/services` as your guide.

Summary

In this hour, we learned the basics of IP firewalling, packet filtering, and forwarding with Linux 2.4 kernels using the `iptables` utility. Specifically, we covered

- The list of kernel options necessary to make use of the `iptables` utility and various types of network address translation.
- The basic logical process behind the functionality of the `iptables` command.
- Construction of a simple yet reasonably secure ruleset that also enables network address translation when a machine is acting as the gateway between an internal network and an external one.
- Simple-case port forwarding, such as when running a Web server from behind the firewall.

Although the script we created here is a simple one, you should now have enough knowledge to construct very complex or very paranoid `iptables` configurations, given patience, determination, and a willingness to refer to the `iptables(8)` manual page often.

Q&A

Q With the use of TCP wrappers described in Hour 6, "TCP/IP Network Security," is the use of `iptables` and packet filtering really necessary?

A In a sense, it's up to you. Certainly if you're running a system that is acting as a router between an internal network and the outside world, you'll need `iptables` to administer network address translation and protect the internal network. If you're using a standalone machine, it isn't strictly necessary, but it does provide one more measure of security and logging.

Q What happened to `ipmasqadm`?

A The `ipmasqadm` utility was used only for 2.2 kernels. With the advent of kernel 2.4 and `iptables`, all functionality related to packet filtering, network address translation, and port forwarding has been moved to a central location—the `iptables` command.

Q An Internet user has told me that the `iptables` script in this hour isn't very secure and that I should use the script from `http://www.foo.bar` instead. It's a lot longer, and I don't really understand it. Should I use it?

A Probably not, for two reasons. First, the script in this hour, although not as paranoid as possible, is really secure enough for smaller systems. This is especially true if all hosts on the internal network are similarly configured and TCP wrappers are installed and properly configured all around.

Second, you should never install a script of this sort that you don't understand from a user you don't personally know. If you understand exactly what the script does, then the decision about whether to use it is up to you, but if not, you might actually be opening your system up to attack without realizing it.

New Terms

chain   A list of rules that are applied for a given context. Three chains are automatically defined at all times: `input`, `forward`, and `output`.

packet filtering   A kernel feature that allows incoming network packets to be discarded based on a number of administrator-supplied criteria.

port forwarding   A method for allowing packets reaching a network port on an external interface to be forwarded to the same port on an internal interface, thereby allowing network services to be provided from behind a firewall.

rule   A list of criteria that, when applied, instruct the kernel to either discard or accept one specific group, family, or source of network packets.

state-based matching   A new kind of rule matching introduced with kernel 2.4 that allows packet filtering based on the context of the packet's use, rather than just on source or destination IP address or protocol or port type.

tables   A way of incorporating the functionality of a number of programs into a single program, `iptables`, by allowing for multiple lists of chains that are applied or not applied based on the filtering or translation task at hand.

Exercises

1. Assume that a second local network is connected to `eth2` and uses the IP addresses `10.1.1.1` through `10.1.1.50`. Add lines to the script to enable the system to act as a router for this second internal network as well.

2. Add a line to the script that prevents any packets from being sent out that seem to have an address belonging to the local network. This offers minimal protection against suspicious activity from local users.

HOUR 12

Securing Apache, FTP, and SMTP Services

This hour, we're going to learn about basic security issues involving three common Internet services often provided to the outside world: HTTP, FTP, and SMTP. The HTTP server we're going to discuss is Apache, the most commonly used Web server for Linux systems. The mail (SMTP) server we're going to discuss is Sendmail, still the most popular SMTP server among Linux users.

Having already configured TCP wrappers correctly and set up basic packet filtering, firewalling, and port forwarding when necessary, your network services are already fairly secure. However, all these general security measures are for naught if gaping holes are left in your daemon configurations.

This chapter doesn't cover SSL-enhanced HTTP server modules, however. Hour 18, "Encrypting Web Data," is dedicated completely to this type of functionality.

Security and the Apache HTTPD Server

The Apache Web server is one of the most famous pieces of open source software, and with good reason: It is fast, stable, and extremely secure out of the box. Therefore, most distributions' Apache installations require few modifications. Rather than spend time recompiling and reinstalling Apache and creating configuration files from scratch, it is more efficient simply to cover a few basic security-oriented concepts to keep in mind when configuring Apache.

> As is the case with all software, different versions of Apache have different capabilities. For the purposes of this text, we're going to assume that you'll be using Apache 1.3.x, currently the most widely used version of Apache in the Linux community.

As we browse through the configuration file, try to follow along. Many of the configuration items we'll discuss might already be present in your default configuration file. It is important that you find existing items and modify them rather than simply adding new ones without checking because, in some cases, the effects of multiple identical configuration items might be cumulative.

Global Basic Security-Related Directives

The `httpd.conf` file is the central configuration file for most Apache installations. Different distributions store the file in different locations, but if you have installed Apache packages, you can find the `httpd.conf` file on your system with a simple command:

```
locate httpd.conf
```

Within this file is a series of directives within scoping (context-oriented) boundaries that are used to control the behavior of nearly every aspect of the HTTPD server. An in-depth description of all possible directives in this file is beyond the scope of this text, but details can be found in the official Apache documentation at `http://httpd.apache.org/docs/`.

A few global directives in the file are very important for the basic security of `httpd.conf` and Apache. The recommended settings shown here are a good starting point for most users:

```
ResourceConfig /dev/null
AccessConfig /dev/null
```

The `ResourceConfig` and `AccessConfig` directives specify locations for configuration files that are now considered obsolete. Just to be sure, it's a good idea to point them to a location that cannot be edited.

The `MaxClients` directive specifies the maximum number of connections that will be enabled at any one time, such as

```
MaxClients 50
```

It is important to understand that, if this number is reached, additional connecting users will receive an error message. Don't set the number too low. On the other hand, a new HTTPD process is started for each connection, so setting the number too high can make your system vulnerable to a simple denial of service attack. A number between 50 and 150 is acceptable for the average Pentium system with 32–64 megabytes of memory.

The `Port` directive

```
Port 80
```

is self-explanatory. The normal HTTP port is port 80, but if you don't want to make your Web server obviously accessible to the average person, you can specify an alternative port. Be sure not to conflict with any ports already used in `/etc/services`!

The `User` and `Group` directives are extremely important. They represent the user and group ownership under which your HTTPD processes will run:

```
User nobody
Group nobody
```

The `nobody` user is a good choice if it exists on your system. If not, create a `nobody` user or a `www` user and specify it with this directive. Never run HTTPD with the permissions of any human user on the system or with the permissions of `root`. To do so is to make all of that person's files completely accessible to the entire world. In the case of `root`, the potential results are disastrous!

The `DocumentRoot` directive specifies the base directory from which Apache will serve pages:

```
DocumentRoot /public/www
```

It corresponds to a Web site's `root` directory for users in the outside world. In the interest of both simplicity and security, it is important to set this directive to a location created specifically to house Web pages, owned by the user and group you specified in the `User` and `Group` directives. All Web content will then be placed in this directory.

12

The `UserDir` directive allows the HTTPD server to also serve files from a per-user location supplied in the URL, such as

```
UserDir public_html
UserDir disabled root
```

Set to `public_html`, the following mappings would occur:

```
http://host.net/~bob -> ~bob/public_html
http://host.net/~bob/funnies/ -> ~bob/public_html/funnies/
```

This sort of thing is convenient for giving multiple users a home page, but can represent a security risk if the server is pointed to the wrong areas. Thus, the `disabled` option enables the `UserDir` directive to exclude certain users from this kind of translation. If you also had, for example, `/home/ftp` and `/home/citadel` directories and their corresponding users, you might want to exclude them at the same time, as follows:

```
UserDir disabled root ftp citadel
```

An alternative, more conservative policy is to disable the `UserDir` feature altogether as a matter of policy and then enable it only for specific users:

```
UserDir disabled
UserDir enabled bob jamie karen laffer
```

> Even when using the `disabled` option, the `UserDir` directive poses some fundamental security risks unless a conservative `root` (`/`) directory directive is also in place in your `httpd.conf` file. Be sure to read and understand the "`Directory` and `DirectoryMatch` Scopes" section later in this hour if you plan to use `UserDir`.

The `UserDir` facility isn't by any means mandatory. On small systems or networks where no user home directories need be accessed, the feature should probably be disabled altogether.

Global Logging Directives

Good logging is critical to good security, and no time is this truer than when dealing with a typically high-traffic area like the HTTPD server. The first two logging directives are straightforward:

The `ErrorLog` and `LogLevel` directives

```
ErrorLog /var/log/httpd/error_log
LogLevel warn
```

aren't explicitly security-related, but can become so if Apache becomes unstable or encounters runtime errors. It is therefore important to log errors and watch the log. The level suggested here is warn, which generates a minimal amount of log traffic, but doesn't let anything critical pass.

The other logging directives are more involved. The LogFormat directive allows the format of log files to be dictated by the administrator. The directive accepts two arguments, a format string enclosed in quotation marks that will be expanded each time an entry is made and a name for the log format specified. The most common special values that can be expanded are shown in Table 12.1.

TABLE 12.1 LogFormat Special Values

String	Expands To
%a	Remote user's IP address
%A	Local HTTPD server's IP address
%b	Non-header bytes sent (common log file format)
%c	Connection status after response:
	X = connection aborted
	+ = response completed, keep alive
	- = response completed, connection closed
%f	Name of file sent
%h	Remote host
%H	The request protocol
%{str}i	The contents of the HTTP header string str
%m	Request method
%l	Remote name as given by identd
%p	Port to which HTTPD server is connected
%P	Process ID of HTTPD serving request
%q	The query string (when applicable)
%>s	Server status
%t	Time (common log file format)
%T	Time elapsed in serving request
%u	Remote name as given by auth
%U	URL requested

12

A number of other values can also be expanded; these are documented fully in the canonical Apache documentation. The idea is to use them to construct a standard log entry format to your tastes or needs. A good starting point might be

```
LogFormat "%h %l %u %t \"%r\" %>s %b" common
CustomLog /var/log/httpd/common_log common
```

This creates a log in common log file format with enough information to keep many administrators satisfied. In the interest of additional security, you might also want to specify

```
LogFormat "%h %t \"%{Referer}i\" \"%{User-Agent}i\"" extra
CustomLog /var/log/httpd/extra_log extra
```

If you feel that you need extra logging information, feel free to create as many logs as you have disk space for.

Directory and DirectoryMatch Scopes

A scope in the httpd.conf file can contain any number of directives, each of which will have effect only within the scope in question. The format for a scope demarcation is as follows:

```
<Scope argument>
    Directive arguments
    Directive arguments
    Directive arguments
    ...
</Scope>
```

The httpd.conf file can contain any number of scopes.

The Directory scope causes the set of directives it contains to apply to the directory mentioned in the scope header. For example, consider the following scope definition that should be present on every system:

```
<Directory />
    Order Deny,Allow
    Deny from all
</Directory>
```

The two directives Order and Deny will be effective for the directory / (root) and all subdirectories, which inherit its properties. The Order directive instructs httpd to consider Deny directives in this scope before Allow directives. The Deny directive blocks access to all files in this scope.

The Deny and Allow directives provide a method to allow system administrators to grant or deny access within a scope based on simple rules. Any Deny or Allow directive can be followed by the word all (to allow or deny *all* requests), a network, or nearly any fragment of an IP number or a hostname. For example, the following are all valid:

```
Deny from all
Deny from 192.168.1.0/24
Deny from 192.168.1.
Deny from .conga.net

Allow from all
Allow from 10.0.0.0/8
Allow from 10.
Allow from .borneo.com
```

Typically, Deny or Allow directives are preceded in a scope by an Order directive, which determines whether all Deny rules will be considered first, followed by Allow rules, or vice versa.

The net effect of the previous scope is to prevent HTTPD from retrieving files anywhere in the file system at all. Clearly, this isn't desirable because a Web server is pointless if it isn't allowed to actually serve any pages. So, exceptions must be created:

```
<Directory /public/www>
    Order Allow,Deny
    Allow from all
</Directory>

<Directory /home/*/public_html>
    Order Allow,Deny
    Allow from all
</Directory>
```

These two scopes create exceptions in a sense to the first Directory scope we defined. We now grant public access to all files in /public/www as well as to all files in users' public_html directories, assuming that account homes are in /home. Notice that simple wildcard characters can be used in scoping. The order of Order has been reversed in the interest of convenience and logic. If we want to create any Deny exceptions to the new Allow rules, they can again come *after* the first rule allowing access to all.

If more wildcard flexibility is desired, the DirectoryMatch scope can be used instead. It functions identically to the Directory scope but allows the use of complete regular expressions in the argument.

12

Additional Scopes

Four other scopes are used at times in addition to the `Directory` and `DirectoryMatch` scopes, although they aren't as broadly useful.

The `Files` and `FilesMatch` scopes perform similar functions, but with respect to a single file, which can be supplied either relatively or with an absolute path. For example, to prevent any file called `private.txt` from being accessed anywhere in the system, you could use

```
<Files private.txt>
    Order Deny,Allow
    Deny from all
</Files>
```

To allow any file that ends in `.public.html` to be displayed, regardless of where it occurs, you would use

```
<Files *.public.html>
    Order Allow,Deny
    Allow from all
</Files>
```

The `FilesMatch` scope is similar, but again enables complete regular expressions to be used as arguments.

Two other scopes, `Location` and `LocationMatch`, perform similar functions, but on the URL location, rather than the local directory paths. In many cases, they can be used in place of `Directory` or `DirectoryMatch` when it is convenient to do so.

The `Location` and `LocationMatch` scopes can sometimes confuse security matters. First, they are slightly more confusing to use than `Directory`, `DirectoryMatch`, `Files`, and `FileMatch`, which allow the administrator to think in terms of local directories and files that should or should not be made public.

More importantly, however, they can also conflict with existing scopes. If a `Location` scope explicitly allows for a URL that otherwise would have been denied because of an existing `Directory` scope, for example, the file will go out to the requester anyway.

Authentication

At times it is necessary to provide some kind of authentication method for accessing a file or directory. For example, you might want to allow access to the directory `/private/projects` via the Web, but only to certain employees. Step one is easy enough:

```
ln -s /private/projects /public/www/employee-projects
```

Now there is a valid URL where the directory can be found. However, the `Directory` scope restricting access to the `root` (`/`) file system still prevents access to the directory. You could then add another scope:

```
<Directory /private/projects>
    Order Allow,Deny
    Allow from all
</Directory>
```

This will allow access to the directory in question, but it will give access to everybody in the world. The proper way to handle a situation like this is via user authentication. By assigning username and password pairs to the group of employees who need to have access to `/private/projects`, you can put the data on the Web without making it completely public.

To do this, we can add the following scope to `httpd.conf`:

```
<Directory /private/projects>
    AuthType Basic
    AuthName "Employee Files"
    AuthUserFile /etc/httpd/employee-users
    Require valid-user
</Directory>
```

The `AuthType` directive instructs HTTPD to use basic authentication (ask for a username and a password) before allowing files in the directory to be served. The `AuthName` directive determines what will be displayed to the remote user when a username and password are requested.

The next two directives require more explanation. The `AuthUserFile` directive dictates that a user and passwords file located at `/etc/httpd/employee-users` be consulted for authentication information. The `Require` directive with the `valid-user` option dictates that a valid username and password pair is required before logins will be allowed. But where does this user and passwords file come from?

The file must be created and maintained using the htpasswd utility. The utility is very easy to use. To begin a new file and add a user to it, use

```
htpasswd -b -c file user password
```

So, for example, to give a user named bob access to `/private/projects` over the Web, you'd create an account for him in a brand new file like this:

```
htpasswd -b -c /etc/httpd/employee-users bob bobspass
```

12

Be careful not to place the password file in the same directory you're protecting with the password. If you do this and don't protect it in some other
way, any user will be able to download the directory after he is inside!

If you then wanted to add `sara` to the existing file, you'd drop the `-c` (create) argument:

```
htpasswd -b /etc/httpd/employee-users sara saraspass
```

Of course, there are some circumstances in which it is undesirable for the user passwords
to appear on the command line and in command history. In order to be prompted for a
password rather than supplying it on the command line, drop the `-b` (batch) argument:

```
# htpasswd -b /etc/httpd/employee-users barney
New password:
Re-type new password:
Adding password for user barney
#
```

The file `/etc/httpd/employee-users` now contains accounts for three users, `bob`, `sara`,
and `barney`, all of whom will have access to the `/private/projects` directory via the
`employee-projects` directory in the URL.

This form of authentication uses a plain-text password file. It's reasonably
secure given permissions that do not allow public reading because the passwords contained inside it are encrypted with `crypt`. It is, however, slow for
large databases of users and passwords.

An alternative authentication system using the database libraries is also
available. Instead of the `htpasswd` command, it uses `dbmmanage`, also relatively simple, to add and remove users, and replaces directives like
`AuthUserFile` and `AuthGroupFile` with `AuthDBMUserFile` and
`AuthDBMGroupFile`, respectively.

Complete details can be found in the official Apache documentation.

To remove users from `/etc/httpd/employee-users`, simply load it into your favorite
text editor and slice them out again; one user occupies each line in the file.

What we've provided here is a simple-case scenario for protecting various directories or
URLs with password authentication using Apache. For complete documentation on each
of these directives and the options available to them, please refer to the official Apache
documentation at `http://httpd.apache.org/docs`.

The `Options` and `AllowOverride` Directives

Now that we're reasonably familiar with scoping, it's important to include discussion of two security-oriented directives. The `Options` directive specifies a set of Web-oriented permissions for a file or directory. The syntax for `Options` is as follows:

```
Options [+|-]option [+|-]option ...
```

There are a number of options available to the `Options` directive, but the most common are shown in Table 12.2.

TABLE 12.2   Options Available to the `Options` Directive

Option	Description
ExecCGI	Enable or disable execution of CGI scripts from this directory.
FollowSymLinks	Enable or disable the following of symbolic links in this directory.
SymLinksIfOwnerMatch	Follow symbolic links only if the owner of the symbolic link matches the owner of the file pointed to by the link.
Indexes	Enable or disable the generation of file indexes in the absence of an `index.html` (or `DirectoryIndex`-specified) file.
Includes	Enable or disable processing of server-side includes.
IncludesNOEXEC	Allow server-side includes, but disallow the `#exec` and `#include` directives.

At this point, it might be a good idea to insert an `Options` directive into your public Web content `Directory` scope in the interest of security. The new scope would look like this:

```
<Directory /public/www>
    Order Allow,Deny
    Allow from all
    Options -ExecCGI -Indexes
</Directory>
```

This way, only directories that you later specifically mark for CGI execution or index generation will allow these tasks to be performed.

`AllowOverride` also changes the security-related behavior in a `Directory` scope, but in a different way—it determines when a local access file (discussed in the next section) will be able to override the settings in `httpd.conf`. There are several legal arguments to `AllowOverride`, but we're only going to concern ourselves with three of them, `AuthConfig`, `Limit`, and `None`.

The `AuthConfig` option allows local access files to override `httpd.conf` restrictions by asking for username and password authentication. The `Limit` argument allows local

12

access files to use the `Order`, `Deny`, and `Allow` directives. The `None` argument never allows any overrides. In order to follow the example in the next section "The Access File," you'll need to amend your `root` `Directory` scope to look like this:

```
<Directory />
    Order Deny,Allow
    Deny from all
    AllowOverride AuthConfig Limit
</Directory>
```

After making this change, the access file we're about to create will be allowed to have an effect.

The Access File

Now we can block access to certain directories while permitting access to others. We can even do this based on criteria such as the host name of the requesting system or whether or not the requester can supply a valid username and password. This is enough information to establish a reasonable level of security. However, we're still having to store all this information in `httpd.conf`. It's clumsy, and, what's more, it can be dangerous if you move public directories around but forget to update `httpd.conf` to reflect their new names and locations.

To solve these problems, Apache includes another global directive that is very commonly used:

```
AccessFileName .htaccess
```

The default name is `.htaccess`, but you can change it to whatever you like. It is a special file that Apache will normally look for in a directory before serving files from it. The access file can contain directives whose scope is limited to the directory tree in which it resides. For example, instead of creating a new `Directory` context for `/private/projects` in the previous section, we could have instead created an `.htaccess` file like the one shown in Listing 12.1.

LISTING 12.1   The `/private/projects/.htaccess` File

```
AuthType Basic
AuthName "Employee Files"
AuthUserFile /etc/httpd/employee-users
Require valid-user
```

This has the same effect as the `Directory` scope from the previous section, but if the `/private/projects` directory is moved elsewhere, its `.htaccess` file will travel with it—no need to remember to update `httpd.conf`.

Other directives can also appear in the access file. For example, if you knew that all the employees who needed access to /private/projects would also be connecting from specific places, you could make the access file even more secure, as shown in Listing 12.2.

LISTING 12.2   Updated Access File

```
Order Deny,Allow
Allow from blarney.castle.net
Allow from 206.13.40.0/24
AuthType Basic
AuthName "Employee Files"
AuthUserFile /etc/httpd/employee-users
Require valid-user
```

Now connecting users will just see a "forbidden" message if they are connecting from any systems other than hosts in the 206.13.40 network or blarney.castle.net. If the connection is from one of the allowed systems, a username and password will be required.

Security and File Transfer Protocol

The file transfer protocol, FTP, is an incredibly useful service, and is one of the most used services on the Internet, behind HTTP, SMTP, and DNS.

The wu-ftpd server is very flexible, and configuration files can become quite complex. However, the vast majority of FTP servers on the Internet do one of two things (or perhaps both of them) on a regular basis: provide anonymous FTP access to everyone or provide private FTP access for a few users. Two short files and a few tips are all that is needed to keep FTP secure under these circumstances, provided you update when security patch releases are made available.

> We're going to discuss the most common FTP server, wu-ftpd, in this section. There are any number of alternative servers, including some like NcFTPd or ProFTPd, which are quite popular. The wu-ftpd server is still king among the Linux distributors, however, and remains one of the easiest and most secure to configure and use.

Anonymous Versus Private FTP

Before editing any FTP-specific configuration files, you should decide whether or not you want to enable anonymous FTP. If you only need a few users with accounts on your system to be able to log in and manipulate their files, then by all means, disable anonymous FTP. The easiest way to do this is to remove the `ftp` user from your `/etc/passwd` and `/etc/shadow` files. So-called "real" users will still be able to log in; `ftp` or anonymous logins will be rejected.

The `/etc/ftpaccess` File

Most distributions ship with a preconfigured `/etc/ftpaccess` file that is already set to handle mundane things like filenames, local email addresses, and so on, so we'll just mention those options that are security-oriented here. If you don't see the recommended entry in your `/etc/ftpaccess` file, consider adding it. All these options are explained in further detail in the `ftpaccess(5)` manual page.

```
loginfails 3
```

`loginfails 3` gives a user three tries to get his username and password pair right before he is booted off.

```
greeting brief
```

`greeting brief` reduces the amount of server-specific information given to connecting users before they have been authenticated. Without this line, `wu-ftpd` will display its version number, among other things, to connecting users.

```
log commands anonymous,guest,real
```

`log commands anonymous,guest,real` causes the FTP server to log all commands entered by users of all types. If you run a high-traffic server, this is probably a bad idea, but in most cases, it's desirable.

```
log transfers anonymous,guest,real inbound,outbound
```

`log transfers anonymous,guest,real inbound,outbound` causes the FTP server to log all transfers initiated by users of all types. Transfers in both directions will be logged. Even for high traffic servers, this option is recommended.

```
log security anonymous,guest,real
```

`log security anonymous,guest,real` causes the FTP server to log all attempted security violations caused by users of all types. Even for high traffic servers, this option is recommended.

The lines

```
chmod no anonymous,guest
delete no anonymous,guest
overwrite no anonymous,guest
rewrite no anonymous,guest
umask no anonymous,guest
```

prevent anonymous and guest users from changing permissionson a file, deleting a file, overwriting a file, rewriting a file, or changing the `umask` value.

```
passwd-check rfc822 enforce
```

`passwd-check rfc822 enforce` forces anonymous and guest users to supply a valid email address as a password when logging in. Invalid passwords will be rejected.

```
deny !nameserved /home/ftp/nodns.txt
```

`deny !nameserved /home/ftp/nodns.txt` causes the FTP server to reject logins from any machine that is not served by a working nameserver or whose name doesn't resolve with its own nameserver. This is a kind of identity check for connecting machines. The file specified will be displayed to users in violation before they are dumped; it should simply contain a message explaining why they are being denied access.

The `/etc/ftpusers` File

The `/etc/ftpusers` file tends to confuse new administrators because it behaves in the opposite way from what they expect. The `/etc/ftpusers` file is simply a list of account names that are not allowed to log in to FTP.

Thus, if you want to prevent an exiting user from logging in to FTP, you should add her account to the end of the list. By default, the file should exclude everybody in `/etc/password` except real users—who should have access—and the `ftp` account—if you want to allow anonymous access.

On a brand-new Linux installation where only one non-`root` user has been created and the `ftp` account exists, this file can be created with a little shell trickery:

```
cut -d: -f1 </etc/passwd | grep -v ftp | \
    head -$[$(wc -l /etc/passwd | \
    awk '{ print $1 }')-2] >/etc/ftpusers
```

This miniscript extracts all users but the most recently created user and the user called `ftp`. It dumps the users, one per line, to the `/etc/ftpusers` file. Note that this won't work after several users have been created or if the `ftp` user has been removed.

Anonymous Upload Permissions

Allowing for anonymous FTP uploads to an `incoming` directory is never a good idea, either legally or with respect to security considerations. However, if you must allow for anonymous uploads, you should at least ensure that you set permissions on this directory:

```
chmod 733 incoming
```

This will prevent users from seeing files that other users have uploaded, giving the system administrator a chance to preview what has been uploaded before it is made public.

Security and `sendmail`

The `sendmail` daemon is an ugly beast, but it is very standard and very flexible. In fact, it is so flexible that its bizarre configuration file format is like a cross between a programming language and an exploding bit bucket.

Because of this, it's not recommended that you reconfigure Sendmail at all—certainly not without the aid of a Sendmail book. Most distribution maintainers do a much better job of constructing Sendmail configuration files than the average small network administrator has time to do. Thus, if you keep up to date with regard to Sendmail packages and updates from your distribution vendor, there's little more you can really do about the configuration of Sendmail.

However, `sendmail` or any mail daemon for that matter can still be made more secure. In organizations of all sizes, the security of SMTP agents is especially vulnerable to unauthorized use, either from spammers or, in a worst-case scenario, by crackers. Luckily, in the case of an SMTP agent, there's never a need to allow for full public access. There will always be some small number of hosts or a specific network that should have access to SMTP and the rest of the world, which should not.

There are thus two basic ways to secure Sendmail: with packet filtering or with TCP wrappers.

Securing Sendmail Through Packet Filtering

Packet filtering, as discussed in Hour 10, "Using `ipchains` for Firewalling and Routing," and Hour 11, "Using `iptables` for Firewalling and Routing," is a method of filtering out unwanted network traffic from untrusted sources using a table of information inside the kernel. Recall that the two basic packet-filtering utilities are `ipchains` for 2.2 kernels and `iptables` for 2.4 kernels.

Using `ipchains` to filter out Sendmail requests from untrusted sources is a simple matter:

```
ipchains -A input -p tcp -s 192.168.1.0/24 \
    -j ACCEPT
ipchains -A input -p tcp -s my.isp.mail.host \
    -d ext.ip.number.here smtp -j ACCEPT
ipchains -A input -p tcp -i ! lo \
    -d ext.ip.number.here smtp -j DENY -l
```

The first two `ipchains` lines allow packets from an internal network (change this to suit your own needs) on the one hand and from a trusted external host on the other hand. The third line drops and logs all SMTP packets not originating in the internal network or with the trusted host. You might have realized that if you have already implemented the set of `ipchains` rules from Hour 10, you won't need the last line because a similar, more all-encompassing rule already exists.

> Remember that ipchains and iptables rules are order-dependent. This
> means that if you already have a set of rules that are active, perhaps started
> by a script when you booted, you can't simply type these new rules in and
> expect them to work at the end of the chain. Insert them into your script
> before any final DENY or DROP rules and reboot in order to activate the filter-
> ing effects given here.

Using iptables, the series of commands is similar, albeit not exactly the same:

```
iptables -t filter -A INPUT -i ! lo -m state \
    --state ESTABLISHED,RELATED -j ACCEPT
iptables -t filter -A INPUT -p tcp -s my.isp.mail.host \
    -d ext.ip.number.here --destination-port smtp \
    -j ACCEPT
iptables -t filter -A INPUT -i ! lo \
    -d ext.ip.number.here -j LOG --log-prefix "iptables: "
iptables -t filter -A INPUT -i ! lo -m state \
    --state NEW,INVALID -d ext.ip.number.here -j DROP
```

The first two iptables lines allow packets from an internal network (again, change this
to suit your own needs) and from a trusted external host. The third line logs all packets
not caught by the first two rules, and the last line drops the bad packets. Here again, if
you have already implemented the set of iptables rules from Hour 11, the last line isn't
necessary because a more stringent rule finished that script.

Securing Sendmail Using TCP Wrappers

You might remember the section on configuring TCP wrappers from Hour 6, "TCP/IP
Network Security." The same TCP wrappers used to start in.ftpd and in.telnetd can
also be used to start a mail transfer agent such as Sendmail. Although a few distributions
do things this way already, most of the major distributions do not.

To start Sendmail using inetd and /usr/sbin/tcpd, you will need to do two things.
First, remove the Sendmail script links from the runlevels in which you want to secure
sendmail. The process of managing init scripts was discussed in Hour 5, "System and
User Fundamentals." After you've stopped Sendmail from automatically being started at
boot time, add the following line to your /etc/inetd.conf file, or uncomment it if it is
present but commented out:

```
smtp stream tcp nowait root /usr/sbin/tcpd /usr/sbin/sendmail -bs
```

This line instructs inetd to start Sendmail only when it is required and to use
/usr/sbin/tcpd, the TCP wrapper, to do it. This way, information in the
/etc/hosts.allow and /etc/hosts.deny files can be used to govern who will be

12

granted permission to use the SMTP service on your host and who will not. Remember to restart `inetd` so that the changes take effect:

```
killall -HUP inetd
```

This technique has one drawback. Because Sendmail isn't running all the time, it can't automatically attempt to resend mail in the queue that failed on first attempt on a periodic basis. To fix this, Sendmail must be explicitly called every now and then to process the queue, if necessary. This is best done with a root cron job. A line like this one will cause Sendmail to attempt to process the queue every half hour:

```
0,30 * * * * /usr/sbin/sendmail -q
```

For details on the format of a cron user file, see `crontab(5)`. For details on editing a cron user file, see `crontab(1)`.

m4 and `sendmail.cf` Configuration Notes

Though `m4` configuration of Sendmail is beyond the scope of this book, there is one security-oriented directive that you should consider adding to your `sendmail.m4` file if you plan to rebuild `sendmail.cf` using `m4`. This directive is

```
define('confPRIVACY_FLAGS','authwarnings,goaway')dnl
```

This directive adds two privacy flags, `authwarnings` and `goaway`, to your Sendmail configuration. The `authwarnings` flag causes `X-Authentication-Warning:` headers to appear in messages in which Sendmail configuration or communication oddities have been detected. The `goaway` flag causes Sendmail to reject all requests for information about your Sendmail server that could potentially be used to do harm.

If you don't plan to reconfigure with `m4`, you can edit your `/etc/sendmail.cf` file directly for the same effect. Search for the line beginning with

```
O PrivacyOptions
```

If it is commented out, uncomment it. Change the line to read

```
O PrivacyOptions=authwarnings,goaway
```

This change will have the same effect as would making the `m4` change above and then regenerating the `sendmail.cf` file.

Summary

This hour, we covered basic security techniques for the three most common network services that must interact with the outside world: Web service (HTTP), File Transfer Protocol (FTP), and Simple Mail Transfer Protocol (SMTP).

For the Apache Web server, we covered global security-oriented directives; the concepts of directory-based, file-based, or location-based scoping; basic username/password authentication techniques; and the local access file to make security administration easier.

For the wu-ftpd FTP server, we covered the difference between anonymous and "real" user FTP access and how to disable the former when necessary. We also discussed a number of recommended security-oriented options for the /etc/ftpaccess file, as well as the format of the /etc/ftpusers file.

Finally, for the sendmail daemon, an SMTP mail transfer agent, we discussed the most common external security risk: unauthorized connection. We covered two basic techniques for stopping unauthorized connections: packet filtering via ipchains or iptables and the conversion of sendmail from a permanently backgrounded daemon to a daemon managed by inetd and started with TCP wrappers.

Q&A

Q I have questions about Apache that aren't covered in this chapter!

A Unfortunately, there just isn't space to cover every Apache directive in-depth. Web servers have become complicated, flexible animals with configuration needs to match. What we've discussed here are the basics. If you plan to run a high-traffic Web server, I heartily recommend that you obtain a text entirely about Apache and use it to guide you through the entire process.

Q What about anonymous FTP write access?

A Write access for anonymous FTP is strongly discouraged for a number of reasons, most of them legal rather than technical. Unfortunately, publicly writable anonymous FTP has become a choice tool for software pirates. Because this isn't a common need anyway, it hasn't been included. You'll find the details you need in ftpaccess(5), however, and should be able to go from there.

Q Isn't Sendmail fundamentally insecure? Isn't it also obsolete? Can I use mail transfer agents foo or bar?

A No, no, and no. Sendmail isn't any more or less secure than any other network daemon out there. It's as secure as the last update you downloaded and the configuration file you're using. As always, it's important to stay on top of updates as they occur and (especially in the case of Sendmail) to use configuration files from canonical sources if you're not ready to create your own.

More importantly, the instructions given will work with most any other SMTP mail transfer agent as well; you'll simply have to adjust the paths to suit your needs.

12

New Terms

directive   A single option element from an Apache configuration file. Some directives are global, whereas others apply only within a given scope.

local access file   A file, usually `.htaccess`, that contains directives that apply to the current directory tree. Often, an `AllowOverride` directive must appear in the master configuration file for an `.htaccess` file to have effect.

scope   A segment of an Apache configuration file, generally referring to one file, directory, URL, or virtual host, which can contain a number of directives.

Exercises

1. After enabling user home directories in Apache, password-protect your own home directory.

2. Try implementing both packet filtering and `inetd` management for `sendmail` or for your SMTP daemon.

HOUR 13

Network Security: DNS with BIND

This hour, we're going to secure the BIND daemon, version 8.x. Actually, this is a little misleading. The BIND daemon is incredibly complex and nuanced; it would be more accurate to say that we're going to improve the security of your BIND installation with a few security tricks.

The BIND daemon used by many Linux distributions supplies domain name service (DNS) and has been victim to more than its fair share of attacks in the past, partly due to the complexity of the task it performs, and partly due to the resultant possibility for complexity in its configuration. Because of this, it has become a common practice to run named in a chroot environment—a kind of jail cell a cracker can't easily penetrate.

If your network is too small to require that you run your own domain name service, you can safely skip this hour. If you ever need to provide any kind of DNS port access on an external network interface, however, you should take the time to secure the BIND daemon before going online. Understand that we're not going to cover general-purpose BIND configuration here; this hour assumes that you either have a working BIND configuration or have resources to assemble one on your own.

Pre-Chroot BIND Security

Of course, there are some basic things that can be done before chrooting `named` to improve the security quotient under which your DNS machine will be operating. There are several aspects of configuration that fall under this umbrella.

First and most importantly, keep your BIND packages up-to-date. There are times when bug fixes for BIND seem to come almost rapid-fire style, and BIND exploits tend to be very popular among script kiddies, so it's important to stay on top of things, especially if your BIND socket will be open to hosts on an external network interface.

Next, implement packet filtering and take care of a few important options and issues in the `named.conf` file. We'll discuss those now.

Packet Filtering for the Domain Port

BIND uses both the TCP and UDP protocols, the former for larger queries and the latter for smaller ones, so to filter out unwanted requests using packet filtering, we'll have to account for both protocol types. Using `ipchains`, a general form is shown in Listing 13.1.

LISTING 13.1   DNS Port Filtering with `ipchains`

```
ipchains -A input -p tcp -s 192.168.1.0/24 \
    -d int.ip.number.here domain -j ACCEPT
ipchains -A input -p udp -s 192.168.1.0/24 \
    -d int.ip.number.here domain -j ACCEPT
#ipchains -A input -p tcp -s trusted.ext.system.ip \
#    -d ext.ip.number.here domain -j ACCEPT
ipchains -A input -p udp -s trusted.ext.system.ip \
    -d ext.ip.number.here domain -j ACCEPT
ipchains -A input -i ! lo \
    -d ext.ip.number.here domain -j DENY -l
```

Notice that one `ipchains` command is commented out. This is the command that allows larger (TCP) transfers on the external interface to a specific trusted host. Uncomment and use this command if you need to for your circumstances (for example, for zone transfers from inside to outside); otherwise you're safer to leave it out. In most cases for small networks, this set of filtering rules will match your needs. A similar set of rules for those using `iptables` is shown in Listing 13.2.

LISTING 13.2   DNS Port Filtering with `iptables`

```
iptables -t filter -A INPUT -p tcp -s 192.168.1.0/24 \
    -d int.ip.number.here --destination-port domain \
    -j ACCEPT
```

LISTING **13.2**   continued

```
iptables -t filter -A INPUT -p udp -s 192.168.1.0/24 \
    -d int.ip.number.here --destination-port domain \
    -j ACCEPT
#iptables -t filter -A INPUT -p tcp -s trusted.ext.sys.ip \
#    -d ext.ip.number.here --destination-port domain \
#    -j ACCEPT
iptables -t filter -A INPUT -p udp -s trusted.ext.sys.ip \
    -d ext.ip.number.here --destination-port domain \
    -j ACCEPT
iptables -t filter -A INPUT -i ! lo \
    -d ext.ip.number.here -j DROP
```

Note that if you need to provide large transfers to a large number of external systems, you may need to adjust these rules for the sake of practicality. Remember also that the last commands in both Listing 13.1 and Listing 13.2 simply filter out all packets not excepted in earlier commands; they should be the last `ipchains` or `iptables` command in your system-wide filtering script and need only be present once. They're listed here for correctness.

Notes on `named.conf`

Though the full format of the `named.conf` file is well beyond the scope of this text, there are a few configuration items in this file to which you should pay particular attention. The first is in the `options` section, and the recommended entry is as follows:

```
options {
    version "Sorry, the version number is not available.";
};
```

This prevents BIND from revealing its version information when asked to do so by a remote party. Why bother? Because information about the specific version of BIND you are running can at times be half the battle in exploiting it. This measure also discourages potential hackers, who will know that you have taken steps to secure your BIND installation.

The other `named.conf` items we need to discuss are the access controls you impose. Even the simplest DNS server configuration on a small network should impose access controls if it will be connected in any way to the outside world. The best policy is to set up conservative defaults in the `options` section and then override these when necessary in your individual zones.

Access control in `named.conf` is implemented with five basic keywords. Brief descriptions of these keywords' functions are shown in Table 13.1.

13

TABLE 13.1   Access Control in `named.conf` Zones

Keyword	Description
allow_query	Determines which host(s) or network(s) will be allowed to make ordinary queries of this server.
allow_transfer	Determines which host(s) or nctwork(s) will be allowed to receive zone transfers from this server.
allow_recursion	Determines which host(s) or network(s) will be allowed to make recursive queries to this server.
allow_updates	Determines which remote hosts will be allowed to submit dynamic DNS updates to this server.
blackhole	Determines which hosts(s) or network(s) will be blocked from having communication of any kind with this server.

The default values for the first three items are the most relaxed defaults possible: Allow queries from everyone, allow everyone to receive zone transfers, and allow recursive queries from everyone. Only updates are restricted; the default is to allow updates from no one. Taken as a whole, this is clearly not the right set of defaults for a small DNS server. `allow_transfer` is especially troublesome because it could allow a potential cracker to map your network. A recommended modified set of default options is shown in Listing 13.3.

LISTING 13.3   New Options with Access Control

```
options {
    version "Sorry, the version number is not available.";
    allow_query {
        localhost;
    };
    allow_transfer {
        none;
    };
    allow_recursion {
        none;
    };
};
```

Each of the access control settings can be overridden within a specific zone, depending on your needs, so that no important one need be left out in the end. After including the options from Listing 13.3 in your `named.conf`, the default behavior is as follows: Allow general queries only from the local host, allow no zone transfers, and allow no recursive queries. To override these defaults in a zone, simply respecify the item with an access control specifier or specifiers inside the braces. The most common specifiers are shown in Table 13.2.

TABLE 13.2 Access Control Specifiers

Specifier	Description
any	Allow from any host anywhere (no access control at all).
none	Allow from no hosts anywhere (all access forbidden).
localhost	Allow from the local host.
localnet	Allow from hosts that reside on a network for which the local host has a hardware interface.
N.N.N.N	Allow from host with matching IP number.
N.N.N.N/N	Allow from the network matching this network/netmask specifier. For example, 192.168.1.0/24 allows from all hosts on the local 192.168.1. network.

The allow_updates and blackhole items, which are to be specified within zones, use the same access control specifier formats.

Running named in a Chroot Environment

Since BIND is a traditional favorite among crackers wanting to gain illegitimate entry into a system, many administrators have taken to running named in a chroot environment. A chroot environment is a way of tricking BIND into thinking that a subdirectory is actually the root file system. For example, to all other processes on the system, named may be running inside /usr/local/bind, but to the named process itself and to its children, the /usr/local/bind directory will actually appear to be the root (/) directory. If someone cracks a chrooted named process, he will be able only to damage or access files in /usr/local/bind.

It is also a good idea to run BIND under a user and group specifically created to hold the named process, rather than running as root, which seems to be the default on many Linux distributions.

Adding User and Group

Because BIND version 8 includes its own chroot functionality, we need only add a user and group for named to the system-wide passwd and group files located in /etc. This is easy to do from the command line:

```
# echo "named::29" >>/etc/group
# echo "named:x:29:29:named:/:" >>/etc/passwd
```

> Remember to use the append redirect (>>) rather than the create redirect (>) when appending lines to a file or you could end up erasing your password and group files!

13

We also need to add the new `named` user to the `/etc/ftpusers` file if the file transfer protocol is going to be running, because there's no good reason to allow `named` login attempts in FTP:

```
# echo named >>/etc/ftpusers
```

Feel free to adjust the user and group ID numbers assigned to `named` if necessary to accommodate the needs of your own system. Try to choose low numbers, though, to indicate that these accounts are system accounts.

Creating the Jail

The first steps in running BIND from a chroot jail are creating the jail "cell" and adding a specific user and group for the `named` process and file ownership. A good location for the cell is `/usr/local/named`, but use your own discretion:

```
# mkdir /usr/local/named
# cd /usr/local/named
# mkdir dev etc etc/named lib usr usr/sbin
```

The `/etc/named` directory (remember, this is chroot) will be used to hold DNS data. Adjust it if necessary to suit your needs or preferences.

> If you're going to copy data and configuration information from an existing `named` setup (we haven't shown this here), remember to change ownership with `chown` to the new `named` user and group. Also remember that `named` will soon be running in a chroot environment, so your `named.conf` will have to be edited to reflect the new paths—as though `/usr/local/named` were really `/`.

Some basic device nodes are also necessary in many instances for BIND to run, so we'll create those as well:

```
# mknod dev/null c 1 3
# mknod dev/zero c 1 5
# mknod dev/random c 1 8
# mknod dev/urandom c 1 9
# mknod dev/tty c 5 0
# chmod 666 dev/null dev/zero dev/tty
```

Now, we need to copy a few files from the system's `/etc` directory to the jail cell. These are basic files that `named` will need to operate properly:

```
# cp /etc/nsswitch.conf /etc/resolv.conf etc
# cp /etc/ld.so.cache /etc/localtime etc
```

Now it's time to copy named and its components:

```
# cp /usr/sbin/named /usr/sbin/named-xfer usr/sbin
```

Because the named and named-xfer binaries are likely statically linked, some libraries will also be required. In order to find out which libraries ought to be copied, you can use the ldd command:

```
# ldd usr/sbin/named
      libc.so.6 => /lib/libc.so.6 (0x40020000)
      /lib/ld-linux.so.2 => /lib/ld-linux.so.2 (0x40000000)
```

Remember to copy the libraries and not just the symbolic links that point to them. The symbolic links are created afterward:

```
# cd lib
# cp /lib/libc-2.1.2.so .
# cp /lib/ld-2.1.2.so .
# ln -s libc-2.1.2.so libc.so.6
# ln -s ld-2.1.2.so ld-linux.so.2
```

Experience demonstrates that in some instances in Linux, a few additional libraries are needed. Adjust to match your own version numbers:

```
# cp /lib/libnss_compat-2.1.2.so .
# cp /lib/libnss_files-2.1.2.so .
# cp /lib/libnsl-2.1.2.so .
# ln -s libnss_compat-2.1.2.so libnss_compat.so.2
# ln -s libnss_files-2.1.2.so libnss_files.so.2
# ln -s libnsl-2.1.2.so libnsl.so.1
```

Be sure to check permissions on all of the configuration files, libraries, and binaries to ensure that none of them are writable by user named or group named and that none of them are running as SUID or SGID to root. Once this is all done, you should (in theory) be almost ready to go.

Setting Up syslogd for Chroot named

Even though named will be running in its own root file system, we want to be able to get logs from named sent to the normal system logger. Newer syslogd daemons have a command-line option that allows us to do so. The option we're interested in is -a, and it is used like this:

```
syslogd -a /usr/local/named/dev/log
```

Starting syslogd this way will cause it to create a listening socket at /usr/local/bind/dev/log, which the chrooted named will conveniently see as /dev/log. In order to make this change permanent, you'll need to edit your /etc/rc.d/init.d/syslog script

13

(or whichever script your system uses to start `syslogd`) and add the necessary options. Then, restart the daemon so that the changes are in effect now as well:

```
# /etc/rc.d/init.d/syslog restart
```

If you need more help with the files in `/etc/rc.d/init.d`, refer to Hour 4, "The Boot Process."

Starting `named` in the Chroot Jail

We're almost ready for a chrooted `named` dry run. If a `named` is already running and your new `named` would be listening on the same port, stop the old `named` before continuing with the correct init script. Some distributions use `/etc/rc.d/init.d/dns`, others use `/etc/rc.d/init.d/named`, and there are other variations as well. Use the one that is correct for your distribution:

```
# /etc/rc.d/init.d/named stop
```

All systems are now go. It's time to test out the new `named`. The `-t` command-line argument allows us to specify the location of the chroot jail. The `-u` and `-g` options allow us to specify the user and group under which this instance of `named` should run:

```
# /usr/local/named/usr/sbin/named -t /usr/local/named -u named -g named
```

If all goes well, your `named` should now function as it did before, only now if it is compromised by a cracker, it's a dead end for further intrusion. To make the change permanent, though, you'll also need to edit your `/etc/rc.d/init.d/named` (or synonymous) script to reflect the new command-line arguments with which `named` must be started.

Summary

This hour, we learned how to make the domain name service provided by BIND a bit more secure than it is in most default Linux installations. We did this with a three-pronged approach:

- First, we make sure to configure packet filtering to prevent connections to the `domain` port from systems we don't have any legitimate business with.
- Next, we implement good access control defaults in the `named.conf` file, paying special attention to disallowing zone transfers to strangers.
- Finally, we alter the standard `named` installation so that the daemon now runs in a chroot jail, preventing crackers from further compromising the system if they manage to break in through `named`.

These basic security measures will make your domain name service daemon much less risky than the standard runs-as-`root` installation found on most Linux systems.

Q&A

Q **I've seen other suggestions for domain name service, including a dual-`named` approach and using other servers instead of BIND. What do you think?**

A There are advantages and disadvantages to using BIND. The largest advantage is that it comes from the Internet Software Consortium and, following that, the degree to which BIND is a *de facto* Internet standard. Using the techniques in this hour can make most BIND installations secure enough for any small to mid-size network.

Q **I tried to install `named` in a chroot environment, but something isn't working! Help!**

A The first place to turn for aid is the log. Check the system logs and if necessary increase the logging level as you start and run the new `named` installation. If logging isn't working, concentrate on getting that running first.

The most common problem when converting from an existing BIND installation involves user oversight—the failure to set new permissions or file ownership on a critical file, or the failure to correctly edit one or more paths in the `named.conf` file.

If you are familiar with `strace`, you can also use it to watch program execution and locate the trouble spot.

New Terms

BIND   The Berkeley Internet Name Domain, an open source implementation of the domain name service (DNS) set of protocols. BIND is the most common DNS implementation among Linux users.

chroot jail   A colloquial term meaning a chroot environment—a substituted `root` file system that is actually a subdirectory in a larger file system. The exterior file system cannot be accessed by processes in the chroot environment.

domain name service (DNS)   A set of protocols and databases used to match a human-readable name to a machine-ready IP address. For example, without DNS, `yahoo.com` would instead be known as `64.58.76.179`, a much less memorable name indeed.

13

HOUR 14

Network Security: NFS and Samba

This hour, we're going to work toward more secure installations of the two most widely used Linux network file system implementations: Samba and the network file system (NFS).

NFS is widely used among Unix and Linux users for sharing traditional Unix-like file systems over TCP/IP networks. It has been around since the very early days of TCP/IP networking, but it has changed little when compared to many other network services.

Samba, more popular than ever and commonly used as a replacement for Windows NT server, is designed to allow Linux to supply file and print services to Windows network users. Configuration of a basic Samba installation tends to be much more complex than configuration of a basic NFS installation, but the resultant system is a cross-platform dream that can outperform Windows. Unless secured properly, however, it can suffer some of the same security problems as Windows.

Network File System (NFS) Security

Because NFS has been around so long, and because NFS, in configuration terms, is so simple, it is a very good security compromise of the type we're seeking in this text. On the one hand, because of its design, NFS can never be perfectly secured. Because of this, it shouldn't be run on extremely sensitive systems or on a primary firewall. Whenever possible, it should be run only for a local network residing behind a primary firewall machine.

On the other hand, with judicious use of packet filtering to keep NFS inside your network, careful construction of the /etc/exports file, and wise choice of your NFS server, NFS can easily be secure enough for most small to mid-size businesses.

Selecting an NFS Server

There are two NFS servers for Linux: an older user space daemon and a newer kernel-based NFS daemon. Both are still widely used and supported, but there are two important reasons why the kernel-based NFS implementation should be the implementation of choice for security-conscious users.

The first and most important reason is for the (admittedly kludgy) capability to operate more or less correctly with file systems that are locally enhanced by the addition of Access Control Lists (ACLs). While the interoperability is far from perfect, the kernel-based version is automatically patched by the ACL patches to make conservative decisions about granting access based on local ACL information and won't choke on ACL data or lose data because of ACLs. The user space NFS daemon, on the other hand, will require additional patches, recompilation, and re-installation; is known not to work correctly in many incarnations with ACLs; and may even lose data or grant access incorrectly to data that ought to have been restricted. The kernel-based daemon also supports NFS version 3, which fixes many of these problems without the need for additional patching.

The second reason for wanting to choose the kernel-based NFS implementation is the speed improvement that many users will see when choosing the kernel-based NFS implementation over many older user space NFS daemons. The user space NFS daemon has traditionally been much slower and CPU bound than kernel-based implementations.

Including Kernel-Based NFS Support

NFS support is included in both the 2.2 and 2.4 versions of the Linux kernel. The options necessary to include kernel-based NFS server support in the Linux 2.2 kernels are found in the Network File Systems submenu of the File Systems section. They are shown in Table 14.1.

TABLE 14.1   Linux 2.2 Kernel-Based NFS Options

Option	Description
CONFIG_NFS_FS	Includes NFS file system support, a logical counterpart to NFS server support.
CONFIG_NFSD	Includes the actual kernel-based NFS server.

In 2.4 kernels, the options related to the kernel-based NFS server are in the Network File Systems submenu of the File Systems section. They are shown in Table 14.2.

TABLE 14.2   Linux 2.4 Kernel-Based NFS Options

Option	Description
CONFIG_NFS_FS	Includes NFS file system support, a logical counterpart to NFS server support.
CONFIG_NFS_V3	Includes support for Linux to act as an NFS version 3 client.
CONFIG_NFSD	Includes the actual kernel-based NFS server.
CONFIG_NFSD_V3	Includes additional code to allow the kernel-based NFS server to work with version 3 clients, the best possible server/client match for systems using ACLs with the local file system.

Of course, you must compile and install the kernel in order to cause the changes to take effect.

> Many Linux distributions already include support for kernel-based NFS service. Use a command such as locate to search for the modules nfsd.o, lockd.o, and sunrpc.o.

Configuring the /etc/exports File

The /etc/exports file is the primary configuration file for the NFS system. Each entry in the file is one line, and the format is very simple:

```
/path/to/export     [host](option,option) ...
```

Each line in the file begins with one directory or subdirectory in the local file system to which the line applies. When an entry for a subdirectory of an already exported directory exists, the more specific entry (the subdirectory) will override the less specific entry, creating a kind of exception.

Following the export path at the beginning of each line is any number of host option specifiers. Each one of these specifiers contains a host (which may be an IP, a hostname, a network with mask, or a wildcard) and a series of options enclosed in parentheses that

14

dictate the type of access, if any, that the host, series of hosts, or network in question is to be granted. Common valid formats for host are shown in Table 14.3; a list of the most common available options is shown in Table 14.4.

TABLE 14.3 Common Valid host Formats

Format	Description
hostname	Specifies that the options in question apply to the host with name hostname.
N.N.N.N	Specifies that the options in question apply to the host with IP number N.N.N.N.
N.N.N.N/M	Specifies that the options in question apply to the network given by N.N.N.N, with subnet mask M.
*.domain.com	Specifies that the options in question apply to all hosts in the domain.com domain. Note that wildcard characters do not match the dots in a fully qualified domain name. For example, *.domain.com would not match my.sys.domain.com, while *.*.domain.com would.

TABLE 14.4 Common Options for Each host

Option	Description
insecure	This option allows client requests from connecting systems to come from source ports above 1024. Because it can be insecure, it should be used only when needed and only for completely public file systems.
rw	Specifies that parties who have permission to mount this exported directory will also be given permission to modify the files and directories it contains.
noaccess	Specifies that no access is to be given to this directory. Useful when creating per-directory exceptions to higher-level directory exports.
root_squash	Modify all client requests that come from the root user (user ID 0, group ID 0) to operate as if they had instead come from the user nobody and group nobody, which should be present in the /etc/passwd and /etc/group files.
no_root_squash	Specifies that client requests from the root user should be accepted as having come from the root user. For security reasons, this option is risky and should not be used for general-purpose exports.
squash_uids=N,N,N,...	Specifies that client requests from the user ID numbers listed should operate as if they had instead come from the user nobody.
squash_gids=N,N,N,...	Specifies that client requests from the group ID numbers listed should operate as if they had instead come from the group nobody.
all_squash	Specifies that all client requests should be mapped to user nobody, group nobody.

TABLE 14.4   continued

Option	Description
map_static=mapfile	Specifies the path to a file that should be used to map remote user and group ID numbers to local user and group ID numbers. The format of the file is very simple and is documented in exports(5).
anonuid=N	Specifies that all client requests should operate as if they had come from the user with user ID N.
anongid=N	Specifies that all client requests should operate as if they had come from the group with group ID N.

By using these options thoughtfully, it is possible to assemble a clear, concise, and relatively secure system of exportable file systems. A sample /etc/exports file is shown in Listing 14.1.

LISTING 14.1   Sample /etc/exports File

```
/fs/work                192.168.1.0/24(root_squash)
/fs/work/public         192.168.1.0/24(rw,root_squash)
/fs/work/private        (noaccess)
/fs/pubrecords          (all_squash)
/usr/local/db           phoenix(rw,no_root_squash)
/usr/local/db-public    *.redux.com(insecure,all_squash)
/scratch                phoenix(rw) newton(rw) hotswap
```

This file says the following to the NFS daemon:

- Export a read-only file system at /fs/work to all systems on the local 192.168.1.0 network, squashing root access attempts.

- Export a writable file system at /fs/work/public to all systems on the local 192.168.1.0 network, squashing root access attempts.

- Do not allow anyone who has mounted the /fs/work file system to access the /fs/work/private directory at all.

- Export a read-only file system at /fs/pubrecords to anyone in the world connecting from a port below 1024. Squash all incoming user and group identification.

- Export a writable, root-capable file system at /usr/local/db to the host on the local network called phoenix.

- Export a public, read-only file system to anyone in the redux.com domain connecting from any port. Squash all incoming user and group identification.

- Export the /scratch directory to the local network hosts phoenix and newton as writable. Export the /scratch directory to the local network host hotswap as read-only.

14

No other configuration of any kind needs to be done for NFS. Once the `/etc/exports` file has been constructed, you are ready to go.

NFS Packet Filtering

Though the `/etc/exports` file provides for some security, in and of itself it may not be enough. Unless you want to provide completely public NFS exports to the entire world, you should impose packet filtering rules to disallow NFS requests from strange hosts or networks.

This is complicated somewhat by the fact that NFS actually requires three ports to operate. Port 111 traditionally is used by the portmapper, `rpc.portmap`, which then calls the mounter, `rpc.mountd`, to mount the file system using the NFS port, 2049. Notice that I didn't mention a port number for `rpc.mountd`. This is the problem; `rpc.mountd` typically uses a dynamic port number the way it is configured in most Linux installations. However, this can be fixed with an addition to the `/etc/services` file:

```
mount        2050/udp    mountd
nfs          2049/udp    nfsd
```

When `rpc.mountd` starts, it will search the `/etc/services` file for the `mount` service (or, in some cases, the `mountd` service, which is why we've created an alias) and if found, will use the port specified there. Notice that we've also added a line for `nfs` in order to simplify things. Now we're ready to filter packets.

> In order to use NFS services, the `rpc.portmap` daemon must be running. If you've disabled it in your init system, you'll have to re-enable it before NFS will work properly. Be sure to start `rpc.portmap` much earlier than services such as `mountd` or `nfsd` that depend on it, or they won't start properly.

Using `ipchains`, an example set of rules for allowing one trusted external system to use NFS while forbidding all other external systems from using these specific ports is shown in Listing 14.2.

LISTING 14.2   NFS Packet Filtering with `ipchains`

```
ipchains -A input -p tcp -s trusted.ext.system.ip \
    -d ext.ip.number.here sunrpc -j ACCEPT
ipchains -A input -p udp -s trusted.ext.system.ip \
    -d ext.ip.number.here sunrpc -j ACCEPT
ipchains -A input -p udp -s trusted.ext.system.ip \
    -d ext.ip.number.here 2049:2050 -j ACCEPT
```

LISTING 14.2 continued

```
ipchains -A input -i ! lo \
    -d ext.ip.number.here sunrpc -j DENY -l
ipchains -A input -i ! lo \
    -d ext.ip.number.here 2049:2050 -j DENY -l
```

Using `iptables`, a similar set of rules can be constructed. A sample set of rules using `iptables` is shown in Listing 14.3.

LISTING 14.3 NFS Packet Filtering with `iptables`

```
iptables -t filter -A INPUT -p tdp -s trusted.ext.sys.ip \
    -d ext.ip.number.here --destination-port sunrpc \
    -j ACCEPT
iptables -t filter -A INPUT -p udp -s trusted.ext.sys.ip \
    -d ext.ip.number.here --destination-port sunrpc \
    -j ACCEPT
iptables -t filter -A INPUT -p udp -s trusted.ext.sys.ip \
    -d ext.ip.number.here --destination-port 2049:2050 \
    -j ACCEPT

iptables -t filter -A INPUT -i ! lo \
    -d ext.ip.number.here --destination-port sunrpc \
    -j DROP
iptables -t filter -A INPUT -i ! lo \
    -d ext.ip.number.here --destination-port 2049:2050 \
    -j DROP
```

> If you plan to use NFS over TCP, be sure to modify the filtering rules to open ports 2049 and 2050 for TCP packets as well.

Assuming you already have packet filtering scripts in place by now, you'll have to edit these rules as necessary to make them fit within your own security framework.

Samba Security

Samba is actually a pair of daemons, `smbd` and `nmbd`, that allow a Linux system to appear to be a Windows NT file or print server to Windows systems using NetBIOS over TCP/IP. Because Samba involves a significant percentage of the Windows networking paradigm in addition to using TCP/IP networking, a complete Samba security guide is beyond the scope of this text. However, basic security options and user management can be managed with the Samba Web Administration Tool (SWAT), which is part of the offi-cial Samba distribution.

14

Starting SWAT

Since SWAT uses its own built-in Web server, you do not need to have Apache or another HTTPD service running in order to use SWAT.

Once it has been installed, you can log in to SWAT on the local host simply by starting your Web browser (usually Netscape) and typing the following into the URL box:

```
http://127.0.0.1:901
```

This URL opens a connection to the local host on port 901, the port used by SWAT. You'll be asked to provide a username and a password; you should log in as root and provide the necessary password. If you find that this isn't working for you, troubleshoot based on the following steps:

1. Make sure that an entry for SWAT exists in the /etc/services file by using grep swat /etc/services.

2. Make sure that an entry for SWAT exists in the /etc/inetd.conf file by using grep swat /etc/inetd.

3. Check to see if you have ipchains or iptables rules that may be preventing connections on the loopback interface on port 901.

4. Make sure that there are no entries in /etc/hosts.allow or /etc/hosts.deny that would prevent SWAT access under your particular circumstances.

If you find that the problem is the first or second item in the preceding list (no SWAT entries in either /etc/services or /etc/inetd), SWAT hasn't been installed on your system. Some distributions separate Samba and SWAT into two separate packages, so look for a SWAT package and install it.

If you're not able to find a SWAT package anywhere for your distribution, there are no SWAT entries in /etc/services or /etc/inetd, and there is no SWAT binary anywhere on your system, you may want to consider downloading Samba from www.samba.org and re-installing it from scratch.

Because SWAT doesn't use a secure (encrypted) connection, you may want to avoid using it from any location outside your internal network. If your network isn't behind a firewall, it's a good idea to prevent access from any remote host altogether.

Regardless of how you decide to use it, it's important to remember to prevent all types of unauthorized access. To do this, edit your /etc/hosts.allow and /etc/hosts.deny files as necessary.

Once you actually log in to SWAT, you'll see the Samba title in the browser window, as shown in Figure 14.1.

FIGURE 14.1

The page you'll see after logging in to SWAT.

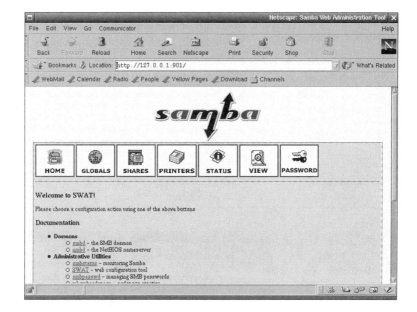

Global Security Options in SWAT

Inside SWAT, notice the row of buttons across the top of the page. These lead to the different administration areas within SWAT. To visit the global options page, click on the button labeled Globals in this row of buttons. Scrolling down a little on the global options page, you'll find a section labeled Security Options, as shown in Figure 14.2.

The important options in the Security Options section are documented in Table 14.5.

TABLE 14.5   Security Options

Option	Description
security	One of Share, User, Server, or Domain. Most small networks will choose Share or User here. Share means that passwords will be assigned to resources; for example, one password for everyone grants access to a specific file system. User means that the same username/password pairs will be used both under Linux and on the remote Windows systems.
encrypt passwords	For both security and compatibility reasons, it is a good idea to choose Yes here.

14

TABLE **14.5**   continued

Option	Description
update encrypted	Samba maintains a separate username/password database from Linux. If an existing unencrypted database exists, choosing Yes here will cause Samba to encrypt passwords automatically as users log in. Unless you have this specific need, set to No.
guest account	This is the account used by users who access guest-allowed services. Normally set to an innocuous account like nobody or ftp.
hosts allow	This specifies which hosts will be allowed to use Samba services. Should be a space-separated list including IP numbers of the form N.N.N.N, networks of the form N.N.N.N/M, or individual host or fully qualified domain names.
hosts deny	A list of hosts explicitly denied access to Samba, usually as exceptions to allowed hosts.

FIGURE **14.2**

Security Options in the Global section.

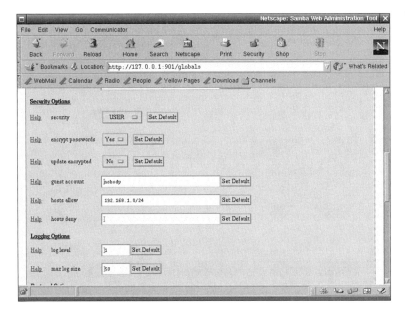

Once these options have been set to your needs, be sure to click the Commit Changes button at the top of the page to save the changes you've made to the Samba configuration files.

Share Security Options in SWAT

To configure security options related to individual Samba shares, click on the Shares button at the top of any SWAT page. Here you'll be offered a choice among the different existing shares you want to administrate. After choosing one, you'll be presented with a list of per-share options, including security options, as shown in Figure 14.3.

FIGURE 14.3

Per-share security options.

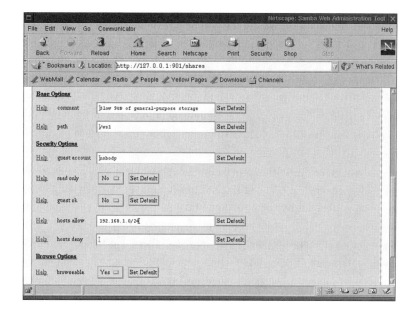

The functions of the security and browse options are documented in Table 14.6.

TABLE 14.6   Per-Share Security and Browse Options

Option	Description
guest account	Name of the guest account to access this share if guest use is allowed.
read only	Specifies whether the share will be exported with read-only access or whether writing will be allowed by validated users as well.
guest ok	Specifies whether guests are allowed to use this share.
hosts allow	Specifies which hosts will be allowed to use this share. Should be a space-separated list including IP numbers of the form N.N.N.N, networks of the form N.N.N.N/M, or individual host or fully qualified domain names.
hosts deny	A list of hosts explicitly denied access to Samba, usually as exceptions to allowed hosts.
browseable	Specifies whether or not this share is hidden. If set to Yes, this share will appear in browse lists obtained from the server.

14

Packet Filtering and Samba

Of course, if you're going to allow any Samba access on an external interface at all, you'll want to impose packet filtering rules that allow only the specific machines that should access Samba and that disallow everyone else. If you search for the `netbios` service in `/etc/services`, you'll find that Samba uses ports 137, 138, and 139:

```
# grep netbios /etc/services
netbios-ns        137/tcp
netbios-ns        137/udp
netbios-dgm       138/tcp
netbios-dgm       138/udp
netbios-ssn       139/tcp
netbios-ssn       139/udp
```

A sample for a filtering ruleset that allows for one external trusted host and that disallows everyone else using `ipchains` is shown in Listing 14.4. A similar sample using `iptables` is shown in Listing 14.5.

LISTING 14.4   Samba Packet Filtering Using `ipchains`

```
ipchains -A input -p tcp -s trusted.ext.system.ip \
    -d ext.ip.number.here 137:139 -j ACCEPT
ipchains -A input -p udp -s trusted.ext.system.ip \
    -d ext.ip.number.here 137:139 -j ACCEPT

ipchains -A input -i ! lo \
    -d ext.ip.number.here 137:139 -j DENY -l
```

LISTING 14.5   Samba Packet Filtering Using `iptables`

```
iptables -t filter -A INPUT -p tdp -s trusted.ext.sys.ip \
    -d ext.ip.number.here --destination-port 137:139 \
    -j ACCEPT
iptables -t filter -A INPUT -p udp -s trusted.ext.sys.ip \
    -d ext.ip.number.here --destination-port 137:139 \
    -j ACCEPT

iptables -t filter -A INPUT -i ! lo \
    -d ext.ip.number.here --destination-port 137:139 \
    -j DROP
```

As always, you'll need to adjust these rulesets to fit within your existing packet filtering framework.

Summary

This hour, we learned about security related to the two most popular networked file systems for Linux users and servers: the network file system (NFS) and Samba, which is used for sharing files with Windows systems.

NFS is a classic Unix service and isn't terribly risky or terribly secure but is somewhere in between the two. If you can avoid having to share files via NFS with the outside world, it's best to run NFS only to serve local systems behind a dedicated firewall.

If you must serve files to the outside world via NFS, be sure to construct packet filtering rules to protect it. It uses port 111 and port 2049, plus a third port for `rpc.mountd` that you must add to `/etc/services` in order for filtering to work.

Always take the time to construct a good `/etc/exports` file. This is the primary means for securing NFS exports. Samba is a service that allows Linux to "speak" NetBIOS over TCP/IP in order to impersonate a Windows NT server and in so doing share files or directories with Windows users.

The easiest way to configure Samba security options is with SWAT, the Samba Web Administration Tool, which can be launched in a browser window by connecting to port 901 on the Samba server. Once inside SWAT, choose between share-based access control, which asks for a password based on the share being requested, and user-based access control, which allows Samba to use username/password pairs just as the Linux server itself does. Samba resides on ports 137–139, so packet filtering rules affecting Samba should focus on these ports.

Q&A

Q If NFS isn't terribly secure for public, untrusted system use, are there any alternatives that offer similar functionality?

A The AFS file system is the reigning *de facto* alternative to the NFS file system. Unfortunately, AFS is a commercial product, and no free Linux version is available. An experimental implementation is under development and is usable, but you'll have to use your own discretion with regard to the security implications of running unstable code. The free, experimental AFS system can be found at `http://www.stacken.kth.se/projekt/arla`.

Q I don't like SWAT. Is there a text-based configuration file for Samba? Where is it stored?

14

A Yes, there is a text-based configuration file for Samba; it uses a format similar to the format used by Windows INI files and is therefore not familiar to longtime Linux or Unix users. It is called `smb.conf` and is often found at `/etc/samba.d/smb.conf`, though a call to the `locate` command will help to find it if it doesn't appear in `/etc/samba.d` on your system. The format of the file is documented in excruciating detail in `smb.conf(5)`. Unless you need the extra flexibility or have a book dedicated to Samba on hand, you'll probably find yourself wanting to use SWAT, which is sufficient for most small to mid-size environments, with Linux acting as the single NetBIOS file server.

New Terms

export   A file system made available to other systems on the network via NFS.

NFS (network file system)   The traditional method for sharing Unix-like file systems over local area networks.

Samba   A set of two daemons that allows Linux to "speak" NetBIOS over TCP/IP and serve shares to Windows clients.

share   A resource (such as a file system or printer) made available to other systems on the network through Samba.

SWAT   The Samba Web Administration Tool, a program designed to automate the administration of a Samba server in a Web browser window.

HOUR 15

Securing X11R6 Access

This hour we're going to focus on securing the use of the X11R6 streaming protocol, with an emphasis on authentication when initiating new remotely connected streams. We'll also take a moment to discuss packet filtering as it relates to X and to the X Display Manager, xdm.

We're going to cover two authentication methods: the simple and less secure host-based authentication mechanism and the more secure magic cookie authentication method.

Why Is X Security an Issue?

X11R6 can be used as a network protocol, though it isn't often used this way in small business or personal Linux installations. When used as a network protocol, X allows applications to run using the CPU and memory of one system while appearing on the display of and accepting input from another system on the network using the system's X server, as shown in Figure 15.1.

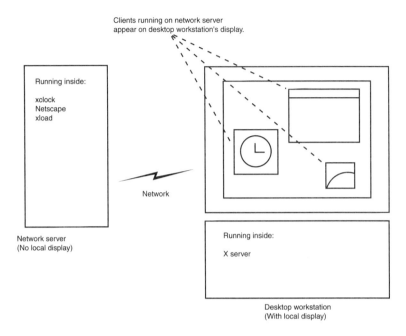

FIGURE 15.1

X clients and server on separate machines.

Clients running on network server appear on desktop workstation's display.

Running inside:

xclock
Netscape
xload

Network server
(No local display)

Network

Running inside:

X server

Desktop workstation
(With local display)

Because of this network-aware functionality, and because X servers typically run with `root` permissions, it is important to have some control over who is allowed to connect to a running X server.

There is often no need to run an X server at all on an important system. Though many combination desktop/small server machines will need an instance of X running on the local console, most dedicated servers are used to supply a limited set of network services and are rarely or never used for desktop applications. If you use a machine in such a role, consider simply omitting X from the machine's Linux installation altogether.

Even if it is necessary to run an X application every now and then, you can make a server system more secure by not running an X server, displaying the applications instead on another X workstation using the network capabilities of X. That way, no X server will be needed, and one more potential security risk will be eliminated.

Host-Based Authentication

Host-based authentication enables the X server to allow or disallow incoming connections based on the network address, domain name, or hostname of the host making the

15

connection request. If the network address, domain name, or hostname appears in a list of allowed hosts, then the connection will be accepted and opened. Otherwise, it will be rejected.

The `/etc/Xn.hosts` File

There are two methods provided for editing the list of allowed hosts that the X server will use for authentication. The first of these is with the `/etc/Xn.hosts` file, where n represents the number of the local display to which a given file will apply. On most Linux systems, there will be only one file called `/etc/X0.hosts`. The format of this file is very simple: Each line contains one IP address, domain name, or hostname. A sample `/etc/X0.hosts` file is shown in Listing 15.1.

LISTING 15.1   A Sample `/etc/X0.hosts` File

```
192.168.1.14
192.168.1.15
station20.bigwing.org
station21.bigwing.org
xclaim.multiply.net
workstation1
workstation2
workstation3
workstation4
station-kathy
station-john
```

Notice that no wildcards are used in Listing 15.1; this is because no wildcards are allowed. Each system that should be allowed must be explicitly listed.

The `xhost` Command

Because the `/etc/Xn.hosts` file is read only once each time the X server is launched, the `/etc/Xn.hosts` file cannot be used to make changes to the authentication list at runtime (as the X server is operating). At times this can be inconvenient. To allow for on-the-fly changes to the authentication list, X developers created the `xhost` command, which manipulates the X server's internal host-based authentication list at runtime.

Using the `xhost` command is also a very simple affair. To add a host to the list of hosts to be authenticated, call `xhost` with the name of the host to add, prepended by a plus symbol (+):

```
$ xhost +host.to.add
host.to.add being added to access control list
$
```

To remove a host from the list of hosts to be authenticated, call xhost with the name of the host to remove, prepended by a minus symbol (-):

```
$ xhost -host.to.remove
host.to.remove being removed from access control list
$
```

This command will remove the named host from the list, preventing future connection attempts from being accepted.

 Manipulation of the host access control list has no effect on connections that are already open. Therefore, removing a host from the list will prevent any future connection attempts from being successful, but all streams that existed at the time of the change will remain active and open after the change until they are shut down by one side or the other.

To see the current list of allowed or forbidden hosts, call the xhost command without any arguments:

```
$ xhost
INET:localhost
INET:192.168.1.14
INET:192.168.1.15
INET:station20.bigwing.org
INET:station21.bigwing.org
INET:xclaim.multiply.net
INET:workstation1
INET:workstation2
INET:workstation3
INET:workstation4
INET:station-kathy
INET:station-john
LOCAL:
$
```

In addition to the capability to add or remove single hosts from the list or display the list to the user, the xhost command also provides the capability to enable or disable host-based authentication altogether. To enable or disable host-based authentication, supply either the minus (-) or plus (+) symbol, respectively, as an argument. For example, to disable host-based authentication, supply the plus symbol as an argument:

```
$ xhost +
access control disabled, clients can connect from any host
$
```

To re-enable host-based authentication after it has been disabled, supply the minus symbol as an argument to the xhost command:

```
$ xhost -
access control enabled, only authorized clients can connect
$
```

There is rarely, if ever, a legitimate reason to disable access control, so use of the plus and minus arguments for the xhost command is strongly discouraged.

> It is important to understand that disabling host-based access control using the method shown here does *not* have the effect of disabling all incoming connections. Instead, it has the exact opposite effect. When access control has been disabled, the X server will accept all incoming connections from any host anywhere. It is therefore never a good idea to disable host-based authentication on any system that is connected to a live network.
>
> Understand also that the plus (+) and minus (-) arguments are reversed with respect to many users' expectations. The plus argument actually *disables* access control, while the minus argument *enables* it. Confusing the two can have serious security consequences!

Host-Based Authentication Problems

There are some important problems with host-based authentication that must be considered for any user who will be running an X server on a live network.

First, host-based authentication is not very secure, for several reasons. Most importantly and obviously, a host or IP address can easily be spoofed, rendering host-based authentication completely impotent in many cases. Even when spoofing doesn't occur, undesired access can be granted in error innocently.

For example, many networks now use Dynamic Host Configuration Protocol (DHCP) to assign IP addresses. This means that one IP address can actually represent a number of different systems over time, and that there may be no way to predict which systems are associated with a given IP address at any time. An IP address added to the host list at noon may refer to a completely different system on the network by half past noon. Because the IP address is in the host list, however, access will be granted to the new system just as if it were the old system, because it resides at the same address.

Host-based authentication also fails to relate directly to user(s); it applies only to entire systems. It is therefore not possible to grant access to one user on a system but deny connection attempts from another user on the same system. Using host-based authentication, all users on a system must have access if one user is to have access. Similarly, to guarantee access to a single important user, access must be given to all hosts on which the user might appear. For an administrative user, a number of systems may be involved. Furthermore, because adding a system to the access control list means that all users on that system can connect, any guarantee of access for a single important user may mean as a side effect the granting of unwanted access to any number of unrelated users.

Clearly, host-based X authentication is not the most desirable type of access control for X11R6 servers.

Token-Based Authentication

To overcome the limitations of host-based authentication, the designers of X also implemented a method of authenticating a remote user based on a system of token exchange. When a remote system makes a connection request, the X server compares a magic cookie (a kind of unique identification code) it supplies with a magic cookie stored on the local system. If the two cookies match, access is granted. If they do not match, access is denied. It is assumed that only users who should have access will have been given the cookie.

Normally, once a user has possession of a cookie, it is stored in a file located at `$HOME/.Xauthority`, and little intervention is then required to interact with the remote X server. Each time a client connection is attempted, the cookie for the remote server will be read automatically and supplied as part of the authentication exchange.

The actual implementation is a little more complex, but with practice, it can seem as easy to manage as the `xhost` method for controlling access.

Using the `xauth` Command

Before you can start an X server with token-based authentication enabled, a magic cookie must first be generated and added to the magic cookie file maintained by the `xauth` command. The command used for manipulating magic cookies and magic cookie files for token-based authentication is `xauth`. To generate a cookie and add it to the file, which is normally found at `$HOME/.Xauthority`, you'd use

```
xauth add host:display . keyvalue
```

The value for `host:display` will normally be the hostname of the system on which the X server is run, followed by the number 0 (zero), unless you are planning to run X servers on multiple displays. The `keyvalue` should be a large random or pseudorandom value with an even number of digits from which the magic cookie will be generated. For example, on a host named `station-john`, using a variation on the current date and time as a key value, you might execute the following command to generate the magic cookie and add it to the authentication file:

```
xauth add station-john:0 . $(date +%S%M%H%y%d%m)
```

If you want to add this cookie to a file other than the file located at $HOME/.Xauthority, you need to supply the -f argument to the xauth command:

```
xauth -f /etc/xac add station-john:0 . $(date +%S%M%H%y%d%m)
```

To remove an existing cookie from an authentication file, use the remove argument along with the string matching an existing entry. For example, to remove the cookie just added for station-john, use

```
xauth -f /etc/xac remove station-john:0
```

It is a very good idea to remove magic cookies from the cookie file when you are done with them. To extract the magic cookie for a given host, use the extract argument. For example, to write the magic cookie for station-john to a file called cookie.auth, use

```
xauth extract cookie.auth station-john:0
```

If the name of the output file is a dash (-), the cookie will be sent to standard output, where it can be redirected or piped as necessary. To merge a supplied cookie into an existing authorization file, use the merge argument. For example, to merge a cookie from the cookie.auth file into the authorization file at /etc/xac, you'd use

```
xauth -f /etc/xac merge cookie.auth
```

If the name of the input file is a dash (-), the cookie will be read from standard input and then incorporated into the authorization file.

Starting the X Server

Once you have created the magic cookie for a system and display, starting the X server with token-based authentication is a simple matter. Simply supply the -auth argument to the server, followed by the name of the file containing the cookie authentication tokens. For example, any of the following may be correct, depending on the particulars of your installation and the circumstances surrounding the server's launch:

```
X -auth /etc/X11/global-cookies
Xwrapper -auth $HOME/.Xauthority
startx -- -auth $HOME/.Xauthority
```

All of these commands have the same effect: They launch the X server and instruct it to use the supplied cookie file for token-based authentication. Once the server has been started this way, it will be able to challenge incoming connection requests for the magic cookie before access is granted.

Distributing the Cookie

Once the server has been started with token-based authentication, it is important that the cookie be supplied to those users or accounts that should have access to the running X server. The easiest way to do this is to use the extract and merge arguments with the xauth command as already discussed. However, it can be a pain to transfer extracted cookie files between hosts. Because of this, there is a shortcut often used for exchanging cookies that may be helpful to you.

Using the xauth command in conjunction with rsh and a pipe, it is possible to transfer a cookie from your account on one host to your account on another host from within an X session. Assuming that the remote host is called foobar, the command would be

```
xauth extract - :0 | rsh foobar xauth merge -
```

This command instructs xauth to place the cookie for the current display on standard output, which is then piped to an xauth command on the remote system ready to merge the cookie from standard input.

> This method for distributing the cookie has two caveats. First, you must have access to use rsh on the remote system. Second, rsh is not a very secure protocol in and of itself, and passing a magic cookie over rsh may be doubly insecure because rsh does not encrypt data as it is transferred.
>
> The solution to this problem is to perform the same function using ssh instead. The ssh service will be detailed in Hour 16, "Encrypting Data Streams." Please install and use ssh instead of rsh for magic cookie exchange whenever possible.

Host-Based and Token-Based Authentication Interaction

There is obviously some tension between host-based and token-based authentication, since it's already been made clear that disabling host-based authentication is a bad idea. If you plan to use token-based authentication, it is essential that you completely empty your host authentication file and list so that there are no hosts that are authenticated based merely on their identity.

This is because host-based authentication supersedes token-based authentication when both are present. If a connecting system appears in the authenticated hosts list, the connection will be opened without any challenge for a magic cookie, even if token-based authentication has also been enabled. It is therefore almost pointless to place hosts (which are easily spoofed) into the host-based access control list and enable token-based authentication at the same time.

The X Display Manager (XDM)

Because the vast majority of X clients will be run on the same machine as the X server to which they connect, it is possible to automate the management of token-based authentication even further. This is done using the X Display Manager, or XDM, which is

15

included with nearly all X installations and is now installed and run by default on many Linux installations.

When launched, XDM automatically generates a magic cookie and starts the X server with token-based authentication enabled. The xdm process then provides a graphical login screen instead of the traditional text-based login. When a user logs in to the X session, his $HOME/.Xauthority file will be updated automatically to contain the magic cookie for the local X server. When he logs out again, the cookie will be removed.

Even remote X sessions can be further automated, using an additional option to the X server, the string -query followed by the name of the host on which xdm is running. For example, nearly all of the clients on your local X server will be connected from the host foobar, which is running xdm. You can start your local X server as follows:

```
X -query foobar
```

This will cause the local X server to initiate cookie exchange with your account at foobar automatically, and you will then be able to log in to the X session securely as if it were running on foobar, as shown in Figure 15.2.

FIGURE 15.2

The X Display Manager in a queried session.

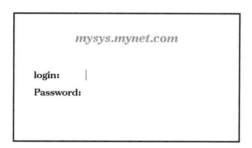

For more information on using xdm, please see xdm(1).

X and Packet Filtering

Many X servers (including the XFree86 server) include no functionality to dictate the ports on which the X server will operate. The XFree86 X server used most commonly on Linux simply begins looking for an unowned port at 6000 and continues upward until it finds one. It is therefore important that you ensure that at least one port in the 6000 range is open for X to use and that your filtering rules take this range into account if you want to allow networked X use on a filtered machine.

Also important for networked X use is port 177, which is used by the XDMCP protocol to manage connection authentication. Packet filtering rules that allow for networked X use via ipchains and iptables are shown in Listings 15.2 and 15.3.

LISTING 15.2   X Packet Filtering Rules with `ipchains`

```
ipchains -A input -p tcp -s trusted.ext.system.ip \
    -d ext.ip.number.here 6000:6100 -j ACCEPT
ipchains -A input -p tcp -s trusted.ext.system.ip \
    -d ext.ip.number.here xdmcp -j ACCEPT
ipchains -A input -p udp -s trusted.ext.system.ip \
    -d ext.ip.number.here xdmcp -j ACCEPT

ipchains -A input -i ! lo \
    -d ext.ip.number.here 6000:6100 -j DENY -l
ipchains -A input -i ! lo \
    -d ext.ip.number.here xdmcp -j DENY -l
```

LISTING 15.3   X Packet Filtering Rules with `iptables`

```
iptables -t filter -A INPUT -p tcp -s trusted.ext.sys.ip \
    -d ext.ip.number.here --destination-port 6000:6100 \
    -j ACCEPT
iptables -t filter -A INPUT -p tcp -s trusted.ext.sys.ip \
    -d ext.ip.number.here --destination-port xdmcp \
    -j ACCEPT
iptables -t filter -A INPUT -p udp -s trusted.ext.sys.ip \
    -d ext.ip.number.here --destination-port xdmcp \
    -j ACCEPT

iptables -t filter -A INPUT -i ! lo \
    -d ext.ip.number.here --destination-port 6000:6100 \
    -j DROP
iptables -t filter -A INPUT -i ! lo \
    -d ext.ip.number.here --destination-port xdmcp \
    -j DROP
```

If you don't plan to run an X server on the machine, there is no need to use rules like these to allow such packets through.

Summary

This hour you have learned about X authentication security, which is needed when X servers on a live network will be accepting connections from remote X applications (clients). There are two major types of X authentication.

Host-based authentication grants or denies access based on the connecting system's presence in or absence from a list of systems allowed to connect to the local X server. Host-based authentication is simplistic and inflexible and provides only minimal security at best. It should be used only on smaller systems behind a dedicated firewall.

15

Token-based authentication grants or denies access based on the connecting user's ability to supply a magic cookie, generated as a kind of connection password. Token-based authentication can be applied on a per-user basis and is much more secure than host-based authentication.

When the two types of authentication are both used, a connecting system is checked against the host list first. If it appears in the list, access is granted, without the token ever being checked. It is therefore advisable to leave the host list blank when token-based authentication is enabled.

The X Display Manager (xdm) can be helpful in automating the token-based authentication process. xdm is capable of automatically generating magic cookies and facilitating their exchange without needing to use the xauth command.

Q&A

Q My system doesn't run xdm, but when I boot it starts kdm (from KDE) or gdm (from GNOME) instead. Do these provide similar functionality?

A Yes, kdm and gdm both implement the XDMCP protocol and perform token management in similar if not identical ways. However, be sure to keep your kdm and gdm versions current; both KDE and GNOME are under heavy development, and both managers have at times been known to have serious bugs.

Q Isn't X always insecure anyway because it is an unencrypted data stream? Isn't it always a bad idea to use X over a network?

A Yes, X is an unencrypted data stream. Thus, it is a good idea to use unencrypted X streams only behind a dedicated firewall. X can be encrypted by tunneling it through ssh, however, making it much more secure. For details on ssh, please see Hour 16.

Q How long does a token-based authentication cookie last before it expires?

A Unfortunately, using the standard MIT-MAGIC-COOKIE mechanism, the cookie does not expire; either side can continue to use it indefinitely, as long as it matches the cookie on the other side. It is therefore a good idea to cycle X sessions periodically and remove old cookies from your authentication file.

New Terms

GNOME Display Manager (gdm)   An xdm-compatible display manager included with the GNU Network Object Model Environment (GNOME).

host-based authentication   A method of authenticating an incoming connection in which the connecting system's address, domain, or hostname is compared against a list of permitted systems.

KDE Display Manager (kdm)   An xdm-compatible display manager included with the K Desktop Environment.

magic cookie   A kind of randomly generated connection password that both sides must know for a connection to be established. Magic cookies are stored in an authentication file and managed by the xauth command.

token-based authentication   A method of authenticating an incoming connection in which the X server challenges the connecting system to provide a magic cookie for the session. If the remote user is unable to supply the correct magic cookie, the connection attempt is rejected.

X Display Manager (xdm)   A daemon that makes management of X access to networks much easier by automating tasks like magic cookie generation and exchange.

X Display Manager Control Protocol (XDMCP)   A protocol used by xdm for administering multiple X client/server sessions.

PART III

Data Encryption

Hour

Hour 16

Encrypting Data Streams

This hour, you'll learn to encrypt data streams of most kinds for increased security during transport. You'll also learn to increase the authentication security of many types of protocols on your network.

Two major software packages are regularly used with Linux to encrypt data streams and provide this increased authentication security. The first is SSH, the Secure Shell. The second, OpenSSH, is an open source implementation of the SSH protocol created by the OpenBSD project to address concerns with the commercial nature of the original SSH, which is free only for non-commercial use.

In this hour, we'll discuss installation and use of both SSH version 2.4.0 and OpenSSH 2.3.0p1. Both are available for download from their respective Internet sites.

What Do SSH and OpenSSH Do?

In the simplest sense, the ssh2 utility, which forms the core of the SSH package, is a replacement for the rsh utility. The rsh utility allows Linux commands to be executed on remote systems, with the capability to pipe the standard input, standard output, or standard error path between systems over the network. The ssh2 command has one important advantage over rsh: with ssh2, all input, output, and other data involved in remote execution can be encrypted.

The SSH package has two additional important capabilities, however. First, SSH can authenticate the systems on both ends of a connection much more securely, using any one of several methods, reducing the chance that data will be stolen from under your nose.

Second, SSH can "tunnel" other common network protocols through its encrypted connection, providing them with the same benefit.

A traditional unencrypted data stream can be a security risk; anyone on the network theoretically can intercept and use information sent in unencrypted form. This applies to unencrypted data of all kinds, from e-mail to file transfer via FTP to remote X11R6 sessions. A packet belonging to an encrypted data stream on the other hand is exceedingly difficult to use even if intercepted, because the intercepting party must have enough information to decrypt it first. Data encryption of network communications is thus a good idea, especially if one of the machines involved in the communication is not behind a dedicated firewall.

The SSH package enables encryption to take place almost transparently for most protocols. As a result, compatibility is excellent, even with protocols like the X11R6 data stream, provided that SSH capability is present on both ends of the connection.

An additional SSH benefit is the capability to improve network speeds in some cases by compressing a data stream using gzip-based compression after it has been encrypted. This is especially helpful with slower modem, ISDN, or low-end DSL connections, where every last bit of bandwidth is valuable.

Installing, Configuring, and Using SSH

The original SSH suite is owned and maintained by SSH Communications Security Corporation, which can be found on the World Wide Web at http://www.ssh.com. Though the source code is freely available for download, SSH cannot properly be called open source software, and the free download applies only to noncommercial users or a short trial period for commercial users, after which SSH must be purchased.

Downloading and Installing SSH

The download page for SSH is located at http://www.ssh.com/products/ssh/ download.html; U.S. users may download SSH from any of the following mirrors:

ftp://ftp.cis.fed.gov/pub/ssh/

ftp://ftp.iodynamics.com/pub/mirror/ssh/

```
ftp://metalab.unc.edu/pub/packages/security/ssh

ftp://ftp.gw.com:/pub/unix/ssh

ftp://herbie.ucs.indiana.edu/pub/security/ssh

ftp://ftp.in-span.net/pub/ftp.ssh.org/

ftp://mirror.chpc.utah.edu/pub/ssh

ftp://ftp.keystealth.org/pub/ssh
```

16

After you've downloaded the SSH tarball from one of these distribution sites, use the GNU `tar` command to extract the tarball and then change to the newly created SSH distribution directory:

```
$ tar -xzf ssh-2.4.0.tar.gz
$ cd ssh-2.4.0
$
```

Inside the `ssh-2.4.0` directory, use the `configure` command to tailor the source code configuration for your own system's circumstances. You'll probably want to supply the `--with-libwrap` option to allow SSH to work with TCP wrappers:

```
$ ./configure --with-libwrap
...[ output of configure ]...
$
```

If you want to change the location of the final SSH installation, use the `--prefix` option to alter the installation path:

```
./configure --with-libwrap --prefix=/opt/ssh2
```

Remember that if you adjust your installation path when configuring the source, you'll need to account for this difference later on when configuring and using SSH. A number of additional options can be used to change some of the properties or behaviors of the final SSH installation; to see a list of these options, use the `--help` option:

```
./configure --help
```

The configure utility will likely take several minutes to finish on early Pentium or older systems. Once it has returned without errors, SSH can be built and installed using `make`. Don't forget to install as superuser or the installation attempt will fail.

```
$ make
...[ output of make ]...
$ su
Password:
# make install
...[ output of make install ]...
# exit
$
```

During installation, the 1024-bit host keys necessary for some aspects of SSH operation will be generated automatically and stored in the /etc/ssh2 directory as hostkey and hostkey.pub. Simply repeat this process on each machine needing an SSH installation so that each of them has its own set of keys. You may see several Error 1 messages as SSH attempts to discover an existing SSH version 2.x installation; as long as the install process continues, these errors can be safely ignored.

After you install the SSH files, it is necessary to make a few changes to the /etc/services and /etc/inetd.conf files. Making these changes will allow inetd and TCP wrappers to manage incoming SSH requests transparently, simplifying some aspects of SSH use and preserving system resources. Add the following lines to /etc/services:

```
ssh2            22/tcp          ssh
ssh2            22/udp          ssh
```

These lines define a new service called ssh2 that will listen on port 22 for incoming connections. If you plan to run SSH on another port, be sure to adjust the port numbers as necessary. To start SSH, add this line to /etc/inetd.conf:

```
ssh2 stream tcp nowait root /usr/sbin/tcpd /usr/local/sbin/sshd2 -i
```

This line allows inetd to start the SSH daemon when required and to use TCP wrappers. This way, you can control access to SSH from the /etc/hosts.allow and /etc/hosts.deny files using sshd2 as the name of the service. Once these changes have been made to the system's network configuration files, you'll want to send the hang-up signal (HUP) to the system's running inetd process:

```
killall -HUP inetd
```

This will restart the inetd program and cause any changes you've made to the /etc/inetd.conf file to become active. For most users, little or no additional SSH configuration is required.

In the past, it was common for system administrators to recommend that SSH be started from an init script like /etc/rc.d/rc.local rather than being started on demand by the inetd process. Administrators avoided using inetd with SSH because of the delays that could be introduced for connecting SSH clients during daemon launch and key generation, both resource-intensive operations.

On a reasonably modern Linux system, however, concern of this kind is no longer warranted except in situations involving very heavily loaded machines. On today's average Linux box, with a 266MHz or faster CPU and a multigigabyte hard drive, the delays introduced by starting sshd2 with inetd are almost undetectable in most cases and will not result in any measurable loss of productivity.

Additional Configuration

The sshd2 binary, located by default at /usr/local/sbin/sshd2, is responsible for handling incoming ssh2-encrypted connections. Though the default behaviors are usually adequate, there are a few additional security-oriented options that can be changed by editing the /etc/ssh2/sshd2_config file.

The format of /etc/ssh2/sshd2_config is familiar to most Linux and Unix users; the file is composed of a number of keyword/value pairs, one pair per line. Empty lines or lines beginning with the hash mark (#) are assumed to be comments and are ignored.

Some additional sshd2 options that may be helpful to you from a security standpoint are shown in Table 16.1. The complete list of sshd2 configuration options is documented exhaustively in sshd2_config(5).

TABLE 16.1 Common Options for the sshd2_config File

Option	Description
AllowGroups	Followed by a comma-separated list of regular expressions, this keyword gives a list of groups that are allowed to use connections controlled by SSH. Users who don't belong to a matching group will not be authenticated. The default is to allow all groups.
DenyGroups	Follows the same format as AllowGroups, but will instead deny authentication to users who belong to a matched group.
AllowHosts	Followed by a comma-separated list of regular expressions, this keyword gives a list of hosts that are allowed to use connections controlled by SSH. Hosts can be given either in text form or by IP number. Users who are connecting from a host not on this list will not be authenticated. The default is to allow all hosts.
DenyHosts	Follows the same format as AllowHosts, but will instead deny authentication to users who connect from a matched host.
AllowUsers	Followed by a comma-separated list of regular expressions in the form user@host, this keyword gives a list of individual users on specific hosts who are allowed to use connections controlled by SSH. Users who do not match an entry in the list will not be authenticated. The default is to allow all users.
DenyUsers	Follows the same format as AllowUsers, but will instead deny authentication to users matching an entry in the list.
MaxConnections	Followed by a number indicating the maximum number of incoming connections that sshd2 will allow at any one time, this option can prevent denial-of-service attacks caused by opening large numbers of simultaneous SSH connections. The default value is 0 (connections not limited).

16

TABLE 16.1   continued

Option	Description
PermitEmptyPasswords	Specifies whether authentication will be provided for accounts with an empty password string. Should be set to no for any secured system.
PermitRootLogin	Specifies whether users claiming to be root will be authenticated. Should be set to no for any secured system.
RequireReverseMapping	Specifies whether a connecting system's IP number must match its DNS entry. Should normally be set to yes for any secured system.

The ssh2 client binary is located by default at /usr/local/bin/ssh2 and is responsible for initiating outbound ssh2-encrypted connections. Though the default set of behaviors is usually adequate, there are a few additional security-oriented options that can be changed by editing the /etc/ssh2/ssh2_config file.

The format of /etc/ssh2/ssh2_config is virtually identical in many ways to the format of the /etc/ssh2/sshd2_config file; the file is composed of a number of keyword/value pairs, one pair per line. Empty lines or lines beginning with the hash mark (#) are assumed to be comments and are ignored.

Some additional ssh2 options that may be helpful to you are shown in Table 16.2. The complete list of ssh2 configuration options is documented exhaustively in ssh2_config(5).

TABLE 16.2   Common Options for the ssh2_config File

Option	Description
Compression	When set to yes, causes the encrypted data stream to be compressed on-the-fly. This option is most useful for low-bandwidth connections, but can also slow things down on machines with very slow CPUs.
EscapeChar	Supplies the character that can be used to interrupt interactive SSH sessions. The word none disables the escape character. Control key combinations can be given by prefixing an alphanumeric character with the caret (^) character. The default is the tilde (~) character.
User	Specifies the default username to supply when connecting to remote SSH servers. Optional; this can be useful if your username on the local machine is different from your username on the remote machine.

Once you have installed SSH on at least two machines and are satisfied with any changes you've made to your SSH configurations, it's time to put SSH to work.

Using SSH for Remote Logins

The first and simplest use for SSH is as a kind of secure replacement for remote login programs like rlogin or Telnet. SSH can perform a similar function to these two protocols, but because SSH encrypts the data stream (including the password as it is being sent during authentication), communication between two systems is much more secure and difficult, if not impossible, to intercept.

To connect to an SSH-enabled server from an SSH-enabled client machine for remote login, simply call the ssh2 client binary and supply the remote hostname as an argument:

```
ssh2 newton
```

When SSH establishes a connection with the remote system, an exchange of host keys takes place. The SSH client checks to see if a key entry for the remote system is already present in the $HOME/.ssh2 directory. If so, the SSH client compares the key on record for the remote system to the key just sent by the remote system. If they match, authentication proceeds.

Since this is your first time connecting to the remote system, there will be no identification information on file for it. SSH will therefore ask you whether or not this system's key should be added to the list of known identifications. A transcript of the first-time connect process is shown in Listing 16.1.

LISTING 16.1 Connecting for the First Time

```
$ ssh2 newton
Host key not found from database.
Key fingerprint:
xopil-nyboh-mynyr-zifeb-zygok-zytam-bokab-potut-femyz-boxox
You can get a public key's fingerprint by running
% ssh-keygen -F publickey.pub
on the keyfile.
Are you sure you want to continue connecting (yes/no)? yes
Host key saved to $HOME/.ssh2/hostkeys/key_22_newton.pub
host key for newton, accepted by joe Sat Jan 06 2001 22:31:23 -0700
joe's password:
Authentication successful.
```

Notice that the host key for the host known as newton was saved to a file in the $HOME/.ssh2 directory. From now on, whenever joe connects to newton with SSH, the key supplied by newton will be compared to the key on file for newton. If the two don't match, SSH will notify joe of this and ask if the new key should be accepted. This provides a basic kind of protection against identity theft on the network.

After the key has been added, joe is prompted for his password. Because this is an SSH connection, joe's password will be encrypted as it is sent across the network, rather than being sent in clear text, an important improvement over programs like rlogin or Telnet. Once the password is successfully entered, a remote shell like any other will be started on the remote host called newton.

> Since the remote login capability of SSH clearly duplicates the functionality of Telnet or rlogin but does so much more securely than either of these other protocols, there is often no good reason to continue to allow incoming Telnet or rlogin requests to an SSH-enabled server.
>
> If you have no specific need for Telnet, for example, consider editing the /etc/inetd.conf file and commenting out the Telnet service once SSH has been installed. Afterward, use SSH for remote logins to the system. If necessary, you can even add an alias to your shell preference files for convenience:
>
> `alias telnet=ssh2`
>
> Assuming you compiled SSH with TCP wrappers support, you can still enforce any existing limits you had on Telnet in /etc/hosts.deny or /etc/hosts.allow by using ssh2 as the service name instead of telnet.

Host-Based Authentication

There are times when it is convenient to be able to connect to a host without needing a password; this was one of the functional strengths of the original rsh tool, though it was also one of the largest security weaknesses. The host-based authentication involving the .rhosts file is extraordinarily weak. SSH improves on this model with its capability to identify systems based on their public keys. However, it is still important to use so-called host-based authentication only for systems that are basically trusted.

In order to allow host-based authentication, you must have write access to the files in /etc/sshd2 on the destination system. Assuming that the local machine's hostname is local and the remote machine's hostname is remote, follow along with these steps:

1. Transfer the local (client) machine's public key to the remote (server) machine. The easiest way to do this is with SSH.

   ```
   cat /etc/ssh2/hostkey.pub | ssh2 remote 'cat > key.pub'
   ```

2. Log back in to the remote host and use su to gain administrative access.

   ```
   user@local$ ssh2 remote.host
   user's password:
   Authentication successful.
   user@remote$ su
   Password:
   user@remote#
   ```

3. Make a directory called knownhosts if one doesn't already exist in /etc/ssh2 and copy the key to the directory using a special name format:

```
user@remote# mkdir /etc/ssh2/knownhosts
user@remote# cp key.pub /etc/ssh2/knownhosts/local.mynet.net.ssh-dss.pub
```

Notice the format of the key file's name. It is the fully qualified domain name of the client host, followed by .ssh-dss.pub.

4. Modify the /etc/sshd2_config file on the destination system using your favorite editor. Search for the AllowedAuthentications keyword and add the option hostbased to the list of allowed authentication types:

```
AllowedAuthentications          hostbased,publickey,password
```

5. Drop out of root-level access, add the necessary client to your .shosts file, and set the file's permissions to 0400.

```
user@remote# exit
user@remote$ echo "local.mynet.net user" >>.shosts
user@remote$ chmod 0400 .shosts
user@remote$ exit
Connection to remote closed.
user@local$
```

Notice that the fully qualified domain name was used in the .shosts file and was followed by the name of the user account.

After these changes are made, user@local.mynet.net will be able to use ssh2 to connect to remote.mynet.net without having to enter a password each time, provided the key files aren't changed.

Public Key Authentication

On the opposite end of the spectrum from host-based authentication is the public key authentication scheme, perhaps the most flexible and certainly a more secure authentication method supported by SSH.

In order to use this authentication scheme, you must generate a personal set of keys and transfer the public key to the remote system. To generate your own key, simply run the ssh-keygen2 utility:

```
ssh-keygen2
```

This program will ask you for an optional passphrase of your choosing and will generate two keys: a public key and a private key for your own personal use, which will be stored in $HOME/.ssh2. After the keys have been generated, write the keyword idkey and the name of the private key (the file without the .pub extension) to the file $HOME/.ssh2/identification. The command to do this will usually be

```
echo "idkey id_dsa_1024_a" >> $HOME/.ssh2/identification
```

Next, copy the public key to the remote system and write the keyword `key` and the name
of the public key file to the file `$HOME/.ssh2/authentication` on that system:

```
$ cd .ssh2
$ cat id_dsa_1024_a.pub | ssh2 remote cat '>' .ssh2/mykey.pub
user's password:
Authentication successful.
$ echo "key mykey.pub" | ssh2 remote cat '>' .ssh2/authentication
user's password:
Authentication successful.
$
```

Now when you connect to the remote system, authentication will take place using your
public key instead of using your password on the remote system.

Using SSH for FTP

The SSH protocol can be used for more than rsh- or Telnet-style functionality. Another
important feature included with SSH is the capability to encrypt file transfers to prevent
data being exchanged from being intercepted or stolen. Though the protocol used is not
compatible with the real FTP protocol, the interface most users are accustomed to in the
standard `ftp` client has been more or less preserved, so the learning curve is low.

The `sftp2` client is the SSH version 2.x file transfer client. To use it, the `sftp2` client
must be present on the local system and the `sftp-server2` binary must be installed on
the remote system. Both of these programs are installed in a standard SSH installation as
described earlier. The remote system must also be configured to allow incoming
`sshd2` connections, just as was necessary for `ssh2` client connections.

Once the requirements have been met, using `sftp2` is easy; simply call `sftp2` using the
destination host as an argument:

```
sftp2 newton
```

The remote system will prompt for the user's password, and if this is the first SSH connection between this client and server, the key exchange as already described will also
occur. Once logged in, any user familiar with the standard `ftp` client will be able to navigate easily, though there is one important difference: He will not have access to files outside his own home directory.

As was the case with Telnet or rlogin, the SSH version of the FTP protocol is
much more secure than is the standard FTP protocol, and there is no real
performance or features penalty in most circumstances.

Unless you need to provide anonymous FTP access or for some reason you
require FTP service that preserves the original FTP protocol, it is probably a

good idea to disable the standard FTP service in /etc/inetd.conf and rely on SSH for file transfer instead, since SSH doesn't send clear text passwords, encrypts transferred files, and provides some means for authenticating a host's identity.

Tunneling TCP Streams Through SSH

16

One of the most important features of SSH is the capability to tunnel TCP data through an encrypted data stream. Using this feature, it is possible to encrypt data streams of all kinds, from the Simple Mail Transfer Protocol (SMTP) used by daemons like Sendmail to the protocol used by the print spooler.

Tunnels of this kind are created by asking SSH to listen for connections of the desired kind on a port on the local machine. When a connection to this port is opened, SSH will then forward this connection to a port on the remote machine through an encrypted channel, thereby securing an otherwise unsecured network protocol.

The syntax for asking SSH to wait in the background and forward TCP streams through an encrypted tunnel is

```
ssh2 host -f -L localport:host:port
```

In general, *host* refers to the destination system to which you want clients to be able to connect, *port* represents the normal port for the TCP stream you want to tunnel, and *localport* represents the new port you want SSH to listen to on the local machine. The best way to illustrate is with a simple example.

Suppose our fictitious user joe regularly brings his e-mail from the host known as newton to the local machine using the Post Office Protocol version 3 (POP3). This protocol is perhaps one of the most commonly used on the Internet today and manages lots of mail for lots of people, including joe. There are some problems with POP3, however. The two most important are that the identity and password information is sent across the network in plain text and that messages are sent this way as well, making any e-mail connection fair game for mischief. To remedy this situation, joe wants to encrypt his POP3 connection to newton.

To do this, joe runs the following command:

```
ssh2 newton -f -L 7501:newton:110
```

Then, he configures his mail client to connect to the host localhost on port 7501 instead of to newton on port 110 as is normally the case with POP3 connections. Now, each time his mail client polls the remote system for new e-mail using the POP3 protocol, all of the communication, including passwords and any mail text, is encrypted by SSH.

The majority of protocols you'll find in the `/etc/services` file can be tunneled through SSH this way. It is a good idea to take advantage of this feature whenever possible.

Improving X Security with SSH

The final security problem we'll tackle while using SSH is the X11R6 data stream. Recall that in the last hour we used a little trick to move an X session's magic cookie from one host to another:

```
xauth extract - :0 | rsh foobar xauth merge -
```

This command copied the X session's magic cookie, designed to improve connection security, from one system to another one. Unfortunately, this introduced a new security vulnerability, since the magic cookie itself was transmitted in clear code and was therefore susceptible to being intercepted and used by unknown parties.

With SSH, we can instantly fix this problem. The command is virtually identical:

```
xauth extract - :0 | ssh2 foobar xauth merge -
```

The difference is that the magic cookie is now encrypted before being sent out across the network, making it much less susceptible to unwanted use by untrusted parties.

Using SSH, X11R6 security can be improved even more. This is done by encoding the X11R6 data stream itself. Tunneling of other network protocols was a little difficult to grasp, but X is such an important protocol that SSH includes special functionality for working with X. The clearest, simplest example requires only a running X server on the local machine.

Assuming that you want to launch clients on a machine called `remote` that will display on the already running local X server, simply issue a command like this:

```
ssh2 remote /usr/X11R6/bin/xterm
```

An `xterm` window running on `remote` appears on your local display, without additional intervention or explicit tunneling or forwarding instructions. From inside this `xterm`, try launching any number of X applications; they will all start on your local display as expected.

In this case, SSH has taken care of all of the details for you; when SSH determines that an X application is to be run, it automatically exchanges the magic cookie from your XDMCP session and sets the `DISPLAY` environment variable in the remote environment correctly. More involved configurations might even call SSH in the `.xinitrc` file to start a window manager on the remote machine:

```
ssh2 remote /usr/local/bin/wmaker
```

In this case, by starting Window Maker as the first client, virtually the entire session would be tunneled through SSH without any need for further intervention.

Installing, Configuring, and Using OpenSSH

Because of the commercial nature of the original SSH protocol implementation, a group of coders began work on an open implementation of the SSH protocol, in cooperation with the OpenBSD project. OpenSSH is fully compatible with the SSH version 2.x protocol, and the version for operating systems other than OpenBSD, Portable OpenSSH, runs well on Linux. The OpenSSH home page can be found at http://www.openssh.com.

16

> OpenSSH has two modes of operation, one compatible with the original SSH protocol and one compatible with the new SSH version 2.x protocol used by ssh2. Because the OpenSSH implementation of the SSH version 2.x protocol isn't yet complete, this text will only discuss OpenSSH and the version 1.x SSH protocol.

Downloading and Installing OpenSSL

Before downloading, compiling, and installing OpenSSH, you'll need to download, compile, and install OpenSSL, an open source encryption library that OpenSSH depends on for operation. The OpenSSL home page can be found at http://www.openssl.org.

The source code download page for OpenSSL can be found at http://www.openssl.org/source/. After downloading the latest source tarball, extract the source code and visit the newly created source directory:

```
$ tar -xzf openssl-0.9.6.tar.gz
$ cd openssl-0.9.6
$
```

Now configure, compile, and install OpenSSH:

```
$ ./config
...[ output of config ]...
$ make
...[ output of make ]...
$ su
Password:
# make install
...[output of make install ]...
# exit
$
```

The default configuration of OpenSSL installs most of its files in the /usr/local tree, with libraries going in /usr/local/ssl/lib.

Downloading and Installing OpenSSH

To download OpenSSH, visit the Portable OpenSSH download page at `http://www.`
`openssh.com/portable.html`. Choose a mirror site near you and download the latest
`.tar.gz` source archive. Extract the source code and visit the newly created directory with
the `cd` command.

```
$ tar -xzf openssh-2.3.0p1.tar.gz
$ cd openssh-2.3.0p1
$
```

Inside the `openssh-2.3.0p1` directory, use the `configure` command to tailor the source
code configuration for your own system's circumstances. You'll probably want to supply
the `--with-tcp-wrappers` option to allow OpenSSH to work with TCP wrappers:

```
$ ./configure --with-tcp-wrappers
...[ output of configure ]...
$
```

If you want to change the location of the final OpenSSH installation, use the `--prefix`
option to alter the installation path:

```
./configure --with-tcp-wrappers --prefix=/opt/openssh2
```

Remember that if you adjust your installation path when configuring the source, you'll
need to account for this difference later when configuring and using OpenSSH. As was
the case with SSH, a number of additional options can be used to change some of the
properties or behaviors of the final OpenSSH installation; to see a list of these options,
use the `--help` option:

```
./configure --help
```

The configure utility will likely take several minutes to finish on early Pentium or older
systems. Once it has returned without errors, OpenSSH can be built and installed using
`make`. Don't forget to install as superuser, or the installation attempt will fail.

```
$ make
...[ output of make ]...
$ su
Password:
# make install
...[ output of make install ]...
# exit
$
```

During installation, the 1024-bit host keys necessary for some aspects of OpenSSH operation will be automatically generated and stored in the `/usr/local/etc` directory as
ssh_host_key and ssh_host_key.pub. Simply repeat this process on each machine
needing an OpenSSH installation so that each of them has its own set of keys.

After installing the OpenSSH files, it is necessary to make a few changes to the /etc/ services and /etc/inetd.conf files. Making these changes will allow inetd and TCP wrappers to manage incoming SSH requests transparently, simplifying some aspects of SSH use and preserving system resources. Add the following lines to /etc/services:

```
ssh          22/tcp          openssh
ssh          22/udp          openssh
```

These lines define a new service called ssh2 that will listen on port 22 for incoming connections. If you plan to run OpenSSH on another port, be sure to adjust the port numbers as necessary. Now add the line to start OpenSSH to /etc/inetd.conf:

```
ssh stream tcp nowait root /usr/sbin/tcpd /usr/local/sbin/sshd -i
```

This line allows inetd to start the OpenSSH daemon when required and to use TCP wrappers. This way, you can control access to SSH from the /etc/hosts.allow and /etc/ hosts.deny files using sshd as the name of the service. Once these changes have been made to the system's network configuration files, you'll want to send the hang-up signal (HUP) to the system's running inetd process:

```
killall -HUP inetd
```

This will restart the inetd program and cause any changes you've made to the /etc/inetd.conf file to become active.

A PAM configuration for the sshd daemon must also be created before OpenSSH will be able to use password authentication. The easiest way to do this is to use the generic PAM configuration file located in the contrib directory in the OpenSSH source tree. Simply copy the file to the /etc/pam.d directory:

```
# cd openssh-2.3.0p1/contrib
# cp sshd.pam.generic /etc/pam.d/sshd
#
```

On systems with a single central PAM configuration file, simply edit the file and copy and paste the configuration from the generic sample, taking care to insert the word sshd at the beginning of each line.

Once these changes have been made, for most users little or no additional OpenSSH configuration is required.

Additional Configuration

The sshd binary, located by default at /usr/local/sbin/sshd, is responsible for handling incoming ssh2-encrypted connections. Though the default set of behaviors is usually adequate, there are a few additional security-oriented options that can be changed by editing the /usr/local/etc/sshd_config file.

The format of `/usr/local/etc/sshd_config` is familiar to most Linux and Unix users; the file is composed of a number of keyword/value pairs, one pair per line. Empty lines or lines beginning with the hash mark (#) are assumed to be comments and are ignored.

Some additional `sshd` options that may be helpful to you from a security standpoint are shown in Table 16.3. The complete list of `sshd` configuration options is documented exhaustively in `sshd(8)`.

TABLE 16.3   Common Options for the `sshd_config` File

Option	Description
AllowGroups	Followed by a comma-separated list of patterns, this keyword gives a list of groups that are allowed to use connections controlled by OpenSSH. Patterns can contain * and ? as wildcard characters. Users who don't belong to a matching group will not be authenticated. The default is to allow all groups.
DenyGroups	Follows the same format as `AllowGroups`, but will instead deny authentication to users who belong to a matched group.
AllowUsers	Followed by a comma-separated list of patterns, this keyword gives a list of individual users who are allowed to use connections controlled by OpenSSH. Patterns can contain * and ? as wildcard characters. Users who do not match an entry in the list will not be authenticated. The default is to allow all users.
DenyUsers	Follows the same format as `AllowUsers`, but will instead deny authentication to users matching an entry in the list.
MaxStartups	Followed by a number indicating the maximum number of as-of-yet unauthenticated incoming connections that `sshd` will allow at any one time. Setting this option can prevent denial-of-service attacks on a backgrounded `sshd` daemon caused by opening large numbers of simultaneous OpenSSH connections. The default value is `10`; set to zero for no limit.
PermitEmptyPasswords	Specifies whether authentication will be provided for accounts with an empty password string. Should be set to `no` for any secured system.
PermitRootLogin	Specifies whether users claiming to be `root` will be authenticated. Should be set to `no` for any secured system.
RequireReverseMapping	Specifies whether a connecting system's IP number must match its DNS entry. Should normally be set to `yes` for any secured system.
X11Forwarding	Should be set to `yes` to allow OpenSSH to tunnel the X11R6 data stream.

The `ssh` client binary is located by default at `/usr/local/bin/ssh` and is responsible for initiating outbound ssh2-encrypted connections. Though the default set of behaviors is usually adequate, there are a few additional security-oriented options that can be changed by editing the /usr/local/etc/ssh_config file.

The format of /usr/local/etc/ssh_config is virtually identical in many ways to the format of the /usr/local/etc/sshd_config file; the file is composed of a number of keyword/value pairs, one pair per line. Empty lines or lines beginning with the hash mark (#) are assumed to be comments and are ignored.

Some additional ssh options that may be helpful to you are shown in Table 16.4. The complete list of ssh configuration options is documented exhaustively in ssh(1).

TABLE 16.4   Common Options for the ssh_config File

Option	Description
Compression	When set to yes, causes the encrypted data stream to be compressed on-the-fly. This option is most useful for low-bandwidth connections, but can also slow down machines with very slow CPUs.
CompressionLevel	Allows the user to control the compression ratio used by ssh when compression is enabled. Set to a digit from 1 (fastest) to 9 (slowest, but with highest compression).
EscapeChar	Supplies the character that can be used to interrupt the interactive OpenSSH sessions. The word none disables the escape character. Control key combinations can be given by prefixing an alphanumeric character with the caret (^) character. The default is the tilde (~) character.
ForwardX11	Should be set to yes to allow OpenSSH to handle X11R6 forwarding, magic cookies, and the DISPLAY environment variable automatically.
User	Specifies the default username to supply when connecting to remote SSH servers. Optional; this can be useful if your username on the local machine is different from your username on the remote machine.

Once you have installed OpenSSH on at least two machines and are satisfied with any changes that you've made to your SSH configurations, it's time to put OpenSSH to work.

Using OpenSSH for Remote Logins

The process of logging on to a remote system using OpenSSH is almost identical to the process of logging on to a remote system using SSH, covered earlier.

To connect to an OpenSSH-enabled server from an OpenSSH-enabled client machine for remote login, simply call the ssh client binary and supply the remote machine's hostname as an argument:

```
ssh newton
```

As was the case with SSH, when OpenSSH establishes a connection with the remote system, an exchange of host keys takes place. The OpenSSH client checks to see if a key entry for the remote system is already present in the $HOME/.ssh directory. If so, the OpenSSH client compares the key on record for the remote system to the key just sent by the remote system. If they match, authentication proceeds.

The first time you connect to a specific remote system using OpenSSH, there will be no identification information on file for it. OpenSSH will therefore ask you whether or not this system's key should be added to the list of known identifications. A transcript of the first-time connect process is shown in Listing 16.2.

LISTING 16.2   Connecting for the First Time

```
$ ssh newton
The authenticity of host 'newton' can't be established.
DSA key fingerprint is cf:af:f4:81:be:32:d0:78:a2:7b:9e:18:34:03:43:88.
Are you sure you want to continue connecting (yes/no)? yes
Warning: Permanently added 'newton,192.168.1.137' (DSA)
to the list of known hosts.
joe@newton's password:
$
```

From now on, whenever joe connects to newton with OpenSSH, the key supplied by newton will be compared to the key on file for newton. If the two don't match, OpenSSH will notify joe of the discrepancy, and joe will be able to take whatever steps he deems necessary.

After the key has been added, joe is prompted for his password. Once again, because this is an OpenSSH connection, joe's password will be encrypted as it is sent across the network, rather than being sent in clear text.

RhostsRSA Authentication

Like SSH, OpenSSH also provides the capability to authenticate connecting systems based on their public host keys. The mechanism for allowing this type of authentication is slightly different in OpenSSH, however, and is known as *RhostsRSA authentication*. As was the case with host-based authentication, RhostsRSA authentication should be used only for generally trusted machines.

In order to enable RhostsRSA authentication, you must have write access to the /usr/local/etc/ssh_known_hosts file on the destination system. To enable a specific client to log in to the server using host-based authentication, you'll need to add a line of the following format to the ssh_known_hosts file:

hostname   bits   exponent   modulus comment

As luck would have it, this format matches very closely the format of the /usr/local/ etc/ssh_host_key.pub file. To add the local client's public host key to the remote machine's ssh_known_hosts file is therefore a simple matter. Simply enter the name of the client host and then paste the entire contents of the client host's ssh_host_key.pub file into ssh_known_hosts on the same line.

Afterward, be sure to add the client host to either the $HOME/.shots or /etc/shosts.equiv file on the server machine so that this type of authentication will be permitted for the client host in question.

User-Based Public Key Authentication

As was the case with SSH, in order to use public key authentication with OpenSSH, you must generate a personal set of keys and transfer the public key to the remote system. To generate your own key, simply run the ssh-keygen utility:

```
ssh-keygen
```

This program will ask you for an optional passphrase of your choosing and will generate two keys: a public key and a private key for your own personal use, which will be stored in $HOME/.ssh/identity.pub and $HOME/.ssh/identity, respectively.

The exchange of keys when using OpenSSH is much simpler than the exchange of keys when using public key authentication with SSH. All that is required is that the key in identity.pub be appended to the $HOME/.ssh/authorized_keys file on the remote system. This can be accomplished easily, given a server host known as remote:

```
$ cd .ssh
$ cat identity.pub | ssh remote cat '>' .ssh/authorized_keys
user@remote's password:
$
```

Once you enter your password and the data is exchanged, your next call to ssh should proceed either without a password request or after asking for your public key passcode, if you chose to supply one when generating your set of keys.

Tunneling TCP Streams Through OpenSSH

Like SSH, OpenSSH also includes a facility for tunneling many common network protocols through an encrypted channel by forwarding a port on the local machine. The syntax for forwarding a port in order to encrypt various kinds of network data using OpenSSH is

```
ssh -L localport:host:port host
```

In general, host refers to the destination system to which you want clients to be able to connect, port represents the normal port for the TCP stream you want to tunnel, and localport represents the new port you want SSH to listen to on the local machine. For example, to tunnel the POP3 mail service through an encrypted channel at port 8100 to a remote machine known as pokey, you might use

```
ssh -L 8100:pokey:110 pokey
```

There is no explicit way to force OpenSSH simply to forward a port in the background as there was with SSH, but a similar effect can be achieved, since OpenSSH won't close a connection until all users of the port have exited. Assuming that the user had already configured fetchmail to contact port 8100 on localhost for his mail, the following command would be suitable for a script that checks mail regularly:

```
ssh -L 8100:pokey:110 pokey sleep 1; fetchmail
```

The call to ssh forwards the port for one second, during which fetchmail starts and connects to the port. OpenSSH will then leave the port open until fetchmail terminates.

Improving X Security with OpenSSH

Like SSH, OpenSSH includes extra functionality to streamline encrypted tunneling of the X11R6 protocol. To use this functionality, you must first enable it in the /usr/local/etc/sshd_config file on the X client (ssh server) machine, since OpenSSH disables this functionality by default.

To enable the X-related features, be sure that the following line appears in the sshd_config file:

```
X11Forwarding    Yes
```

Once you've added this line, launching X applications with OpenSSH is just as easy as it was with SSH:

```
ssh remote-host /usr/X11R6/bin/xterm &
ssh remote-host /usr/X11R6/bin/xclock &
ssh remote-host /usr/local/bin/netscape &
```

As was the case with SSH, OpenSSH has taken care of all of the details for you; when OpenSSH determines that an X application is to be run, it automatically exchanges the magic cookie from your XDMCP session and sets the DISPLAY environment variable in the remote environment correctly.

Summary

In this hour, you learned to install, configure, and use your network encryption tool of choice: Secure Shell (SSH), for those who can afford or who prefer a commercial license, and the SSH version 2 protocol or OpenSSH, an open source implementation of the SSH protocol.

You learned how to use either one of these tools for a number of purposes:

- As a general-purpose replacement for rsh, rlogin, Telnet, and other aging protocols that don't protect any of the data they send across the network, including things like passwords and other account-oriented information.
- As a multipurpose network stream encryption tool, using port forwarding from the local machine to a remote destination.
- As a more secure and more convenient method for handling the X11R6 magic cookie authentication exchange.
- As a more secure and more convenient method for handling X11R6 data streams representing multiple X clients.

16

Though SSH may seem daunting at first, once mastered it quickly becomes as convenient and easy to use as familiar commands like rsh. The convenience of some functions (such as those used by network-oriented X) is greatly enhanced through the use of SSH.

Q&A

Q Why didn't you discuss the SSH version 2 protocol support in OpenSSH?

A Because it isn't really done yet as this text is being written. Specifically, host-based authentication isn't yet supported at all (RhostsRSA is not a part of SSH-2) and there have been some compatibility problems between the official SSH 2.x components and the OpenSSH components when running in SSH-2 mode.

At this point, there is no substantial loss to most small business or small network users forced to use SSH-1 instead of SSH-2; the original SSH protocol remains a mainstay of the networked world and provides most of the functionality of the SSH-2 protocol.

Q Aren't there import or export restrictions on OpenSSH or SSH? Won't I get into trouble if I use them?

A No. The commercial SSH has never been subject to U.S. export restrictions because it is not developed in the U.S. but in Europe. There has never been an import restriction on cryptographic tools. The main issue for a number of years with SSH was the fact that the RSA encryption algorithm was patented by a U.S. company, and thus, free distribution of SSH was in violation of that patent. However, the patent expired in 2000, and there are no known legal entanglements for using either SSH or OpenSSH in the U.S. at this time.

Q I have installed SSH on an older computer system, and each time a connection attempt is made, it seems to take forever for sshd (or sshd2) to respond. What's going on?

A This is because the daemon launch and key generation are using most of your limited resources each time a connection is opened. The solution in cases of old or very slow hardware is to start `sshd` or `sshd2` once from an init script of your choice or construction as the machine boots, rather than to have it started by inetd each time a new connection is requested.

New Terms

keys (public and private) A special kind of code used for encryption. Each authenticatable entity in the SSH world has two keys: a public key and a private key. Both keys yield the same encryption result, but the keys are different and one key cannot be derived from another. The public key is known by everyone and shared upon request. The private key is secret and is never shared. Authentication takes place when data encoded by a second party using the public key is correctly decoded by the original party with the secret private key, thereby proving the identity of a user or host on the network.

OpenSSH An open source implementation of the secure shell protocol based on early releases of the "official" SSH software, which were also open source.

Secure Shell (SSH) A kind of Swiss Army Knife replacement for the original `rsh` command. The chief benefits of SSH (indeed, the reasons for its name) are its capability to perform much more secure types of authentication than `rsh` ever could and its capability to encrypt network data streams, making them harder to intercept and use maliciously.

tunneling A way of describing what occurs when SSH forwards a local port to a remote destination or vice versa and encrypts the packets while they are in transit for increased security.

Hour 17

Introduction to Kerberos

This hour, you're going to learn how to use an open source implementation of the Kerberos authentication system to secure authentication and encrypt connections made on your local network. More specifically, you're going to install and configure a key distribution center (KDC) and add principal hosts and users to its database.

The home page for the Kerberos 5 implementation we're going to cover here can be found at http://web.mit.edu/kerberos/www.

> Because Kerberos is still export restricted, this hour applies to users inside the U.S. and Canada only. An exportable alternative to Kerberos version 4 known as eBones is available to users outside of the U.S. and Canada. One set of eBones sources can be found at http://www.pdc.kth.se/kth-krb/.

What Is Kerberos?

First and foremost, Kerberos is a more secure authentication system than the one normally employed by most network-aware operating systems. It is needed because of a fundamental shortcoming in the way standard authentication takes place.

Put simply, standard protocols like Telnet are very trusting. When Telnet accepts an incoming connection, it asks only for a password before granting access. It assumes that the remote user really is who he claims to be, rather than a stranger using a stolen password. It furthermore assumes that the remote system is who it claims to be, rather than a rogue system hiding behind a stolen address. Similarly, the telneting user has no way of knowing if he is telneting into the actual system he intended to reach, or if the address has been hijacked by a rogue system, ready to steal his password or do something even worse.

Kerberos tries to solve this identity problem in a simple way: One system on the local area network becomes the key distribution center (KDC), a kind of master database of credentials. When a user employs a Kerberos-enabled protocol to connect from one system to another, all parties involved—the user and both hosts—request that the KDC check out everyone's credentials. The KDC then gathers identification information in the form of encryption keys from the user and from both hosts. If these keys are correct according to the database of users and hosts on file at the KDC, the KDC then informs each party that the others are really who they claim to be, and the connection is established.

Though this method is relatively complex and is by no means foolproof, it is among the most secure methods for authentication currently in widespread use.

Building a Key Distribution Center

The key distribution center, or KDC, is the machine on which the central database of credentials is stored. Once Kerberos authentication is made active on your network, any Kerberos-enabled connection will have to go through your KDC in order to be opened. It is therefore important that this machine be as secure and as stable as possible, because if the KDC goes down, the entire network can grind to a screeching halt.

It is a good idea to dedicate an entire system to the KDC role. All other services and ports on the KDC machine will be disabled, and no logins or other types of activity will be performed on the KDC machine, either locally or remotely. Because a KDC on smaller networks won't handle huge amounts of traffic or streaming data, even an older, smaller computer system can suffice as long as it has a network interface and a reasonable amount of free disk storage.

Perform a minimal Linux installation on the KDC machine. Neither XFree86 nor any user application is required for operation as a KDC.

Downloading and Installing Kerberos 5

The Kerberos 5 download page can be found at `http://web.mit.edu/network/`
`kerberos-form.html`. You'll need to read each question and answer truthfully to satisfy
the export restriction conditions. Once you have filled out and submitted the form, you'll
be able to download Kerberos 5 in various forms. For Linux, download the source code
to the latest version (1.2.1 as this is being written) and save it to your hard drive.

The source is packaged as a tarball containing several tarballs. To extract the distribution
tarball, which is uncompressed, use `tar -xvf`:

```
$ tar -xvf krb5-1.2.1.tar
krb5-1.2.1.crypto.tar.gz
krb5-1.2.1.crypto.tar.gz.asc
krb5-1.2.1.doc.tar.gz
krb5-1.2.1.doc.tar.gz.asc
krb5-1.2.1.src.tar.gz
krb5-1.2.1.src.tar.gz.asc
$
```

Now, extract the additional tarballs created when the distribution tarball was extracted.
They all overlay into the `krb5-1.2.1` source directory. Afterward, visit the directory containing the source.

```
$ tar -xzf krb5-1.2.1.src.tar.gz
$ tar -xzf krb5-1.2.1.crypto.tar.gz
$ tar -xzf krb5-1.2.1.doc.tar.gz
$ cd krb5-1.2.1/src
$
```

Building the source is a straightforward process on most Linux systems. The Kerberos 5
sources use the GNU autoconf utilities, so configuration is generally as easy as running
the `configure` script. However, most Linux users will want to include the `--enable-`
`shared` option to build shared libraries instead of static ones, and in this hour, we're also
going to assume that you've used the `--prefix=/usr/local/kerberos` option in order to
isolate the Kerberos installation and make things more clear.

```
$ ./configure --enable-shared --prefix=/usr/local/kerberos
...[ output of configure script ]...
$
```

Once `configure` has run successfully, building is simple. Just run a `make` followed by a
`make install` as root. The actual build time will vary, but you should expect it to be
similar to that required to build a Linux kernel.

```
$ make
...[ output of make ]...
$ su
Password:
# make install
```

17

```
...[ output of make install ]...
# exit
$
```

Once you have followed these steps, you have a complete installation of the Kerberos
binaries in the /usr/local/kerberos tree. It's time to proceed to configuration.

Configuring Kerberos 5

Kerberos uses a few ports for key distribution and administration, among other things, so
the first order of business is to add a few lines to the end of the /etc/services file.
Rather than entering them by hand, it is easiest to use the services.append file, located
in the src/config-files directory of the Kerberos source tree:

```
# cat config-files/services.append >>/etc/services
```

Some Linux distributions include existing entries in /etc/services for Kerberos, but
these are often incorrect or are for Kerberos 4, so be sure to remove any existing entries
that match either port or protocol name before adding these new entries.

Next, you need to create a few extra directories in the /usr/local/kerberos hierarchy
that are necessary for Kerberos configuration:

```
# cd /usr/local/kerberos
# mkdir etc var var/krb5kdc
#
```

In the newly created /usr/local/kerberos/etc directory, you're going to create two configuration files: krb5.conf and kdc.conf. You'll need to know the name of your domain and
the realm name you plan to use. For example, if your current host is kdc.mynet.net, then
your domain is mynet.net, and your realm, by convention, is MYNET.NET (case-sensitive).
Two sample configuration files are shown in Listings 17.1 and 17.2.

LISTING 17.1   Sample /usr/local/kerberos/etc/krb5.conf

```
# These are some defaults. Change the default_realm to
# match your own realm (your domain in uppercase). See
# krb5.conf(5) in /usr/local/kerberos/man for more
# details on this file's format.

[libdefaults]
     ticket_lifetime = 600
     default_realm = MYNET.NET
     default_tkt_enctypes = des3-hmac-sha1 des-cbc-crc
     default_tgs_enctypes = des3-hmac-sha1 des-cbc-crc

# Use the IP address of your KDC machine here. Do not change
# the ports (88,749) because they are standard for Keberos.
# default_domain should be set to your domain.
```

LISTING 17.1   continued

```
[realms]
    MYNET.NET = {
        kdc = kdc.mynet.net:88
        admin_server = kdc.mynet.net:749
        default_domain = mynet.net
    }

# These equivalencies just help Kerberos to figure out which
# hosts belong to which domain. Adjust for your situation.

[domain_realm]
    .mynet.net = MYNET.NET
    mynet.net = MYNET.NET

# These are the paths to log data. They are placed in
# /var/log in this case so that all system logs are in the
# same place.

[logging]
    kdc = FILE:/var/log/kdc.log
    admin_server = FILE:/var/log/kadmin.log
    default = FILE:/var/log/kerberos.log
```

17

LISTING 17.2   Sample /usr/local/kerberos/etc/kdc.conf

```
# Only two changes should really be necessary in this file: change
# both instances of MYNET.NET to match your realm. This file is
# documented at kdc.conf(5) in /usr/local/kerberos/man.

[kdcdefaults]
    kdc_ports = 88, 750
# It is important not to change any of the paths below if you installed
# in /usr/local/kerberos; the Kerberos code has some interesting bugs
# with these options. Specifically, some parts of the paths are hard-
# coded, so these paths must match the hard-coded segments.

[realms]
    MYNET.NET = {
        database_name = /usr/local/kerberos/var/krb5kdc/principal
        admin_keytab = /usr/local/kerberos/var/krb5kdc/kadm5.keytab
        acl_file = /usr/local/kerberos/var/krb5kdc/kadm5.acl
        dict_file = /usr/local/kerberos/var/krb5kdc/kadm5.dict
        key_stash_file = /usr/local/kerberos/var/krb5kdc/.k5.MYNET.NET
        kadmind_port = 749
        max_life = 12h 0m 0s
        max_renewable_life = 7d 0h 0m 0s
        master_key_type = des3-hmac-sha1
        supported_enctypes = des3-hmac-sha1:normal des-cbc-crc:normal
    }
```

Before we proceed, you may want to add the /usr/local/kerberos/bin and /usr/local/kerberos/sbin directories to your PATH environment variable. You should probably also do this on a permanent basis by editing /etc/profile or a similar shell configuration script.

```
# PATH=/usr/local/kerberos/bin:$PATH
# PATH=/usr/local/kerberos/sbin:$PATH
# echo "PATH=/usr/local/kerberos/bin:$PATH" >>/etc/profile
# echo "PATH=/usr/local/kerberos/sbin:$PATH" >>/etc/profile
#
```

Now it's time to initialize the database. This is done with the kdb5_util program located in /usr/local/kerberos/sbin. Using the create command with kdb5_util initializes the database so that we can run the KDC server later. The -r option should be followed by your realm name as an argument. You'll be asked for a password; this is the master password for your KDC database and will rarely be used in the course of normal operation. Choose a *very* difficult password for maximum security.

```
# kdb5_util create -r MYNET.NET -s
Initializing database
'/usr/local/kerberos/var/krb5kdc/principal'
for realm 'MYNET.NET', master key name 'K/M@MYNET.NET'
You will be prompted for the database Master Password.
It is important that you NOT FORGET this password.
Enter KDC database master key:
Re-enter KDC database master key to verify:
#
```

You are now ready to launch the KDC server, krb5kdc, located in /usr/local/kerberos/sbin. This program will automatically background itself once it has successfully started.

```
# krb5kdc
#
```

Now the server needs to be tested to see if it is distributing keys properly. Before this can occur, a test principal must be added. A principal can be a user, a host, an administrator, or anything the KDC may someday be asked to identify. Normally, principals are added with the kadmin utility, which will be discussed later in this hour, but since no administrator principals have been created yet, something else must be done instead to allow principals to be added. The kadmin.local program is a modified version of kadmin that will run only on the KDC itself and thus doesn't need any existing principals to run. Inside kadmin.local, use the add_principal command to create a user called testuser and give testuser a password. Then, exit from kadmin.local.

```
# kadmin.local
kadmin.local: add_principal testuser
Enter password for principal "testuser@MYNET.NET":
Re-enter password for principal "testuser@MYNET.NET":
```

```
Principal "testuser@MYNET.NET" created.
kadmin.local: exit
#
```

Now a user principal called `testuser` has been created. To test the KDC server, use the kinit utility, which we'll discuss in more detail later in this hour, to get a ticket for `testuser`. Then, use klist to display the ticket information.

```
# kinit testuser
Password for testuser@MYNET.NET:
# klist testuser
Ticket cache: FILE:/tmp/krb5cc_0
Default principal: testuser@MYNET.NET

Valid starting      Expires              Service principal
01/08/01 12:25:01 01/08/01 22:24:56    krbtgt/MYNET.NET@MYNET.NET

Kerberos 4 ticket cache: /tmp/tkt0
klist: You have no tickets cached
# kdestroy
#
```

The output of klist shows that one Kerberos 5 ticket has now been cached, for the user known to Kerberos as `testuser@MYNET.NET`. This demonstrates that the KDC server is running and that the `krb5.conf` and `kdc.conf` files are correct. Notice that `kdestroy` was run afterward. This erases the ticket just granted to `testuser` with kinit.

The second part of a standard KDC host is the administrative server, which must be running for Kerberos administration to be possible from hosts other than the KDC itself. To get the administrative server `kadmind` running, you'll need to add a couple of entries to a special file called `kadm5.acl`, located in `/usr/local/kerberos/var/krb5kdc` by our configuration files. To do this, start `kadmin.local` once again and use the `ktadd` command to add keys for `kadmin/admin` and `kadmin/changepw`.

```
# kadmin.local
kadmin.local: ktadd -k /usr/local/kerberos/var/krb5kdc/kadm5.keytab
➥kadmin/admin kadmin/changepw
...[ Output from ktadd command ]...
kadmin.local: exit
#
```

You should now be able to start the `kadmind` server, which will also background itself immediately, just as `krb5kdc` did.

```
# kadmind
#
```

If both `krb5kdc` and `kadmind` were launched successfully, your KDC machine is virtually ready to use. The only task remaining is to start `krb5kdc` and `kadmind` from your init scripts somewhere. The easiest place to do this may be the `/etc/rc.d/rc.local` file. A few lines like these should suffice:

17

```
# Start the Kerberos services

PATH=$PATH:/usr/local/kerberos/bin:/usr/local/kerberos/sbin
krb5kdc
kadmind
```

With these changes made, your KDC host will automatically start Kerberos services each time it starts.

> If possible, you should make every attempt to create a kerberos script for your /etc/rc.d/init.d directory instead of starting Kerberos from rc.local. Use your existing scripts as a template. This will give you more control over the run-levels at which Kerberos will be started and how it will be started and stopped.

Administrating Kerberos 5

Now that your KDC is running, most of the battle is won. Most of the information you still need is related to various tasks you'll encounter while administrating Kerberos services on your network.

Adding Administrator Principals

Though you have a working KDC, you have no administrators at the moment, making your KDC almost useless, since administrator access is required to add hosts. To add an administrator, first start kadmin.local (or kadmin once you have at least one administrator account to work from) and use the add_principal command to add the user principal who will be given administrator access:

```
# kadmin.local
kadmin.local: add_principal jake
Enter password for principal "jake@MYNET.NET":
Re-enter password for principal "jake@MYNET.NET":
Principal "jake@MYNET.NET" created.
kadmin.local:
```

Now there is a principal for the user jake. However, we also want to give jake administrator access, so we create a second principal with the /admin suffix. Generally, it is easiest for jake if the same password is used for both accounts, though this isn't required.

```
kadmin.local: add_principal jake/admin
Enter password for principal "jake/admin@MYNET.NET":
Re-enter password for principal "jake/admin@MYNET.NET":
Principal "jake/admin@MYNET.NET" created.
kadmin.local: exit
#
```

Now jake is classified as an administrator and will be able to start the kadmin program. However, the administrator called jake still has no privileges once inside kadmin. The set of privileges given to each administrator is controlled with an access control list file called kadm5.acl located in /usr/local/kerberos/var/krb5kdc. Each line in the file contains the fully qualified Kerberos name of an administrator and the permissions he is to have. These permissions are shown in Table 17.1.

TABLE 17.1 Kerberos Administrator ACL Permissions

Permission	Description
a	Allowed to add principals or policies.
d	Allowed to delete principals or policies.
m	Allowed to modify principals or policies.
c	Allowed to change passwords for principals.
i	Allowed to run database inquiries.
l	Allowed to list principals in the database.
* or x	Short for admcil (all permissions).

To give full permissions to jake, add the following line to /usr/local/kerberos/var/krb5kdc/kadm5.acl:

```
jake/admin@MYNET.NET      admcil
```

The same effect could also have been achieved by adding this:

```
jake/admin@MYNET.NET      *
```

> The default set of ACL permissions for an administrator is no permissions at all. Therefore, if you don't add an entry to the ACL file for a newly created administrator, that administrator will be able to start kadmin but won't be able to do anything once inside.

After editing the ACL file, you'll have to restart kadmind for changes to take effect. Unfortunately, the -HUP signal doesn't have the expected effect on kadmind, so the only option is to kill it and restart it:

```
# killall kadmind; kadmind
#
```

The user jake should now be able to use kadmind from any host in the realm, provided he has a valid Kerberos ticket.

Adding and Configuring Host Principals

Before any host on your network can fully participate in services that have been
Kerberos enabled, the host must be added to the KDC database and properly configured
to use the new set of services.

First, download and install Kerberos, following the same instructions that you used for the
KDC but stopping after the make install step. Once the Kerberos tree has been installed
in /usr/local/kerberos with make install, create the /usr/local/kerberos/etc directory and copy the krb5.conf and kdc.conf files from your KDC host's /usr/local/
kerberos/etc directory. Add the /usr/local/kerberos/bin and /usr/local/kerberos/
sbin directories to your PATH variable.

Now, become the superuser on the new host and use the kinit command to get a ticket
for an administrator account. For example, remembering that we already created an
administrator account for jake, enter the command kinit jake on the new host and
enter the password for jake.

```
newhost$ su
Password:
newhost# kinit jake
Password for jake@MYNET.NET:
newhost#
```

After a ticket has been acquired, launch the kadmin utility and use the
add_principal command to add a principal for the current host, in the form
host/f.q.d.n, where f.q.d.n is replaced with the fully qualified domain name of the
host you're adding. Be sure to choose an unguessable password for each host you add.

```
newhost# kadmin
Authenticating as principal jake/admin@MYNET.NET with password:
Enter password:
kadmin: add_principal host/gfxstation.mynet.net
Enter password for principal "host/gfxstation.mynet.net@MYNET.NET":
Re-enter password for principal "host/gfxstation.mynet.net@MYNET.NET":
Principal "host/gfxstation.mynet.net@MYNET.NET" created.
kadmin:
```

The final step inside kadmin is to add a keytab file entry for the current host. This is
done with the ktadd command:

```
kadmin: ktadd host/gfxstation.mynet.net
...[ Output of ktadd operation ]...
kadmin: exit
newhost#
```

The current host has now been added to the KDC host's database of known hosts in the
realm, and a keytab file on the new host has been created at /etc/krb5.keytab.

Though the KDC database information is all in place, all of the original (non-Kerberized) services are still active on the new host. In order to make the host secure, the host must stop honoring requests from the old (insecure) protocols. They must instead be replaced with new, Kerberos-only versions.

Again add the extra protocol information to /etc/services, taking care to eliminate entries with duplicate port numbers or duplicate service names:

```
newhost# cd $HOME/krb5-1.2.1/src/config-files
newhost# cat services.append >>/etc/services
newhost#
```

The /etc/inetd.conf file must now be edited. Add the lines in Listing 17.3 to the file, and comment out any lines already in the file with matching service names.

LISTING 17.3   Additions/Changes for /etc/inetd.conf

```
klogin stream tcp nowait root /usr/sbin/tcpd /usr/local/kerberos/sbin/klogind
➥ -ki
eklogin stream tcp nowait root /usr/sbin/tcpd /usr/local/kerberos/sbin/klogind
➥ -eki
kshell stream tcp nowait root /usr/sbin/tcpd /usr/local/kerberos/sbin/kshd -ki
telnet stream tcp nowait root /usr/sbin/tcpd /usr/local/kerberos/sbin/telnetd
➥ -a user
ftp stream tcp nowait root /usr/sbin/tcpd /usr/local/kerberos/sbin/ftpd -a
```

Be sure to at least comment out the standard login, shell, telnet, and ftp services in your /etc/inetd.conf file, since they are being replaced with these new, Kerberos-only services.

Once you've made all of the desired changes to /etc/inetd.conf, restart your Internet daemon so that the new changes take effect:

```
newhost# killall -HUP inetd
newhost# exit
newhost$
```

The new host is now Kerberized and active to the KDC, and it is known to other Kerberos-enabled hosts in your realm. Users who cannot be authenticated with Kerberos will no longer be allowed to use protocols like rlogin, ftp, or telnet; other Kerberos-compatible software you install on this host will be able to take advantage of its realm membership for Kerberos authentication.

Adding User Principals

The user principal, which roughly corresponds to the concept of an "account" on a traditional Unix-like system, is the easiest type of principal to add. Any ticketed administrator with the capability to add can do so simply by starting kadmin and using the add_principal command.

```
$ kinit jake
Password for jake@MYNET.NET:
$ kadmin
Authenticating as principal jake/admin@MYNET.NET with password.
Enter password:
kadmin:  add_principal lucy
Enter password for principal "lucy@MYNET.NET":
Re-enter password for principal "lucy@MYNET.NET":
Principal "lucy@MYNET.NET" created.
kadmin: exit
$
```

The administrator jake has now created a user called lucy. This can be done from any host in the realm on which jake has access to execute the kadmin utility.

More on Kadmin

So far, we haven't discussed the kadmin utility in great detail. This is because it's really a very simple utility. There are three operations you should concern yourself with in a small Kerberos realm when starting out.

The first is the add_principal command with which you are already familiar. The add_principal command is used to add new principals (administrators, hosts, or users) to the KDC's authentication database.

The next is the delete_principal command, which works largely the same way, but has the opposite effect. It deletes whichever principal you supply from the KDC's database, meaning that the principal in question will no longer be authenticatable.

The third is the list_principals command, which does just that. It displays all principals in the KDC database, one per line. Wildcards can also be used; for example, to list all of the hosts in the realm that are known to the KDC, supply a pattern like host/*@MYNET.NET as an argument.

A few other operations are also supported, such as password changes and more complex per-user control using a technique called a policy. These are actually quite simple to use and are documented fully in kadmin(8), located in /usr/local/kerberos/man/man8.

Using Kerberos 5

After you have a KDC up and running in your local area network and at least two hosts are "registered" with the KDC and prepared for Kerberos-enabled operation, it's time to learn how to use Kerberos for authentication. Using Kerberos in a non-administrative capacity is quite simple, and most users adjust to it almost immediately.

Because Kerberos is a time-sensitive system, it is important that clocks on the KDC and various client and server machines on your network all be perfectly synchronized. The easiest way to do this is via the network time protocol (NTP) used by many Linux distributions.

Getting a Ticket

A "ticket" in Kerberos is just what it sounds like—a small piece of identification, supplied by the KDC, that will essentially "admit" you to a Kerberos-enabled service or host. To obtain a ticket, you must have a principal account in the KDC's database; you then use the `kinit` command to request a ticket from the KDC.

For example, recall that a few moments ago, `jake` (an administrator) was kind enough to add a principal user account for `lucy` to the KDC's database. `lucy` can now get her ticket like this:

```
lucy@somehost.mynet.net$ kinit lucy
Password for lucy@MYNET.NET:
lucy@somehost.mynet.net$
```

After her password has been entered, `lucy`'s ticket has been obtained. To list the tickets `lucy` has in her ticket cache, she uses the `klist` command:

```
lucy@somehost.mynet.net$ klist
Ticket cache: FILE:/tmp/krb5cc_100
Default principal: lucy@MYNET.NET

Valid starting     Expires            Service principal
01/11/01 14:22:25 01/11/01 00:22:20   krbtgt/MYNET.NET@MYNET.NET


Kerberos 4 ticket cache: /tmp/tkt100
klist: You have no tickets cached
lucy@somehost.mynet.net$
```

`lucy` is now ready to connect to another Kerberos-enabled host using any "Kerberized" protocol. For example, `ftp`:

```
lucy@somehost.mynet.net$ ftp anotherhost
Connected to anotherhost.mynet.net.
220 anotherhost.mynet.net FTP server (Version 5.60) ready.
334 Using authentication type GSSAPI; ADAT must follow
GSSAPI accepted as authentication type
GSSAPI authentication succeeded
Name (anotherhost:lucy):
232 GSSAPI user lucy@MYNET.NET is authorized as lucy
Remote system type is UNIX
Using binary mode to transfer files.
ftp>
```

The same ticket is valid for all Kerberos-enabled services. A new ticket is not needed for each connection (the same one will do), though a ticket will need to be "refreshed" every few hours because it will expire for security reasons.

The new Kerberos-enabled protocols require new Kerberos-enabled clients. New ftp, telnet, rlogin, rsh, and other clients are found in the /usr/local/kerberos/bin directory, and these should be used instead of the originals (which will no longer work with the Kerberos-enabled hosts).

You may want to disable the original binaries for ftp, telnet, and so forth by doing a chmod a-x to them. Failure to do this can result in extreme user confusion!

Note also that the new binaries in the Kerberos installation are backward-compatible with non-Kerberized systems, so the telnet in /usr/local/kerberos/bin will work with systems both inside and outside your network, while the original one in /usr/bin will now work only with hosts outside your network.

There is a minor bug in the telnet client included with Kerberos 5 that causes it to fail on some Linux systems unless either the -l or -x option is supplied. The -l argument simply specifies the user's account on the remote system:

telnet anotherhost -l lucy

The -x option enables data stream encryption and is described in the "Encrypting Data Streams" section, later in this hour.

Destroying a Ticket

Every Kerberos ticket will eventually expire, but if a ticket will no longer be used, it is a good idea from a security perspective to destroy it so that there is no chance at all that any malicious use can occur. Ticket destruction is performed with the kdestroy command, which will destroy all currently active tickets:

```
lucy@somehost.mynet.net$ kdestroy
lucy@somehost.mynet.net$ klist
klist: No credentials cache file found
lucy@somehost.mynet.net$
```

Tickets will also expire automatically when a user logs out completely, meaning that a ticket will never be left over long after its user has gone.

Changing Your Password

Any principal can change his password using the kpasswd utility.

```
lucy@somehost.mynet.net$ kpasswd lucy
Password for lucy@MYNET.NET:
Enter new password:
Enter it again:
Password changed.
lucy@somehost.mynet.net$
```

Since Kerberos passwords are stored centrally on the KDC, any new password will be effective on any host in the realm, not just on the host in which it was entered. It is also important to understand that the Kerberos password has no relationship to the login password on any host.

Encrypting Data Streams

17

Most of the client replacements included with Keberos 5, including `telnet`, `rlogin`, `rsh`, and `ftp`, include built-in encryption options that will make them even more secure. To encrypt such a session completely, use the `-x` argument:

```
lucy@somehost.mynet.net$ rlogin -x anotherhost
This rlogin session is using DES encryption for all
data transmissions.
Last login: Fri Jan 12 14:46:53 from somehost
lucy@anotherhost.mynet.net$
```

Though the Kerberos documentation warns about slowdowns due to encryption, this warning doesn't really apply to modern PC hardware running Linux, on which the encryption algorithm requires only a fraction of the CPU's time.

Summary

In this hour, you learned to compile and install Kerberos 5 in order to configure a KDC for your local realm. You also learned basic Kerberos administration tasks, such as adding administrator, additional host, and user principals to your realm's KDC database.

Finally, you learned the basics of working with Kerberos once it is installed, including how to obtain and subsequently destroy a ticket, how to change a Kerberos password, and how to encrypt the data streams of standard protocol clients included with Kerberos 5.

Q&A

Q I can't get krb5kdc to start.
I can't get kadmind to start.

A Go back through the instructions and double-check everything to make sure you've followed all the steps. Did you use `kdb5_util create` to create a database for your realm? Did you remember to use the `-s` option to stash the key? Did you remember to use `ktadd` to add `kadmin/admin` and `kadmin/changepw` to the `kadm5.keytab` file before trying to start `kadmind`? As a last resort, start `krb5kdc` or `kadmind` with `strace`; this should give you some indication of the reason for the failure.

Q **I installed Kerberos on one or more hosts, and now `telnet`, `ftp`, `rlogin`, or some other protocol is not working. What happened?**

A You must be running the special Kerberos-enabled client binaries in order to connect to systems requiring Kerberos authentication. Be sure that you're calling the protocol from the `/usr/local/kerberos/bin` directory and not the binaries from `/usr/bin` instead.

Q **Is there a way to make other protocols and services use Kerberos?**

A Absolutely. Many Linux software packages support Kerberos, usually either with configuration file changes or (at worst) a recompile supplying a Kerberos-oriented option. For example, SSH version 2 (discussed in Hour 16, "Encrypting Data Streams") can be compiled for Kerberos authentication support with an option to the `configure` command before compiling.

Unfortunately, there's no standard way to turn on Kerberos support for every program out there. Your best bet is to RTFM (Read The Friendly Manual) in each case for information on Kerberos support.

Q **Isn't the single, central KDC a vulnerability?**

A Yes. This is why it's important that you secure your KDC as much as possible, run no additional services on it at all, ensure that its hardware is in good condition, and make frequent backups of the KDC's hard drive.

There is also a provision for secondary KDC systems to act as backups when needed. This functionality is discussed in more detail in the Kerberos documentation.

New Terms

eBones   An alternative implementation of the Kerberos protocol for use outside the U.S. to circumvent export restrictions placed on the MIT Kerberos code by the U.S. government.

Kerberized   Enjoying the state of being Kerberos-enabled. A Kerberized system or service is capable of handling Kerberos authentication.

key distribution center (KDC)   The system responsible for maintaining information about all primaries in a Kerberos realm and for handling authentication exchanges.

primary   In a sense, another word for "account." A primary is an entry in the KDC's database that refers to a user, an administrator, or a host in the realm. Each primary has a password and, if so configured, additional policy information describing the primary's properties and privileges.

realm   The area of influence of a Kerberos network or, more specifically, usually a single KDC. Inside a Kerberos realm, one typically finds a number of users, administrators, and hosts. By convention, a realm is the network's domain, converted to ALL CAPS.

ticket   A small unit of identification given to a primary that is then used, in conjunction with the KDC, to authenticate that primary to other primaries in the realm.

17

HOUR **18**

Encrypting Web Data

This hour, you'll learn how to compile and configure minimally an Apache Web server that has been enhanced with the mod_ssl package, making it capable of handling SSL (Secure Sockets Layer) communications for increased security. You'll also learn how to create a self-signed certificate for use in such communications, so that you can immediately begin accepting https:// connections with your Web browser.

Understand, however, that Web security is a large and complex field of study, well beyond the scope of a book like this one in many respects. This hour will not discuss the underlying mechanism of SSL or the process involved in certifying your Web server with a well-known Certificate Authority (CA) such as VeriSign or Xcert.

For a preliminary understanding of SSL and some of the many issues involved, the mod_ssl user manual is an excellent place to begin. It can be found at http://www.modssl.org/docs/2.7/.

Compiling and Installing `Apache+mod_ssl`

Unfortunately, the process of upgrading your Apache installation to support SSL means recompiling and reinstalling the Apache binaries. Because of this, it's simplest to start over with Apache rather than trying to drop new components into old locations.

It is therefore recommended that before you begin, you back up your existing Apache configuration and data files, if necessary, and then use your distribution's package manager to remove the `apache` or `httpd` series of packages. It is not necessary to remove your actual Web documents tree; this can remain in place, and your new configuration file can be updated to reflect its location.

> With the lifting of export restrictions on SSL in recent months, some Linux distributors have started shipping `Apache+mod_ssl` as a standard distribution component.
>
> Before following the steps in this chapter, you may want to check to see if `Apache+mod_ssl` is a standard component of your Linux distribution already.

Downloading Apache, OpenSSL, and `mod_ssl`

To compile and install `mod_ssl`, you'll actually need to download and compile three software tarballs: one for Apache, one for OpenSSL, and one for `mod_ssl`.

The home page for OpenSSL can be found at `http://www.openssl.org`. The latest version of the OpenSSL source code can be downloaded from `http://www.openssl.org/source/`.

The home page for `mod_ssl` can be found at `http://www.modssl.org`; the latest version of the `mod_ssl` source code can be downloaded from `http://www.modssl.org/source/`. You'll notice that each of the `mod_ssl` source tarballs has two version numbers, separated by a dash. For example, consider the following names from the `mod_ssl` Web site:

```
mod_ssl-2.7.1-1.3.14.tar.gz
mod_ssl-2.6.6-1.3.12.tar.gz
mod_ssl-2.5.1-1.3.11.tar.gz
mod_ssl-2.4.10-1.3.9.tar.gz
```

In each of these names, the version number before the second dash (`2.7.1`, `2.6.6`, `2.5.1`, `2.4.10`) represents the `mod_ssl` version number, while the version number after the second dash (`1.3.14`, `1.3.12`, `1.3.11`, `1.3.9`) represents the Apache version with which this `mod_ssl` tarball is meant to work. Be sure to get the `mod_ssl` tarball matching the version of Apache you plan to use, or vice versa.

The home page for the Apache Web server can be found at `http://httpd.apache.org`; the latest version of the Apache Web server source code can be downloaded from `http://httpd.apache.org/dist/`. For this project, download the 1.3 release of the Apache Web server that matches your `mod_ssl` tarball, rather than a newer Apache 2.0 release. This is necessary because `mod_ssl` doesn't yet support Apache 2.0 or later.

Extracting and Compiling OpenSSL

For this installation, it is necessary to begin by extracting and compiling OpenSSL. If you already completed this installation during Hour 16, "Encrypting Data Streams," and you still have the source code directory available, you can skip this step.

Extract the source code and visit the newly created source directory:

```
$ tar -xzf openssl-0.9.6.tar.gz
$ cd openssl-0.9.6
$
```

Now configure, compile, and install OpenSSL:

```
$ ./config
...[ output of config ]...
$ make
...[ output of make ]...
$ su
Password:
# make install
...[output of make install ]...
# exit
$
```

The default configuration of OpenSSL installs most of its files in the `/usr/local` tree, with libraries going in `/usr/local/ssl/lib`.

Extracting, Configuring, and Compiling `mod_ssl` and Apache

The next step in the process is the extraction and configuration of both the Apache and the `mod_ssl` source code. After both have been extracted, visit the newly created `mod_ssl` source directory tree.

```
$ tar -xzf mod_ssl-2.7.1-1.3.14.tar.gz
$ tar -xzf apache_1.3.14.tar.gz
$ cd mod_ssl-2.7.1-1.3.14
$
```

Use the `configure` script in the `mod_ssl` directory along with the `--with-apache` option to tell `mod_ssl` where the Apache sources are located, relative to the `mod_ssl` source directory tree.

```
$ ./configure --with-apache=../apache_1.3.14
Configuring mod_ssl/2.7.1 for Apache/1.3.14
 + Apache location: ../apache_1.3.14 (Version 1.3.14)
 + Auxiliary patch tool: ./etc/patch/patch (local)
 + Applying packages to Apache source tree:
   o Extended API (EAPI)
   o Distribution Documents
   o SSL Module Source
   o SSL Support
   o SSL Configuration Additions
   o SSL Module Documentation
   o Addons
Done: source extension and patches successfully applied.
$
```

Now, visit the Apache directory and run the `configure` script there, setting the `SSL_BASE` environment variable to point to the location of the OpenSSL sources and supplying the `--enable-module=ssl` and `--enabled-shared=ssl` arguments. In this hour, we're also going to supply the `--prefix=/usr/local/apache` argument so that Apache is correctly installed into its own directory tree.

```
$ cd ..
$ cd apache_1.3.14
$ SSL_BASE=../openssl-0.9.6 ./configure \
> --enable-module=ssl --enable-shared=ssl \
> --prefix=/usr/local/apache
...[ Output of configure ]...
$
```

If the `configure` script exits normally, indicating that all is well, build the modified Apache sources.

```
$ make
...[ Output of make ]...
$
```

A complete build of Apache is fairly fast; you can expect a 486 machine to be done in just a few minutes. A Pentium-class system or an even more modern system will be done in less than a minute, even on a loaded system.

Making a Self-Signed Certificate

Before installing the Apache tree, you'll want to configure Apache for your server's certificate. In this hour, we're simply going to build a self-signed certificate for general-purpose use without having to work with a commercial Certificate Authority.

To do this, use the `make certificate` command, setting the variable `TYPE` to the value `custom`. You'll be asked a number of questions; answer to the best of your ability, using the default answers whenever you're unsure. Some of the output in Listing 18.1 has been condensed, but you should still be able to follow along. Items in bold indicate your input and should be changed to match your needs or information.

LISTING 18.1   Generating a Self-Signed Certificate

```
$ make certificate TYPE=custom
make[1]: Entering directory '$HOME/apache_1.3.14/src'

STEP 0: Decide the signature algorithm used for certificates
The generated X.509 certificates can contain either
RSA or DSA based ingredients.
Select the one you want to use.
Signature Algorithm ((R)SA or (D)SA) [R]:r

STEP 1: Generating RSA private key for CA (1024 bit)

STEP 2: Generating X.509 certificate signing request for CA
You are about to be asked to enter information that will be
incorporated into your certificate request.
1. Country Name            [XY]:us
2. State or Province Name   [Snake Desert]:Utah
3. Locality Name           [Snake Town]:Salt Lake City
4. Organization Name       [Snake Oil, Ltd]:Brine Inc.
5. Organizational Unit Name [Certificate Authority]:[enter]
6. Common Name             [Snake Oil CA]:Brine Inc.
7. Email Address           [ca@snakeoil.dom]:joe@brine.com
8. Certificate Validity    [365]:[enter]

STEP 3: Generating X.509 certificate for CA signed by itself
Certificate Version (1 or 3) [3]:3

STEP 4: Generating RSA private key for SERVER (1024 bit)

STEP 5: Generating X.509 certificate signing request for server
You are about to be asked to enter information that will be
incorporated into your certificate request.
1. Country Name            [XY]:us
2. State or Province Name   [Snake Desert]:Utah
3. Locality Name           [Snake Town]:Salt Lake City
4. Organization Name       [Snake Oil, Ltd]:Brine Inc.
5. Organizational Unit Name [Web Server Team]:[enter]
6. Common Name             [Snake Oil CA]:www.brine.com
7. Email Address           [ca@snakeoil.dom]:joe@brine.com
8. Certificate Validity    [365]:[enter]
STEP 6: Generating X.509 certificate signed by own CA
Certificate Version (1 or 3) [3]:3

STEP 7: Encrypting RSA private key of CA with a pass phrase
Encrypt the private key now? [Y/n]:y
Enter PEM pass phrase:[enter desired password]
Verifying password - Enter PEM pass phrase:[re-enter desired password]
```

18

LISTING 18.1   continued

```
STEP 8: Encrypting RSA private key of SERVER with a pass phrase
Encrypt the private key now? [Y/n]:y
Enter PEM pass phrase:[enter desired password]
Verifying password - Enter PEM pass phrase:[re-enter desired password]

Congratulations that you establish your server with real certificates.
make[1]: Leaving directory '$HOME/apache_1.3.14/src'
$
```

You have now created your own small Certificate Authority and a self-signed server certificate. This will allow you to accept `https://` connections from visitors to your Web site. However, it will not provide you with the protection against impersonation that you would enjoy were you established with a well-known Certificate Authority like VeriSign or Xcert.

Installing and Configuring the Apache Tree

Now that you've compiled the source code and created a set of self-signed certificates, it's time to install the Apache tree.

```
$ su
Password:
#  make install
...[ Output of make install ]...
#
```

Assuming you supplied the `--prefix=/usr/local/apache` argument to the `configure` script during source configuration, the Apache files, including your site certificates, will be installed into the `/usr/local/apache` tree.

For the most part, we're going to ignore Apache configuration in this hour, since general-purpose Apache security has already been covered in Hour 12, "Securing Apache, FTP, and SMTP Services." However, there are a few changes that need to be made for the average system before launching this new, improved Apache and trying it out. Search through the `/usr/local/apache/conf/httpd.conf` file, locate each indicated keyword, and make the change(s) suggested.

```
DocumentRoot "/usr/local/apache/htdocs"
<Directory "/usr/local/apache/htdocs">
```

If this is a new Apache installation from the ground up, feel free to leave these directives as they appear and install your Web document trees in the `/usr/local/apache/htdocs` directory. If you have an existing Web document tree elsewhere, however, you should update these directives to reflect the path to your existing Web documents.

```
Port 8080
Listen 8080
```

These ports are not standard for `http` service. In most instances, you'll want to configure them to port 80 instead of port 8080 so that this instance of Apache will respond to standard `http://` requests without connecting users needing to supply a port number in addition to your Web address.

```
Listen 8443
<VirtualHost _default_:8443>
```

Both of these ports refer to the SSL-enhanced port needed for operation of the secure channel. Here again, the default configuration is not standard and should be changed to port 443 instead of port 8443 for standard operation.

Starting the SSL-Enabled Apache Server

Once you've made the necessary preliminary changes to the default Apache configuration, it's time for a test run to ensure that everything is working before you proceed to the real task of configuring your Apache as a production Web server.

To start the new Apache server, use the apachectl program located in the binaries directory of the Apache installation, in this case `/usr/local/apache/bin/apachectl`. Pass to it the `startssl` argument to instruct it to start the Apache server with SSL enabled. You will be required to enter the password you supplied when creating your keys.

```
# /usr/local/apache/bin/apachectl startssl
Apache/1.3.14 mod_ssl/2.7.1 (Pass Phrase Dialog)
Some of your private key files are encrypted for
security reasons. In order to read them you have to
provide us with the pass phrases.

Server www.brine.net:443 (RSA)
Enter pass phrase:

Ok: Pass Phrase Dialog successful.
/usr/local/apache/bin/apachectl startssl: httpd started
#
```

Once you have entered the password, the Apache server will be started. Notice that it has been started with the `-DSSL` argument:

```
# ps ax | grep httpd
23439 ?        S        0:00 /usr/local/apache/bin/httpd -DSSL
23440 ?        S        0:00 /usr/local/apache/bin/httpd -DSSL
23441 ?        S        0:00 /usr/local/apache/bin/httpd -DSSL
23442 ?        S        0:00 /usr/local/apache/bin/httpd -DSSL
23443 ?        S        0:00 /usr/local/apache/bin/httpd -DSSL
23444 ?        S        0:00 /usr/local/apache/bin/httpd -DSSL
23445 ?        S        0:00 /usr/local/apache/bin/httpd -DSSL
23446 ?        S        0:00 /usr/local/apache/bin/httpd -DSSL
#
```

18

You should be able to launch a Web browser and visit your Web server from another system on your network, both with `http://` and with `https://`, though at this point both types of connection share the same document root tree. Check to see that you can connect both ways and that, when connected securely, the Web browser can verify that the connection is secure.

When connecting with SSL enabled, you may notice that Netscape (or another browser if you're not using Netscape to connect) asks you about the certificate being supplied by your server, as is shown in Figure 18.1.

FIGURE 18.1

Netscape may ask about your certificate.

The browser asks how you want to proceed because the certificate your site is using is self-signed, meaning that there is no trusted third party to verify the authenticity of your server. This shortcoming does limit security to some degree, because there is no way for a connecting user to be sure that he is really talking to your server.

However, once the browser has been instructed to accept the certificate in spite of the fact that it is self-signed, the connection will be encrypted with full 128-bit RSA encryption (if your browser supports it). Assuming that both the connecting client and the server are who they claim to be (and in this particular case, you know for a fact that they are), the data flowing back and forth through the connection is very secure.

Summary

In this hour, you learned about using the `mod_ssl` addition to Apache to enable your Linux Web server to operate with encrypted SSL Web connections for increased security.

You learned how to download and compile an enhanced Apache server with `mod_ssl` included and to install and configure the enhanced server enough that it can be launched and tested successfully. Your server is now ready for full configuration before going online as a secure server.

Q&A

Q **Aren't there times when I can use a self-signed certificate without potential bad effects?**

A Yes, and you've already seen it. When you know for a fact that both client and server are who they claim to be—for example, when both machines are located in the same internal network—a self-signed certificate is perfectly adequate.

Even when not used in the local network or the intranet context, many sites on the Internet use Apache with self-signed certificates to avoid the costs involved in being certified by a commercial Certificate Authority. However, if you will be doing a large volume of e-commerce or handling very sensitive data across the Internet, you should definitely look into using a commercial Certificate Authority.

Q **I followed the instructions in this hour and Apache is now running enough for me to visit it from my other machine. Isn't that enough configuration?**

A No! Please at least see Hour 12 for a little more information on configuring Apache securely. If you seriously plan to use SSL for e-commerce or other sensitive purposes, however, you should definitely invest your dollars in comprehensive Apache documentation and a significant amount of time in ensuring that your Apache configuration is both correct and functional.

To put it another way, SSL isn't really so wonderful if there are gaping security holes and configuration-related stability problems throughout the rest of your Apache configuration.

Q **I can't get the new Apache server to start.**

I can't get the new Apache server to connect with SSL.

Check your log files to see what sort of error is occurring. These are located at /usr/local/apache/logs in this case.

If your logs are showing garbage when SSL connections are requested, double-check your httpd.conf file, taking care to ensure that you replace all instances of port 8080 with port 80 and all instances of port 8443 with 443. Also, be sure that you are starting Apache with /usr/local/apache/bin/apachectl startssl. Using start instead of startssl will start the server, but with SSL functionality disabled.

If your logs all appear to be empty, check the default log locations in /usr/local/apache/logs, regardless of where your log directives are set in httpd.conf. Unfortunately, Apache+mod_ssl seems to have some bugs in the form of hard-coded paths.

18

New Terms

Certificate Authority (CA)   A trusted third party with a well-known public key who can vouch for the validity of a Web server's identity certificate. In general, listing a Web server with a Certificate Authority is a costly step, so many smaller sites choose instead to use a self-signed certificate, which is less secure.

mod_ssl   An addition to the Apache source code that relies on the OpenSSL library and implements SSL capability in the Apache Web server.

Secure Sockets Layer (SSL)   A group of protocols and specific interactions implemented by Web browsers and Web servers to allow for the authentication of the hosts involved and the negotiation of an encrypted data stream.

site certificate   A block of data used for encryption and identification purposes by an SSL-enabled Web site and any party connecting to it. For best security, a site certificate should be signed by a Certificate Authority so that the authority's public key can be used to verify the validity of the certificate.

HOUR 19

Encrypting File System Data

This hour, you'll learn to encrypt file system data using the Transparent Cryptographic File System (TCFS) for Linux. TCFS can be found at http://www.tcfs.it. Because TCFS is based on NFS, it is suitable for encrypting network file system data for transport. Since it stores file system data on the server in encrypted form as well, it is also well suited to local file system encryption.

Because TCFS requires a patched kernel and a number of patched file system utilities, it would normally be considered a fairly intrusive tool to install. This chapter, however, takes a few extra steps to isolate the TCFS installation in its own branch of the file system tree.

TCFS currently is not available for the 2.4 kernel series. Two TCFS versions exist now: a stable version (TCFS 2.2.x) for the 2.0 series of kernels and a beta-test version (TCFS 3.x) for the 2.2 series of kernels. Though the TCFS 3 releases are currently not officially stable, they're the versions covered in this chapter, largely because of the age of the 2.0 kernel series.

A Brief Overview of TCFS

TCFS is an unusual tool in the Linux world because of the way it is constructed. Rather than running on the server or implementing some form of client/server key exchange, TCFS functions exclusively on the client host.

It is the kernel on the client that is patched for TCFS operation. An NFS share from any NFS-capable server is then mounted on the client machine as file system type TCFS. To the NFS server, this operation is transparent.

The user on the client system has a private encryption key that is used to encrypt the data to be stored. After being encrypted, the data is transmitted via NFS to the server and stored in encrypted form on the server's drive. When the data is read back, it is transmitted in encrypted form to the client once more, where it is decrypted by the user's key. No encryption keys of any kind are ever transmitted across the network, and there is no way to decrypt the data stored on the server in isolation. Data stored this way can be decrypted only on a client machine by the user who generated the data in the first place.

For local file system encryption, the server and client simply become one. A directory or volume is exported via NFS; it is then mounted on the same machine via TCFS, and encrypted data is written to the new mount point, where it is encrypted before being written to the hard drive.

Because of this client-based mode of operation, all of the configuration and installation done in this chapter will occur on a TCFS client machine rather than an NFS server.

Preparing to Install TCFS

Before installing TCFS, you should ensure that you have a number of things prepared. Because of the intrusive nature of a TCFS installation, it will be easy to make mistakes if you haven't taken care of the following things in advance.

An Empty EXT2 Partition

Because TCFS is beta-level code and because it uses raw data storage, it is a good idea to isolate your encrypted files on a separate file system on the NFS server in question for export and mount, just in case. Normally, this means having created an empty partition and using mke2fs to create an EXT2 file system on it.

If you don't have a spare partition or don't want the hassle of creating one, you can use the Linux loopback driver if you don't mind the extra overhead. For example, to create a 50-megabyte virtual disk and mount it at /mnt/virtual, you would do something like this:

```
# dd if=/dev/zero of=/virtual.image bs=1k count=50000
50000+0 records in
50000+0 records out
# losetup /dev/loop0 /virtual.image
# mke2fs /dev/loop0
...[ Output of mke2fs ]...
# mount -t ext2 /dev/loop0 /mnt/virtual
#
```

Whether you use a real partition or a virtual image, remember to take the extra steps necessary to preserve the new volume through reboots. For example, remember to add the new partition to /etc/fstab or to initialize the loopback device in an init script if necessary.

A Working NFS Installation

You should be able to verify that NFS is working on the server you plan to use to hold the encrypted file system, and you should modify /etc/exports to export the partition or virtual disk in question and grant read/write access (instead of read-only access) to the user(s) and host(s) who will be using the encrypted volume.

A Kernel 2.2.16– or 2.2.17–Ready System

You should have either a Linux system that is already running kernel 2.2.17 or one that is capable of installing and running kernel 2.2.17 successfully without too many additional patches. Information on requirements for using kernel 2.2.17 can be found in the Documentation/Changes file in the kernel 2.2.17 source tree.

Additional patches should be kept to a minimum, though TCFS has been known to work with patches to some extent (for example, Ingo Molnar's backported RAID code).

Downloading and Installing TCFS

When you're ready to take the plunge, it's time to download the 2.2.17 kernel source and TCFS and install them on the client host in question. Source code for the 2.2.16 and 2.2.17 kernels can be found at http://www.kernel.org/pub/linux/kernel/v2.2. In this chapter, we focus on 2.2.17, but if you have some need for 2.2.16, it will work as well.

Source code for TCFS version 3.0b (the latest version as this book went to press) can be found at http://www.tcfs.it/tcfs30b.html. A small, almost hidden link will enable you to download the entire distribution of TCFS in a single file called tcfs-3.0b-distrib.tar.gz rather than requiring you to download it in pieces.

Extract Sources and Apply Patches

The process of extracting and compiling TCFS and the 2.2.17 kernel can be a complicated one and is made more so by our desire to install TCFS nondestructively in

19

/usr/local/tcfs rather than destructively by overwriting existing utilities. Follow along closely.

First, visit the /usr/src directory and become root. Extract the source for both the kernel distribution and the TCFS distribution there. The details below assume that the source distributions were saved in the /tmp directory; adjust as necessary. Remember to preserve your existing kernel source tree if necessary.

```
client:~$ su
Password:
client:/home/joe# cd /usr/src
client:/usr/src# mv linux linux.old
client:/usr/src# tar -xzf /tmp/tcfs-3.0b-distrib.tar.gz
client:/usr/src# tar -xzf /tmp/linux-2.2.17.tar.gz
client:/usr/src#
```

Now gunzip the kernel patch in the TCFS source tree and apply it to the kernel source. Afterward, extract the main TCFS source tarball in the TCFS distribution tree.

```
client:/usr/src# gunzip tcfs-3.0b/patch-linux-2.2.16.gz
client:/usr/src# patch -p0 <tcfs-3.0b/patch-linux-2.2.16
client:/usr/src# tar -xzf tcfs-3.0b/tcfs-3.0b.tar.gz
client:/usr/src#
```

The newly extracted Linux kernel source has now been modified for TCFS operation. Before compiling the new kernel, however, we're going to compile and install much of the rest of TCFS.

Compile and Install the TCFS Distribution

Visit the utils/ directory in the TCFS source tree and extract the TCFS library code.

```
client:/usr/src# cd tcfs-3.0b/utils
client:tcfs-3.0b/utils# tar -xzf tcfslib-1.0.0.tar.gz
client:tcfs-3.0b/utils# cd tcfslib-1.0.0
client:utils/tcfslib-1.0.0#
```

Now, using your favorite editor, edit the Makefile in the tcfslib-1.0.0 directory. Toward the top of the file, change the installation paths from /usr/local/lib, /usr/local/man, and so on to /usr/local/tcfs/lib, /usr/local/tcfs/man, and so on. This will keep the TCFS files and libraries separate from the rest of the /usr/local tree to some degree.

After changing the Makefile, make the directories for the /usr/local/tcfs hierarchy, then run make all and make install to install the newly built libraries and manuals. Once the libraries are built and installed, add the /usr/local/tcfs/lib directory to your system library cache.

```
client:utils/tcfslib-1.0.0# mkdir /usr/local/tcfs
client:utils/tcfslib-1.0.0# cd /usr/local/tcfs
client:local/tcfs# mkdir bin lib man
client:local/tcfs# cd man
client:tcfs/man# for nm in 1 2 3 4 5 6 7 8; do
> mkdir man$nm
> done
client:tcfs/man# cd /usr/src/tcfs-3.0b/utils/tcfslib-1.0.0
client:utils/tcfslib-1.0.0# make all
...[ Output of make all ]...
client:utils/tcfslib-1.0.0# make install
...[ Output of make install ]...
client:utils/tcfslib-1.0.0# echo "/usr/local/tcfs/lib" >> \
> /etc/ld.so.conf
client:utils/tcfslib-1.0.0# ldconfig
client:utils/tcfslib-1.0.0#
```

If this is the first time you have installed kernel 2.2.17, you may experience some problems with missing include files. If this happens to you while compiling the TCFS libraries, try issuing the following commands and then rebuilding the libraries:

```
# cd /usr/src/linux/include
# ln -s asm-i386 asm
```

This will create a symbolic link for /usr/include/asm that normally exists only after a kernel has been built once.

Once the TCFS libraries have been successfully installed, revisit the utils/ directory and extract the TCFS utilities source code.

```
client:utils/tcfslib-1.0.0# cd ..
client:tcfs-3.0b/utils# tar -xzf tcfsutils-2.0.0.tar.gz
client:utils/tcfsutils-2.0.0#
```

Here again, you will need to edit the Makefile to change all occurrences of /usr/local/* to /usr/local/tcfs/* so that our TCFS installation doesn't mingle with the existing /usr/local tree. This time, the Makefile in tcfsutils-2.0.0/src/ also has a bug. Edit this file and search for the two lines near the top beginning with BINDIR= and SBINDIR= and simply delete them altogether. Once both Makefile files have been fixed, build the utilities with make all and install them with make install.

```
client:utils/tcfsutils-2.0.0# make all
...[ Output of make all ]...
client:utils/tcfsutils-2.0.0# make install
...[ Output of make install ]...
client:utils/tcfsutils-2.0.0#
```

19

> Because of different library versions in use among the various Linux distribu-
> tions, some users may get a number of errors about "undefined references"
> while attempting to complete the `make all`. If this happens to you, it is
> likely because your system requires that the `gdbm` and `dl` libraries be linked
> in explicitly.
>
> Reopen the `src/Makefile` file and search for the following line in the file:
>
> `LOADLIBES=-ltcfs`
>
> Change this line to read
>
> `LOADLIBES=-ltcfs -lgdbm -ldl`
>
> Now, in the `tcfsutils-2.0.0` directory, run a `make clean` and then try again
> with `make all` followed by `make install`.

Once the utilities have been installed, modified `mount` and `umount` binaries as well as
modified EXT2 tools are required for the TCFS file system. Visit the `tcfs-3.0b/conrib`
directory and extract the replacement `util-linux-2.10m` source code. Since only the
`mount` and `umount` programs are required, we can partially compile the `util-linux` package and install the new binaries in `/usr/local/tcfs/sbin`. Follow along closely.

```
client:utils/tcfsutils-2.0.0# cd ../../contrib
client:tcfs-3.0b/contrib# tar -xzf util-linux-2.10m-tcfs.tar.gz
client:tcfs-3.0b/contrib# cd util-linux-2.10m-tcfs
client:contrib/util-linux-2.10m-tcfs# cd lib
client:util-linux-2.10m-tcfs/lib# make
...[ Output of make ]...
client:util-linux-2.10m-tcfs/lib# cd ../mount
client:util-linux-2.10m-tcfs/mount# make
...[ Output of make ]...
client:util-linux-2.10m-tcfs/mount# chmod 4755 mount umount
client:util-linux-2.10m-tcfs/mount# mv mount umount /usr/local/tcfs/sbin
client:util-linux-2.10m-tcfs/mount#
```

The final order of business in the TCFS source code tree is to compile the new set of
EXT2 file system tools. These are also in the `contrib/` directory.

```
client:util-linux-2.10m-tcfs/mount# cd ../..
client:tcfs-3.0b/contrib# tar -xzf e2fsprogs-1.19-tcfs.tar.gz
client:tcfs-3.0b/contrib# cd e2fsprogs-1.19-tcfs
client:contrib/e2fsprogs-1.19-tcfs# ./configure --prefix=/usr/local/tcfs
...[ Output of configure ]...
client:contrib/e2fsprogs-1.19-tcfs# make
...[ Output of make ]...
client:contrib/e2fsprogs-1.19-tcfs# make install
...[ Output of make install ]...
client:contrib/e2fsprogs-1.19-tcfs#
```

The entire TCFS distribution has now been compiled and installed and resides in /usr/local/tcfs. Special versions of mount, umount, e2fsck, chattr, and lsattr, which are required to operate TCFS file systems, are also located in the /usr/local/tcfs tree, in /usr/local/tcfs/bin and /usr/local/tcfs/sbin.

Compile the Patched Kernel

Now visit the patched kernel source tree and configure and compile your kernel, taking care to enable the configuration options listed in Table 19.1.

TABLE 19.1 Kernel Options for TCFS Operation

Option	Location
CONFIG_EXPERIMENTAL=y	Code maturity level options
CONFIG_MODULES=y	Loadable module support
CONFIG_TCFS_FS=m	File Systems, Network File Systems menu

After compiling the kernel, you may want to copy the kernel image to a new file and add a new label to your /etc/lilo.conf file so that you can boot into TCFS explicitly while preserving your existing kernel as well.

Don't forget to compile and install the modules after the kernel image has been built:

```
# cd /usr/src/linux
# make modules; make modules_install
#
```

After installing the modules and a new LILO boot sector with the capability to boot from your new kernel, reboot your system and start using the new kernel.

Building the Encryption Module and Enabling TCFS

Once you have successfully booted into your new kernel, one last task remains; you must revisit the TCFS source tree and build the 3DES encryption module that will be used to encrypt the file system data. Don't forget to rebuild your module dependencies once the module has been built.

```
client:~$ su
Password:
client:/home/joe# cd /usr/src/tcfs-3.0b/modules/3desmodule
client:modules/3desmodule# make
...[ Output of make ]...
client:mdoules/3desmodule# cp tcfs_default_cipher.o \
> /lib/modules/2.2.17/fs
client:modules/3desmodule# /sbin/depmod -a
client:modules/3desmodule# cd
client:~#
```

19

You are now ready to load the TCFS modules so that the client's kernel will be ready to operate with TCFS.

```
client:~# modprobe tcfs
client:~# modprobe tcfs_default_cipher
client:~#
```

If you plan to use TCFS on this client regularly, you will want to edit your init scripts to load these modules automatically at boot time.

Using TCFS

Before any regular use can take place, the volume in question must be mounted somewhere on the client machine. Remember also that any user who is going to use the volume to store encrypted data must have write access to some directory on the mounted volume. This must all be done on the NFS server.

For example, let's assume that a user named joe wants to be able to store encrypted data on the server in question, and that the server is exporting a directory at /exp/crypt for this type of storage. Assuming that joe has the same UID and GID on both server and client, an administrator on the server would need to give joe a "home directory" on the encrypted volume:

```
# cd /exp/crypt
# mkdir joe
# chown joe.users joe
#
```

Once this is done, joe will be able to write somewhere.

Enabling TCFS Access (Administrative Tasks)

Let's assume now that on the client machine joe is using, an administrator has mounted the encrypted volume at /mnt/priv. Remember, this must be done with the new mount command with knowledge of TCFS

```
# /usr/local/tcfs/bin/mount -t tcfs server:/exp/crypt /mnt/priv
#
```

Once the volume has been successfully mounted, users, including joe, will find the encrypted volume at /mnt/priv. This means that joe's directory on the encrypted volume is at /mnt/priv/joe.

Before joe can manipulate any encrypted files, an account must also be configured for him in the TCFS user database. This is done with the tcfsadduser command:

```
# /usr/local/tcfs/sbin/tcfsadduser

TCFS Utilities: version 2.0.0
Insert the user name to add in the tcfs key's file: joe
```

```
Entry for user <joe> was inserted.

#
```

The administrative tasks associated with getting joe's files encrypted are now complete.

Taking Advantage of Encryption (User Tasks)

Before joe will have permission to access files on the TCFS volume (even files to which he has access permissions), he must generate a key for himself. This is done with the tcfsgenkey utility, which will ask joe to enter his password and will then ask for 10 random keystrokes to seed the key.

```
client:~$ /usr/local/tcfs/bin/tcfsgenkey

TCFS Utilities: version 2.0.0
Insert your password, please:
Press 10 random keys, please: **********
Updating completed: key successfully generated.

client:~$
```

Now that joe has created his key, he's nearly ready to use the TCFS volume. One last task must be attended to, however: The key must be made active with tcfsputkey.

```
client:~$ /usr/local/tcfs/bin/tcfsputkey

TCFS Utilities: version 2.0.0
Insert your password, please:
Passing completed.

client:~$
```

Each time joe logs in, he must use tcfsputkey to activate his key. When he logs out, he should use tcfsrmkey to disable it.

Encrypting Files

The actual process of encrypting files is fairly simple. The new chattr command in /usr/local/tcfs/bin supports an additional attribute, +X (capital letter) for encrypted or -X for not encrypted. If joe had a file that he wanted to encryptcalled myfile.txt in /mnt/priv/joe, he would use chattr as follows:

```
client:~$ cd /mnt/priv/joe
client:priv/joe$ /usr/local/tcfs/bin/chattr +X myfile.txt
client:priv/joe$
```

The lsattr command can demonstrate that the change has indeed been made:

```
client:priv/joe$ /usr/local/tcfs/bin/lsattr
----------RX-- ./myfile.txt
client:priv/joe$
```

19

The encoding of entire directory trees is also a simple matter. For example, `joe` could do the following:

```
client:priv/joe$ /usr/local/tcfs/bin/chattr +X /mnt/priv/joe
client:priv/joe$
```

Now any new files created in `/mnt/priv/joe` will inherit the +X attribute and will be encrypted themselves.

Summary

This hour, you learned to install and use the Transparent Cryptographic File System (TCFS) to encrypt file system data using 3DES encryption on an NFS host from a TCFS-enabled client.

You compiled a 2.2.17 kernel with the TCFS modifications and performed a custom installation of TCFS, placing it in the `/usr/local/tcfs` tree to give you as an administrator a little more control over the way in which TCFS is used.

Q&A

Q This chapter describes how to use TCFS over a network to an NFS host. How do I do it locally on a single machine?

A The concept is the same. Just export the file system to yourself and mount it using NFS. Of course, you must have a running NFS server to do this.

For example, if you wanted an encrypted file system under `/usr/private` on the `/dev/hda4` partition, you would make an EXT2 file system on `/dev/hda4`, mount it somewhere else (for example, at `/mnt/private`), and then mount `/mnt/private` via TCFS to `/usr/private`:

```
mount -t tcfs localhost:/mnt/private /usr/private
```

The `/usr/private` directory will hold the accessible data, `/mnt/private` will hold raw (encrypted) data, and the entire exchange will take place over the local NFS server.

Q How do I know the data is really encrypted?

A Take a look at the directory containing the raw data. For example, considering our earlier example, an `ls` of the `/exp/crypt` directory on the NFS server might look like this:

```
$ ls -1 /exp/crypt
g2jb40th5cJ9Uxw7lnKzUgAA=
g2jb40th5cJQaO#i+PkXkAAA=
g2jb40th5cJgCzDcaiRL3wAA=
g2jb40th5cJxotD56hc7vAAA=
g2jb40th5cLpbHFH7RveIAAA=
$
```

At the same time, the mounted volume on the client appears in unencrypted form:

```
$ ls -1 /mnt/priv
textfile-1.txt
textfile-2.txt
textfile-3.txt
textfile-4.txt
textfile-5.txt
```

Try viewing any of these encrypted files on the server. You'll get a lot of garbage printed on your terminal.

Note that on the client, encrypted files are visible only to their owner. For example, any user other than joe looking at /mnt/priv/joe might see zero files listed, though joe has several hundred encrypted files stored there.

Q The TCFS file system is very slow! What can I do to improve speed?

A Unfortunately, not much. It's not just the overhead of NFS you're experiencing. It's the overhead of the encryption itself, which doesn't seem like a slowdown when using an SSH session interactively, but becomes very obvious when compared to the speed of raw disk access.

Q I can't seem to mount the TCFS volume. Why?

I can't get the extended attributes to work. Why?

I ran e2fsck, and it corrupted my encrypted file system. Why?

A Please remember to use the modified utilities in /usr/local/tcfs/bin and /usr/local/tcfs/sbin when dealing with a TCFS file system. The normal utilities will not work.

Q My modified chattr doesn't seem to know about +X. How can I fix this?

A Actually, it does. It's not documented, and it doesn't show up with usage information on the command line, but try it—it works.

New Terms

3DES An older, reasonably fast encryption algorithm that is less complex than some newer algorithms but remains in widespread use, especially on mature networks like those serving automated teller machines (ATMs).

network file system (NFS) The standard method for networked file exchange between Unix-like machines, similar in purpose to the type of file system sharing managed by Samba for communicating with Windows machines.

Transparent Cryptographic File System (TCFS) A method of encrypting file system data for transport over an NFS connection and for secure storage.

HOUR 20

Encrypting E-Mail Data

This hour, you'll learn to use the Free Software Foundation's implementation of the Pretty Good Privacy (PGP) method for general-purpose data security. The name of this implementation is the GNU Privacy Guard (GPG).

Though PGP and more specifically GPG can be used for encrypting many kinds of data, PGP really became an international success because of its capability to do quick-and-dirty encryption with many popular e-mail clients. The encryption of e-mail remains PGP's most common function.

A Quick PGP Overview

Like many of the other encryption methods we've covered so far, PGP works with a two-key encryption system. Every person using PGP creates a key pair for himself. One key in the pair is a public key; the other is a private key. The public key is circulated as widely as possible and may even be listed in any one of several public key databases, where other Internet users around the world can find it. The private key is a closely guarded personal secret and is never transmitted or copied anywhere or to anyone.

These two keys work together to encrypt and decrypt data. Data encrypted with the public key can be decrypted only with the private key, and conversely, data encrypted with the private key can be decrypted only with the public key. This enables two kinds of verification to take place.

First, the members of the public at large who want to send a message to a specific person can encrypt the message or data in question with the person's public key before sending it. Since only the person's private key can decrypt the message or data, the sender is guaranteed that no one other than the intended recipient, who has the private key, will see it in unencrypted form.

In the other direction, a sender can also validate (sign) a message or data using his private key and send it to his friends or various members of the public at large. When the recipients are able to decode the signature using the supposed sender's public key, they can be assured that the message or the data did indeed come from the sender the message or data claims to be from.

Though there are really many more twists, turns, and features than this, this is the basic idea behind public key cryptography. PGP represents a kind of brute force, simple implementation of this concept.

Getting and Installing GNU Privacy Guard (GPG)

The GNU Privacy Guard implementation of PGP is largely compatible with the various encryption algorithms implemented by commercial versions of PGP, with the exception of the IDEA algorithm, which remains under patent until the year 2007. RSA encryption, whose patent has recently expired, is now included in the standard GPG distribution. The GPG home page can be found at `http://www.gpg.org`.

GPG can be downloaded from `http://www.gpg.org/download.html`. As this text goes to press, the most recent version of GPG is 1.0.4, and one important security patch has been released. To install GPG, download both the `gnupg-1.0.4.tar.gz` file and the patch file, `gnupg-1.0.4.security-patch1.diff`.

Extract the GPG sources and apply the patch, then run the `configure` script in the GPG source tree. The default installation options are adequate for most users. After running `configure` on the patched sources, run `make` and then `make install` to install the GPG binaries and other components.

```
$ tar -xzf gnupg-1.0.4.tar.gz
$ cd gnupg-1.0.4
$ patch -p1 <../gnupg-1.0.4.security-patch1.diff
patching file g10/mainproc.c
```

```
patching file g10/plaintext.c
patching file g10/openfile.c
$ ./configure
...[ Output of configure ]...
$ make
...[ Output of make ]...
$ su
Password:
# make install
...[ Output of make install ]...
# exit
$
```

Assuming everything installed cleanly, you can proceed to the next step, setting yourself up with a pair of keys and learning how to use the software. If you are unable to compile and install GPG, a number of prebuilt packages are available for many distributions, including Debian and many RPM-based distributions.

Generating Your Keys

Before you can send or receive any data encrypted by or for you specifically, you need to generate a pair of keys, one private and one public. This is done by calling the GnuPG tool with the --gen-key command. If this is your first time using GPG (let's assume that it is), GPG will simply create the $HOME/.gnupg directory on its first run. You must then call it a second time with the --gen-key argument to continue. The second time, your keys will be generated after GPG asks you a series of questions. Simply answer all of them with the default answers for now, providing personal information where required, as shown in Listing 20.1.

LISTING 20.1   Key Generation

```
$ gpg --gen-key
Please select what kind of key you want:
   (1) DSA and ElGamal (default)
   (2) DSA (sign only)
   (4) ElGamal (sign and encrypt)
Your selection? 1
DSA keypair will have 1024 bits.
About to generate a new ELG-E keypair.
              minimum keysize is  768 bits
              default keysize is 1024 bits
    highest suggested keysize is 2048 bits
What keysize do you want? (1024) 1024
Requested keysize is 1024 bits
Please specify how long the key should be valid.
        0 = key does not expire
      <n>  = key expires in n days
      <n>w = key expires in n weeks
```

20

LISTING 20.1   continued

```
        <n>m = key expires in n months
        <n>y = key expires in n years
Key is valid for? (0) 0
Key does not expire at all
Is this correct (y/n)? y

You need a User-ID to identify your key; the software
constructs the user id from Real Name, Comment and
Email Address in this form:
    "Heinrich Heine (Der Dichter) <heinrichh@dusseldorf.de>"

Real name: Joe User
Email address: joe@mynet.net
Comment: PGP Rules!
You selected this USER-ID:
    "Joe User (PGP Rules!) <joe@mynet.net>"

Change (N)ame, (C)omment, (E)mail or (O)kay/(Q)uit? o
You need a Passphrase to protect your secret key.

Enter passphrase:
Repeat passphrase:
```

> Be sure to choose a good passphrase for your private key. The same rules
> that apply to good password selection also apply here: Use at least one
> numeric digit, avoid using words or combinations of whole words, and defi-
> nitely avoid using any personal information about yourself that might be
> obvious. Birthdays, last names, children's names, weight, favorite actor or
> actress, and so on are bad ideas because they are easy to guess.

At this point, GPG will set about trying to generate your keys. However, it needs a small
but steady stream of random numbers in order to do this. It normally gets these from the
`/dev/random` device in Linux, but this device requires entropy, a kind of measure of disorder in a system, to work reliably. If your system doesn't have enough entropy, you may
see a message like this one:

```
Not enough random bytes available. Please do some other
work to give the OS a chance to collect more entropy!
```

If this occurs, moving the mouse around or hitting the Shift or Ctrl key a few times will
usually generate the disorder needed to finish the task. Eventually, you'll be told that
GPG has successfully created your keys:

```
public and secret key created and signed.
```

You're now ready to begin learning to use GPG.

Working with Keys

Before you can encrypt or decrypt any messages, files, or other data, you'll need to learn to collect, use, and validate GPG keys to ensure the integrity of the data you'll be exchanging. The primary tools for working with keys that we'll discuss here are key listing, key importing, key exporting, key signing, and user trust.

Listing Keys

Throughout the rest of this hour, it will be very helpful to you to be able to list the keys in your own public key database. To obtain a list of keys in your "keyring" and the matching names and e-mail addresses of their owners, use the following:

```
$ gpg --list-keys
/home/joe/.gnupg/pubring.gpg
pub 1024D/D9BAC463 2001-01-03 Joe User (PGP Rules!) <joe@mynet.net>
sub 1024g/5EE5D252 2001-01-03

pub 1024D/4F03BD39 2001-01-15 Pipi Socks (I'm WIRED) <pipi@hairnet.org>
sub 1024g/FDBB477D 2001-01-15

$
```

Each entry in the list represents a public key that you have on file and that can be used to encrypt data sent to the matching e-mail address.

Importing and Exporting Keys

The process of importing and exporting public keys is the meat-and-potatoes of the PGP world, because it is only when a potential recipient has your public key that you are able to make use of PGP in messages or data sent to him. Likewise, any number of potential senders may want you to have their keys so that they can send you secure information.

The first step is to learn to export your own key, so that you can provide it to others. This is done with the --export argument. For example, if you're joe, you can export your own public key to the file mykey.gpg like this:

```
$ gpg --export joe@mynet.net >mykey.gpg
$
```

The public key for joe@mynet.net is now stored in mykey.gpg and can be supplied to friends, family, or co-workers that joe may want to communicate with in a secure way. Unfortunately, the key is not in an easily readable format; it looks like a lot of garbage and isn't pleasant at all. It is therefore common practice to communicate keys and other types of PGP information in ASCII format, suitable for inclusion in an e-mail message. This is done with the -a argument:

```
$ gpg -a --export joe@mynet.net >mykey.gpg
$
```

20

The new `mykey.gpg` is very nicely formatted and contains the same information—joe's public key and general identification strings. Keys can be imported in similar fashion:

```
$ gpg --import pipiskey.gpg
$
```

Once `pipi`'s key has been imported, `joe` can send encrypted messages to `pipi` or receive signed messages from `pipi` using her public key. The same holds true for `pipi`, assuming that she imports the copy of `joe`'s key that `joe` exported.

Signatures and Trust

If you're following along and experimenting, you may have noticed that GPG isn't so quick to trust an imported key—there's actually quite a bit more output than is shown in the examples in the previous section. This is because the PGP scheme depends on the validity of public keys. That is, if lots of fake public keys start being passed around so that, for instance, a public key that claims to be from `pipi` is really from `joan`, the whole security model breaks.

Therefore, GPG includes a complex trust system designed to help you decide which keys are real and which aren't, based on evidence included with the key. This trust system involves the signing of keys by other individuals who believe the key to be authentic.

When you receive a new public key from someone you know and GPG informs you that there isn't any solid trust information available for the key you've received, the first thing you should do is fingerprint the key. To illustrate, let's suppose that you have just imported `pipi`'s key, and GPG has informed you that no trust information for this new key exists.

The first thing you need to do is run a fingerprint on the new key:

```
$ gpg --fingerprint pipi@hairnet.org
pub 1024D/4F03BD39 2001-01-15 Pipi Socks (I'm WIRED) <pipi@hairnet.org>
    Key fingerprint = B121 5431 8DE4 E3A8 4AA7 737D 20BE 0DB8 4F03 BD39
sub 1024g/FDBB477D 2001-01-15

$
```

This fingerprint is generated from the data in the key and is reasonably unique. You then phone `pipi` to ask her two questions. First, has she just sent you a key, and next, what is the fingerprint of her public key.

If `pipi` answers that she has indeed just sent you a key and the fingerprint matches the one you've generated, you know that the key is valid. You can then sign the key, in effect stating that this key is `pipi`'s and you trust her.

```
$ gpg --sign-key pipi@hairnet.org

pub 1024D/4F03BD39 created: 2001-01-15 expires: never
sub 1024g/FDBB477D created: 2001-01-15 expires: never
```

```
(1) Pipi Socks (I'm WIRED) <pipi@hairnet.org>

pub 1024D/4F03BD39 created: 2001-01-15 expires: never
Fingerprint = B121 5431 8DE4 E3A8 4AA7 737D 20BE 0DB8 4F03 BD39

Pipi Socks (I'm WIRED) <pipi@hairnet.org>

Are you really sure that you want to sign this key
with your key: "Ima User (I'm just ME) <me@mynet.org>"

Really sign? y
You need a passphrase to unlock the secret key for
user: "Ima User (I'm just ME) <me@mynet.org>"
1024-bit DSA key, ID D9BAC463, created 2001-01-03

Enter passphrase:
$
```

This key has now been signed with your private key; anyone holding your public key can verify that the signature is yours. The signature you have added to `pipi`'s public key will travel with it anywhere it goes, your personal guarantee that this is `pipi`'s key.

To get a list of the signatures associated with a public key in your personal keyring, use the `--check-sigs` argument:

```
gpg --check-sigs pipi@hairnet.org
```

The longer the list of signatures, the more valid a key can be assumed to be. It is this system of signatures that provides key verification. Suppose you receive a key that has been signed by `pipi`. You know that it is really her signature because it can be verified with her public key, which you have just signed as authentic. Assuming you trust `pipi`, you can then trust as real any key `pipi` has signed. This web of trust, as it is called, can continue much further than any one e-mail user can reach, ensuring that people are who they claim to be.

What happens, however, when a key has only a small number of signatures, or even just one signature, from a signer who is either questionable in his own identity or is too lax with his signatures, simply signing any key that passes through?

To combat trust dilution, GPG includes one additional resource, the trust level. With it, you can indicate the degree to which you trust the owner of any key you have. For example, suppose that even though you know `pipi`'s public key is authentic, you don't actually trust her judgment when it comes to signing other keys. You think that `pipi` may just sign a few keys without checking them out. You can set the trust level with the `--edit-key` command.

```
$ gpg --edit-key pipi@hairnet.org
```

```
pub 1024D/4F03BD39 created: 2001-01-15 expires: never trust: -/f
```

20

```
sub 1024g/FDBB477D created: 2001-01-15 expires: never
(1) Pipi Socks (I'm WIRED) <pipi@hairnet.org>

Command> trust

  1 = Don't know
  2 = I do NOT trust
  3 = I trust marginally
  4 = I trust fully
  s = please show me more information
  m = back to the main menu

Your decision? 2
Command> quit
$
```

By using the `trust` command in the key editor and selecting trust level 2 (I do NOT trust), you have invalidated any trust chain that must pass through `pipi`'s signatures.

Of course, when GPG asks you about a questionable key, you will always be able to force GPG to use it, regardless of the degree to which it can be trusted. However, the trust system provides a way for you as a GPG user to know which keys are *certainly* valid, which keys *may* be valid, and which keys are almost certainly *not* valid.

Using GPG: Nuts and Bolts

So far, there's been a lot of discussion about keys and key exchanges. Now we finally begin to get into the actual day-to-day use of GPG for sending and receiving data.

There are two kinds of exchanges that are routinely made with GPG: signed data and encrypted data. In the first case, the sender uses a private key and the receiver a public key. In the second case, the opposite is true.

Signatures for Data

Data signatures are created for data you're sending out. A signature is generated using your private key; any user receiving this data who has your public key and trusts it can use it to validate the integrity of the data you've sent. He can then be sure that the information being received comes straight from you and hasn't been tampered with.

The simplest way to sign a piece of data is to use the ASCII-ready `--clearsign` command. This causes GPG to produce a nice, human-readable signature suitable for sending via e-mail.

```
$ gpg --clearsign mymessage.txt

You need a passphrase to unlock the secret key for
user: "Ima User (I'm just ME) <me@mynet.net>"
```

```
1024-bit DSA key, ID D9BAC463, created 2001-01-15

Enter passphrase:
$
```

After entering the passphrase, you'll notice that a new file with the `.asc` extension has been created, in this case `mymessage.txt.asc`. This file contains the original contents of `mymessage.txt` plus a signature similar to the one shown in Listing 20.2.

LISTING 20.2   A GPG-Generated PGP Signature

```
-----BEGIN PGP SIGNATURE-----
Version: GnuPG v1.0.1 (GNU/Linux)
Comment: For info see http://www.gnupg.org

iD8DBQE6YouhU87DFNm6xGMRAiwqAJ4mnviKz5wA9HFhCW9PG6z17A2LPACgk0SB
n+yWiCt4SCTVkSSgezGKIUk=
=WnX/
-----END PGP SIGNATURE-----
```

When the file or message containing this signature is received, the recipient who has your public key on file can verify the message's integrity by issuing the `--verify` command to GPG:

```
$ gpg --verify message.txt.asc
gpg: Signature made Sat Jan 13 22:33:21 2001 MST using DSA key D9BAC463
gpg: Good signature from "Ima User (I'm just ME) <me@mynet.net>"
$
```

A verified signature indicates that the message or file really does come from the source it claims to be from and that it hasn't been modified in any way.

Encrypting and Decrypting Data

GPG is also useful when a message, file, or other unit of data is for one person's eyes only. At such times, GPG can use the person's public key to encrypt the file, making it unreadable until it is decrypted by the person holding the matching private key (presumably the intended recipient).

To encrypt a data file using the recipient's public key, use the `-r` argument to specify a recipient and the `--encrypt` command to instruct GPG to encrypt the file in question:

```
$ gpg -r pipi@hairnet.org -a --encrypt message.txt
$
```

It's as simple as that; GPG uses the public key on file for `pipi@hairnet.org` to encrypt `message.txt` and writes the output to `message.txt.asc`. The resulting file is shown in Listing 20.3.

20

LISTING 20.3   An Encrypted File for `pipi`

```
-----BEGIN PGP MESSAGE-----
Version: GnuPG v1.0.1 (GNU/Linux)
Comment: For info see http://www.gnupg.org

hQEOA/Yj7lT9u0d9EAQAhE+KaGfMzvRfCdrfW2EYzuu+YeaKdoJksHB16CO7RsZC
Dk1lV/uma/rMj5PiDzFoV8PGjqdq9M+n9YXOVnuG3XITWhuvfFqm1KWxK9e0UDoS
7Tb2cm+k8UK18HBI/EaNrV+a3A5YQr6nVY0OCXheohg3+9ursFc8uOBQma64/VUD
/io0EQiIxEmERy2UsN7e+OB1/w4FUcRt7FFWCTVMGdUuQPY8UkeStH7u43NlPsf5
6uPPjaTxCOjjQoCf17XnfxqJPm9c0uyPDj1jXYmp74XroT+lHvGcaKK56t0agGVo
i5nMflXoCIA2n/KDALzTjy7cIzLnUeYVU4NrBt7pV4TTyelxYB70mW94Wlr5BlLj
S+FYueR31i790QO+265iS4QPA+zxXIT5KCF8TT1gVPaZOJxmo0wRKuoOYrCd7LQD
Oz3exhCgeKKjfZRwJtqvl/QVamFJWSyhAiuTlA60IHyxIqAZlwLoYoXs9oOIs49g
HLYG6hSemJEW+fTX8xipOOfDXzHrJjUE897igeW62Mf6HLr4aNb1kwrlH7d7Xdr8
29+sckZlSRtBvL3/dSw5FcRCFYbS51AHstdywYvNu4rqSOljv5C6dXEw9Gre+wPS
5S7k0KoTLK4VOZJI2byBTZxgjQNr7ytpu1QMN2+10tpHx6MLkUFV/BJZbAtJ3C0v
auS4xskoSlZgbuX/8Veqhx4GC0lSRLqn14M9CP/tzZN0dIZSTbM2aq58zk0wZZVB
Tmb06HdYvkLrcLkmyNBt3/PUlDIIdeXNCkqN5bjGD/elTtkaMmHN9OIIDHWA9olR
tcXoLJPF4kgg1q6y6pgy2sklYQhI8A4q8VoQNJDzF/SbKvlnGji5HyF6rvKDCF0m
/l0heQEMn4AyFbJ7LZt2zh4i3jSwyV4Ff+tWJD09xaNziKi791FaSBVMxsPhT4SD
w+R75JR/FV0IRpMsy8kdJw/+kejQwCmRqDbm3EHOESCOouxsL8JB39vX+1h32p1b
EdVyQIHZA+TomHsp/y3i+EX52MC8+8XmCukHfT0dCVcnfk2H0hKvFueBkW8Y2JGd
FJZb+CDX33Aapr6FW9CIXvI+1NFOz+cIWVZIYYECnUZe4l3Jikjw3rY2To4E/WUy
MN+ZKsMb6x1hMSoRa9qHWY+S/pp9D8qiqweOLg4cnCjZBZWVOMf4dMcDWNjsW3mX
GgYVmPf52WxvVFtp1yjNbHBu+is8/ZR1P04efD+kOg1WtwpfRdHKQ1o1fn/OxYX1
oP7PVR5BK05HaQYmI0Vlwkcv59RyeYqqOQOiEfL0hEWdGy1gdj0R0eHYuZLnBLfb
SHJ20tRpcqHuXB27EU3C4OR/N++7ExhG/MNB8WPFb82cbIP8xDF9q+3b73b7myTn
JpAYj4p2ocv9Zf1DH9HHaT7bYD37hvjLlNXe07kYOlMWB9+48meO/o+Yjn5oEj60
wipRdCiP4TUoAwC9EDFED64qLXST9MBycLrc5DwiMYzfdyauiHU3MNhUfErXVaRJ
/5ljtJUGHA/P/ouqbSCleHQ=
=2Sgq
-----END PGP MESSAGE-----
```

An encrypted message can be signed as well. To do this, include the `-s` argument in addition to the others when encrypting using GPG.

To decrypt an encrypted file like this one, `pipi` will need to use the `--decrypt` command and redirect standard output to where she'd like the message to go.

```
$ gpg --decrypt message.txt.asc > message.txt

You need a passphrase to unlock the secret key for
user: "Pipi Socks (I'm WIRED) <pipi@hairnet.org>"
1024-bit ELG-E key, ID FDBB477D, created 2001-01-15

Enter passphrase:
$
```

Once `pipi` has entered the passphrase for her secret key, the message you sent will be decrypted and sent to the file `message.txt`. You have now securely transmitted a message to `pipi` using GPG.

Summary

In this hour, you downloaded and installed the GNU Privacy Guard, GnuPG or GPG for short, a free implementation of Pretty Good Privacy (PGP).

You learned to create your own public/private key pair, import and export public keys, fingerprint new public keys for verification, and sign keys you can positively verify. You learned to indicate to GPG whether or not signatures from other users whose keys you have on file ought to be trusted as though you had signed the keys yourself.

Finally, you learned to use GPG to sign messages or data using your private key, to verify signed messages that others have sent you, to encrypt outbound messages that are for the receiver's eyes only, and to decrypt inbound messages that are for your eyes only.

Q&A

Q What about subkeys, revocation certificates, alternative algorithms, e-mail client integration…

A This hour is intended only as a primer for a very large and flexible protocol and application system. If you plan to use GPG/PGP on a regular basis (and you should), it is strongly advised that you visit the GnuPG home page and read the online documentation. Afterward, scour the `gpg` manual page and learn about the various options and commands.

Q I want to encrypt only data I send to others. Can't I just use the keys they send me in e-mail and ignore all of this "trust" stuff?

A Not really. You see, if you want to encrypt the data you send to others, there's probably a reason—the data is too sensitive to be seen by just anyone.

Because a key contains nothing more than encryption data, name, and e-mail address, it is possible for you to receive a completely forged key from someone other than the person it appears to be from. Whoever made the bogus key also has the matching private key that can decrypt its output. If you encrypt and send without verifying a key's authenticity, you may be revealing sensitive information to a malicious third party.

You should therefore always verify a public key before you use it to send sensitive encrypted data to anyone.

20

New Terms

entropy   A quantity of work-related disorder or activity present in a running system that is used to generate random numbers.

GNU Privacy Guard (GnuPG, GPG)   An implementation of PGP from the Free Software Foundation that is mostly compatible with commercial PGP implementations. The IDEA algorithm, which remains under patent until 2007, is not officially supported by GPG.

Pretty Good Privacy (PGP)   A general-purpose method of exchanging encrypted or signed data of nearly any type based on public key cryptography.

private key   The second half of an encryption key pair, the private key must be kept under strict secrecy and encrypted with a passcode and should be known only to its owner.

public key   One half of an encryption key pair, the public key can be circulated widely, signed by other users, and used to encode messages to the key's owner.

signature   Validation information created using the source's private key that can be verified as having come from the source in question using the source's matching public key. Data and other public keys can be signed as valid.

web of trust   A measure of the degree to which the validity of a key is certain. Trust is determined by the number of trusted individuals who have signed a public key and whose signatures on the key can be verified using their own trusted public keys.

PART IV

Intrusion Detection, Auditing, and Recovery

Hour

HOUR 21

Auditing and Monitoring

This hour you'll learn to download, install, and use two tools, one for auditing and one for monitoring, that together are enough to keep most small networks reasonably safe from attack.

For auditing hosts on your network, you'll learn the basics of using SAINT, the Security Administrator's Integrated Network Tool. SAINT's easy-to-use interface and powerful vulnerability-finding capability combine to make SAINT the tool of champions for small network security.

For monitoring your host and server logs, you'll install and use SWATCH, the Simple WATCHer, which will lurk in the background watching logs. When something questionable happens in one of the monitored logs, you'll be the first to know.

Putting SAINT to Work

Security Administrator's Integrated Network Tool (SAINT) is an incredibly useful tool for administrators of small networks. It single-handedly scans any hosts on your network and checks them against a database of vulnerabilities known for your operating system type (in this case, Linux). It then compiles a report with enough information to help you hunt down and close nearly every vulnerability or potential vulnerability it finds.

SAINT is based on SATAN, the Security Administrator's Tool for Analyzing Networks, but it has been updated to include a much friendlier user interface and wider operating system support.

The SAINT home page can be found at `http://www.wwdsi.com/saint/`.

Downloading and Installing SAINT

Before downloading and installing SAINT, you need to make sure that you have a fairly recent (5.0 or later) version of Perl installed. Most current Linux distributions include a new enough version, but you may need to visit `http://www.cpan.org` to download and install a new one. Be sure that your distribution has installed `flex` and `bison` as well. You can check for the presence of their manual pages to see if they have been installed.

If you have Windows clients or servers on your network, you'll also want to be sure to install Samba, since this will make a number of Windows-style networking tools available to SAINT. That way, even Windows-based clients can be scanned for vulnerabilities.

You'll also need to install `nmap`, a tool commonly referred to as a port scanner. SAINT will use `nmap` to check many of the network ports on your system to see how open to attack they are. To download `nmap`, visit `http://www.insecure.org/nmap/` and grab the latest source tarball. Then extract, configure, compile, and install it in the usual manner.

```
$ tar -xzf nmap-2.53.tgz
$ cd nmap-2.53
$ ./configure
...[ Output of configure ]...
$ make
...[ Output of make ]...
$ su
Password:
# make install
...[ Output of make install ]...
# exit
$
```

Once `nmap` has been installed, you're ready to get on with the installation and use of SAINT itself. The latest version of SAINT can be downloaded anonymously and at no charge from `http://www.wwdsi.com/saint/downloads/`. After you have downloaded the source tarball to your hard drive, installation is very easy, because Linux is one of the primary platforms for which SAINT is developed.

Extract the source code, configure, and compile. You can run a `make install` if you want, but this will only install a manual page for SAINT; the program itself will remain in the source directory.

```
$ tar -xzf saint-3.1.2.tar.gz
$ cd saint-3.1.2
$ ./configure
...[ Output of configure ]...
$ make
...[ Output of make ]...
$ su
Password:
# make install
mkdir -p /usr/local/man/man1
install -c -o root -g 0 -m 444 saint.1 /usr/man/man1/saint.1
#
```

> SAINT isn't meant to be released in a "stable version" and then installed and used that way for years on end. This is because network vulnerabilities and attacks are constantly evolving. You can and should regard any installation of SAINT as temporary, ready to be replaced with a new version or updated with new information the next time you run an audit.
>
> Audits should be run regularly, at least once a month with the latest version of SAINT available if you are on a small network. On larger networks, this should be done even more often.

Assuming that SAINT has compiled without errors, you're ready to put it to work.

Using SAINT

You must be the superuser and have access to an X display in order to run SAINT, because it runs in a Netscape window. To start SAINT, run the `saint` executable in the source directory.

```
./saint
```

Within a few moments, you'll be greeted by a Netscape window displaying the SAINT title page, along with some basic information and a list of options. This page is shown in Figure 21.1.

21

FIGURE 21.1
The SAINT title page.

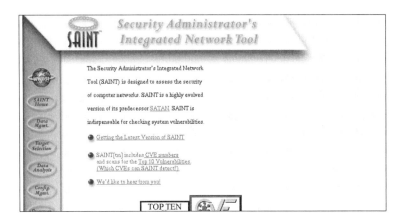

To begin scanning for vulnerabilities, choose the Target Selection option along the left side of the browser window. This will bring up a page in which you can input the hostname(s) or IP number(s) of the target or targets to be scanned by SAINT, as shown in Figure 21.2.

FIGURE 21.2
Tell SAINT which hosts to scan.

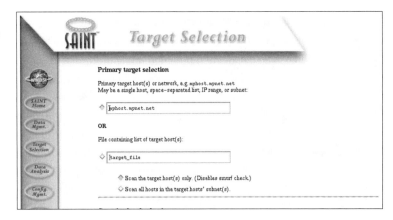

Normally a scan is conducted on the local host, but you may also specify more than one host by separating the names of hosts, or even entire subnets to be scanned, with spaces.

When you have input the host or hosts that will be scanned, scroll down to the bottom of the page to select the scanning intensity. In general, especially for a first scan, you want to select the most intense type of check possible. You should therefore select the Heavy+ scan to have SAINT check everything it knows how to check, as is shown in Figure 21.3.

FIGURE 21.3

SAINT should scan very heavily.

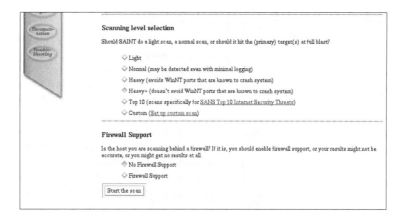

> **Scanning level selection**
>
> Should SAINT do a light scan, a normal scan, or should it hit the (primary) target(s) at full blast?
>
> ◇ Light
> ◇ Normal (may be detected even with minimal logging)
> ◇ Heavy (avoids WinNT ports that are known to crash system)
> ◆ Heavy+ (doesn't avoid WinNT ports that are known to crash system)
> ◇ Top 10 (scans specifically for SANS Top 10 Internet Security Threats)
> ◇ Custom (Set up custom scan)
>
> **Firewall Support**
>
> Is the host you are scanning behind a firewall? If it is, you should enable firewall support, or your results might not be accurate, or you might get no results at all.
> ◆ No Firewall Support
> ◇ Firewall Support
>
> Start the scan

When you are ready to proceed, click the Start the Scan button at the bottom of the form. SAINT will display the warning shown in Figure 21.4, instructing you *not* to use the open Web browser to visit any sites outside your network from this instance of Netscape, which has been started by SAINT. Heed this warning—SAINT is running with root-level access and storing runtime information using Netscape.

FIGURE 21.4

Don't use this browser for anything else!

> **Warning – SAINT Password Disclosure**
>
> Your Hypertext viewer may reveal confidential information when you contact remote WWW servers from within SAINT.
>
> For this reason, SAINT advises you to not contact other WWW servers from within SAINT.
>
> For more information, see the SAINT vulnerability tutorial.
>
> This message will appear only once per SAINT session.
>
> In order to proceed, send a *reload* command (Ctrl–R with Lynx), or go back to the previous screen and select the same link or button again.

To proceed, click the Reload button in the Netscape window, and choose Yes when Netscape asks if you want to repost the most recent form data. SAINT will then begin the scan of the hosts you specified. The output of one such scan is shown in Figure 21.5.

When the check is complete, you can scroll through the output to study the things SAINT has checked and verified. Near the bottom of the page, SAINT will also tell you how many hosts were checked in this scan. When you are ready to see the problems or potential problems that SAINT found on your host or network, scroll to the bottom of the page and click the Continue with Report and Analysis link.

21

FIGURE 21.5

*A SAINT vulnerability
check in progress.*

SAINT data collection

Data collection in progress...

```
01/15/01 -10:42:31 bin/timeout 60 bin/fping myhost.mynet.net
01/15/01 -10:42:31 bin/timeout 60 bin/tcpscan.saint 12754,15104,16660,20432,27665,1 -9999 myhost.mynet.net .PLUS
01/15/01 -10:42:31 bin/timeout 20 bin/ddos.saint myhost.mynet.net .PLUS
01/15/01 -10:42:32 bin/timeout 20 bin/ostype.saint myhost.mynet.net .PLUS
01/15/01 -10:42:32 bin/timeout 20 bin/finger.saint myhost.mynet.net .PLUS
01/15/01 -10:42:32 bin/timeout 60 bin/udpscan.saint
19,53,69,111,137-139,161-162,177,8999,1-18,20-52,54-68,70-110,112-136,140-160,163-176,178-1760,1763-2050,32767-33500 myhost.mynet.net
.PLUS
01/15/01 -10:42:32 bin/timeout 20 bin/dns.saint myhost.mynet.net .PLUS
01/15/01 -10:42:33 bin/timeout 20 bin/rpc.saint myhost.mynet.net .PLUS
01/15/01 -10:42:54 bin/timeout 20 bin/ostype.saint myhost.mynet.net .PLUS
01/15/01 -10:43:14 bin/timeout 20 bin/xhost.saint -d myhost.mynet.net:2 myhost.mynet.net .PLUS
01/15/01 -10:43:14 bin/timeout 20 bin/xhost.saint -d myhost.mynet.net:3 myhost.mynet.net .PLUS
01/15/01 -10:43:14 bin/timeout 20 bin/xhost.saint -d myhost.mynet.net:4 myhost.mynet.net .PLUS
01/15/01 -10:43:14 bin/timeout 20 bin/xhost.saint -d myhost.mynet.net:6 myhost.mynet.net .PLUS
01/15/01 -10:43:14 bin/timeout 20 bin/xhost.saint -d myhost.mynet.net:5 myhost.mynet.net .PLUS
01/15/01 -10:43:20 bin/timeout 20 bin/xhost.saint -d myhost.mynet.net:7 myhost.mynet.net .PLUS
01/15/01 -10:43:21 bin/timeout 20 bin/xhost.saint -d myhost.mynet.net:8 myhost.mynet.net .PLUS
01/15/01 -10:43:21 bin/timeout 20 bin/xhost.saint -d myhost.mynet.net:9 myhost.mynet.net .PLUS
01/15/01 -10:43:21 bin/timeout 20 bin/sendmail.saint smtp myhost.mynet.net .PLUS
01/15/01 -10:43:21 bin/timeout 20 bin/imap.sara myhost.mynet.net .PLUS
01/15/01 -10:43:21 bin/timeout 20 bin/showmount.saint myhost.mynet.net .PLUS
01/15/01 -10:43:21 bin/timeout 20 bin/xhost.saint -d myhost.mynet.net:10 myhost.mynet.net .PLUS
01/15/01 -10:43:21 bin/timeout 20 bin/xhost.saint -d myhost.mynet.net:11 myhost.mynet.net .PLUS
```

You'll now see a page labeled Data Analysis, which gives you a series of options, each of which will display information about vulnerabilities or potential vulnerabilities that SAINT found on the hosts that it scanned. This page is shown in Figure 21.6.

FIGURE 21.6

*The SAINT Data
Analysis page.*

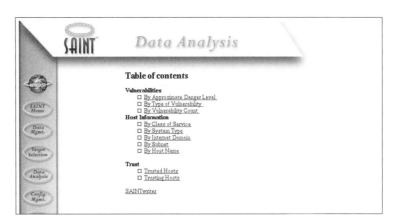

The first link to check is the By Approximate Danger Level link under the Vulnerabilities heading. This link will take you to a list of the vulnerabilities or potential vulnerabilities SAINT found that are most likely to be a problem to you or your network.

Clicking the link will bring up a page that may be filled with links. Each link refers to one vulnerability or potential vulnerability that SAINT found. Those that have been most commonly exploited in the real world are marked with a Top 10 graphic, as shown in Figure 21.7.

FIGURE **21.7**

*Vulnerabilities plus
some Top 10s.*

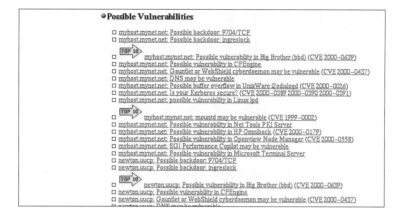

Each vulnerability is listed by host and title. You should visit each of these links in succession, paying special attention to those marked with the Top 10 graphic. These are the ones most likely to cause you trouble. Each time you click a link, SAINT will display an information page giving you some or all of the following details:

- The common name of the vulnerability and links to other detailed information about the vulnerability at security organizations around the world.

- Information on how to determine whether or not the vulnerability affects you.

- The danger level it represents.

- The types and versions of operating systems or other software known to be affected by the vulnerability.

- Possible solutions or correct steps that should be taken to eliminate the vulnerability or recover from an attack.

Once such page is shown in Figure 21.8. Note the large traffic signal in the upper-right corner of the page; this is a very easily identifiable indicator of the level of vulnerability. A yellow light means that you *may* be affected, and a red light means that you *are* or *have already* been affected by a vulnerability.

Each yellow-light vulnerability should be studied carefully to see if it affects your host. If you can determine that it doesn't, you can safely ignore the warning. All red-light notices must be taken care of immediately, or you will certainly suffer the consequences sooner or later, assuming that you haven't already.

For the small network administrator, that's all there is to using SAINT. There are a number of other capabilities to the Web front end; feel free to explore the Web interface and study all that it has to offer. More details about command-line SAINT operation can be found in the SAINT manual page (assuming you have installed it) at saint(1).

21

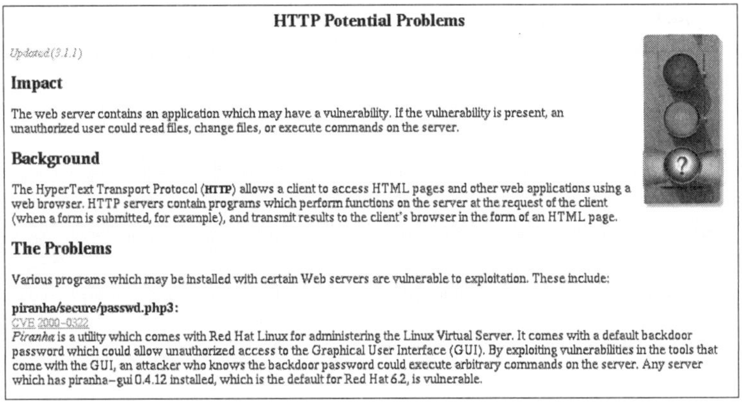

FIGURE 21.8

*An information page
with a yellow light.*

HTTP Potential Problems

Updated (3.1.1)

Impact

The web server contains an application which may have a vulnerability. If the vulnerability is present, an unauthorized user could read files, change files, or execute commands on the server.

Background

The HyperText Transport Protocol (**HTTP**) allows a client to access HTML pages and other web applications using a web browser. HTTP servers contain programs which perform functions on the server at the request of the client (when a form is submitted, for example), and transmit results to the client's browser in the form of an HTML page.

The Problems

Various programs which may be installed with certain Web servers are vulnerable to exploitation. These include:

piranha/secure/passwd.php3:
CVE 2000-0322
Piranha is a utility which comes with Red Hat Linux for administering the Linux Virtual Server. It comes with a default backdoor password which could allow unauthorized access to the Graphical User Interface (GUI). By exploiting vulnerabilities in the tools that come with the GUI, an attacker who knows the backdoor password could execute arbitrary commands on the server. Any server which has piranha-gui 0.4.12 installed, which is the default for Red Hat 6.2, is vulnerable.

Staying Alert with SWATCH

SWATCH is a very simple tool written in Perl that performs a very simple task: It watches whichever logs you tell it to watch, searching for log activity you've described. When such log activity appears, SWATCH takes whatever action you have ordered. Because SWATCH can execute any command in response to a specific kind of log activity, it's incredibly flexible. You can even have it page you on your beeper or send you a fax if you have those tools installed on your system.

Our SWATCH treatment will be fairly short and sweet. It'll be up to you to configure SWATCH to suit your own needs and circumstances and to perform the types of actions you need it to perform in response to log activity.

Downloading and Installing SWATCH

The SWATCH utility can be downloaded from its fairly Spartan home page, located at `http://www.stanford.edu/~atkins/swatch/`. It's available only as a `.tar` file representing the current release.

Once you have downloaded SWATCH, extract it, visit the directory created during extraction to hold the source, and run the `Makefile.PL` script using the Perl interpreter. Note that you will need to have Perl 5.0 or later installed; earlier versions will not work.

```
$ tar -xf swatch.tar
$ cd swatch-3.0.1
$ perl Makefile.PL
...[ Output of perl ]...
$
```

> SWATCH also needs a number of additional Perl modules to run. Many Linux operating systems install these modules or at least make them available as part of a Perl module kit package.
>
> If SWATCH is unable to find these modules, it will ask if you would like to contact www.cpan.org or one of its mirrors automatically and install the modules. This will work, but you will first need to interrupt the process, enter su to become the superuser, and then restart the process again so that the modules can be correctly installed.

After SWATCH has been built, you can install it with a simple make followed by a make install; this will install both the main Perl script and the manual page.

```
$ make
...[ Output of make ]...
$ su
Password:
# make install
...[ Output of make install ]...
#
```

Assuming that you have a working Perl installation and that all of the required Perl modules were also installed correctly, you now have a working SWATCH installation.

Using SWATCH to Watch Logs

Use of the swatch command isvery simple. Though there are a number of arguments documented in swatch(1), the basic form of operation is

```
swatch -c matchfile --tail logfile
```

The logfile is the path to one of your system logs. This can be a log maintained by syslogd or it can be some other kind of log altogether; SWATCH doesn't care. The SWATCH program is willing to watch any text file and treat it as an active log.

The matchfile is a short, simple file describing a series of text strings SWATCH is to look for in the file and the actions SWATCH should take each time any of these strings is matched.

The Match File Format

The SWATCH match file is a text file that begins with a watchfor keyword followed by a regular expression indicating a pattern or series of patterns with which SWATCH is to be concerned. The following is an example:

```
watchfor /ROOT LOGIN|uid=0/
```

21

This line will cause SWATCH to watch the log in question for the strings ROOT LOGIN or uid=0 in order to stay abreast of root-level activity occurring on the system responsible for the log being watched. After each watchfor line is a series of lines describing the actions that are to occur when the pattern is matched. For example, after the watchfor pattern, you might see the following:

```
echo red
mail addresses=admin@mynet.net:jz@w1x.org,subject=".SW.ROOT"
bell 3
```

These lines cause SWATCH to display the relevant log entry in red on the terminal controlling SWATCH. Then, SWATCH will mail the log entry to two addresses—admin@mynet.net and jz@w1x.org—with the easily identifiable subject .SW.ROOT. Finally, SWATCH will ring the terminal bell three times.

The list of actions continues on until the next watchfor line, which begins anew with a different pattern to watch for. The actions SWATCH can be instructed to take are listed in Table 21.1.

TABLE 21.1 Actions for the SWATCH Match File

Action	Description
echo [mode]	Displays the matching log entry to the controlling terminal. Optional mode can be one of bold, underscore, blink, inverse, black, red, green, yellow, blue, cyan, white, black_h (highlighted), red_h, green_h, yellow_h, blue_h, cyan_h, or white_h.
bell [count]	Rings the terminal bell. Optional count describes the number of times the bell should sound.
exec command [args]	Executes the specified command, with any supplied arguments. $N in arguments will be expanded to whitespace-separated field N in the log entry. $0 will be expanded to the entire log entry.
mail [addr],[subj]	Sends the related log entry to the invoking user's e-mail address. If addresses=addr:addr:... is supplied, sends mail to the listed address(es). If subject="subject text..." is supplied, uses the supplied subject as the subject for the message(s) being sent.
pipe command	Sends the log entry to the standard input of command.
write [user]	Writes the related log entry to the terminal of user. More than one user can be listed by separating with a colon (:) character.
throttle h:m:s	Specifies that if the log entry is repeated more than once in the supplied time period (in hours:minutes:seconds), the action(s) for the match should be carried out only once during that period of time.
continue	Instructs SWATCH to attempt to match this log entry to other watchfor patterns in the match file after actions for this pattern are complete.

Using these actions and well-constructed `watchfor` lines, you can have SWATCH monitor your logs for almost any type of activity. A very simple file is shown in Listing 21.1.

LISTING 21.1 A Simple General-Purpose Match File

```
watchfor     /ROOT LOGIN|uid=0/
echo red
mail addresses=admin@mynet.net,subject=".SW.Root Activity"
bell 2

watchfor     /REPEATED|repeated/
echo red
mail addresses=admin@mynet.net,subject=".SW.Repeat Activity"
bell 2

watchfor     /FAILED|INVALID|authentication failure|Unauthorized/
echo
mail addresses=admin@mynet.net
bell 1

watchfor     /changed by/
echo blue
mail addresses=admin@mynet.net,subject=".SW.Password Change"
bell 2

watchfor     /caught signal|exiting|abnormal|aborted|restart|registered/
echo blink
mail addresses=admin@mynet.net,subject=".SW.Unknown"
bell 2

watchfor     /kernel:|init:/
echo blink
mail addresses=admin@mynet.net,subject=".SW.System"
bell 2

watchfor     /LOGIN FROM/
echo
```

The match file in Listing 21.1 attempts to track a general group of common but questionable log entry types on many Linux systems and display them locally, notify an administrator, or both.

When you have SWATCH configured to suit your needs, you might consider starting it somewhere in the background during the boot process for important log monitoring. You also might dedicate a central log machine to logging all machines on your network and monitoring those logs with SWATCH.

21

Summary

In this hour, you learned to use SAINT and its Netscape-based graphical interface to perform a basic security audit on your system. You then learned how to search the information provided by SAINT and use it to eliminate vulnerabilities found on your host or around your network.

You also learned to install and use SWATCH, a simple but very useful tool for watching system logs as they are written. Using SWATCH, you can continuously monitor logs for certain important patterns and either notify an administrator(s) or take action based on the matching entries occurring.

Q&A

Q I have a file or configuration issue that SAINT says may represent a vulnerability, but I think it's supposed to be there. Should I remove it anyway?

A It depends on a number of factors. First, if SAINT says that a given file may indicate the presence of a backdoor or root kit but you are sure the file is original, there is an easy way to be sure. Compare the file's checksum, size, and date against the original from your distribution package. If they match, the file is original. This does not necessarily mean that it is safe. Be sure to check for updates from your distribution maintainer in case the original file contains a vulnerability.

If SAINT is warning you about a configuration issue, you will need to apply some critical thinking to the issues SAINT is raising. Is there another way to accomplish the same thing in a less vulnerable way? If the issue is an enabled service or open port, is it needed at all or can it be removed?

Remember, software programs like SAINT are only tools. You are the administrator, and in the end the call—and consequences—are yours.

Q How do I know which strings to match in SWATCH?

Some of the strings in the sample SWATCH match file have never appeared in my logs.

Shouldn't you also include string "N" in your match file?

A There are almost as many different daemon and `syslogd` versions as there are Linux distributions, so strings will vary from one system to the next, depending on vendor and date of assembly. Even such basic things as the `init` binary can be based on completely different code bases from system to system.

Your SWATCH match file will have to be based on experience. That is not to say that you have to be hacked in advance in order to build a good file. There is a simple way to learn about the types of log entries you ought to watch for: behave badly yourself!

By mounting your own series of "attacks" or at least "interesting" behavior on your own network, you can see how each action will appear in your log, and you can monitor for those strings. Running software like SAINT can generate a number of log entries that may indicate to you that bad things are going on. Furthermore, you actually have control over the logging of some system components—TCP Wrappers and Apache, for example. Since you decide on the strings that will be logged in the first place, it should be easy for you to match them with SWATCH.

Q My logs are very inactive, or empty.

A There are a few possible reasons for this.

First, empty or nearly empty logs that were once very active are an almost certain indication that some sort of attack has taken place. Run SAINT to check for problems and look carefully at your old logs, paying special attention to the point at which they stop. You may find that your system is already compromised.

Second, you may simply need to reconfigure your daemons to be more verbose in their logging. This will have to be fixed in your init scripts, in /etc/inetd.conf, and in your /etc configuration files on a case-by-case basis. You may want to consider reinstalling or switching to a different distribution that does more logging.

There is one more slightly obvious reason that your logs may be empty. Have you checked to ensure that your disk isn't full and hasn't recently been full? Syslog will stop when it encounters a full disk and will not restart again on its own, even if space once again becomes available.

New Terms

Security Administrator's Integrated Network Tool (SAINT)   An incredibly useful scanner and vulnerability analyzer that is popular with system administrators. SAINT tests a system for vulnerability to a large number of standard or common attacks and generates a report that the administrator can then use to make his system or network more secure.

Security Administrator's Tool for Analyzing Networks (SATAN)   An older piece of software for analyzing security, upon which the newer SAINT application is based.

Simple WATCHer (SWATCH)   A simple but powerful Perl script used to watch any text or log file as it progresses and take action or make reports based on the information that appears there.

vulnerability   A term used to describe any way in which a malicious user or program might violate your system. Default Linux installations usually have a number of vulnerabilities at first. It is your job as the system administrator to systematically try to eliminate as many of them as you can.

21

HOUR **22**

Detecting Attacks in Progress

This hour, you'll learn to use a program called Snort to monitor all traffic on your network actively and in real time to discover and report malicious packets as they are in transit. Though probably too resource-intensive for very small installations (one or two machines), medium-size networks can certainly benefit from such monitoring.

You'll also learn about a quick-and-dirty tool for formatting and tabulating Snort's alert output to make it more readable for administrators with a limited amount of free time.

What Is Snort?

In the simplest sense, Snort is simply a packet sniffing tool, designed to grab packets as they travel across a network, so that they can be used for one purpose or another. The strength of Snort, however, and what makes it so popular among system administrators, is its capability to search through this network traffic and make decisions based on rule-matching with respect to the sniffed packets.

Since the Snort user community is continually compiling rulesets about various classes of attacks that have occurred on some network somewhere, every Snort user has the benefit of thousands of man-hours of experience when he downloads one of the public rulesets from the Snort community.

Using Snort, all of these attacks can be logged and, if the system administrator is vigilant, stopped. More details can be found on the Snort home page at `http://www.snort.org`.

Special Snort Requirements

Because Snort is a very intrusive tool with respect to the network on which it is running, there are some very specific guidelines that most users will want to adhere to when deciding whether or not to run Snort.

It is generally a good idea to run Snort only when you can dedicate an entire machine on your network to it. There are two reasons for this. First of all, Snort's rule-matching capability is not without overhead; it takes resources to compare high-speed network traffic to a large set of attack signatures continuously. A dedicated machine is therefore the best candidate for Snort operation. Second, Snort's packet-sniffing core capability places any network interface it listens on into promiscuous mode, so in the interest of isolating such an interface to the greatest degree possible, it should be run on a separate host.

Snort is best suited to operation on an internal network protected by a firewall. There's a lot of network traffic out there as a general rule, and the number of false positives (innocent matches that appear to be attacks) that you'll receive with an external Snort machine makes for a large time investment. It simply isn't practical for anyone on a small network to dedicate as much time or energy to Snort as would be required when watching packets outside a firewall.

If your network is very small—for example, if you can afford a firewall or a Snort sniffer but not both—buy the firewall and pass on the Snort box. A firewall is a much more essential defensive measure.

Also notable is the fact that Snort is most helpful on mixed networks, those that contain both Linux and Windows machines. This is because Snort can catch many types of attacks or compromises that many desktop versions of Windows can't defend against or even detect.

Downloading and Installing Snort

The process of downloading, compiling, and installing Snort involves several components, and not all of it is straightforward. You'll need to be comfortable installing a few files by hand on the machine where Snort will be installed.

Installing `libpcap`

The `pcap` library is required for Snort to operate. This library is standard on BSD Unix systems, but must be separately downloaded and installed on Linux systems. The `pcap` library can be found on the `ftp://ftp.ee.lbl.gov` FTP site. The latest version of `pcap` will generally be symlinked to the name `libpcap.tar.Z` (filename is case sensitive).

After downloading the source code, extract it, run the `configure` script, and run a `make` followed by a `make install`.

```
$ tar -xzf libpcap.tar.Z
$ cd libpcap-0.4
$ ./configure --prefix=/usr
...[ Output of configure ]...
$ make
...[ Output of make ]...
$ su
Password:
# make install
/usr/bin/install -c -m 444 -o bin -g bin libpcap.a /usr/lib/libpcap.a
ranlib /usr/lib/libpcap.a
#
```

The `pcap` library is now installed. Notice, however, that no include files were installed. There is an `install-incl` target in the `Makefile`, but in order to give the `pcap` includes their own directory, they can be copied by hand to `/usr/include/pcap` and `/usr/include/pcap/net`. A manual page can be installed with the `install-man` target.

```
# mkdir /usr/include/pcap
# cp *.h /usr/include/pcap
# mkdir /usr/include/pcap/net
# cp bpf/net/*.h /usr/include/pcap/net
# make install-man
/usr/bin/install -c -m 444 -o bin -g bin ./pcap.3 \
    /usr/man/man3/pcap.3
# exit
$
```

The `pcap` library and the related include files have now been installed. It is possible to compile Snort without installing the `pcap` library completely by adjusting some of the Snort configuration options, described in the "Installing Snort" section later in this hour. Several other popular network tools also use `pcap`, so it may be to your benefit to install it anyway.

Installing `libnet`

The latest version of the `net` library is found at `http://www.packetfactory.net/Projects/Libnet/dist/`. As this book goes to press, the latest version present is `libnet-1.0.1b.tar.gz`.

Installation of `libnet` is fairly straightforward. Extract the sources with `tar`, run the configure script, `make`, and then `make install`.

```
$ tar -xzf libnet-1.0.1b.tar.gz
$ cd Libnet-1.0.1b
$ ./configure --prefix=/usr/local
...[ Output of configure ]...
$ make
...[ Output of make ]...
$ su
Password:
# make install
...[ Output of make install ]...
# exit
$
```

No special file copies are required to install the `net` library.

Installing Snort

The latest version of Snort can be downloaded from the Snort download page, which can be found at `http://www.snort.org/snort-files.html`. After downloading the source code, you can extract, compile, and install it in more or less the usual way. Note, however, the additional options used in the following code. They adjust the paths for the `pcap` library installation, which otherwise won't be found correctly, and add Samba and flexible response support to Snort.

```
$ tar -xzf snort-1.7.tar.gz
$ cd snort-1.7
$ ./configure --prefix=/usr/local \
> --with-libpcap-includes=/usr/include/pcap \
> --with-libpcap-libraries=/usr/lib \
> --enable-smbalerts \
> --enable-flexresp
...[ Output of configure ]...
$ make
...[ Output of make ]...
$ su
Password:
# make install
...[ Output of make install ]...
# exit
$
```

Support for other features, including the capability to log information to databases like Oracle, MySQL, or PostgreSQL, can be compiled in if you need such functionality. For a complete list of options, call `configure` with the `--help` argument.

Using Snort

Before you can tell Snort to watch network traffic for certain patterns, you must have rulesets containing patterns that match common attacks. Luckily, you don't have to build all of these rulesets yourself. A number of large, comprehensive rulesets have been compiled by the Snort community for machines operating in various roles.

To download one or several of these rulesets, visit `http://www.snort.org/snort-files.htm#Rules`. Here you will find a list of text files that are ready for drop-in ruleset operation with Snort. Table 22.1 gives details on some of these rulesets and when they might be appropriate for Linux users.

TABLE 22.1   Using Snort Rulesets

Ruleset	Appropriateness
Backdoor Activity	Most useful for Windows hosts; generates a lot of false alarms. Not recommended.
Backdoor Attempts	Most useful for Windows hosts; generates a lot of false alarms. Not recommended.
Backdoor (Sig.)	Most useful for Windows hosts. Recommended for mixed environments.
DDoS	Recommended for all installations.
Exploits	Essential for all installations.
Finger	Recommended for all installations.
FTP	Essential when FTP service will be available on the network.
ICMP	Recommended for all installations.
MISC	Recommended for all installations.
NetBios	Essential when running Samba on a Linux host or when Windows hosts are present on the network.
RPC	Recommended for all installations.
Rservices	Recommended for all installations.
Scans	Recommended for all installations.
SMTP	Essential when SMTP service will be available on the network.
Telnet	Essential when standard Telnet service will be available on the network.
Virus	Most useful for Windows hosts; recommended when local Windows hosts will be using e-mail clients.
Web-cgi	Essential when Web service will be available on the network.
Web-ColdFusion	Essential when ColdFusion-based Web service will be available on the network.

TABLE 22.1 continued

Ruleset	Appropriateness
Web-FrontPage	Most useful for Windows hosts; essential when a Windows host will be providing FrontPage-based Web service on the network.
Web-IIS	Most useful for Windows hosts; essential when a Windows host will be providing Web service on the network from an IIS server.
High False Alerts	Miscellaneous rules that generate a lot of false alarms. Not recommended.

To compile your final ruleset, download all of the rulesets you want to use and simply `cat` them together into a single file.

```
# cd downloaded_rules
# cat ddos finger rpc telnet exploits ftp misc scans \
> web-cgi web-misc icmp netbios > /etc/snort.rules
#
```

This file becomes your master ruleset. Be sure to check the Snort community often for updated rulesets so that you'll be prepared for the latest attacks and exploits.

To start Snort with your ruleset as a daemon that will watch in the background and log alerts to a single log-style file suitable for watching with a program like SWATCH, start Snort with this:

```
snort -D -A alert -c /etc/snort.rules
```

The default log file is located at `/var/log/snort.alert`. To make sure that Snort is running and listening correctly, run `ifconfig` and supply your network device as an argument; ensure that `ifconfig` reports that the device is in promiscuous mode.

As long as you keep Snort running, keep the rulesets you use current, monitor the Snort log, and check out all reports of suspicious or malicious activity, you're up and running. For more information on using Snort, consult the manual page for `snort(8)` and the Snort Web page.

Pretty Snort Reports

For some, the default Snort format may be a bit difficult to work with. More information and statistics in a central location can certainly be helpful under certain circumstances. Silicon Defense has created a program for such concerns known as SnortSnarf, which can be found at `http://www.silicondefense.com/snortsnarf/`.

SnortSnarf is designed to be run from a CRON job or some other periodic execution tool. It chews up the output from Snort, digests it, and creates very readable Web documents containing alert tabulations and links to more details about many of the alerts Snort produces.

Since SnortSnarf is a preconfigured Perl script, no building or installation is required *per se*. Simply place the SnortSnarf distribution where you want it and run `snortsnarf.pl` from there.

Practical SnortSnarf Use

SnortSnarf is best called with a script from a CRON job or some other type of periodic execution daemon. A number of options are described at the top of the `snortsnarf.pl` file itself, but the simplest and most common syntax is

```
snortsnarf.pl -d outputdirectory snortfile
```

outputdirectory is the directory that should contain all of the generated HTML files. In this directory, the file `index.html` will be the root document for SnortSnarf's statistics and analysis. The *snortfile* argument refers to the Snort alerts file.

Though the number of potential deployment methods is nearly infinite, a simple script that could be called from a CRON job to rotate and update Snort alert data and SnortSnarf output is shown in Listing 22.1.

LISTING 22.1   A Sample SnortSnarf Script

```
#!/bin/bash

DATE=$(date +%m%d%y)
mkdir /var/log/snortsnarf/$DATE

/usr/local/snortsnarf/snortsnarf.pl \
    -d /var/log/snortsnarf/$DATE \
    /var/log/snort.alert

mv /var/log/snort.alert /var/log/snort/alert.$DATE
gzip -9 /var/log/snort/alert.$DATE
```

The script in Listing 22.1 is a simple one. It can be run daily or even weekly. It simply creates a new directory for the current day in `/var/log/snortsnarf` that will contain the HTML output. Then it saves the current batch of Snort alerts in the `/var/log/snort` directory to make way for the new day's or new week's alerts.

Summary

This hour you learned how to install and use a network sniffing system called Snort, which has the capability to detect and log attacks as they occur and vulnerabilities as they appear. When combined with a tool like SWATCH, Snort provides a potent one-two punch in network defense.

You learned which rulesets maintained by the Snort community are appropriate under various circumstances. Remember to keep these rulesets updated with the latest information from the Snort community if Snort is to remain an effective tool for you.

Finally, you learned how to use the Web-based tool called SnortSnarf to tabulate and analyze the Snort alert logs on a regular basis.

Q&A

Q I have a very fast machine that is behind a firewall. Can't I use it to run Snort and a number of other services as well?

A If you have reasonably trusted users on your internal network, this might be an option. Trial and error will quickly let you know whether or not the resource requirements of Snort will hurt the performance of other daemons.

While certainly not the ideal solution, on smaller networks with limited financial resources, it can be necessary at times to run many services, including Snort, on a small number of machines or even on a single machine.

Q I want to watch for Snort activity with SWATCH. What alerts do I pay attention to and what alerts do I ignore?

A This is where your job as system administrator comes in. Every Snort installation will generate false alarms. If you choose to have SWATCH notify you in a very paranoid fashion of every little bit of Snort activity, you'll quickly learn to ignore the warnings. Later on, when it's not just "crying wolf," you'll regret that you made SWATCH so noisy with respect to Snort alerts.

Since the false alarms generated by Snort will vary from installation to installation, it will be up to you to work with your Snort rulesets and your SWATCH monitoring until you get the balance right. This can be done only through experience.

New Terms

packet sniffer A program that can see all data traveling across a network and record or analyze it. Packet sniffing can be used either for good (as is the case with Snort) or malicious purposes (such as data or password theft).

promiscuous mode A mode of operation for an ethernet device in which it will accept and process all packets it receives, rather than silently dropping packets that are not specifically addressed to it.

22

ruleset   A complex group of patterns consisting of packet types, network ports, sources and destinations, and even text data strings. These patterns can be used to uniquely identify various types of attacks and suspicious or malicious behavior on a network.

Snort   A packet sniffer and rule matching program designed to monitor network traffic and log attacks or various suspicious events as they occur.

SnortSnarf   A Web-based tabulation and analysis tool for making more effective use of Snort's alert output.

HOUR 23

Preserving Data

This hour, you'll learn some of the basics of making timely backups under Linux. You'll learn about `tar` and `afio` and be given a brief overview of some of the more popular commercial backup solutions for Linux systems.

When you're done, you should have enough information to make timely and complete backups and to protect them well.

Data Backups and Security

What do system backups have to do with Linux security? Everything. Backups and security are intimately related because of the potential effect that an intruder or malicious user can have on the data stored in your system(s).

The information presented thus far in this book has been designed to help you to ward off potential threats—to protect your system from crackers, sniffers, script kiddies, and thieves. However, it is almost inevitable that at some point, no matter how vigilant you are, at least some part of your system will be compromised. This is simply the nature of a networked world. Just as crime in the real world will eventually touch every citizen in some way, crime in the data world will eventually touch every citizen in some way.

Preserving Your Valuable Data

When your system is compromised, a malicious intruder or Trojan horse program may gain write access to some or all of the data on your system. A primary worry, of course, is that such an intruder may gain access to data that is intended to be private. Another worry that is no less valid, however, should be that the intruder or malicious program may simply delete in an unrecoverable way vast amounts of irreplaceable data. This can happen only if you don't have well-maintained backups stored somewhere away from the system or network that was compromised.

Modified System Binaries

It's not only your data that is vulnerable, however. Believe it or not, your program binaries and configuration files are just as vulnerable and represent an even bigger problem—the threat of future vulnerability. This is because any intruder who gains write permission to the program binaries in your system will have the capability to replace any of them in a clandestine fashion with modified binaries. These modified binaries will often bear all the hallmarks of the originals, including things like size and date. They may even appear to function identically. However, the modified binary inserted by a cracker or malicious user will usually contain a back door of some kind.

A back door is a hidden way—such as a secret password, listening on a secret port, or recognizing a secret series of network packets—for the malicious user to re-enter your system without your knowledge, even after you have analyzed his attack and tried to secure your system.

The Root Kit

In the Linux world, one of the most common discoveries about a compromised system is that a root kit has been installed. A *root kit* is a group of modified binaries that can replace things like login, ls, syslogd, and other system-level tools.

A root kit is particularly dangerous because it is designed in such a way as to prevent its own discovery. For example, the modified login program in a root kit might accept the intruder's secret password for root access—a back door. A modified ls might then be programmed not to display extra files or system modifications introduced by the intruder. Other modified programs and configuration files participate in the deception while possibly even introducing other back doors.

Because of this danger, it is almost never safe to continue to use a compromised system on a network. There are only two ways to ensure that every system binary and every configuration file is restored to an uncompromised state. One way is to wipe the hard drive clean and reinstall Linux from your installation CD. The other is to wipe the hard drive clean and restore from a series of backups made before the system was compromised. Most users prefer the latter.

Using `tar` and `afio` for Backups

Despite the proliferation of user-friendly backup solutions, `tar` and `afio` remain the two most commonly used standbys for Linux data storage and retrieval. This is probably because `tar` and `afio` are both small enough to fit on a rescue floppy, and neither requires any support infrastructure in the form of additional libraries, configuration files, or graphics support.

Simple Backup and Restore with `tar`

The `tar` command can write archive data to a file or to a tape or raw disk device. The syntax for a typical `tar` command is as follows:

```
tar -[c|x|t] [-pv] -f device path1 path2 ...
```

Each invocation of `tar` requires a command, usually c for *create*, x for *extract*, or t for *test*. The p option instructs `tar` to preserve original file ownership and permissions when extracting. The v option instructs `tar` to operate verbosely. The f option and the argument that follows specify that `tar` should write to the given device. All arguments to `tar` given by path1, path2, and so on are directory trees or files that are to be added to the archive.

For example, to write the /usr tree to the tape in the drive located at /dev/st0, the command is

```
tar -cf /dev/st0 /usr
```

At first glance, it appears that a simple command to back up an entire Linux file system to tape is

```
tar -cf /dev/st0 /
```

However, be aware that this command is generally not what you mean to do. First of all, this command will attempt to back up the /proc directory as well. Depending on your kernel version, this may add hundreds of megabytes of unwanted kernel runtime data to your backup or even cause `tar` to freeze or segmentation fault.

Backing up the root directory (/) also backs up the /mnt directory, where things like mounted CD-ROM data are often found, and any mounted network file systems (which can be a good thing or a bad thing, depending on what you intended to do).

To back up your root directory but except the /proc and /mnt directories, try constructing a command like this one:

```
tar -cf /dev/st0 $(ls -1 / | grep -v -e proc -e mnt)
```

This will back up all directories in the root directory but leave out the /proc and /mnt trees.

When a tar archive is created, the leading slash (/) will normally be removed from each filename. This means that when the files are restored, they will be restored relative to the working directory in which tar is being run. For example, to restore files from the tape in /dev/st0 to their original location, the command is

```
cd /; tar -xpf /dev/st0
```

During extract (restore) operations, additional paths can be specified. These paths then represent the limited list of files that are to be extracted. Wildcards are permitted. To restore only the /usr/X11R6 and /usr/local trees to their original location from the tape in /dev/st0, use

```
cd /; tar -xpf /dev/st0 'usr/X11R6/*' 'usr/local/*'
```

To restore the data stored on the SCSI magneto-optical drive at /dev/sdc relative to the /usr/local tree on the local machine, preserving all permissions and ownership and displaying the names of files as they are restored, use

```
cd /usr/local; tar -xpvf /dev/sdc
```

You can use the tee command to display the list of processed files to the terminal while at the same time writing the list to a file:

```
cd /; tar -xpvf /dev/sdc | tee /var/log/restored.files
```

Additional information on using tar for more complex operations, including multivolume or incremental backup and restore, can be found in tar(1).

There's a reason the z option for tar hasn't been mentioned here. While it's true that, for example, tar -cz will create a compressed tar archive, the compression of the tar command is stream based.

This means that if you are storing to magnetic tape, which is often affected by high error rates, and an unrecoverable bit error isencountered, you will not lose only that file. You'll lose the entire tape.

Because of this, use of the z option with tar is recommended only for low-error media such as magneto-optical. Note that this problem is not related to tape drives that employ hardware-based compression, thereby making software compression unnecessary.

Simple Backup and Restore with `afio`

The `afio` command is a similarly simple alternative to `tar` that is favored by some users for one of two main reasons. First, `afio` archives can be made interoperable with systems that support the `cpio` command. Second, `afio` supports per-file compression, making it much more suitable for making compressed backups to magnetic tapes that don't employ their own hardware-based compression.

23

> Your distribution may not ship with an `afio` package. If so, you can get the `afio` source code in the classic Metalab Linux archive at `ftp://metalab.unc.edu/pub/Linux/system/backup`.

Because `afio` accepts the list of files to archive as a standard input stream, the basic syntax for using `afio` as an archive tool involves two commands:

```
find path1 path2 ... [-opts] | afio -[i|o|t] [-vZ] device
```

The `-i` command restores (inputs from) a tape or archive, the `-o` command writes (outputs to) a tape or archive, and the `-t` command tests a tape or archive. The `-v` option causes files to be listed as they are processed, and the `-Z` option causes each file to be compressed with `gzip` before being written to tape.

Since the `find` command is generally used to provide `afio` with its list of files on which to operate, it is possible to construct a much more specific and flexible file-archiving scheme with `afio` by using the special capabilities of `find`.

In the simplest case, however, things remain short and sweet. To write the `/usr` tree to the tape inserted in the drive at `/dev/st0`, use

```
find /usr | afio -o /dev/st0
```

To write the same archive, but compress it before writing each file to tape, use the following:

```
find /usr | afio -o -Z /dev/st0
```

To restore the archive relative to the root (`/`) directory, use the `-i` command instead of the `-o` command:

```
cd /; afio -i /dev/st0
```

To restore an archive that was compressed, remember to include the `-Z` option:

```
cd /; afio -i -Z /dev/st0
```

Verbose operation has the same effect as it did using the `tar` command. To restore the
archive while displaying the list of processed files to the terminal and to a file in
`/var/log`, use

```
afio -i -Z -v /dev/st0 | tee /var/log/restored.files
```

> The method for restricting the list of files to be processed is a little more
> complicated in `afio` than it is in `tar`, so we won't go into it much here.
>
> The `-y` option and an argument in the form of a shell pattern cause files
> matching the supplied pattern to be processed and files not matching the
> pattern to be excluded.
>
> The `-Y` option and an argument in the form of a shell pattern cause files not
> matching the supplied pattern to be processed and files that do match to be
> excluded.

Additional information on using `afio` for more complex operations, including multivolume (multi-tape) support and double-buffering for speed, can be found in the `afio` manual page at `afio(1)`.

Using mt to Operate Tape Devices

While `tar` and `afio` are used for writing to and reading from data storage devices, magnetic tape drives generally require more intervention than simple read or write commands. Functions such as tape loading and unloading, rewind, retensioning, density
configuration, and fast file searching are not supported by `tar` or `afio`.

The `mt` command is used to control tape devices. The basic syntax used in common situations with `mt` is

```
mt -f device operation_command [arguments]
```

A list of the most common operation commands and their arguments is shown in Table 23.1.

TABLE 23.1   Common mt Operation Commands

Command	Description
rewind	Rewinds the tape.
offline	Rewinds and ejects the tape.
status	Shows the current status of the tape drive, including whether or not a tape is present and, if so, the density being used to write to the tape.

TABLE 23.1 continued

Command	Description
retension	On streamer devices (whose tapes require periodic retensioning), causes the tape to be wound completely onto the second reel, then back to the first reel.
erase	Blanks the tape. Note that this is not the same thing as formatting; floppy-interface tapes must be formatted before a successful erasure can take place.
datcompression n	If n is 0, turns compression off for the specified device. If n is 1, turns on compression for the specified device.
fsf n, bsf n	Searches forward or backward n archive files on the tape device.
fsr n, bsr n	Searches forward or backward n records in the current archive file on the tape device.
eod	Positions the tape immediately after the end of the last archive file stored on the tape, so that a new file may be appended to the tape.

Using mt and tar or mt and afio together creates a reasonably complete backup and restore solution for working with magnetic tape devices that can fit on a single floppy or run on memory-limited systems.

More information on using the mt command, including advanced features like density selection, can be found in mt(1).

Using mtx to Operate Changer Devices

Low-end magnetic tape changer devices have dropped radically in price over the last few years and have thus become much more popular on smaller networks. Tape changers have the advantage of flexibility: The multiple tapes in the changer can either be used to hold a great deal more data at one backup cycle or they can be used to implement intervention-free rotating backups.

The command needed for control of tape changer devices in Linux is the mtx command. Note that mtx controls only the robot in the changer device; the read/write mechanism itself is controlled by the mt command. The mtx command can be downloaded from http://mtx.sourceforge.net.

The syntax for mtx is as follows:

```
mtx -f generic-device command [args]
```

generic-device is one of the Linux SCSI generic device nodes: /dev/sg0-sgn on some systems and /dev/sga-sgz on others. Check your own /dev directory and the information in /proc/scsi to determine the /dev/sg device that refers to your changer. Though there are a number of different commands understood by `mtx`, the most important clearly are `load` and `unload`, which are self-explanatory.

To load the tape in slot 2 from the changer pointed to by `/dev/changer` into the drive, use

```
mtx -f /dev/changer load 2
```

The command exits normally if the tape is successfully loaded or with a nonzero exit status on error. To unload the tape back to slot 2, use

```
mtx -f /dev/changer unload 2
```

The `next` and `unload` (no arguments) commands simply load the next tape found in the changer or unload the current tape into the slot from which it came, respectively:

```
mtx -f /dev/changer next
mtx -f /dev/changer unload
```

Other commands understood by the `mtx` command can be found by consulting the `mtx` manual page at `mtx(1)`.

Scheduling, Rotating, and Preserving Backups

It is not enough to write all of the data on your hard drive or on the NFS file systems on your network to tape once and assume your backup problem to be solved.

If you do any kind of real work at all, data on your systems is constantly changing. Furthermore, tape media gradually deteriorate, so it's helpful to have more than one backup around. One set of tapes might be inadequate—if you overwrite your only backup tape each night, what happens if you want to recover a file that was accidentally deleted last Thursday? Finally, what happens if the entire place burns down? Will your tapes be safe, or will they go up in smoke with your systems and hard drives?

Thinking ahead can be more than half the battle when it comes to maintaining useful backups.

Scheduling Backups

Because your data is constantly changing, you should back up often. If your system is hacked and you are forced to restore from tape, you probably won't find a backup tape you made four months ago to be of much help. Even a one-month-old backup can be next to useless, depending on the freshness of the data you work with.

It is therefore important to schedule your backups. This isn't always as difficult as it sounds. There's no need to write a "backup date" in your Palm scheduler so that you can remember to insert a tape and run `tar` once every Thursday. A simple CRON job involving a call to `mt` and a call to `tar` can be more than enough to make your DAT drive work for you.

Consider the following:

```
mt -f /dev/st0 eod; tar -cf /dev/st0 /home
```

This simple command spaces to the end of existing data and writes a new `tar` archive to the tape using the contents of the `/home` directory. Assuming your DAT drive holds 12 gigabytes uncompressed and your `/home` tree is about 2 gigabytes, you could use this command as a weekly CRON job and have to switch tapes only every month or so.

If you need nightly backups and can enable DAT compression, you may find that you can replace the tape once every Monday morning, automatically keeping a week's worth of backups going all the time.

Rotating Backups

Under ideal circumstances, when your month (or your week) of scheduled backups is up, you will simply eject the tape, label it with the week (or month) it contains, and file it away safely, never to be written to again. It will then always be on file should you need data it contains.

If you absolutely must reuse tape media, don't use the same tape over and over again. Keep at least three or four media units on hand; that way, on Monday morning you won't eliminate your only existing backups when you begin writing to the start of the tape again.

When you're finished with the first tape at the end of the week, insert tape two. At the end of that week, insert tape three. Only after the third week do you reinsert the first tape again. That way, you'll always have yesterday's backup and last Friday's backup available as well.

Tape changers can be especially useful in this regard. For example, assume for a moment that you are using a six-tape changer and that you can afford to fill all six slots with media. Consider the extremely simple script shown in Listing 23.1, which takes advantage of the `date` command and the built-in math capabilities of `bash`.

LISTING 23.1 Simple Rotating Changer Script

```
#!/bin/bash

# This line sets the SLOT variable to contain the remainder
# of the current week number (0-52) of the year divided by
# the number of slots in the changer (6).
SLOT=$[$(date +%U)%6]

# This line makes sure that no tape is already loaded
mtx -f /dev/changer unload

# This line loads the correct tape for this week
```

LISTING 23.1   continued

```
mtx -f /dev/changer load $SLOT

# This line searches to the end of data
mt -f /dev/st0 eod

# And this line writes the /home tree to tape
tar -cf /dev/st0 /home
```

A script like the one in Listing 23.1 can automatically rotate the tapes in your changer on a weekly basis, meaning that you can have rotating scheduled backups indefinitely without any intervention at all.

Of course, in your own scripts, you'll want to include some error condition checking, archive verification, and so forth—but the possibilities are clear.

Backups at Multiple Locations

What about that fire we mentioned, or a malicious intruder who gains access to your server's tape changer, in which all of your rotated backups are sitting? Now we're getting into escalating costs, but it's still possible for many small businesses.

At the very least, buy a fire- and waterproof safe and put your rotated tapes into it for safekeeping. Though they still won't necessarily make it through a calamity, their chances will be greatly improved, and they will be under lock and key as well.

Even better, however, is to make multiple simultaneous or near-simultaneous backups in multiple locations. If you can afford to do so and have the equipment to do so, buy two streamers or two changers. Keep one in the office and one in the other office or, if you can afford a reasonably fast pipe, at home. In your scripts or CRON jobs, run the backup twice—once to the local drive and once to an identical or similar drive on a remote machine. Your data is now reasonably well protected against catastrophic loss.

For those who can afford not to be do-it-yourself backup artists, commercial network backup services exist that allow you to store your data safely under lock and key in fire-proof, guarded installations with lots of insurance protection.

Proprietary Backup Software

Though the combination of tar/mt/mtx or afio/mt/mtx will work well for many users, some users simply aren't comfortable with command-line tools, and still others require more sophistication and network-readiness than tar or afio can provide. Because of these needs, two very popular commercial Linux backup solutions should be mentioned here.

Backup and Restore Utility (BRU)

The BRU application is perhaps the most popular GUI-based backup and recovery utility available for Linux. It is shipping or has shipped as a standard part of several retail Linux distributions.

BRU supports backup of live file systems and a number of different types of network file systems, as well as per-user backups and restores even in NIS-enabled environments. BRU also supports crash recovery features designed to help bring a system back online from catastrophic data loss as quickly as is possible. BRU archives are portable across a wide range of BRU-supported platforms, including Windows NT.

More information about BRU can be found at `http://www.estinc.com`.

23

Arkeia

Arkeia is perhaps the most celebrated of Linux backup solutions, and with good reason— it's designed to handle the backup needs of the largest of networks.

With extensive multiplatform, multiprotocol, and robustness features, Arkeia is the first choice for many Linux users. Arkeia sports a flexible, smart implementation, including sophisticated network monitoring and choice of client-side or server-side compression to preserve resources of all kinds optimally.

Perhaps more interestingly, a full license to use Arkeia on a small network (one Linux server and two clients) is free. More information on Arkeia can be found at `http://www.knox-software.com`.

Summary

This hour you learned about the importance of maintaining multiple current backups in as secure an environment as is possible, in order to be able to recover more fully from malicious attacks of all kinds.

To help you to achieve this goal, you have learned the basics of using your choice of `tar` or `afio` in conjunction with `mt` and `mtx` (for magnetic tape devices) to maintain backups, including scheduled, rotating backups using CRON jobs.

Finally, you learned briefly about two popular Linux backup solutions for those who are uncomfortable using command-line tools like `afio`, `tar`, `mtx`, and `mt` or for those who find the standard tools lacking in some fashion.

Q&A

Q Is there a way to support the advanced random access and fast search features of my DAT drive?

A A variety of tools for KDE, GNOME, and the command line exist for DAT devices—too many to list here. Unfortunately, there is no *de facto* standard or even common favorite among these software packages; they all have their strengths and weaknesses.

To find some of them, visit a Linux application site such as `http://linuxapps.com` or `http://freshmeat.net` and search for the strings `dds` and `dat`.

Q Can I back up to a raw Zip disk?

What device do I use to back up to a raw MO disk?

Can I back up to a file?

A Writing using `tar` or `afio` to raw devices like unpartitioned Zip disks or MO disks is simple; use the device name for the drive in question. For example, if your IDE Zip drive is `/dev/hdc`, insert a disk and tell `tar` or `afio` to write to `/dev/hdc` instead of a tape device like `/dev/st0`.

To write to a file, just provide a file instead of a device. For example, consider the following:

```
tar -cf /mnt/net/home.tar /home
```

This command would back up the `/home` tree on the local system to the file `/mnt/net/home.tar`. The restore operation would be identical—just supply the name of the `tar` or `afio` file instead of a device node.

Q What is the best media for long-term archiving?

A The best media for long-term data storage is optical media like CD-R, CD-RW, DVD-R, or magneto-optical. CD and DVD formats have an especially long life—some types of CD and DVD media boast a 300-year data life expectancy. However, since the CD and DVD formats generally do not support random writes or variable-speed streaming, they are unsuitable for use as general-purpose backup devices. Magneto-optical (MO), on the other hand, can be used with `afio`, `tar`, and other backup software just as you would use any other removable storage device. Though data life expectancy on MO disks is somewhat shorter (on the order of 50 years), it is significantly longer than the data life expectancy of magnetic media.

Magnetic media such as DAT tapes or Zip and Jaz disks, while very popular, are among the worst for long-term storage. Magnetic media have an expected data life of 2–5 years. In a sense, many traditional paper documents have a better life expectancy. Be sure to account for this when designing your backup and data preservation procedures.

New Terms

back door   A secret vulnerability put in place by an intruder who has compromised your system. This vulnerability can then be used in the future to gain access to your system again.

root kit   In a sense, a root kit is like a complicated back door. It is a series of files put in place by an intruder for devious ends, often in such a way as to disguise the changes that have occurred.

rotating backup   Scheduled backups occurring not only on a single tape but on a series of tapes in rotation.

scheduled backup   A periodic backup run by CRON or some other periodic execution daemon.

23

Hour 24

Recovering from Attacks

In the final hour of this book, you'll learn what to do if in spite of your best efforts you find that your system has been violated. You'll learn the steps to take to protect yourself and your network against further harm, and how to get back online quickly, safely, and without risk of further mischief from the same intruder.

The Telltale Signs

Three tools have been covered in this book that provide your best notification mechanism for illicit activity on your system or network:

- SAINT, when run as a weekly audit, is able to detect the telltale signs left over from many kinds of attacks and point you to the files that have likely been compromised under such circumstances.

- SWATCH monitors your logs and can report suspicious activity to you. By paying attention to your logs using SWATCH and checking out each notification or warning it gives you, you'll know when something is about to happen or already has.

- Snort monitors for a large variety of attacks, back doors, and distributed denial-of-service evidence and records an alert for all such activity. When a Snort alarm goes off that you are unable to discount, you'll often find that you have been the victim of an attack.

In addition, there are a few telltale signs that you may have been compromised in some way. You should watch for these carefully:

- The sudden presence of a new account that you didn't create in the /etc/passwd file. If you find one of these, your system has been compromised.
- The failure or odd behavior of system binaries that are normally nearly invisible. For example, if you are suddenly unable to log in to your system from a console, or your system logs suddenly go silent, there is a good chance that a root kit has been installed on your machine. Check the integrity of the related binaries (such as login or syslogd) against known good binaries on another system, and run SAINT to see if it discovers anything.
- Lots of unexplained network traffic is also good evidence that all is not well. Sometimes it is even more obvious than simply "lots of traffic." If a call to netstat reports lots of open connections to a system you're not familiar with on rarely used and high-numbered ports, you've likely been compromised. This is especially true if these connections are "magically" opened again without your help every time you reboot.

In general, anything unusual and unexplainable should cause you to take a closer look. Examples include heavy CPU load that can't be accounted for, files or directories that can't be read even by root, or the failure of your system to ask for a password when you log in at a console.

Be vigilant!

Worst-Case Scenario

This is it. You saw some weird behavior in your system and checked it out, or you got an alert from Snort or SWATCH. Your system has been compromised.

What now?

Pull Offline Immediately

The first order of business is to get the system disconnected from the network. Any user malicious enough to break into your system is not likely to stop and follow the law immediately afterward. Chances are that he is proceeding with additional illegal behavior, most likely against other systems, and your system may be one hop in his path, potentially implicating you in his crimes. There is no time to waste.

Unplug the network cable. If you are unable to do this safely for some reason for a single host in your network, disconnect your network from the firewall/router unit so that the outside world is no longer a threat.

Disentangle the machines as quickly as possible and isolate the compromised machines from the others. There isn't a long history of viruses or worm-like attacks with Linux, but it isn't out of the question by any means, so you'll need to try to quickly break the link between the compromised system and other systems on your internal network.

When administering large networks with large amounts of resources, there may be time for romantic ideas like stealthily watching a criminal in your logs and gathering information until you suddenly spring on him with law enforcement at your back. However, this is the real world, and most mom-and-pop operations with one to five machines or even a few more just can't afford to waste time. Better to get things moving along toward recovery; you won't catch this guy single-handedly.

Stop Linux

Because malicious software installed by crackers can do some very nasty things, you don't want to leave this system running while you try to analyze what went wrong. You could lose data or hardware (yes, even *hardware*) in the process as destructive programs dance through your drive space or your system's various flash ROM units.

Become `root` using the `su` command, if possible, and issue the reboot command:

```
shutdown -r now
```

If you are unable to use the `root` account for some reason (for example, the `su` binary and `login` binary have both been compromised to lock out legitimate `root` use) and you have Magic SysRq key functionality installed in your kernel, do an emergency sync.

Whether you can emergency sync or not, if you are unable to shut down legitimately, use the reset button immediately.

> The Magic SysRq key is really a series of special keystrokes that instruct the Linux kernel to perform specific tasks if a system has become unstable.
>
> The SysRq key can be enabled with a compile-time kernel option (the last option in the kernel configuration process) or by writing 1 to the `/proc/sys/kernel/sysrq` file as the superuser:
>
> ```
> echo 1 >/proc/sys/kernel/sysrq
> ```

> If you suspect your system has been violated and your SysRq key is enabled, use the Alt+SysRq+U keystroke combination to remount all file systems as read-only and then use the Alt+SysRq+S keystroke combination to sync all file systems. It may be a good idea to repeat these keystrokes several times, waiting a second each time, to ensure that they take effect.
>
> Once you have remounted your file systems as read-only and performed an emergency sync, you can safely hit the reset button on the front of your case.

Boot Cautiously

Enter the BIOS setup utility for both your motherboard and any additional controllers you have in your system in the process of restarting. Ensure that all of the settings still look correct and that nothing is out of place before you attempt to continue booting. If something seems to have been changed, change it back. If you notice anything really suspicious, it may be to your benefit to power down the system entirely and move the hard drive to a secondary role on another machine so that you can get to the data there instead.

If you can get a `LILO:` prompt, boot into single-user mode by supplying the word **single** as an argument to the Linux kernel on the command line:

```
linux single
```

If you are unable to get to a `LILO:` prompt (meaning that either your boot sector or your BIOS has been modified past the point of recovery), get a rescue floppy of some kind. One set of convenient and relatively complete floppies can be found with the Slackware Linux distribution at `http://www.slackware.com`.

The goal is to get the data on your hard drive(s) mounted in the safest way possible, either in the single-user read-only context or read-only on a file system tree other than `root` on a separate system.

Archive What's Left

Before attempting to discover what went wrong, who hacked in and how, or any other details, it's important that you preserve what exists at the moment you took the system down. This has several functions:

- It ensures that no matter what happens during discovery and restoration, you will be able to get to data files (databases, word processing files, e-mail, spreadsheets, and so on) that aren't damaged by restoring them from a backup medium.

- In cases in which the system must be brought online again as soon as possible, it provides some way for you to inspect the files that were on the system and try to determine where and how the attack happened.

- It covers you legally, at least to some extent. Law enforcement hasn't quite caught up to the digital age yet in all respects; you might be able to get your local police department or the FBI to file a report on the crime, but you'd better not hold your breath. Having a backup of a compromised system is proof that your system was attacked and is some measure of defense if the cracker used your system in some kind of illegal activity when he was in.

If possible, make two copies of the system, one as a backup or in case it is subpoenaed at some future date as evidence. Label them clearly and lock them away in a safe.

Understanding What Happened

In spite of the cracker's success in compromising the system, you'll often find that it's relatively easy to determine what went wrong. The vast majority of the crackers loose on the Internet today are script kiddies, relatively unsophisticated crackers who use scripts or vulnerabilities developed by others to break into networked computer systems matching certain predefined criteria.

Script kiddies are successful far too often but, more often than not, they also leave behind a number of telltale footprints. If you know what you are looking for, it can often be a simple task to find them.

By far the most common types of attack against Linux systems are buffer overflow attacks against various daemons or network services. These are usually easy to spot because one of the most recent log entries or SWATCH alerts will read as an error message from the daemon in question, often filling the log with garbage as well.

Physically connect the root drive as a second drive to another system, if possible, and do a search using find for files or directories (especially binaries) that have been recently modified. Often, these will be hidden or disguised with correct dates and modification times, but a good percentage of the time they will not.

If your system has package management, restore the package management databases from a backup made before the compromise took place, along with the package manager itself. For example, many systems store the rpm database in /var/lib/rpm. Restore these from your backup, along with the rpm program. Then, verify all packages:

```
rpm -Va
```

Note the differences. There shouldn't be many, and any differences to critical system binaries like login, ls, and so on will at least let you know which files were compromised by the attack.

The primary reason to want to understand what happened is so that you can fix it next time. If the log shows that the user got in through named, check your DNS configuration next time. Make it more paranoid, and check for a package update with a later version of BIND from your distribution maintainer. Once you understand that a particular aspect of the system is vulnerable, you'll be less vulnerable to the same attack again.

Notify the Authorities

In this case, the authorities means other Internet users, rather than law enforcement. Specifically, it means trying to determine the source of the attack using your logs and login information. A host number or network number is what you're looking for, something to identify which machine was connected to your machine at the time the attack took place.

Remember that the system on the other end may not necessarily be some dark criminal organization. It may simply be that the system from which the cracker entered yours was a system that he had previously cracked. The administrators of the other system may not even be aware that it has been compromised.

If you can get an IP address from your logs or SWATCH alerts, the first step is to notify the host directly. For example, if the attack came from 24.13.131.162, send mail to root@24.13.131.162 and carbon copy abuse@24.13.131.162, describing what happened and informing the administrator that the attack came from his host.

This alone doesn't guarantee that your message will reach human eyes, however. The host may be a dynamic address in an ISP dialup pool or a Windows host. Try to get information about who the host is from the IP address you collected. The simplest way to do this is with nslookup, which should be installed by default on most Linux systems or sometimes can be installed as part of the DNS package.

```
$ nslookup 24.13.131.162
Server: newton.mynet.net
Address: 192.168.1.100

Name:   c1333337-a.saltlk1.ut.home.com
Address: 24.13.131.162
$
```

Judging by the hostname associated with this IP address, it is indeed a line at an ISP whose domain is home.com. Now that you have the provider of the IP address from which the attack came, notify them at the abuse address (in this case, abuse@home.com) that your system was compromised and that the attack came from a host within their domain. Be sure to include the IP number of the attack source and the exact date and time of the attack.

If you are unable to get a response, it is time to call /usr/sbin/traceroute, supplying the guilty IP number as an argument (in this case, 24.13.131.162). A list of hops will be printed out, many of them with domain names. At the bottom of your list is the IP address in question. Move up the list one line at a time, mailing to abuse@ for each domain until someone says that he will look into the abuse or until you reach your own domain. Include a copy of the traceroute output and the exact date and time of the attack with each message.

In all likelihood, the cracker involved will get booted from his current ISP and simply move to another one, free to crack another day. However, at least you've caused the cracker some inconvenience. On the other hand, you may actually help to catch a major criminal instead of a mere script kiddie. At the very least, you will be helping to protect others upstream of the cracker's IP from legal trouble.

Getting Back Online

Once you've determined where your system's weakness was (if possible), made a full backup copy of the compromised system for archival purposes, and contacted the authorities about the abuse (if possible), you're ready to begin working toward bringing the system back online again.

Reformat and Reinstall

It's inconvenient to reformat and reinstall, but it's necessary to ensure that no compromised binaries remain on your system. If possible, it may even be best to do a low-level or controller-run format of the drive, to eliminate any shenanigans that may have gone on with the drive's boot sector or partition table. Don't think of it as a lost system, think of it as a chance to upgrade your operating system or clean out all of those old scattered files that have been laying around for two or three years.

Once the drive has been blanked and repartitioned for use, install Linux from a canonical source, such as your original CD. If you have an archive of additions and modifications, such as a /usr/local/src archive on MO disk, reinstall those cleanly as well.

Restore Important Data

Now you can go about restoring your important data. If possible, restore from a tape or backup media that was written before the compromise took place. If you must, retrieve only user data files from the most recent tape made of the compromised system.

If you need to reinstall binaries and configuration files as well, do so from the early backup, not the archival backup of the compromised system, and avoid overwriting any existing binaries from your fresh installation. Both `tar` and `afio` support modes of operation that will refuse to overwrite existing files; most other backup software programs have similar modes of functionality.

After you have restored the files you intend to restore, thoroughly inspect your `/etc/passwd`, `/etc/shadow`, `/etc/group`, and security-oriented configuration files to ensure that they were not tampered with earlier than you realized.

Require all users, including `root`, to change their passwords. Consider issuing new account names as well, if you are able.

Take Care of the Vulnerability

Before bringing the system back online for full operation, be sure to repair the vulnerability that caused your headaches in the first place!

The first place to check is with your distribution vendor. See if updated libraries, kernels, daemons, or other packages are available that have fixed the weakness exploited by the malicious individual who attacked your system. For an even better solution, simply download the entire updates tree if possible and install it. Each of the updates is there for a reason.

If no package can be found that seems to repair the vulnerability you encountered, report it to your distribution vendor through official channels and go in search of an unpackaged version of the compromised piece of code. For example, if the attacker entered your system through BIND, and there are no BIND updates from your vendor, go to the home page of the BIND daemon and see if there is a new release version that fixes the weakness the attacker exploited but that your vendor hasn't yet packaged.

If you can find no way to fix the problem, it may be time to consider disabling the service altogether. Ask yourself: Is the service really important? Is it absolutely essential to the functioning of my network? If the answer is no, switch it off and do without.

If you can't find a fix and you can't afford to switch it off, there is only one other way to deal with the problem: Isolate the service on its own machine. Do almost nothing else on that machine and store as little account and network data as is possible on the machine until the problem can be fixed and the weakness eliminated.

 If nobody appears to be aware that there is a vulnerability in a software package that as far as you can tell has been exploited in your case, be sure to submit a report of exactly what happened, along with the related log information, to the programmers responsible for the piece of code involved.

Nearly all Linux components are free software maintained by open source developers who depend on problem reports from real-world users to keep the software functioning and safe. They'll be happy to hear from you, and you may get the problem fixed more quickly than it otherwise would have been.

Pay Special Attention to Repeat Visitors

Before taking the system back online again, there is one last step you may want to take: snoop a little more on the port of entry involved in the attack. Though many script kiddies will never return, some will, and you may be able to get additional information on them a second time. For example, you might get an IP number you weren't able to get the first time, which will help you put an end to their activities.

Configure TCP wrappers or Snort with some very strict logging rules. In the case of TCP wrappers, you may even want to consider booby trapping the port or service involved so that attempts from certain hosts or networks result in identification attempts on your part. More information on these types of tactics and techniques can be found in the `snort(1)` and `hosts.deny(5)` manual pages.

Go Back Online

Once everything is in place again, it's time to take the system back online. Be sure that all of the security tools are in place, if applicable, and consider making a backup of this clean system as a final step, in case there are any unforeseen problems (damaged disk flash BIOS memory, for instance) that force you to start yet again.

Try to play the optimist. You may have been compromised, but you have also gained valuable experience. In addition, by contacting the violator's provider and the software developers involved, you've helped out others who may have been subject to the same attack.

Summary

This hour, you studied a basic roadmap that you need to follow if you find that a system under your administration has been violated:

- Pull the system offline immediately so that no further damage can occur and any criminal activity your system may be involved with is stopped.
- Reboot Linux into single-user mode. Even with the network down, bad things can still be running and happening. Put and end to them and get the machine restarted.

- Make an archival copy (two if possible) of the compromised system so that you will have information and evidence in the future if the need should arise for such things.

- Study the logs and anything else in the system that may be relevant so that you can find out what went wrong and who carried out the attack.

- If you can get an IP address, or even better a hostname, use it to contact the perpetrator's ISP or even his ISP's upstream providers to report the abuse. It's not just about you, it's about helping others who may have been violated as well.

- Reformat to make the hard drive pristine if possible and reinstall Linux from a canonical source. Reinstall any pristine source archives you've maintained on separate media as well.

- Cautiously restore recent data and configuration files from tapes. Avoid restoring binaries of any kind. Inspect restored account data and configuration files closely.

- Require all users, including `root`, to change passwords. Consider changing account names as well.

- Take care of the vulnerability by obtaining and installing the necessary updates. If they don't seem to exist, report the exploit to your distribution vendor and to the developers of the software in which the hole was found.

- Consider extra security measures or extra logging on the related ports or services.

- Take the system back online, making a full backup first if you are able so that you will have a pristine starting point on media once again, just in case.

Of course, these steps are just a guideline; each case and each small network is different. Most of all, don't get discouraged or let things slide.

Hopefully, the previous 23 hours of this book will help you to avoid this situation altogether. Unfortunately, security is an ongoing battle between the good guys and the bad guys that isn't likely to end soon. Always secure your system to the best of your ability, follow the steps in this hour if your preparation should prove to be inadequate, but most of all remember to stay vigilant!

Q&A

Q **My system was root-kitted and now the drive's file system isn't working properly; I can't get access to data or back up the drive.**

A Hook the drive up to a separate host and mount it somewhere other than as the `root` file system. In most cases, this will allow you to access the file system correctly with tools like `ls`, `cp`, and so on.

There may be cases, however (such as when malicious programs have been run or Trojans introduced), in which data is simply not recoverable through means available to the average home user or small business owner.

Q I got the IP address of the intruder, found his domain, and reported him to his ISP. They didn't care. So I reported to the upstream provider. They didn't seem to care either. What can I do if nobody cares?

A Unfortunately, there are some large providers out there who are notoriously nonchalant about what their users may or may not be doing, whether it is illegal, harmful, or just ethically troubling. Some of them receive thousands of complaints a year, but commerce is commerce and there isn't much that can be done if the powers that be aren't interested in hearing about abuse cases.

One drastic move that you can make is to use packet filtering like `iptables` or `ipchains` to simply block all network traffic of all kinds from the IP ranges or domains responsible.

Understand, however, that if you are running a public service on your machine, such as a Web server or an anonymous FTP server, such drastic measures could prevent hundreds or even thousands of legitimate users from taking advantage of your services.

There's often no point in blocking the single IP where the attack came from, since a large percentage of attacks come from rotating dynamic IP addresses in ISP pools.

Q I got compromised, but my network isn't behind a firewall or anything of that sort. Would a dedicated firewall help to prevent such occurrences in the future?

A Yes!

There is no better security investment that you can make, especially if you are a small network. Consider purchasing a dedicated firewall immediately. If you can't afford one but have a PC laying around, you can construct one with Linux and packet filtering, or you can download a system like Freesco, which can be found at `http://www.freesco.org`, that will transform the PC into a reasonably robust firewall/router for you.

New Terms

abuse An e-mail box that exists on most domains that provide Net access or service of any kind to others. The `abuse` box is where reports of spamming, hacking, cracking, and general nastiness should go.

traceroute   A utility that shows the network path between your host and another host in a series of machine-to-machine "hops," including all of the upstream providers met along the way.

upstream provider   The service provider one step up from any given machine. Even most ISPs have service providers. Often, even if nobody is interested in hearing abuse reports on a given host or at a given network, the upstream provider will be.

PART V

Appendixes

APPENDIX **A**

Configuration Files Important to Security

Tables A.1 through A.7 list the standard security-oriented configuration files that have been covered over the course of this text.

TABLE A.1   Files Related to Booting

File Location	Description, Contents, Uses
/etc/lilo.conf	LILO boot sector configuration; controls access to boot images, including password protection. Documented in lilo.conf(5).
/etc/inittab	Master control for the init daemon and therefore the boot process. Default runlevel and open consoles are configured here. Documented in inittab(5).
/etc/rc.d/init.d/*	Start/stop/restart scripts for most of the services available on Linux systems.
/etc/rc.d/rcN.d/*	Symbolic links to cause a subgroup of start/stop/restart scripts to be called for runlevel N.

TABLE A.1   continued

File Location	Description, Contents, Uses
/etc/rc.d/rc.local	Init script where local additions to the boot process normally are made.
/etc/fstab	Controls mounting of file systems at boot time and afterward. Flags set in /etc/fstab can prevent write access, SUID execution, execution of any kind, and mount/umounting of entire file systems. Documented in fstab(5).

TABLE A.2   Files Related to Accounts and Login

Filename	Description, Contents, Uses
/etc/securetty	List of terminal devices that allow root logins. Documented in securetty(5).
/etc/shells	Lists login shells available to normal users. Documented in shells(5).
/etc/passwd	User accounts (sans passwords) are stored here. Not normally edited by hand. Documented in passwd(5).
/etc/shadow	Passwords matching the account entries in /etc/passwd are stored here. Documented in shadow(5).
/etc/group	Group accounts and membership are stored here. Documented in group(5).

TABLE A.3   Files Related to TCP/IP

Filename	Description, Contents, Uses
/etc/services	Contains bindings between human-readable protocol names and the ports on which the protocols are used. Documented in services(5).
/etc/inetd.conf	Configuration for the Internet daemon, inetd, containing bindings between a protocol name from /etc/services and a matching service daemon. Documented in inetd(8).
/etc/hosts.allow	List of hosts and protocols that are to be allowed by the TCP wrappers support. Documented in hosts_access(5).
/etc/hosts.deny	List of hosts and protocols that are not to be allowed by the TCP wrappers support. Documented in hosts_access(5).

TABLE A.4   Files Related to Services and Daemons

Filename	Description, Contents, Uses
/etc/syslog.conf	File that determines the behavior of the system logger, which handles logs for a variety of services and daemons. Documented in syslog.conf(5).
httpd.conf	The main Apache configuration file, containing nearly all aspects of operation related to Apache.

TABLE A.4 continued

Filename	Description, Contents, Uses
.htaccess	Special file containing additional Apache access control information for the files in the directory in which it appears.
/etc/ftpaccess	Configuration file for the FTP daemon, including aspects such as logging and traffic control. Documented in ftpaccess(5).
/etc/ftpusers	The list of users who are *not* allowed to log in to FTP. Documented in ftpd(8).
/etc/sendmail.cf	Complex control file for the Sendmail SMTP daemon, usually generated not by humans but by the M4 macroprocessor, using one of a few predeveloped input files.
/etc/named.conf	The primary configuration file for the BIND DNS server, version 8. Defines all zones and operation options and gives the paths to supporting files. Documented in named.conf(5).
/etc/exports	List of the file systems that are to be made available via NFS, the hosts to which they will be made available, and the permissions that will be granted upon mounting. Documented in exports(5).

TABLE A.5 Files Related to X11R6

Filename	Description, Contents, Uses
/etc/X*n*.hosts	List of hosts that will be granted permission to place X11R6 clients on the local display, where *n* is the number of the display related to a given file. Documented in Xserver(1).
$HOME/.Xauthority	Storage file for an X11R6 display's magic cookie, used for token-based (per user) rather than host-based authentication.

TABLE A.6 Files Related to SSH

Filename	Description, Contents, Uses
/etc/ssh2/sshd2_config	Configuration file for the SSH2 daemon used for incoming Secure Shell connections. Documented in sshd2_config(5).
/etc/ssh2/ssh2_config	Configuration file for the SSH2 client used for outbound Secure Shell connections. Documented in ssh2_config(5).
/usr/local/etc/sshd_config	Configuration file for the OpenSSH daemon used for incoming Secure Shell connections. Documented in sshd(8).
/usr/local/etc/ssh_config	Configuration file for the OpenSSH client used for incoming Secure Shell connections. Documented in ssh(1).

A

TABLE A.7   Files Related to Authentication Services

Filename	Description, Contents, Uses
`/etc/pam.d/*`	PAM authentication configuration for supported services, one file per service.
`/etc/pam.conf`	PAM authentication configuration, old format (made obsolete by `/etc/pam.d/*`). Documented in `pam(8)`.
`krb5.conf`	Configuration file for all hosts on which Kerberos will run. Defines default realm, included domains, and ticket properties. By convention located either in the `/etc` directory or in the `etc/` subtree of the Kerberos install tree. Documented in `krb5.conf(5)`.
`kdc.conf`	Configuration file for the Kerberos key distribution center (KDC). Defines additional properties of the key distribution center, including location of KDC support files. By convention located either in the `/etc` directory or in the `etc/` subtree of the Kerberos install tree. Documented in `kdc.conf(5)`.
`kadm5.acl`	Access control list for Kerberos key distribution center database administrators. By convention located in the `var/krb5kdc/` subtree of the Kerberos install tree. Documented in `kadmind(8)`.

APPENDIX B

System Account File Formats

Tables B.1 through B.3 describe the formats of the /etc/passwd, /etc/shadow, and /etc/group files.

TABLE B.1 Fields in /etc/passwd

Field Number	Description
1	Name of the account that the user will use to log in to the system, all lowercase. Also known as the user's login.
2	Lowercase letter x on systems with shadow passwords installed; encrypted password on systems without shadow passwords installed.
3	The numeric user ID of this account, typically in either the 500 or 1000 range for normal users, though convention varies.
4	The numeric group ID referring to the user's primary group membership. On systems without user-private groups, usually a number referring to the group users. On systems with user-private groups, this number generally matches the numeric user ID and refers to a private group.

TABLE B.1 continued

Field Number	Description
5	Comment or information about the user. By convention, contains the user's full human-readable name.
6	Path to the user's home directory and files, usually a subdirectory of /home on Linux systems.
7	The user's login shell. By default on Linux systems, /bin/bash is used, but it can be changed by the user to any shell listed in /etc/shells.

TABLE B.2 Fields in /etc/shadow

Field Number	Description
1	Name of the account that the user will use to log in to the system, all lower-case. Also known as the user's login.
2	User's encrypted password.
3	The number of days since epoch (January 1, 1970) that had passed when the user last changed his password.
4	The number of days that must pass before the password can be changed again.
5	The number of days before the user's current password expires and a new password must be selected.
6	The number of days in advance to warn a user about an expiring password.
7	The number of days to wait after a password has expired before disabling a user account if no new password is provided.
8	The number of days since epoch that have passed on the day the user's account becomes disabled.
9	Reserved (if present).

TABLE B.3 Fields in /etc/group

Field Number	Description
1	The name of the group to which this line refers. If the system supports user-private groups, many of these names will match names in the /etc/passwd file.
2	The encrypted group password. If no data is present in this field, no users will be allowed to use newgrp to join the group. No password will be required of explicitly named group members.
3	The numeric ID of this group. If the system supports user-private groups, many of these ID numbers will match ID numbers in the /etc/passwd file.
4	A list of all the users who can be considered members of this group. Account names in the list are separated by commas.

APPENDIX C

Security Web Sites of Note

There are a number of security-oriented Web sites that should be of note to Linux users interested in pursuing system security diligently. A list of those sites follows.

General Security

Computer Emergency Response Team—
`http://www.cert.org`

Originally hosted by DARPA, CERT is now at Carnegie Mellon University's software engineering department and tracks the latest vulnerabilities and exploits on multiple operating systems.

CERT also hosts a wealth of security-related information, links to security tools, and research and white papers related to security topics.

Computer Incident Advisory Capability—
`http://www.ciac.org`

This site, hosted at the U.S Department of Energy, posts monthly reports on the most recently discovered exploits for multiple operating systems, including Linux. Also at the site are links to various tools and other security-oriented U.S. government sites.

The Cypherpunks Home Page—`ftp://ftp.csua.`
`berkeley.edu/pub/cypherpunks/Home.html`

This site at the University of California, Berkeley, is the quintessential export-restricted home page, containing large doses of papers, research, and tutorial information about cryptography. To cap it all off, there is a rather extensive FTP archive full of cryptography-related Linux/UNIX software and a list of other FTP sites containing cryptographic tools.

SecurityFocus.com—`http://www.securityfocus.com`

SecurityFocus.com tracks vulnerabilities across a number of operating systems, almost in real time, it sometimes seems. In addition to the latest vulnerability reports, SecurityFocus.com contains articles, tutorials, and links to security-related software, organized by operating system.

Linux-Specific Security

The Debian GNU/Linux Security Site—`http://`
`security.debian.org`

This site is extensive and up to date, promising to rectify any discovered vulnerability with 48 hours of it being reported.

Red Hat Linux Errata Page—
`http://www.redhat.com/support/errata/`

Security advisories for the latest version of Red Hat Linux are always available from the Red Hat Linux errata page, which falls under the Red Hat support department.

Caldera Systems—
`http://www.calderasystems.com/support/security/`

Caldera Systems' security page contains advisories by year and product, including the latest eDesktop and eServer platforms and related products.

Linux-Mandrake—`http://www.linux-mandrake.com/en/security/`

This URL leads to the security advisories archive for various versions of Linux-Mandrake (more commonly known as Mandrake Linux).

SuSE Linux—`http://www.suse.com/us/support/security/`

This page contains the latest security announcements and advisories for the users of SuSE Linux. Links to SuSE security mailing lists can also be found here.

TurboLinux—`http://www.turbolinux.com/security/`

All of the most recent security updates for users of the TurboLinux distribution can be found on this page, which is formatted for quick package downloads.

LinuxPPC—`http://linuxppc.org/security/advisories/`

Users of LinuxPPC for PowerPC-based machines such as the Power Macintosh G3 and G4 systems will find security advisories for the latest LinuxPPC distribution here.

C

APPENDIX D

Quick Security Checklist

This security checklist quickly goes over the major points covered in each of the hour lessons in this book. Not every hour will apply to every need, depending on the role of the machine in question. However, a concise checklist like this makes it much easier to see many of the security concerns in one place.

Hour 1: Selecting and Installing a Linux Distribution

1.__ The role of the machine in question has been clearly defined and an appropriate Linux distribution has been chosen.

2.__ The distribution has been obtained from a canonical source.

3.__ The file system tree has been split across multiple partitions to isolate security risks, and the root file system has been made read-only–capable.

4.__ All current security updates from the distribution vendor have been downloaded and installed.

Hour 2: BIOS and Motherboards

5.__ A BIOS password has been installed.

6.__ Boot order has been changed to first hard drive only.

Hour 3: Physical Security

7.__ The system has been installed in a location that limits physical access to the greatest degree possible.

8.__ The power switch has been set to permanently on and the reset switch has been disabled.

9.__ The system has been physically secured (locked or cabled down).

10.__ An access auditing system for the physical environment has been put into play.

Hour 4: The Boot Process

11.__ LILO passwords and restrictions for boot images have been enabled.

(`/etc/lilo.conf`)

12.__ The default runlevel has been set correctly, and the Ctrl+Alt+Del sequence has been disabled.

(`/etc/inittab`)

Hour 5: System and User Fundamentals

13.__ Consoles available for root logins have been minimized or restricted.

(`/etc/securetty`)

14.__ Shells available to users have been minimized or restricted.

(`/etc/shells`)

15.__ Service startups have been audited; unnecessary services have been switched off.

(`/etc/rc.d/rc`n`.d`)

16.__ Shadow passwords have been installed if necessary.

17.__ All users have been added with user-private groups, and the importance of strong passwords has been explained.

Hour 6: TCP/IP Network Security

18.___ All unneeded services normally controlled by the Internet daemon have been disabled.

(`/etc/inetd.conf`)

19.___ TCP wrappers are enabled, and the hosts access files have been configured for security.

(`/etc/inetd.conf,/etc/hosts.deny,/etc/hosts.allow`)

20.___ The system logging daemon has been configured for the desired level and location of logging activity.

(`/etc/syslog.conf`)

Hour 7: File System Security

21.___ All disk device nodes have been set to permissions 0600 with `chmod`.

22.___ An audit has been performed of all SUID/SGID binaries on the system, and the unneeded ones have had the SUID and/or SGID bit(s) cleared.

23.___ Changes have been made to the boot process in order to mount the root file system read-only automatically.

Hour 8: Extra File System Security Tools

24.___ Posix Access Control Lists for Linux have been installed for greater permissions control.

25.___ A secure file deletion tool has been installed.

Hour 9: Making the Most of Pluggable Authentication Modules (PAM)

26.___ A `wheel` group has been created and will be enforced with respect to `su` availability.

(`/etc/pam.d/*`)

27.___ The `other` authentication in PAM has been audited for security.

(`/etc/pam.d/*`)

28.___ Strong password enforcement and periodic password expiration have been enabled.

(`/etc/pam.d/*`)

D

Hour 10: Using `ipchains` for Firewalling and Routing

29.___ A default set of packet-filtering policies has been implemented based on the role of this machine and the needs of the local network.

Hour 11: Using `iptables` for Firewalling and Routing

30.___ A default set of packet-filtering policies has been implemented based on the role of this machine and the needs of the local network.

Hour 12: Securing Apache, FTP, and SMTP Services

31.___ Apache: User home pages have been disabled as a general policy and enabled only for those users who need them.

(httpd.conf)

32.___ Apache: Logging rules have been audited and updated as necessary.

(httpd.conf)

33.___ Apache: Password authentication has been enabled to protect sensitive areas that must still be available to some users.

(httpd.conf)

34.___ FTP: Strong e-mail address checking has been implemented for anonymous FTP access.

(/etc/ftpaccess)

35.___ FTP: Reverse DNS lookups are now required for any user connecting via anonymous FTP.

(/etc/ftpaccess)

36.___ FTP: All users who don't absolutely need login FTP access have been forbidden from authenticating.

(/etc/ftpusers)

37.___ Sendmail: Strong packet-filtering rules have been put in place to protect the SMTP mailer against outside abuse.

Hour 13: Network Security: DNS with BIND

38.__ Strong packet filtering rules have been put in place to drop packets from hosts this nameserver doesn't serve.

39.__ BIND version information has been made unavailable.

(/etc/named.conf)

40.__ Zone transfers and recursive queries have been disabled.

(/etc/named.conf)

41.__ BIND has been placed in a chroot jail.

Hour 14: Network Security: NFS and Samba

42.__ The userspace NFS daemon, if present, has been replaced with the kernel-based NFS service to enhance ACL compatibility.

43.__ The list of exported file systems has been audited, and unnecessary exports or unnecessary hosts have been removed or disallowed, respectively.

(/etc/exports)

44.__ SWAT has been installed, and an audit of the security paradigm and other settings has been completed.

Hour 15: Securing X11R6 Access

45.__ The host-level access controls have been completely disabled so that no host is allowed to connect solely on the basis of its claimed identity.

(/etc/X*n*.hosts)

46.__ Magic cookie access control has been put in place, most likely using XDM.

Hour 16: Encrypting Data Streams

47.__ SSH has been installed for stream encryption capability.

48.__ Traditional services that can be replaced by SSH (telnet, rlogin, rsh, and so on) have been disabled.

(/etc/inetd.conf)

D

Hour 17: Introduction to Kerberos

49.__ Kerberos 5 has been installed on all clients and a key distribution center has been constructed.

50.__ Traditional services such as `telnet`, `rlogin`, and `rsh` have been enhanced with Kerberos and the original binaries for these services have been disabled.

(`/etc/inetd.conf`)

51.__ As many systems and services as possible have been reconfigured or recompiled to be Kerberos-aware.

Hour 18: Encrypting Web Data

52.__ Apache has been recompiled to be SSL-capable, and a self-signed certificate has been created.

Hour 19: Encrypting File System Data

53.__ The Transparent Cryptographic File System has been installed, and volumes that are to be encrypted have been created or converted.

Hour 20: Encrypting E-Mail Data

54.__ The GNU Privacy Guard system for PGP encryption and signatures has been made available to users on this host.

Hour 21: Auditing and Monitoring

55.__ SAINT has been installed and run, and a regular regime of SAINT audits has been implemented.

56.__ Any possible vulnerabilities reported by SAINT on its first pass have been thoroughly checked out and will be for all future SAINT passes as well.

57.__ SWATCH has been installed, and an initial match file has been constructed. It will be monitored vigilantly and expanded based on experience and observation of the system logs.

Hour 22: Detecting Attacks in Progress

58.__ Snort has been installed using a collection of rulesets from the Snort community that will be updated regularly.

Hour 23: Preserving Data

59.__ A system of periodic backups has been implemented using CRON or another scheduling daemon.

60.__ A scheme for media rotation in periodic backups has been implemented.

Hour 24: Recovering from Attacks— A Mini-Checklist

__ Take system offline.

__ Reboot Linux into single-user mode.

__ Make an archival full backup.

__ Study logs, SWATCH alerts, Snort alerts.

__ Report attacker to ISP or upstream providers.

__ Reformat and reinstall Linux.

__ Cautiously restore important data from tape.

__ Require all groups and users to change passwords.

__ Watch closer on compromised ports.

__ Take system back online.

D

APPENDIX E

Web Links to Documented Software

Table E.1 gives a summary of the Web locations of software documented in this book that must normally be downloaded.

TABLE E.1 Web Links to Documented Software

Name	URL
OpenSSL	http://www.openssl.org
OpenSSH	http://www.openssh.com
Posix ACLs	http://acl.bestbits.at
BCWipe	http://www.jetico.com
Wipe	http://wipe.sourceforge.net
Overwrite	http://www.kyuzz.org/antirez/overwrite/
Kerberos 5	http://web.mit.edu/kerberos/www/
eBones	http://www.pdc.kth.se/kth-krb/
mod_ssl	http://www.modssl.org
Apache	http://httpd.apache.org

TABLE E.1 continued

Name	URL
TCFS	http://www.tcfs.it
GnuPG	http://www.gnupg.org
SAINT	http://www.wwdsi.com/saint/
Nmap	http://www.insecure.org/nmap/
SWATCH	http://www.stanford.edu/~atkins/swatch/
Snort	http://www.snort.org
libpcap	http://ftp.ee.lbl.gov
libnet	http://www.packetfactory.net/Projects/Libnet/

INDEX

E

-E (--rename-chain) command (iptables utility), 169

-E argument (chage command), 80

e2fsproqs patch, 123

e2fsproqs source, 123

eBones, 259, 383

echo [model] action (SWATCH), 322

eDesktop (Caldera OpenLinux), 14-15

editing
/etc/fstab file, 23-26
/etc/group file, 78
/etc/inittab file, 64
host lists (X server authentication), 225
init processes, 72
permissions, 104
chmod command (numeric mode), 106
chmod command (symbolic mode), 105
setting default (umask command), 107-108
shell scripts, 72

e-mail encryption, 299
GPG, 300-302
encrypting/decrypting data, 307-308
importing/exporting GPG keys, 303
listing GPG keys, 303-304
signed data, 306
PGP, 299
signatures and trust, 305

enabling
disabled services, 76
host-based authentication (SSH), 244

IP forwarding, 157
public key authentication (SSH), 245
SysRq key, 353
TCFS, 293
TCFS administrative tasks, 294

encrypt passwords option (SWAT), 217

encrypting data. *See also* Kerberos
e-mail, 299
GPG, 300-302, 307-308
GPG signed data, 306
importing/exporting GPG keys, 303
listing GPG keys, 303-304
PGP, 299
signatures and trust, 304-305
encrypted file systems, 289
encryption key, 288
file system data, 287
Kerberos, 273
MD5, 77
need for, 238
RSA encryption, 300
SSH, 247-248
TCFS, 295
3DES encryption module, 293
administrative tasks (TCFS), 294
compiling, 290
compiling the patched kernel, 293
EXT2 partitions, 289
file access, 295
installing, 288-292
kernel options, 293

mounting volume on client machine, 294
system requirements, 289
encryption keys, 288

enforcing wheel group (PAM), 141-143

entering BIOS setup program, 33

entries (log), 95-96

environments (security), 46

eod command (mt command), 343

equipment (physical security), 45-46
access auditing, 51-52
boot devices, 49-50
boxes, locking down, 50-51
location strategies, 47-51
locations, 46-47
power cycles, 47-49

erase command (mt command), 343

ErrorLog directive, 182

errors, library version issues, 292

errors=N option (fstab command), 117

EscapeChar option (ssh2_config file), 242

EscapeChar option (ssh_config file), 253

eServer (Caldera OpenLinux), 14-15

ESTABLISHED packet state, 171

/etc/exports file, 367
configuring, 211-212
listing, 213

/etc/fstab file, 366
creating, 23-24
editing, 23-26